THE STRUGGLE FOR PEACE

The Struggle for Peace:
Israelis and Palestinians

EDITED BY
Elizabeth Warnock Fernea
AND
Mary Evelyn Hocking

PHOTOGRAPHS BY
Heather L. Taylor

UNIVERSITY OF TEXAS PRESS

AUSTIN

The essay by Augustus Richard Norton, "Toward Enduring Peace in the Middle East," is partially adapted from an article, "Breaking through the Wall of Fear," also by the author, which appeared in *Current History* (January 1992). Adapted with permission.

The essay by Robert Rubinstein, "Culture and Negotiation," copyright © 1992 by Robert Rubinstein.

∞ The paper used in this publication meets the minimum requirements of American National Standard for Information Sciences —Permanence of Paper for Printed Library Materials, ANSI Z39.48-1984.

Funding for this book provided in part by a grant from The United States Outreach Program of the Middle East Institute.

All photographs are by Heather L. Taylor except those on pp. 158 and 160 by David H. Wells, and on p. 159 by Yesh G'Vul.

Cover photograph: Runners for Peace is a group of Israelis and Palestinians who regularly jog together, sometimes in Jerusalem and sometimes in the West Bank. Photograph by Heather L. Taylor.

Maps drawn by Susan Long.

LIBRARY OF CONGRESS CATALOGING-IN-PUBLICATION DATA

The Struggle for peace : Israelis and Palestinians / edited by
    Elizabeth Warnock Fernea and Mary Evelyn Hocking. — 1st ed.
        p.   cm.
    Includes bibliographical references and index.
    ISBN 0-292-76541-X. — ISBN 0-292-73071-3 (pbk.)
        1. Jewish-Arab relations—1917–   2. Israelis—Interviews.
    3. Palestinian Arabs—Interviews.   4. Jewish-Arab relations—
    Forecasting.   I. Fernea, Elizabeth Warnock.   II. Hocking, Mary
    Evelyn.
    DS119.7.S77   1992
    956—dc20

                                                          91-43509
                                                          CIP

Contents

IV. Future Possibilities

V. Concluding Comment

Acknowledgments

THE BOOK that follows is part of a larger educational project, "Perspectives on Peace: The Middle East," funded by the John D. and Catherine T. MacArthur Foundation, the Ford Foundation, and the Greenville Foundation with assistance from ARAMCO Services Company and the James R. Dougherty, Jr., Foundation. The project also includes a one-hour documentary film, a study guide, and a teleconference.

The book itself is funded partially through a grant from the United States Outreach Fund of the Middle East Institute, Washington, D.C.

For help and support, we are also indebted to the Center for Middle Eastern Studies, University of Texas at Austin, and its directors, Ian Manners (1987–1991) and Robert Holz (1991–   ). Virginia Howell, Persis Karim, Sascha Cohen, and Roberta Micallef all helped with editing, proofreading, and typing various versions of the manuscript. Our editor at U.T. Press, Frankie Westbrook, has been a model of persuasion, and we appreciate her intelligence and her patience. We thank our husbands, Robert Fernea and Joseph Dodge, who put up with the outlandish arrangements and unusual hours which proved necessary in order to finish the manuscript six months ahead of time—to coordinate with the appearance of the film, *The Struggle for Peace: Israelis and Palestinians*.

Elizabeth Warnock Fernea
Mary Evelyn Hocking

Mao was wrong. Power does not come out of the barrel of a gun. Power comes from shared ideas, shared hope, shared ambitions, shared actions. When such sharing goes deep enough in enough people, soldiers don't fire, tank commanders don't obey orders, prisons won't take prisoners.

That is history, again and again.

—MICHAEL VENTURA

THE STRUGGLE FOR PEACE

Introduction

THIS book attempts to open up a discussion of one of the longest and most difficult contemporary conflicts, a conflict that has ramifications far beyond its own parameters and affects relations among people throughout the world. This is the conflict between Israelis and Palestinians over the ancient land northeast of Egypt, called historically by different peoples Judea, Samaria, Israel, and Palestine. Over the last half-century, academic and journalistic views toward the conflict, particularly in the West, have hardened into a single view that might be summarized as follows: The conflict is intractable, unsolvable, and irrational, the product of ancient tribal rivalries between peoples who have been fighting each other for millennia.

Such a view, which impedes efforts at resolution, persists, although the peoples and cultures of the Middle East have been changing in important ways since the establishment of Israel. And Western policies toward the Middle East have also begun to change. This collection of readings is designed to challenge the accepted view that the protagonists in the conflict stand in fixed and unchanging positions. It places together a series of different kinds of texts: interviews with individual Israelis and Palestinians; original essays in several disciplinary discourses; a historical chronology, photos, and maps; and personal biographies. All these texts are related to the conflict, but in different ways; they are expressed in varied and sometimes contradictory voices.

Three historical essays on the background of the contemporary situation set the stage for the discussion that follows. The first is by Avraham Zilkha, an Israeli; the second by Muhammad Muslih, a Palestinian, and the third, on revisionist history, by Joel Beinin, an American historian. The three essays are important representations of the background of the conflict as perceived from different intellectual as well as personal positions. Each presents his own view, one with which the others may disagree.

The remaining sections of the book deal with the possibility of resolution and can be seen as commentaries on and reactions to the opening section. Part II, for example, presents "The View from Outside," three essays by Edward Sherman, a lawyer; Robert Rubinstein, an anthropologist; and Christian Harleman, an international peacekeeper. All three are concerned with the general issue of mediation raised by efforts to resolve the conflict, both abstractly (Sherman and Rubinstein) and in terms of practical matters (Colonel Harleman, who has been directly involved in peacekeeping efforts in several areas of the world).

Part III offers "The View from Inside," introduced by Steve Talley's essay, "Making a Film about Mideast Peacemakers." Talley, a filmmaker who has directed documentaries on ethnic conflict in the United States, suggests how the subject, the realities of the medium, and the preconceptions of the audience and the film crew shape the way writers and filmmakers choose images and words to present the conflict. When beginning the film, I (as the producer) and Talley (as the director) decided to go beyond the usual media approach, involving discussions and stand-up interviews with political leaders. We decided to focus instead on those who seldom "spoke" outside their own societies, ordinary people on both sides who were directly involved in the conflict itself. We discovered that large numbers of Israelis and Palestinians had been working for peace for a long time. This was contrary to our own expectations, which were of course influenced by the media and the fixed academic view outlined above. Here was clear evidence that the conflict was not perceived as unsolvable. We were not looking at a marginalized minority of "peaceniks," but rather at people from all walks of life who demonstrated together in protest marches and on an individual basis in the Israeli community or in the Palestinian community, people who worked together in dialogue groups, vigils, and regular discussions. We asked ourselves what animated these people, whose actions broke open the fixed view we had when we arrived in the area in 1990. It was clearly not political or economic gain, since working for peace either as a Palestinian or as an Israeli put one at odds with the mainstream of one's own community. Did they serve as role models for others? Was their example important in influencing larger, less committed groups? How did their efforts affect public opinion in the Israeli and Palestinian communities?

The lives and beliefs, then, of this diverse group of Israelis and Palestinians came to constitute for us and for the film crew an incontrovertible body of evidence that the fixed view of the conflict, so accepted in the West, was wrong. Even while we were filming, events changed and so did people's relationships. By the time this book was going to press in November 1991, the first face-to-face peace talks between Israelis and Palestinians had taken place in Madrid. Clearly, the situation in the area is far different from that perceived by those living in other parts of the world.

The twenty-five Israelis and Palestinians profiled in Part IV by Martha

Diase, a young scholar of the peace movement in Israel and herself of Palestinian descent, appear also in the film. They represent men and women from many different socio-economic positions: a school principal, a translator, a factory worker, civil servants, an agriculturalist, a pharmacist, child-care workers, journalists. A separate essay by Roberta Micallef, a scholar in comparative literature at the University of Texas at Austin, details one particular response of Israeli and Palestinian women to the peace process. These statements are a remarkable series of diverse texts—insiders' comments on the need for peace, the ways to achieve peace, the problems of peace, and the personal risks involved in holding such views.

The final two essays in the section attempt to go beyond the current situation and speculate about the future. Yehoshafat Harkabi, an Israeli political scientist as well as a former army general, analyzes Israelis' changing attitudes since the Gulf War. Salim Tamari, a Palestinian sociologist, raises some of the issues that a new two-state solution would pose for Palestinian leadership.

The essay "The Palestinian-Israeli Conflict: Options and Scenarios for Peace," by Robert Vitalis, an American political scientist, balances the opening sections of the book and grows out of all the book's textual evidence. Vitalis summarizes, from the point of view of a scholar outside the immediate scene, the options available to both parties in the conflict. He lays out in some detail the consequences, not only for both sides, but for the international community as well.

Augustus Richard Norton, an American social scientist who has also worked with the UN International Peacekeeping Force, offers a final comment. Since the international scene has changed so quickly and unexpectedly that academicians and political leaders are already talking about a new world order, he argues, perhaps the Middle East is also emerging into a new phase—one of hope, or at least realism, about the need for making peace between Israelis and Palestinians. This, he suggests, will contribute not only to improving the welfare of Israelis and Palestinians, but to improving that of all citizens of the world.

It is important to note that we have not attempted to force these essays into a single narrative style. On the contrary, we have welcomed the expressions of different voices, for those forms of expression add an important dimension to the meaning of the material and the understanding of the conflict. The styles are also informative; they reveal something about the variety of the backgrounds of their authors and their expectations about you, their readers. The differences among the authors, both in what they say and in how they say it, demonstrate an intrinsic part of the problem facing those who wish to resolve the Israeli-Palestinian conflict. The collection raises issues in new ways, offers evidence to factor into any contemporary study of the Israeli-Palestinian conflict, and suggests that a new vision of the conflict may be in order.

Elizabeth Warnock Fernea
Professor, Middle Eastern Studies and English
University of Texas at Austin

PART I. BACKGROUND

History of the Israeli-Palestinian Conflict

Avraham Zilkha was born in Iraq and grew up in Israel. Upon receiving his degrees in Hebrew, Arabic, and Middle Eastern Studies from the Hebrew University of Jerusalem, he came to the United States to study linguistics at the University of Texas at Austin. He received a doctorate in 1971 and taught at Indiana and Ohio State universities. In 1974 he returned to the University of Texas, where he has been teaching in the Hebrew Studies Program. He also teaches courses on Israel at the Center for Middle Eastern Studies. He is the editor and translator of a book on the history of the Jewish community of Iraq and the author of a Hebrew-English dictionary.

He has served as president of the Texas Association of Middle East Scholars, and he is presently the associate director of the Center for Middle Eastern Studies at the University of Texas at Austin.

The Emergence of Zionism

At the turn of the century, the boundaries of the Middle East had not yet been drawn. Under Ottoman rule, which lasted four hundred years, Palestine did not constitute a political entity. It was divided administratively into three separate districts, and was, according to Arab sources, inhabited by people who were considered Syrians.[1] In the last decade of the nineteenth century, major events began to reshape the land and the people that would ultimately determine the area's political future.

The turning point in the modern history of Palestine was the birth of political Zionism, a movement launched in Europe by Theodor Herzl, a Hungarian-born Viennese playwright and journalist, whose ultimate objective was the establishment of a Jewish national home in the Holy Land. Zionism, in essence a belief in the return of the Jews to the biblical land of Zion,[2] had existed for many centuries as a religious-Messianic idea based on biblical prophecies. Contrary to that traditional form of Zionism, which was by nature passive, since it relied on divine deliverance, modern Zionism came into being as a political, pragmatic ideology. Moreover, although Palestine was chosen because of its religious and historical significance to Judaism, the Zionist movement was, by and large, secular.

Herzl conceived his ideas about Jewish nationalism as he watched socio-political conditions unfolding in Europe and their effects on Jews. He was particularly shaken by the trial of Alfred Dreyfus, a captain in the French army who was accused of treason. In a climate of anti-Semitism that was sweeping France, Dreyfus was tried not as a Frenchman, but as a Jew. Upon his conviction he was stripped of his rank, dismissed dishonorably from the army, and sentenced to life imprisonment.[3] After witnessing the trial, Herzl realized that political emancipation did not solve the age-old problem of anti-Semitism. His conclusion was that the solution to the Jewish question had to be sought on a political basis. Jews should leave countries where they were not wanted and should establish their own state, a state that would, ideally, be free from discrimination and persecution.

Herzl published his plan in 1896 in a book titled *Der Judenstaat* (*The Jewish State*),[4] in which he described the structure of the state-to-be and its institutions, as well as the necessary means to build it. With regard to the territory in which the Jews would settle, he initially posed the question "Palestine or Argentina?", although he seemed to favor the former as the "unforgettable historic homeland."[5]

Undeterred by the ridicule that he encountered, Herzl convened the First Zionist Congress in Basel, Switzerland, a year later. Despite a great degree of skepticism, participants adopted his plan and set up the necessary apparatus to carry out its implementation. The resolution that was passed contained unambiguous wording: "The aim of Zionism is to create for the Jewish people a home in Palestine secured by public law." It was a triumph for Herzl, who wrote in his diary, "In Basel I founded the Jewish State . . . In five years, perhaps, and certainly in fifty, everyone will see it."[6] Indeed, exactly 50 years later the United Nations voted to create a Jewish state in Palestine. Herzl's untimely death in 1904 prevented him from seeing the realization of his dream.[7]

The Zionist plan required diplomatic efforts to mobilize the support of the major powers, particularly Britain, Germany, Russia, and Turkey, a task that Herzl himself undertook. International support was needed not only to secure the free flow of Jewish immigrants to Palestine, but also to convince skeptics who doubted Herzl's claim that establishing a Jewish state was indeed feasible. The net result of Herzl's diplomacy, including his meetings with the emperor of Germany and the Ottoman sultan, was insignificant.[8] The Zionist plan was also challenged from within. Many Western Jewish leaders, including Baron Edmond de Rothschild,[9] a generous supporter of Jewish settlements in Palestine, opposed it. Some Jewish leaders contested the notion that Jews constituted one nation regardless of their place of residence. They feared that the Zionist claim would jeopardize their position as loyal citizens of their respective countries.[10] Religious groups in western Europe were particularly displeased with the

Zionist challenge to the ancient belief in Messianic redemption. Paradoxically, some of the most zealous opponents of Zionism were the leaders of Jewish labor organizations in Russia, the same country in which Zionism also had its greatest support.[11]

Although Zionist groups such as Hovevei Zion and Bilu (the latter organized immigration to Palestine in the 1880s and established the first colonies)[12] had existed before 1897, none were as powerful and effective as the organizations founded by Herzl. Subsequent meetings of the Zionist Congress, held almost every year, together with continuous fund-raising to secure donations from wealthy European Jews such as the Rothschilds,[13] created the machinery to purchase land in Palestine, assist relocating immigrants, and support newly constructed settlements. Although local Zionist organizations were outlawed in Russia, they were spreading all over eastern Europe, adding to the vitality of the movement and serving as recruitment centers for immigrants bound for Palestine. Despite the harsh conditions that forced many immigrants to leave Europe, by 1914 the Jews in Palestine numbered only 85,000 out of a total population of 500,000.[14]

At the turn of the century, Russian Zionists became actively involved in their country's politics, a factor that shaped the character of the second wave of immigration.[15] The new immigrants to Palestine were, for the most part, young, highly motivated Socialists whose intention was to create not only a Jewish national home, but a new society based on an ideological mixture of Zionism and socialism. They declared equality and manual labor to be the moral and economic foundations of Zionism. They built communes (*kibbutzim*); revived the ancient, but for centuries unspoken, Hebrew language; established modern school systems; created political parties and other democratically elected bodies; and, eventually, laid the foundation for the Jewish military forces. By the end of the 1930s the infrastructure of the state-to-be was already in place, and for all practical purposes, the Jews of Palestine were ready for nationhood.

The Arab Reaction

The fact that Herzl's Zionism was born outside the designated country made it unique among modern national movements, and set the conditions for conflict with the local population. While the Jews felt that they were going home to their ancestral land, the Arab inhabitants of Palestine viewed the Zionist plan as a form of European colonialism.

Arab opposition to Jewish immigration appeared as early as 1886, when Arab residents attacked Petah Tivka, the first Jewish colony, in a dispute over grazing access.[16] Sporadic incidents of this nature continued, and increased in frequency and intensity with the breakdown of Ottoman local government that followed the revolution of the Young Turks in 1908. Zionist leaders, however, believed that there was no conflict of interest with the indigenous population. Because they expected that the Arabs of Palestine would reap a great benefit from the immigration of Jews and the flow of capital into the country, they played down the significance of those incidents, and attributed them to local elements unhappy with the transfer of land ownership.[17] At this early stage of the conflict the Zionists failed to see the wider picture of rising Arab nationalism. Thus, they underestimated the dangers that outbreaks of violence, however limited, posed for the Zionist objectives. In fact, at the eleventh Zionist Congress held in Vienna in 1913, speakers, including Chaim Weizmann, gave an optimistic prognosis based on their understanding of the common ancestry between Jews and Arabs and the development programs for Palestine that they believed would benefit both parties. Gradually, however, it became evident that the Arab opposition, directed primarily at immigration and land purchases by Jews, was assuming a nationalistic character and paralleled the rise of Arab nationalism throughout the region.

Neither the Arabs nor the Jews were masters of the land. Their fate rested in the hands of foreign governments that had the power to draw maps of the region based on their own interests. To consolidate their power and define spheres of influence in the Middle East, the Allies made a deal in 1916, known as the Sykes-Picot agreement, to partition the Middle East among themselves. According to the agreement, France would gain control over Syria (which included today's Lebanon) and land southward to the Galilee, while Britain was to receive the Negev desert and Transjordan, which was designated as an Arab state under British influence. The area between Hebron and the Sea of Galilee, which included the holy sites in Jerusalem and in other locations, was intended to be ruled jointly by the British, French, and Russians. Linked with that arrangement, Britain proposed legal Jewish immigration and settlement in Palestine. Zionist leaders, however, objected to the dissection of Palestine and demanded that the land be placed under the authority of a single power, an arrangement that coincided with British interests in the region. Toward the end of the World War I, Britain received the consent of the French premier, Georges Clemenceau, to revise the 1916 agreement with France, conceding the entire territory of Palestine to British control in return for allowing France to retain control of Syria.

The defeat of the Turks in World War I and the resulting dismantling of the Ottoman Empire were greeted with satisfaction by Zionist leaders. Turkish authorities had been far from supportive and often showed hostility toward Zionist activities in Palestine, despite the financial rewards that were offered to them. Moreover, the British takeover of the land raised expectations about the Zionist plan, based on the good relations Zionists such as Chaim Weizmann had with British leaders. Toward the completion of their conquest of Palestine, the British issued the Balfour Declaration (on November 2, 1917), a decree promising to support "the establishment of a Jewish national home in Palestine."[18] That commitment constituted both a diplomatic and political victory for the Zionist movement, because Britain controlled the land in question. The declaration also appeared to grant Zionism international legitimacy and encouraged American Jews, whose attitude toward the Zionist program had been lukewarm, to step to the forefront of it supporters.

The San Remo Conference of the Allies in April 1920 upheld the Anglo-French agreement, placed Iraq and Palestine under a British mandate, and recognized France as a mandatory power in Syria and Lebanon. Reaffirming the principles of the Balfour Declaration, the conference stated that "An appropriate Jewish agency shall be recognized as a public body . . . in such economic, social, and other matters as may affect the establishment of the Jewish national home and the interests of the Jewish population in Palestine."[19] In 1921, the British carved out the area east of the Jordan River to create Transjordan, and, subject to their supervision, installed Emir Abdullah as the ruler.

The success of Zionism led to a collision with its fiercest enemy: Arab nationalism. The national awakening of the Arabs began before World War I, but intensified in the aftermath of the Turkish defeat. Although the notion that Palestinian nationalism emerged as a reaction to Zionism is disputed by Arabs, it definitely crystallized in opposition to Jewish immigration and land acquisition. Najib Azuri, a Syrian, warned of the strife to come between Jews and Arabs by saying early in the conflict that the Arab and Jewish national movements, although similar in nature, "are destined to a continuous struggle, until one of the two prevails over the other."[20]

The Arabs generally regarded the Balfour Declaration as an act of betrayal because it contradicted earlier pledges made by Britain to them. In October 1915, in a letter from the British high commissioner in Egypt, Henry McMahon, to Hussein, sherif of Mecca, Britain promised to "recognize and support the independence of the Arabs in all the regions within the limits demanded by the sherif of Mecca."[21] The British gesture was evidently made to lure the Arabs into the Allied camp and to secure their assistance in the war against the Turks. The Arabs understood those promises to mean a commitment to include Palestine in a future independent Arab state. The establishment of a Jewish national home in that territory was viewed as a violation of that commitment.

Early Arab reaction to the Zionist advances in Palestine was characterized by lack of organization, and consisted initially of verbal assaults in the press.[22] The protest was directed both at land purchases and at the influx of immigrants that created a labor surplus. This meant that Arab workers had little opportunity to work in the Jewish sector. Land was of particular importance, because the practice of absentee landlords selling their land to Jews caused the dislocation of Arab farmers. In several cases, cultivated fields and grazing lands were lost because farmers did not register them properly with the Turkish authorities. But eventually the political fate of Palestine became the primary concern, as the Arabs gradually realized that the Jews were striving relentlessly, locally as well as internationally, to achieve the ultimate Zionist goal of statehood.

An effort to organize the opposition began in 1913 with the establishment of Palestinian organizations in various locations in the Ottoman Empire. These efforts marked the first expression of a distinct Palestinian identity.[23] The call for firm action, however, was not always heeded, and the Arab conference in Paris that year failed to confront the issue of Jewish immigration. In addition, a number of Arabs were willing to consider that the overall economy of Palestine might derive some benefit from the Zionist enterprise. Some statements friendly to the Zionist cause appeared in the Egyptian press[24] and words of welcome came from Hussein, sherif of Mecca. But when the first Palestinian-Arab Congress convened in January 1919, and declared Palestine part of Syria, Arab oppposition to Zionism had already solidified. Conciliatory pronouncements about Zionism were no longer heard. The Congress, from which the Arab Higher Committee later emerged, demanded retraction of the Balfour Declaration.

The most serious attempt to settle the dispute between the parties took place in May 1918, when Weizmann met in Aqaba with Faisal, Sherif Hussein's son. At that meeting, and on several occasions thereafter, Faisal appeared sympathetic toward the Zionist goals and expressed his belief in Arab-Jewish friendship. In the agreement that was signed by the two leaders in January 1919, Faisal in effect renounced the Arab claim to Palestine, and pledged his support for the Balfour Declaration, which promised a Jewish homeland.[25] Of particular significance in the agreement was the statement that "All necessary measures shall be taken to encourage and stimulate immigration of Jews into Palestine on a large scale, and as quickly as possible to settle Jewish immigrants upon the land."[26] In return for his concessions, Faisal was promised the assistance of the Zionist Organization in developing the economy of an Arab state (of which he was to become king). As the Zionists were praising this new beginning of cooperation with the Arabs, Faisal was having a change of heart. By the time he arrived at the peace conference in Versailles in November 1919, he had already reneged and demanded the inclusion of Palestine in an independent Arab state, as had previously been promised by the Allies. Despite the collapse of his agreement with Faisal, Weizmann continued for many years to seek contacts with Arab dignitaries.[27]

The British Mandate

Soon after assuming the duties of its mandate over Palestine, which was formalized in 1922 by the newly established League of Nations, Britain discovered that it had a serious problem with the Arabs. Moreover, there were officials within the British government who did not approve of the Balfour Declaration, although it had the support of France, the United States, and other countries. British officials expressed their discontentment by trying to water down the promises that they had made to the Zionists. An early sign of erosion in the commitment of Britain to the Zionist cause appeared in 1922, when Colonial Secretary Winston Churchill issued a White Paper (a government report) stating that the number of Jewish immigrants should be limited to a figure determined on the basis of the Palestinian economy's ability to absorb them. Additional White Papers were issued in 1931 and 1939, although Britain continued to claim that they did not constitute a reversal of her position in favor of a Jewish national home. The establishment of a quota system for the immigration of Jews became a major component of the British policy in Palestine. Britain's efforts to pacify the Arabs by barring Jewish immigrants incurred the wrath of the Zionist movement, as immigration was considered its lifeline.

The British administration in Palestine, under High Commissioner Herbert Samuel,[28] soon realized the extent of Arab opposition to the creation of a Jewish national home. In March 1920, the first attack on Jewish settlements occurred, followed in April by Arab riots against Jews in Jerusalem.[29] The attacks constituted a serious escalation of the conflict, and marked the beginning of a path of violence that led to an all-out civil war between Arabs and Jews in the 1940s.

The Jewish reaction to Arab violence went in two directions. A minority of Zionist intellectuals suggested a bi-national state, in the belief that it might win the support of both the Arabs and the British administration. The majority, on the other hand, continued to demand Jewish independence. The revisionists, under the leadership of Vladimir Ze'ev Jabotinsky, called for the creation of a strong military force and for Jewish settlements throughout the land, including Transjordan. Zionist leaders in both Europe and the United States confronted the British on the issue of immigration and other matters that were seen as anti-Zionist. The moderates eventually established the Ihud (Union) Association in 1942, but remained a small minority.[30] The majority, on the other hand, adopted an aggressive policy by establishing local defensive forces, which were consolidated as the Hagana, while the extremists founded the Irgun and Lehi (or Stern) military organizations. To bypass the restrictions of the White Papers, Jews were smuggled into Palestine illegally. By 1937, an estimated 50,000 Jews had entered the country clandestinely, in an ongoing operation that reached its peak in the 1940s.[31]

Zionist efforts during the British Mandate concentrated on three main areas: increasing immigration and strengthening the political and economic foundation of the Yishuv[32] toward independence, training and arming the Jewish population to withstand Arab attacks while trying to deal with the Arabs politically, and mobilizing international support to gain recognition and increase the pressure on Britain.

The flow of immigrants allowed expansion of both urban and rural communities. The city of Tel Aviv became the main Jewish urban center, while the kibbutzim were the center of rural Jewish life. Vigorous economic activity and the formation of labor organizations and health and education systems based upon modern models facilitated the absorption and employment of newcomers. Elective bodies, such as the Va'ad Leumi (National Committee), the Jewish Agency, and various political executives, laid the groundwork for the democratic structure of the Jewish political entity.

The creation of well-trained and organized paramilitary forces gave the Jewish minority protection from the Arabs, who outnumbered them. The kibbutzim were crucial in providing military training away from the watchful eye of the British authorities, as well as hiding places for arms caches.[33] The British unintentionally assisted the Zionists in their military efforts when they trained a Jewish brigade to fight the Germans in World War II.[34]

In the international arena, Zionist diplomacy was aimed at guaranteeing sympathy for the Jews in a final showdown that would determine the fate of Palestine. The reliance on religious-historical claims to establish moral rights struck a chord with Christians, who believed in the validity of biblical promises. The biggest achievement of Zionist diplomacy was the emergence of the United States after World War II as a major supporter of the Zionist cause. This support was not only based on humanitarian grounds; it was principally because of the influence of the American Jewish community.[35] American help was invaluable in exerting pressure on Britain to relax its restrictions on Jewish immigration, and crucial in the diplomatic battle that ensued at the twilight of the British Mandate.

Compared to the dedicated, sophisticated Zionist leadership, ineffectual, rival heads of clans controlled the Arab population of Palestine. Four major families competed over power in Jerusalem alone: Husseini, Khalidi, Nashashibi, and Nusseiba.[36] Haj Amin al-Husseini, the mufti of Jerusalem and the president of the Supreme Moslem Council, who emerged as the prominent leader of the Arabs, was an extremist who so antagonized the British authorities that he had to sneak out of the country to escape arrest.[37]

The Arab strategy against the Yishuv during the British Mandate was based primarily on riots, strikes, and attacks on Jewish communities throughout the land.[38] The violent incidents, although sometimes spontaneous, created confrontations not only with Jews, but also with British authorities, who were trying to maintain law and order. Aside from causing Jewish casualties, the policy of violent resistance did not achieve any political gains. It did, however, strengthen the hands of militant Jewish groups such as the Irgun that believed less in compromise and more in the use of force.[39]

Violence escalated in August 1929, when a procession of young Jews near the Western Wall in Jerusalem triggered an Arab riot in and outside the city that resulted in many casualties. Incited by Muslim agitators calling for the protection of al-Aqsa Mosque against a feared Jewish attack, Arabs rioted throughout the country. In an assault on the ancient Jewish quarter in Hebron, 60 residents were murdered and 50 were wounded.[40] A British commission of inquiry, headed by Walter Shaw, issued a report condemning the Arabs as the instigators of the disturbances but identified the source of the problem as Arab fear brought on by Jewish immigration and land purchases. A recommendation of the Shaw Report to limit the flow of Jews to the country and to restrict their right to buy land caused an uproar among Jewish leaders. Chaim Weizmann, the chief advocate of cooperation with the British, resigned his position as head of the Zionist Organization and Jewish Agency. The resignation of Weizmann and other Jewish moderates, coupled with sharp criticism in Britain itself toward the mandate administration, persuaded the British government to reconsider the recommendations of the Shaw Report.

Another wave of disturbances began in 1936 and continued through 1939. Fueled by Britain's weak posture and the influx of Jewish immigrants from Germany, due to Hitler's ascent to power, Arab violence erupted in various locations in Palestine. Unlike previous riots perpetrated by disorganized groups of Arabs, these attacks, under the command of a Syrian officer, Fawzi al-Qawuqji,[41] were aimed at disrupting Jewish work and transportation lines. Soon the disturbances turned into a general strike and an Arab armed rebellion against the authorities.[42] With twenty thousand troops in the country and the pretext of economic hardship caused by the strike, the British used military force to put an end to the disturbances in October 1936.[43]

The Search for Solutions

To study the situation, a royal commission headed by Lord Robert Peel was dispatched to Palestine in November 1936. Testifying as the head of the Jewish Agency, Chaim Weizmann stated that the Jewish problem was that of "homelessness," because there were 6,000,000 unwanted European Jews. A certificate for entry to Palestine, he added, was a "certificate for freedom."⁴⁴ The Arab Higher Committee, which was founded by the mufti of Jerusalem in April 1936, initially boycotted the Peel Commission, but later changed its position under pressure from Arab governments. In a memorandum submitted to the commission, the Arabs defined their objectives as "an end to the Jewish immigration and the termination of the mandate," to be followed by the establishment of a national, i.e., Arab government.⁴⁵

In July 1937 the Peel Commission issued a report recommending the partition of Palestine, creating a Jewish state in the north and the coastal areas, and an Arab state in the majority of the country, extending from the Lower Galilee southward to the Gulf of Aqaba. The plan would also grant Britain a mandate over an area stretching from Jerusalem to Jaffa on the Mediterranean coast. Bethlehem, Nazareth, and Haifa would also be under British control.⁴⁶

Jewish reaction to the Peel Report was mixed. Although the idea of a Jewish state, albeit small, was received with satisfaction by Jewish moderates, several segments of the Yishuv accused Britain of trying to reduce the national home into a ghetto. The twentieth Zionist Congress, which met in the summer of 1937, turned down the plan but accepted the principle of partition. The Palestinian Arabs rejected the idea of partition out of hand and demanded Britain's withdrawal from Palestine and an end to Jewish immigration. Similar rejection of the British plan came from the Arab countries, with the exception of Transjordan, which tried unsuccessfully to convince the other Arabs to study the partition plan. As a result of Arab objections, a number of clashes occurred in August 1937 between Arab and British forces. At a conference convened in Syria a month later, delegates from four Arab countries declared Palestine an indivisible part of the Arab nation and rejected any compromise based on the recognition of national rights for the Jews.⁴⁷

Faced with mounting Arab violence, Britain dispatched another commission to Palestine, headed by Sir John Woodhead, to reexamine the issue of partition. The committee held its hearings in the shadow of growing Nazi persecution of German and Austrian Jews, adding weight to the Zionist arguments for a homeland. On the other hand, the conflict with the Axis powers in Europe made it necessary for Britain to seek the friendship of the Arab nations. As a result, the British retreated from the idea of partition, and instead adopted the Woodhead Commission's recommendation to establish two states linked together, with each one deprived of economic sovereignty. Finally, Britain abandoned the idea of partition altogether.⁴⁸

After the plan to divide Palestine was discarded, in February 1939 Britain attempted to bring the Jews and Arabs together at a roundtable conference to attain a mutually acceptable solution. But following the British refusal to admit 10,000 Jewish children from Europe, and their acceptance of the Arab states as parties to the negotiations, Jewish sentiment against participating in the conference intensified. The Arabs, for their part, refused to sit face-to-face with Jewish representatives. In March of that same year, compelled to hold separate meetings with each side, the British proposed turning Palestine into an independent state that would be linked to Britain by a treaty. Although both Arabs and Jews rejected the plan, Britain declared its intention to unilaterally implement it. The League of Nations challenged this plan, stating that it was a deviation from the provisions of the mandate. The debate was interrupted by the outbreak of World War II, and instead of a resolution, Britain maintained its policy of restricting Jewish immigration and land purchases.

The breakdown of Britain's commitment to the Zionist cause brought about an escalation in the activities of the Jewish extremist groups, Stern and Irgun, against British targets. While the main Jewish military force, the Hagana, directed its operations in defending against Arab attacks, Irgun and Stern embarked on an aggressive policy of violence aimed at driving the British out of Palestine. These groups also simultaneously engaged in fierce clashes with the Arabs, resulting in numerous deaths on both sides. The British sought to quell violence and resistance by capturing members of opposition groups, particularly those of the Irgun and Stern. Cooperation between British authorities and the more moderate Jewish organizations gradually came to a halt in the aftermath of the 1939 White Paper. Jewish opposition to restrictions on immigration, particularly as Jewish refugees were fleeing Nazi-occupied Europe, grew into a revolt. The Hagana abandonded its policy of working with the government and became an underground force. In defiance of British policy, a large-scale operation was launched to smuggle immigrants by boat. Those captured by the British were detained and turned back. As resistance to British rule increased, the government imposed collective punitive measures, such as curfews and mass arrests of its leaders, on the entire Jewish community.[49] These measures turned the operations of the Irgun and Stern bands into anti-British guerilla warfare. British military installations were blown up, and members of the security forces were abducted and hanged.[50] The British retaliated by executing members of the Jewish groups.

Relations between the mandate government and the Arab population were equally strained. Arab attacks on British institutions and personnel were met with harsh retribution. The Arab Higher Committee was outlawed, and prominent leaders such as the mufti of Jerusalem, were either imprisoned or expelled. The Arab uprising continued in full force until the outbreak of World War II, when the region became preoccupied with the German advance into North Africa and the threat it posed to the Middle East.[51]

During the final years of the mandate, a growing militancy became apparent not only among Jewish leaders in Palestine, but among Zionists in the United States as well. The leadership had passed from the diplomat, Chaim Weizmann, to the charismatic pragmatist, David Ben-Gurion, who was head of the Labor camp and chairman of the Jewish Agency. This new militancy was apparent at the Biltmore Conference that took place in New York in May 1942, when a call was issued to repeal the 1939 White Paper and return to what the Jewish leaders saw as the original framework of the Balfour Declaration. The delegates concluded with a demand that "Palestine be established as a Jewish commonwealth integrated in the structure of the new democratic world."[52] In Palestine, the breakdown of relations with the mandate government was imminent. The appointment of Ernest Bevin, considered anti-Zionist, as foreign secretary of Britain, only accelerated this process.[53]

On the international front, a massive campaign was launched against the British restrictions on Jewish immigration. The misery of the refugees surviving the Nazi death camps who were denied entrance to Palestine made a powerful impression in Western countries. Under U.S. President Harry Truman, who demanded the admission of 100,000 Jews into Palestine, the United States had become an active ally of Zionism. In December 1945, the U.S. Congress passed a resolution recommending free immigration to develop Palestine in the direction of Jewish statehood. At the same time, the United States and several other countries refused to open their doors to Jewish refugees.

In response to mounting criticism, Britain proposed in December 1945 the formation of an Anglo-American committee to study the Palestine problem. The committee deliberated under the shadow of the Nazi Holocaust in Europe and the inability of Britain to maintain law and order in Palestine. In a report presented in April 1946, the committee recommended the repeal of the 1939 White Paper, the admission of 100,000 Jewish refugees, and the establishment of a UN trusteeship. After stating that "Jew shall not dominate Arab and Arab shall not dominate Jew," the committee concluded that "Palestine shall be neither a Jewish state nor an Arab state."[54]

While President Truman was satisfied with the proposed relaxation of the immigration ban, Britain regarded the recommendations as a single package, requiring both the dismantling of Arab and Jewish military organizations and a large American financial contribution. The Jewish reaction was negative, particularly in Palestine, where a quasi-government headed by Ben-Gurion had already been instituted. The Arabs rejected the plan as well, and refused to attend an exploratory conference in London later that year. To represent the Palestinians, Arab delegates from several Arab countries took part in the discussions. This change in representation underscored the fact that Arab governments had assumed responsibility for the Palestine issue since the establishment of the Arab League in 1945.[55] Although Jewish leaders had also officially boycotted the London conference, they did hold discussions with Foreign Secretary Ernest Bevin, who was emerging as a strong opponent of the idea of a Jewish state in Palestine.[56]

To break the diplomatic deadlock, the United States and Britain formed another joint committee in July 1946. Under consideration was the Morrison Plan, a British proposal that called for the division of Palestine into two autonomous regions, with Britain retaining its status as the highest authority in the land. Taking into account Jewish aspirations for statehood, which had the sympathy of many non-Jewish Americans, President Truman rejected the Morrison Plan. In a statement in October 1946, Truman expressed his belief that an independent Jewish state in part of Palestine "would command the support of public opinion in the United States."[57] The Arabs, who also rejected the British plan, submitted their own proposal, based on the establishment of an independent Palestine and a "total ban on immigration."[58]

The Establishment of Israel

By early 1947, the impasse in Palestine indicated a failure on the part of Britain to bridge the gap between Arabs and Jews. There was virtually a civil war in Palestine, with British troops caught in the middle, often on the receiving end of violence. Britain's international reputation was tainted by the sight of tens of thousands of Jewish refugees who had survived the Nazi horrors only to be turned back or detained behind barbed wire. Pressure was mounting from the United States, whose financial assistance was needed to rebuild the postwar economy of Britain. With no solution in sight, the British government conceded its inability to cope with the situation and in April 1947 asked the United Nations to include Palestine in the agenda of the upcoming session of the General Assembly. In response, a commission of inquiry, which came to be known as UNSCOP (United Nations Special Committee on Palestine), was chosen from eleven countries that were not permanently represented at the Security Council.[59]

The commission recognized the Jewish Agency on the one hand, and the Arab Higher Committee on the other, as representatives of the Palestinian population. But in contrast to the elaborate testimony submitted by the Zionist delegation,[60] the Arab Higher Committee, which received its directives from the exiled mufti, Amin al-Husseini, boycotted UNSCOP and threatened violence.[61] Representatives of the Arab League were to speak for the Palestinians.[62]

In its report of August 1947, UNSCOP unanimously recommended the termination of the British Mandate, an immediate solution to the Jew-

ish refugee problem, and preservation of the holy places in Jerusalem, with
a guarantee of free access. But the commission was divided on the question
of the political future of Palestine. A majority (Canada, Czechoslovakia,
Guatemala, the Netherlands, Peru, Sweden, and Uruguay, with Australia
abstaining) suggested partition; a minority (India, Iran, and Yugoslavia)
proposed a federation between an Arab canton and a Jewish one, with
Jerusalem as the capital.[63] Under the partition plan, the Arabs would receive the western Galilee, the central region (excluding Jerusalem) from
Nazareth to Beersheba, and the coastal strip from Ashdod to the Egyptian
border. The rest of Palestine, including the whole Negev desert, was allocated to the Jews. Jerusalem was to be internationalized. The two states
would be linked by an economic union, with the Jews providing a subsidy
for the Arab state. For an interim period of two years, the British administration would remain in Palestine under the supervision of the United
Nations. During that time, Jewish immigration would be subject to a
quota, allowing a total of 150,000 immigrants in the first two years and
60,000 per year thereafter.[64]

   With some reservations, the reaction of the Jews was favorable. Although they were dissatisfied with the division of the territory, Jewish
leaders saw two positive elements in the report; independence and a steady
flow of immigrants. The Arabs expressed dismay and took to the streets to
demonstrate against partition. The Arab Higher Committee in Palestine
issued a statement condemning the recommendations of UNSCOP. It
called upon Arabs to volunteer for a *jihad* (holy war), to thwart by force
any attempt to give part of Palestine to the Jews.[65]

   The U.S. administration was divided on the issue of partition. Although President Truman had a pro-Zionist record, the State Department
opposed the idea of a Jewish state that was unacceptable to the Arabs. As
the UN debate over the UNSCOP proposal approached, pressure on the
White House from prominent American Jews and from Democratic and
Republican leaders increased. There was concern that Truman might lose
the 1948 election if he failed to support a Jewish state. Loy Henderson,
head of the State Department's Middle East desk, wrote to former Secretary of State Dean Rusk that "The Zionists had almost the full support of
the Congress, the U.S. media, and most of the American people."[66] Henderson, himself, opposed a Jewish state, and had to defend his views,
which were those of the State Department, before the president and senior
White House aides.[67] In October 1947, at the United Nations, the United
States announced its position in favor of the partition plan.[68] Britain, on
the other hand, rejected the plan and informed the UN Subcommittee on
Partition that it did not intend to make its troops in Palestine available to
enforce the partition plan. The Russian UN delegate proclaimed his country's support for partition. In the aftermath of Jewish suffering in Europe,
he declared that "It would not be just to deny the Jewish people the right

to fulfill their desire. The creation of the Jewish state is a wholly mature and urgent problem."[69]

The Arab ambassadors to the United Nations made it clear that their governments would not allow the creation of a Jewish state in Palestine. This intransigent position was summarized in a statement by the Iraqi representative, Fadil al-Jamali, who declared that "The Arabs will reject partition in any form. They will oppose and fight it sooner or later, because the Arab World cannot compromise in the matter of a Jewish state, regardless of its shape or size. The Arabs have never been so united on any issue."[70]

In November 1947, with the United States, the Soviet bloc, and France voting in favor, and Britain abstaining, the UN General Assembly approved the partition of Palestine into an Arab state and a Jewish state.[71] A last-minute attempt by the Arab countries to introduce a proposal favoring a federated state was defeated by a joint American-Soviet demand that a vote on the partition plan be taken first. The implementation of the partition plan, however, was far less certain. The violent reaction of the Arabs and the refusal of Britain to keep its troops in Palestine to guarantee a peaceful transition cast a shadow of a doubt at the United Nations. The United States, which had already imposed an arms embargo on the area and declared its unwillingness to send military forces to carry out the UN resolution, proposed the establishment of a temporary trusteeship. Although some Jewish leaders were inclined to support trusteeship because of the danger of war, the majority, under the leadership of Ben-Gurion, feared a renewed UN debate, and insisted on unilaterally proclaiming Jewish statehood.[72] Uncertain about their ability to survive, the 650,000 Jews[73] in Palestine declared their independence on May 14, 1948, a few hours after the last British soldiers left the country.[74] A provisional government was immediately installed, with Ben-Gurion as the premier and Moshe Shertock (Sharett) as foreign minister.[75] Shortly thereafter, the state of Israel was recognized by the United States and the Soviet Union.

The War of 1948

The war in which Israel gained its independence evolved in two phases: The first phase lasted from the partition resolution of November 1947 to the British withdrawal in May 1948, and the second phase, from Israel's declaration of independence to the signing of the armistice agreements in July 1949. During the first period, fighting escalated from guerrilla warfare to full-scale battles between the forces of the Yishuv and Arab groups supported by volunteers from abroad. In the second phase, the war took place between Israel's newly organized army and the invading regular armies of several Arab countries.

In the final months of the British Mandate, as it became evident that

Britain was abdicating, each side of the conflict tried to strengthen its military position. The Arabs claimed that the British forces were evacuating strategic places and handing them over to the Jews.[76] The Jews, on the other hand, complained about the uninterrupted flow of men and materiel from across the borders, while their own supply lines were limited to the British-controlled sea routes.[77] The total Jewish force, including reserves, was 15,000 fighters and 30,000 guards.[78] The latter, which included large numbers of women, were confined to the defense of Jewish towns and rural settlements. The Arab commanders had at their disposal several thousand fighters, of whom the best-trained was the 2,000-strong "Army of Salvation," backed by a total of 35,000 troops from the armies of Syria, Lebanon, Jordan, Iraq, and Egypt. By all accounts, with total aerial and naval superiority, the balance of power seemed to favor the Arabs.[79]

Soon after the vote on the partition plan, the Arabs launched a wide-scale offensive aimed at cutting off roads and destroying Jewish settlements, particularly those built in predominantly Arab areas. Jewish residents in mixed cities also came under heavy attack. In Jerusalem, the Jewish commercial center was burned down; Ben-Yehuda Street, located in the heart of the city, was bombed; and the administrative complex of the semi-governmental Jewish Agency was heavily damaged in an explosion. Jerusalem's Jewish neighborhoods were besieged and shelled, and the city was eventually cut off when the only access road to the coastal region was blocked. The Arabs achieved a major victory when Jordanian forces, under the Jerusalem district commander, Abdullah al-Tal, captured and destroyed the Gush Etzion settlements near Jerusalem.[80] In the north, settlements were attacked by Syrian officer Fawzi al-Qawuqji's "Army of Salvation," supported by Syrian and Iraqi troops.

A Jewish counterattack began two months before the British withdrawal. The intention was to break the siege of Jerusalem and take over areas across the land that were being evacuated by the British forces. In the ensuing battle for Jerusalem, Jewish forces cut an alternative road across the mountainous terrain to avert fighting in the strategic hills that controlled access to the main highway. Jewish forces scored a significant victory at that time when two high-ranking Arab commanders were killed. The death of Abdel-Qader al-Husseini, a cousin of the mufti, dealt a particularly painful blow to Arab morale.[81] Throughout Palestine, one city after another fell into Jewish hands. In the six weeks that preceded the British withdrawal, Jews took control of Haifa, Jaffa, Tiberia, Safed, and nearly a hundred Arab villages.

The morning after Israel declared its independence, the armies of Lebanon, Syria, Iraq, Jordan, and Egypt invaded Palestine. According to a plan that had been worked out in April 1948, the first four armies were to cut off Jewish access to the sea by taking over the coastal area, including the vital port of Haifa and the oil refineries. The Egyptian army was to pin down large Jewish forces protecting Tel Aviv. In the final stage of the plan, the armies would divide Palestine horizontally north of Tel Aviv.[82]

In the north, Syrians attacked by shelling settlements in the Jordan Valley and bombing them from the air. They succeeded in conquering Israeli villages south of the Sea of Galilee, but their advance was halted by a counterattack. The Iraqis operated in the area between Nazareth and Nablus, in close proximity to the British-trained Jordanian Legion. Engaging Israeli forces in heavy battles, the Egyptians moved from the south toward Tel Aviv, coming within twenty miles of the city. Other Egyptian troops advanced toward Jerusalem and took over a kibbutz in the outskirts of the city. The Jordanian Legion, under the command of Sir John Glubb, moved through Jericho and attacked Jerusalem and the surrounding area, unleashing some of the heaviest battles of the war. With their sector of Jerusalem under siege, the Jews sent reinforcements to defend the Jewish Quarter of the Old City, but failed to hold out. Following their surrender, the residents of the ancient quarter evacuated their neighborhood and moved to the New City outside the walls.[83]

While battles were raging in Palestine, efforts were made at the United Nations to stop the bloodshed. Count Folke Bernadotte of Sweden was dispatched to the area to serve as a mediator in the conflict. On June 11, 1948, a four-week cease-fire was declared, but with no progress for peace in sight. The Israelis took advantage of the lull in the fighting to consolidate their forces. Pre-state military groups were reorganized to create the Israel Defense Forces, administered under Ben-Gurion's tight control.[84] Despite the embargo, both sides managed to bring in fresh supplies and new military equipment.[85] In a deal worked out with the Soviets, Israel received weapons from Czechoslovakia.[86]

The attempts at diplomacy failed and fighting resumed with even greater intensity. In a period of ten days, Israeli forces went on the offensive against the Jordanian Legion, conquering the Arab cities of Ramla and Lod (containing the country's primary airport), and opening the road to Jerusalem. The capture of Nazareth of the Galilee forced Qawuqji, who led the only remaining force of Palestinian Arabs, to retreat closer to the Syrian border. The Egyptians were pushed out of Jerusalem and withdrew to the south.

At the United Nations, Bernadotte continued his diplomatic efforts and pushed for a second cease-fire, ordered by the Security Council on July 15.[87] Having achieved the compliance of all sides, despite some serious truce violations, Bernadotte called for the immediate demilitarization of Jerusalem and submitted a proposal to resolve the dispute by modifying the partition plan. His ideas for modification consisted of giving the Negev desert to the Arabs and the Galilee to Israel, providing for the use of

Lod airport and the Haifa harbor by both parties, internationalizing Jerusalem and Bethlehem, and allowing Arab refugees displaced by the war to return to Palestine. But before Bernadotte's suggestions could even be discussed, he and a French aide were assassinated during a visit to Jerusalem in September 1948. Although the perpetrators were never caught, they were assumed to be members of the Stern organization.[88]

The cease-fire broke down when a skirmish erupted on October 15 between Egyptian and Israeli forces in the Negev. The Israelis launched a major offensive and succeeded in capturing Beersheba and encircling an Egyptian division nearby.[89] By the time the Security Council ordered another cease-fire five days later, the Jordanian Legion had replaced the remaining Egyptians, who were cut off south of Jerusalem. Meanwhile, the Israelis expanded their control west of the city. As the United Nations debated the territorial issues, fighting continued on and off on all fronts. In the north, the remaining forces of Qawuqji's "Army of Salvation" were pushed back across the border, and several Lebanese villages fell into Israeli hands. Egyptian preparations for an armored offensive in the south were foiled by an Israeli attack that drove them out of the Negev and ended with the capture of El-Arish inside Egypt. In March 1949, Israeli forces swept through the Negev and reached the Gulf of Aqaba, where they established the port city of Eilat.

As the Israelis increasingly gained the upper hand, the Arab countries agreed to negotiate a truce under the auspices of the United Nations. With American representative Ralph Bunche serving as a mediator at the armistice negotiations in Rhodes, the neighboring countries separately signed permanent cease-fire agreements with Israel. Syria was the last Arab country to sign in March 1949. A Security Council resolution in August 1949 called on the parties to safeguard the provisions of the cease-fire as a prelude to permanent peace. It also called for the establishment of a team of UN observers with headquarters in Jerusalem to guarantee compliance by all signatories. Joint armistice commissions were also set up to deal with bilateral issues between Israel and the other signatories to the agreements.[90]

In the following years, the United Nations continued its involvement with the Arab-Israeli dispute, with very few positive results. The Conciliation Commission, established to help negotiate a permanent peace, failed to bring the Arabs and Israelis together. Territorial issues, the fate of the refugees, and the refusal of the Arabs to recognize Israel were never resolved at the United Nations. The impasse grew worse when member states aligned themselves in blocs that reflected the cold war between the major powers.

For the Jews, the outcome of the 1948 war was the establishment of their state and its survival in the face of a much greater power. The greatest priority was the admission of the European Jewish refugees who had been denied entry by British authorities.[91] At the end of the 1940s, Jews were also immigrating from Arab and Muslim countries, adding credence to the Zionist claim that Palestine was the only place where Jews could live in safety. When the cease-fire lines were recognized by all signatory parties as de facto boundaries, Israel gained 20 percent more land than originally allocated in the partition plan. Much of that land had belonged to Arabs who fled during the war, and was distributed among Israeli farming settlements. Jewish squatters, some of whom were refugees from Arab countries, moved into abandoned Arab homes and towns.

When Israel was admitted to the United Nations in 1949 and moved to establish diplomatic relations with most countries, international legitimacy became a matter of fact. Israel did not, however, win the recognition of the Arab nations. The country was not only boycotted politically and economically by the surrounding Arabs, but was also vulnerable militarily to its neighbors. Along the 600-mile border, towns and settlements were within the reach of Arab gunners and infiltrators. With only a corridor to Jerusalem and a width of nine miles near Netanya, the country could have easily been divided by an invading force. In the south, where the port of Eilat was the only outlet, the Egyptians controlled freedom of passage. Added to this were the enormous problems of rebuilding a shattered economy, absorbing hundreds of thousands of immigrants, and maintaining a sufficient army for defense.

The Arab countries that invaded Palestine made no gains, with the exception of Jordan. When the war ended, the Jordanian Legion, under British command, was in control of the West Bank of the Jordan River and the Old City of Jerusalem. Rather than establish an autonomous Palestinian Arab entity, King Abdullah opted to annex the territory adjacent to Jordan that had not been taken by Israel. The remaining area, the Gaza Strip on the southern coast, was retained by Egypt without a clear definition of its status. The Jordanian takeover of the West Bank was initiated in a conference in Jericho in December 1948, where Palestinian leaders declared the unification of Palestine with Jordan and asked Abdullah to be king of the united country. After Abdullah " thankfully accepted," he informed the Arab League of the unification.[92] The Jordanian-Palestinian joint parliament formally annexed the West Bank and granted its residents Jordanian citizenship.

To secure his grip on parts of Palestine, the Jordanian monarch negotiated with the Jews before the end of the mandate.[93] In an ongoing dialogue with Israeli leaders, including Moshe Shertock and Golda Meir (then Meyerson),[94] Abdullah sought to reach a peace agreement with Israel in exchange for recognition of Jordan's sovereignty over the Arab parts of Palestine and a port on the Mediterranean Sea.[95] Most importantly,

Abdullah wanted East Jerusalem with its Muslim holy shrines. His desire to occupy the Holy City motivated the king to side with the Israelis in opposing an international rule in Jerusalem. But before the talks with Israel could reach a successful conclusion, Abdullah was assassinated in July 1951, during the Friday prayer at the al-Aqsa Mosque in Jerusalem.[96] The king was succeeded by his son, Talal, who was soon replaced, due to Talal's mental illness, by his grandson, Hussein.

Once the war rhetoric and jubilation over imaginary victories died down, the Arabs realized that they had lost Palestine.[97] The leadership had failed to understand the commitment of the Jews to the goals of Zionism and had missed many chances for compromise. When the conflict developed into a full-scale war between Israel and the Arab countries, it became clear that the Palestinian Arabs no longer controlled their fate. Their "saviors," the Arab armies, proved ineffective in confronting Israel's war machine and the dedication of the Jews. Despite attempts by Arab countries to blame the defeat on "Jewish deception" and "imperialist double-crossing," the outcome proved most disastrous for Palestinian Arabs. Not only were they unable to exercise the right of self-determination granted to them under the partition plan, they had also lost most of their land.

In the wake of the 1948 war Palestinian Arab society was shattered, not only politically and economically, but in very real human terms. Mass departure from territory captured by the Jews represented the most devastating aspect of their defeat. One of the controversial points in Bernadotte's plan was the right of the Arab refugees to return to their homes. It was estimated that by August 1948, close to half a million Arabs had already left the Israeli-held territory, with only about 70,000 remaining within the state's borders.[98] Arabs and Israelis disagree on the circumstances under which the mass exodus of the Palestinian Arabs occurred. The Israelis claim that they left voluntarily (sometimes at the urging of their leaders and despite pleas to stay); the Arabs contend that refugees were expelled by the Jews, who often used terroristic methods to force them to leave.[99] Regardless of the reasons why the Arabs had left, the Israelis were pleased and refused to allow them to return.[100] Citing national security and demographic considerations,[101] Israel rejected a UN resolution to repatriate refugees, who numbered, by the end of the war, nearly three-quarters of a million.[102] The refugees were scattered in camps in neighboring countries, on the West Bank, and in the Gaza Strip. Aid from the international community has been provided by the UN Relief and Works Agency (UNRWA). Palestinians did not take part in the events that took place in the Middle East between 1949 and the 1967 Six-Day War. The Jordanians kept them under tight control and violently suppressed any expression of Palestinian nationalism. The establishment of Ahmad Shuqeiri's "Palestine Liberation Army" in the Gaza Strip, destroyed in a matter of hours by the Israelis in 1967, did not alter the balance of power in favor of the Palestinians.

The Arab-Israeli Wars, 1956–1973

Contrary to expectations, the armistice agreements of 1949 did not serve as a prelude to peace. Technically, a state of war between Israel and the Arab countries continued to exist. The plight of the Arab refugees, who were neither taken back by Israel nor absorbed by the host countries, kept the dispute on the agenda of the international community while deepening the animosity of the Arab world toward the Jewish state. Jewish hope that Arab rulers who maintained close ties with the West might show flexibility and settle the conflict with Israel peacefully remained unfulfilled as a series of coups toppled pro-Western regimes.[103] In the military coups in Egypt in 1952 and in Iraq in 1958, Western-oriented monarchies were overthrown. Gamal Abdul-Nasser's rise to power in Egypt increased anti-Western tendencies in the Arab world. Nasser's political ideology, developed in the aftermath of the defeat in Palestine and spelled out in his book, *Falsafat al-Thawra* (*The Philosophy of the Revolution*), was saturated with hostility toward the West, particularly Britain, and also toward Israel.

A conflict that was initially a dispute over land between the Arabs of Palestine and the Jewish immigrants became, for many Arabs, a confrontation between them and Western imperialism represented by its creation, Israel. The Arab people, inflamed by Nasser's calls for pan-Arabism, saw Israel as an agent of the West, planted in their midst as part of an imperialistic conspiracy to dominate the region.[104] Israel's collaboration with Britain and France in attacking Egypt in 1956 only strengthened that conviction. The Soviet Union, by refusing to recognize Israel and supplying an abundance of arms to the new Arab regimes, succeeded in establishing a foothold in the oil-rich Middle East. By allying with the Arabs, the Russians managed to exploit the Arab-Israeli conflict to undermine Western interests.[105] As the U.S. Eisenhower administration assembled the Baghdad Pact alignment against the Communist bloc, the region was drawn deeper into the East-West rivalry of the cold war.

From 1950 to 1956, at a time when Israel was absorbing immigrants and expanding the economy, numerous clashes occurred with the neighboring countries. Infiltrations by Arabs from Syria and Jordan, some of which resulted in heavy casualties among civilians, led to massive Israeli retaliations. A dispute with Syria over water resources, caused by Israel's drying the Hula swamps and building a national water network, nearly caused a war between the two countries. The UN team of observers, whose task was to assure compliance with the terms of the armistice agreements, was ineffective in putting an end to border clashes. The Security Council debated the situation numerous times, often condemning Israel for attacks the Israelis saw as acts of legitimate self-defense. The Middle East was once more moving toward war, with Egypt emerging as Israel's main antagonist.

Ben-Gurion discounted statements by Nasser about possible recognition of Israel under certain conditions;[106] he was convinced that Egypt, heavily armed with advanced Soviet weapons, was becoming a serious threat to Israel's survival. Nasser's call for pan-Arab nationalism, along with his drive to unite the Arab countries against Israel, [107] strengthened the belief among Israeli strategists that he had to be dealt with by force, and that a preemptive strike against Egypt was inevitably necessary.[108] Frequent attacks on Israeli highways and civilian settlements by Egyptian-controlled *fedayeen* infiltrators, coupled with large-scale border clashes, heightened the tension between the two countries. On the diplomatic front, Israel was trying unsuccessfully to achieve the implementation of a Security Council resolution guaranteeing free passage in the Suez Canal.[109] In July 1956 Nasser nationalized the Suez Canal and demanded the evacuation of British military bases near the waterway, a matter which concerned Israel. France, which shared Britain's strategic interests in the Suez Canal, also was annoyed by Nasser's support of the Algerian revolt against French rule. As Israel was assessing the threat of a mutual defense treaty signed by Egypt, Jordan, and Syria, Nasser declared a blockade of the Israeli port of Eilat on the Gulf of Aqaba and escalated his threats against the Jewish state.

These factors brought together Britain, France, and Israel in a scheme to topple Nasser by military means.[110] In accordance with the plan, Israel sent her army across the southern cease-fire line on October 29, 1956, sweeping through the Gaza Strip and the Sinai Peninsula in four days. An infantry brigade marched south and took over Sharm al-Sheikh, overlooking the Straits of Tiran, thus lifting the blockade on the port of Eilat. By the time Israeli forces defeated the Egyptian army and reached the canal, Britain and France had bombed Egyptian airfields and landed troops near the waterway, under the pretext of protecting it from the combatants.

International reaction to the operation was swift and harsh. Condemnation came not only from the Soviet bloc and the nonaligned camp, but from the Eisenhower administration as well. Secretary of State John Foster Dulles was particularly dismayed by the actions of the two NATO members, Britain and France, at a time when he was trying to lure the Arabs into joining anti-Communist alliances. The Russians, while extending full diplomatic support to Egypt, declined to intervene militarily for fear of risking a global war. Likewise, Nasser's allies, Jordan and Syria, failed to honor their military pact with Egypt, preferring to stay on the sidelines. In the end, it was public opinion and heavy pressure from President

Dwight Eisenhower that brought about the withdrawal of the British and French forces, who had performed poorly anyway. For the Israelis, the American president reserved the heavy stick of economic sanctions, a threat that forced Ben-Gurion to withdraw from the Sinai and the Gaza Strip in 1957. In return, the United States committed itself to guaranteeing freedom of navigation in international waterways, including the Gulf of Aqaba. Additionally, to serve as a buffer between Egypt and Israel and to prevent incursions of the fedayeen, the United Nations stationed an emergency force in the Sinai and the Gaza area.

The indecisive conclusion of the Sinai war, so far as the Israelis were concerned, planted the seeds for the next battle. They soon realized that the defeat had not led to Nasser's downfall, but actually had increased his stature both internally and in the Arab world, because he had stood up to an attack by two major European powers. Amid one government crisis after another, Israeli leaders apprehensively watched developments in the Middle East. In July 1958, the Iraqi royal family was murdered in a bloody military coup led by Abdul-Karim Qassem, who established a revolutionary regime. Soon after, as the Soviets achieved a foothold in Iraq, Britain sent troops to Jordan to protect King Hussein from the possibility of a similar coup attempt. In Lebanon, the outbreak of civil war prompted the United States to land marines to prevent the collapse of the predominantly Christian government.[111] It was widely believed that Nasser was the instigator of the unrest in the region, in an attempt to bring down what he considered reactionary Arab regimes in order to fulfill his revolutionary ideas.[112] The rise of the socialist Ba'ath party in Syria brought about a unification with Egypt; the two countries merged in February 1958 under the name United Arab Republic (UAR).[113]

Despite the political turmoil in the region and Nasser's inflammatory rhetoric against Israel, the Egyptian-Israeli border remained relatively quiet. But the tension had merely shifted to the Jordanian, and even more, to the Syrian fronts. Israel carried out major retaliatory operations against Jordan in May and September of 1965, destroying several Jordanian installations and training bases belonging to the newly established Fatah Palestinian group.[114] In the north, from their dominant positions on the Golan Heights, Syrian gunners frequently shelled the Israeli settlements below, and fishermen in the Sea of Galilee came under fire as well. The Israeli air force, often used to carry out reprisals, was unable to inflict significant damage on the Syrians because of the formidable trenches and fortifications that they had built on the plateau. But in a dispute over water, to prevent Syria from diverting the sources of the Jordan River, Israel did utilize the air force effectively in November 1964.[115]

The friction on the Syrian border eventually triggered a chain of events that led to the Six-Day War of 1967. The continued Syrian shelling of Israeli farming settlements, as well as Syrian-backed infiltrations from Jordan and Lebanon, prompted Israel to send its air force to attack artillery positions in Syria in April 1967. In the ensuing dogfight with Russian-made Syrian MIGs, the Israeli pilots shot down six Syrian planes. The incident was followed by a warning from Israeli Chief of Staff Yitzhak Rabin that the Syrian regime would be at risk if attacks on Israel continued.

The Syrians immediately sought help from the Soviets—their military suppliers—and from Egypt. To exploit the propaganda benefit of appearing as protectors of the Arabs, the Russians heightened the tension by claiming that an Israeli attack on Syria was imminent. They sent a delegation to Cairo on May 13 to warn Nasser about a massive Israeli buildup along the Syrian border, but the Soviet ambassador in Tel Aviv refused an invitation from Prime Minster Levi Eshkol to tour the area and see that the allegations were false.[116] The Syrian request for help from Nasser came as he was experiencing serious difficulties. His troops had been bogged down in a long war in the Yemen, supporting a revolution against the ruling imam. Egypt's intervention provoked the animosity of Saudi Arabia, which was supporting the royal family in the five-year tribal war. Nasser's relations with King Hussein of Jordan, whom he labeled "a slave of the imperialists and a prostitute," were at a low point. Perhaps to regain his prestige, particularly after the demise of the UAR, and to pull his army out of the quagmire in Yemen, Nasser took a number of miscalculated steps that set in motion a series of events that made war inevitable.

In response to Syria's appeal, Egypt declared a state of alert on May 16, and warned Israel against launching an attack on her ally.[117] Two days later, Egyptian troops marched through the streets of Cairo on their way to the Sinai, triggering a war hysteria that soon engulfed the whole Arab world. On May 17, Nasser demanded the withdrawal of the international peacekeeping force from the Sinai. Although they had been stationed by UN action in 1957, the troops were promptly pulled out by Secretary General U Thant, who did not consult the Security Council. The UN positions in the Gaza Strip were immediately taken over by the growing group that called itself the Palestine Liberation Army, under the command of Ahmad Shuqeiri. By May 20, more than 100,000 Egyptian troops and 1,000 tanks had crossed the Sinai, deploying on Israel's border.[118] To counter the massive concentration of forces, Israel reacted by mobilizing military reserves. Then, ignoring repeated Israeli warnings that the closure of the Straits of Tiran would be considered *casus belli,* Nasser declared on May 22 that the waterway was closed to Israeli shipping, thus reinstating the blockade on Eilat.[119]

Against the background of mass demonstrations in Egypt urging war with Israel, the closure of the straits convinced Israeli leaders and others around the world that the crisis was real. U.S. President Lyndon B. Johnson declared the Egyptian act "illegal and potentially disastrous to the cause of peace."[120] Intense diplomatic activity began in Israel and in the United States to try to solve the crisis by peaceful means. At the urging of the American administration, the Israelis refrained from military action and sent Foreign Minister Abba Eban to Western capitals to seek support, but he returned home empty-handed. He discovered that even France, Israel's main ally, had changed its Middle East policy under President Charles de Gaulle and no longer supported Israel.[121] At the United Nations, the Soviets employed delay tactics to prevent an intervention by the international body to lift the blockade and ease the tension. Following the failure of President Johnson to mobilize an international maritime force, members of the U.S. Congress objected to a unilateral American move.[122] The U.S. Sixth Fleet in the Mediterranean and the NATO command in Europe were put on a state of alert to handle developments that might involve the Soviets.

As Israel mobilized and waited for a solution to the crisis, concern arose that Prime Minister Levi Eshkol was too weak to handle the situation decisively. To boost public morale, Eshkol appointed Moshe Dayan, army chief of staff in the 1956 war, as minister of defense. Menachem Begin, leader of the right-wing opposition, was invited to join the Labor cabinet as minister without portfolio. In Cairo, Nasser added fuel to the war hysteria by declaring in a speech before the Arab Trade Union on May 22 that the destruction of Israel was the ultimate goal. His statement was backed by a combined Arab force of a quarter of a million men, 2,000 tanks, and 700 aircraft.[123] The mood in Israel turned gloomier when King Hussein flew to Cairo, reconciled his feud with Nasser, and on May 30 signed a defense pact that placed the Jordanian army under Egyptian command. The king returned to Amman to a hero's welcome, accompanied by the Egyptian joint commander, Abdul-Mun'im Riyad, and by Ahmad Shuqeiri, the leader of the Palestine Liberation Organization, who had been beating the drums of war since the crisis began.[124]

A final meeting between Foreign Minister Abba Eban and President Johnson on May 26 convinced the Israelis that the United States was unwilling to offer anything but good advice.[125] Pressure mounted on the Israeli cabinet to launch an immediate, preemptive strike, to deny the joint Arab command the time it needed to consolidate its forces and complete the encirclement of Israel.[126] As the Israeli public believed that an impending Arab attack was imminent, it was not surprised when an official communiqué announced on June 5 that "Israeli forces were engaged in a battle with Egyptian units that were moving toward Israel."[127] In fact, Israel had already launched a massive air strike that almost completely destroyed the Egyptian air force while most of it was still on the ground.[128] In a three-pronged attack, Israeli troops punched through Egyptian lines in the Gaza

Strip and the Sinai. With air supremacy guaranteed, they reached the banks of the Suez Canal on June 8, on their way destroying or capturing Egyptian armor and infantry divisions. In a last-minute operation, the Egyptians sank several ships to prevent passage through the canal.

To avoid a wider conflict, particularly in Jerusalem, her "soft belly," Israel had sent messages to King Hussein through diplomatic channels, assuring him that it had no hostile intentions against Jordan. The United States tried to persuade the king not to join the fighting, but he entered the conflict, citing moral obligations as well as commitments under a pan-Arab military pact.[129] Dean Rusk considered that a grave mistake: "I think we could have gotten the Israelis to stay their hand, but Hussein insisted on getting into it . . . it certainly was not in Jordan's interest to attack Israel, then lose the West Bank and the Old City of Jerusalem."[130] Hussein's decisions may have also been affected by the fact that he was misled by Nasser, who was unaware of the destruction of the Egyptian air force in the early hours of the war. In a telephone conversation, Nasser told Hussein that the Egyptians were attacking Israeli bases and airfields, inflicting heavy damage.[131] Impressed by euphoric reports coming out of Cairo about great victories, Hussein may have felt a need to share in the victory in order to bolster his standing among the Arabs. Thus, on June 5 the Jordanians opened an artillery barrage on the Israeli sector of Jerusalem, and sent a unit into the city's demilitarized zone to occupy the UN observers' headquarters. Simultaneously, they fired from positions along their border with Israel, reaching as far as the city of Tel Aviv. Well-prepared for such an eventuality, the Israelis activated their contingency plans and launched an all-out attack on East Jerusalem and the whole West Bank. After destroying the Jordanian air force, together with some Iraqi aircraft, the Israelis engaged the Jordanians in heavy battles that ended with a complete takeover of all parts of Palestine that had been under Jordanian rule. For the Israelis, the capstone of their victory was the capture of the Old City of Jerusalem on June 7, and with it the Western Wall of the biblical temple, Judaism's holiest site.[132] On that day, King Hussein appeared on television and made a plea to his people to fight "to the last drop of blood," but before the day was over he accepted a UN-sponsored cease-fire.[133]

With the defeat of the Egyptians and the Jordanians, the Israelis could focus their attention on Syria. Although the Syrians were behind the Egyptian mobilization that began the crisis, they did very little to help their ally. Contrary to their bombastic war communiqués, they limited their activities to a static bombardment of Israeli positions. King Hussein called the Syrian failure to send troops to help their neighbor Jordan "treachery." Fearing Russian intervention, Israel's Defense Minister Dayan was reluctant to attack Syria, but under pressure from the settlements that had been subjected to Syrian shelling for years, he gave the order to attack the Golan Heights on June 9. Having lost the bulk of its air force after it attacked the oil refineries in Haifa, the Syrian army had to fight without air cover. The Israelis rushed to climb hundreds of feet of steep terrain under heavy fire to dislodge the Syrians from their fortifications, hoping to complete the operation before the United Nations imposed a cease-fire. When the order finally came from the Security Council, the Israelis had penetrated the Syrian lines and taken over the plateau on June 11, suffering heavy casualties.[134]

The Six-Day War changed the map of the Middle East, with Israel for the first time occupying all of Palestine, in addition to the Sinai and the Golan Heights. In Israel, some assumptions that were made in the euphoria created by the swift and decisive victory proved to be wrong. The Israelis immediately expected that the humiliating defeat would convince the Arabs that Israel was invincible, and they would sit down and talk peace. When Defense Minister Dayan was asked in a BBC television interview what Israel's next step would be, he replied that "We are waiting for a telephone call from the Arabs."[135] But publicly that call never came,[136] either because the Arabs did not want to acknowledge defeat or for reasons of pride.[137] Remembering the pressure in 1957 to return the territories taken in the 1956 war, many Israelis believed that the world community would not allow them to hold on to the newly acquired land. Israel's intention to return the occupied areas was made public in a television interview with Prime Minister Eshkol on the first day of the war. In reply to a question concerning Israeli territorial claims against the Arabs, he declared: "None. All we want is security within our own frontiers."[138] Furthermore, on June 19 the Israeli cabinet voted unanimously to give back the Sinai to Egypt and the Golan Heights to Syria in return for demilitarization and peace. With regard to Jordan, Israel demanded border adjustments, citing security reasons, but the status of Jerusalem was considered non-negotiable; the city was unified and declared an indivisible part of Israel. The general response from the Arab countries to Israel's proposals was negative. At an Arab summit conference in Khartoum, Sudan, in September 1967, the participants had already voted "no" to recognition of Israel and "no" to negotiation or peace with Israel.[139]

At the United Nations the intense debate reflected East-West division, with the nonaligned bloc supporting the Arab-Soviet position. The Russians, after deciding with their Communist allies to sever relations with Israel, insisted on a Security Council resolution that would condemn Israel as the aggressor, demand unconditional withdrawal to the 1949 cease-fire lines, and require the payment of restitutions for the damage inflicted on the Arabs. Realizing that their proposal had little support on the Security Council, the Soviets pushed for a special session of the General Assembly.

But they were unable to muster the required two-thirds majority. Israel adamantly refused to withdraw unless direct peace talks with the Arabs were guaranteed. While the diplomatic maneuvering was under way, tension rose due to the sinking of an Israeli destroyer by Egypt, which was followed by a reprisal attack against Egyptian oil refineries in the city of Suez. The debate moved back to the Security Council, which, after lengthy deliberations, unanimously adopted Resolution 242 on November 22, 1967. The compromise resolution, which has since become the formula for peace, called for Israeli withdrawal from territories captured in 1967,[140] termination of the state of belligerency, and guarantees for the sovereignty, integrity, and independence of every state in the area.[141] It further affirmed the freedom of navigation through international waterways, and the necessity to achieve a just settlement of the refugee problem.

Resolution 242 required the UN secretary general to dispatch an envoy to the Middle East to mediate between the parties. Accordingly, Gunnar Jarring, a Swedish diplomat, was designated. But after numerous trips to the Middle East, it became clear by 1969 that Jarring's mission was not leading to a resolution. Israel, objecting to a complete withdrawal in any case, would not evacuate captured land before a peace treaty was signed, whereas Egypt and Jordan refused to conclude peace agreements until Israel withdrew. Syria, which had not accepted the UN resolution, refused to deal with Jarring. As the Jarring mission dragged on, with no results, the United States stepped in and dispatched Secretary of State William Rogers to the region to submit his own plan. Its main points included a total Israeli withdrawal, a negotiated peace accord, and a solution to the problem of the Palestinians on the basis of freedom of choice between repatriation and compensation. The Israelis, always fearful of a solution imposed by the major powers, turned down the American proposals, as did the Egyptians, although not in clear terms.

During these diplomatic activities, cease-fire lines were far from quiet. Incursions into Israel from Jordan, Lebanon, and Syria, with the predictable Israeli retaliations, had become routine. The heaviest battles took place along the Suez Canal. What began as cease-fire violations and exchanges of fire across the waterway escalated into a war of attrition, in which Egypt counted on the assumption that Israel could not sustain a prolonged war with heavy casualties.[142] By the summer of 1968, Nasser had concluded that diplomatic means alone would not force Israel to leave the Sinai.[143] In September, the Egyptians opened a massive artillery and tank fire barrage along the entire 65-mile length of the canal. Israeli soldiers, many of whom were caught in the open, suffered serious casualties. To sustain their positions, the Israelis began to build a fortified defense system on the canal's eastern bank, which become known as the "Bar-Lev Line." The Egyptian shelling was repeated on a regular basis, with occasional infiltrations into Israeli-held territory. Israel retaliated by launching commando operations inside Egypt, as well as air strikes, which escalated into the bombing of targets in Cairo and the Nile Valley. In the wake of the deep penetrations by Israeli bombers, the Russians rushed to build up Egypt's air defenses. With the heavy supply of surface-to-air missiles (SAMs) and radar installations came Russian advisers. Following a sudden visit by Nasser to Moscow in January 1970, the Soviet Union increased its involvement in Egypt's defense by sending new equipment and thousands of military personnel. Nasser made another trip to the Soviet capital before he announced his acceptance of the Rogers Plan and of the American proposal to stop the fighting. Terms were negotiated through the United Nations, and a cease-fire went into effect in August 1970.[144] By then it became evident that the Russians had strengthened their presence in Egypt substantially. To counter that buildup, the United States increased its shipment of heavy weapons to Israel, including squadrons of Phantom jets.[145]

While mediating an end to the fighting between King Hussein's army and the Palestinian guerillas operating in Jordan, Nasser died of a heart attack in September 1970, and was succeeded by his deputy, Anwar Sadat. Eight months later Sadat signed a treaty with the Soviet Union that required the Egyptians to follow a socialist line and to coordinate their foreign policy with Moscow, in return for Soviet equipment and training of their armed forces. Washington reacted to what was seen as the establishment of a Soviet base in Egypt by boosting Israel's air power as a counter to the Soviet presence. But Sadat soon became disillusioned with the Soviets, at least partly because of their inability to force an Israeli withdrawal. In a surprise move, he expelled the Russian military advisers and instructors in July 1972.

By removing the threat of Russian intervention, the Soviet departure from Egypt increased Israel's sense of security. The memory of the 1967 victory and the sophisticated weapons given by U.S. President Richard Nixon made the Israeli leaders, civilian and military alike, overconfident. Sadat followed his expulsion of the Russians with a plan to regain the Sinai by force, in collaboration with the Syrians, who wanted the Golan Heights back. But he also needed the military assistance of the Soviets, who agreed to ship large quantities of heavy weapons to Egypt and Syria to support an operation that might break the military and diplomatic impasse. In addition to tanks, SAMs, and jets, they also supplied SCUD missiles capable of reaching Israel's population centers.

After careful preparations and an effective political camouflage, Egypt and Syria launched an all-out war in the afternoon of October 6, 1973, catching the Israelis off-guard. That date was the Jewish holy day of Yom Kippur, chosen, among other reasons, in anticipation of a low-level Israeli preparedness.[146] Israeli intelligence reports had warned of large-scale military movements across the borders, but the leadership dismissed them as false alarms. When signs of an impending attack became indisputable, Prime Minister Golda Meir informed the two superpowers that Israel had no intention of striking first, and asked them to relay the message to Egypt and Syria. By the time the Israelis had mobilized their reserves, the Egyptians had managed to cross the Suez Canal, force their way through the sand barriers, and overrun the Bar-Lev Line. By the next morning, 90,000 Egyptian soldiers, 850 tanks, and 11,000 military vehicles had made their way into the Sinai.[147] Simultaneously, the Syrians broke through the cease-fire lines in the north and invaded the Golan Heights.

In addition to the element of surprise, the Egyptians and the Syrians had a clear superiority in men and matériel. With a combined total of 750,000 soldiers (compared to Israel's 250,000), 860 frontline planes, 3,200 tanks, 3,300 pieces of artillery, and large quantities of surface-to-air and anti-tank missiles, they commanded a formidable force.[148] Consequently, the Israelis, unprepared and on the defensive for the first time in their history, suffered a serious setback. In what Herzog describes as a "barrage of inferno," Israeli soldiers along the Bar-Lev Line, subjected to a massive Egyptian onslaught, incurred high casualties. The gravity of the situation was underscored by Dayan's suggestion to withdraw to a new defensive line, an idea that was unacceptable to the cabinet. Due to confusion, bickering among the generals, low morale, and heavy losses (not to mention a surprising Egyptian performance), it took the Israelis several days to recover. The heavy fighting took its toll, draining Israeli military equipment and ammunition to dangerously low levels. In response to an urgent appeal from Prime Minister Meir, President Nixon approved an airlift of military hardware to Israel. On October 16, the Israeli army launched a counterattack led by Reserve General Ariel Sharon, crossed the west bank of the Suez Canal, and succeeded in establishing a bridgehead. By transferring the battle into the Egyptian heartland, the Israelis managed to turn the tide in their favor. For that reason, and to secure the release of their prisoners of war, they were slow in accepting a cease-fire arrangement that was being worked out by U.S. Secretary of State Henry Kissinger. As the Israelis were encircling the Egyptian Third Army and cutting off its supply lines, the Soviet Union threatened intervention. When intelligence reports indicated the Soviets were preparing to airlift troops to the battle zone, President Nixon ordered a nuclear alert, which may have deterred the Russians.

On the Golan Heights a massive Syrian attack proved costly to the Israelis.[149] After the Syrians made initial gains on the ground, their advance was repelled when Israeli reserve units were sent to the front. Jordanian forces dispatched to assist Syria participated in some battles, but an Iraqi reinforcement was later accused of incompetence. The Israeli air force bombed strategic targets inside Syria, causing civilian casualties and protests at the United Nations. By October 12 the Israelis had established a new line, deeper in Syrian territory and closer to Damascus, the capital.

Intense negotiations at the United Nations were coordinated by Henry Kissinger. On October 22 they finally produced a unanimous agreement, Resolution 338, which called for a cease-fire and reiterated Resolution 242 of 1967. The terms of the cease-fire included provisions for face-to-face discussions between Egyptian and Israeli officers to work out the details of the agreement. That first direct contact between the antagonists was an important step toward establishing a limited working relationship between the two countries. Kissinger decided to take advantage of the momentum and try to broaden the cease-fire agreement to include other bilateral matters. Through his shuttle diplomacy he succeeded in arranging disengagement agreements in stages that included limited Israeli withdrawal as well as a separation of the armies, both on the Golan Heights and in the Sinai. A peace conference in Geneva was convened to negotiate a permanent solution, but it ended in futility.

Although Israel could claim military victory, the 1973 war was politically costly. The lack of preparedness and the high number of dead and wounded soldiers caused a public uproar that forced the Israeli government to appoint a commission of inquiry. The Agranat Commission, which questioned military and civilian leaders at all levels, concluded that mistakes were made by the military, but exonerated the political leaders. The public rejected the commission's conclusions that did not hold members of the cabinet responsible, particularly Defense Minister Dayan.[150] Israel's international relations were also damaged. African nations, with whom the Israelis had cultivated ties for years, succumbed to Arab diplomatic and economic pressure and severed relations with Israel. Even the countries of western Europe, Israel's traditional friends, had refused to assist the United States in shipping badly needed arms to Israel during the war. The one exception, Holland, lost oil supplies from Arab countries for assisting Israel. The Arabs imposed their ultimate weapon, an oil embargo, on all countries accused of helping Israel, particularly the United States.[151] Israel's isolation in the international arena, as evidenced by the numerous condemnations at the United Nations, increased her dependence on the United States, both politically and economically. The high cost of the war devastated the Israeli economy and required continuous U.S. aid, which made the country even more dependent.

Perhaps most frustrating for the Israelis was their continuing inability to convert hard-won military victories into political gains. Even after being badly beaten by the Israelis, the Arabs refused to accept peace on Israeli terms. Such was the case after the 1973 war, when the diplomatic stalemate

continued, despite the efforts of Henry Kissinger and others to break the
deadlock. But all that changed suddenly in 1977. In a bold move that
stunned the world, President Sadat decided to break out of the web of
futile diplomatic maneuvering and go to Jerusalem to address the Israeli
parliament. He was received by Menachem Begin, the newly elected prime
minister. Begin and Sadat agreed on the issue of returning the Sinai to
Egypt, which required the dismantling of Israeli settlements, in return for
a peace treaty and full diplomatic relations. But the two leaders could not
reach a consensus on the question of the Gaza Strip and the West Bank,
and on the political future of the Palestinians. After U.S. President Jimmy
Carter stepped in and devoted his energy to the peace negotiations, an
agreement was signed at Camp David, Maryland, which led to the signing
of a peace treaty between Egypt and Israel in March 1979. The Camp
David accords settled the territorial and political issues between the two
countries, but left a final settlement of the Palestinian issue to future negotiations that would include Jordan. As an interim arrangement, the Palestinians would be granted autonomy under Israeli rule for a period of five
years. But discussions on implementing the autonomy plan never took
place, due to several factors: the refusal of King Hussein to take part as
long as the Palestinians objected to the framework; the assassination of
Sadat in October 1980; the war in Lebanon, followed by Begin's resignation 1984; and the reluctance of an increasingly right-wing Israeli government to make territorial concessions.

The Israeli-Palestinian Confrontation

From the early years of Zionist settlement, the relationship between
Arabs and Jews in Palestine was characterized by antagonism and violence.
Although on a person-to-person basis friendship developed here and there
between individuals, the institutions and leaders of the two communities
did not communicate with each other. The Zionist leadership did not expect opposition from the Arabs, and did not understand the nationalistic
nature of their objection to Jewish immigration. What seemed, at the time,
to be a dispute over land was in reality a clash between two emerging
national movements competing over the same territory, with little chance
for mutual accommodation.

Because Zionism was imported from the outside, its growth and expansion came at the expense of the local population, historical or other
rights notwithstanding. The indigenous Arabs inevitably saw Jewish immigrants as alien invaders, all the more so because they came from a different part of the world. The European origin of the settlers made matters
worse, because the Arabs had grudges against colonialism and feared
Western domination. Thus developed the common belief among the Ar-

abs, still prevalent today, that Israel is an agent of Western imperialism.[152] This association only intensified Arab hostility toward Zionism and added an ideological, anti-Western dimension to the conflict.

The first phase of the resistance to Jewish settlement in Palestine climaxed in civil war toward the end of the British Mandate, as described earlier. The rejection of the UN partition plan by the Arabs and the decision of the Jews to declare statehood together led to the 1948 war. The intervention of several Arab countries in the war turned the conflict into a pan-Arab problem, taking the option of reaching a settlement out of the hands of the Palestinians. Instead, the war ended with a cease-fire between Israel and its neighboring Arab countries, leaving the Palestinians, many in refugee camps, on the sidelines. Consequently, being under Egyptian and Jordanian rule, the Palestinians had no influence on the course of events from 1949 to 1967. Attacks across the demarcation lines into Israel by the fedayeen in the 1950s and by Fatah and other groups in the 1960s were a serious problem to the Israelis, but not a threat to their existence. On the other hand, they exposed the host countries to Israeli retaliations. In fact, the objective behind those incursions often was not to score victories, but to provoke Israel into a confrontation with its Arab neighbors. Of all possible shortcomings, an indefinite continuation of the status quo was seen by the Palestinians as most detrimental to their cause.

The establishment of the Palestine Liberation Organization (PLO), under the auspices of the Arab governments in May 1964, did not make the desired defeat of Israel any more possible. From its beginning the organization was fragmented,[153] assembling under one umbrella several factions that were at odds with one another.[154] The fact that the character of the PLO ranged from plain revolutionary to Marxist evoked caution and suspicion among traditionalist Arab rulers. In 1967 there was a transition of power in the leadership of the organization, when Yasir Arafat became the chairman of the organization. In addition to escalating guerrilla activities, he developed a political strategy based on consolidating the power of the PLO vis-à-vis the Arab nations as one among equals. On the international scene, he turned to world opinion and presented the plight of the Palestinians. His major international success came when he was embraced by the Soviet Union, and when the PLO was granted observer status at the United Nations. Arafat gained personal recognition as well, when he was invited to speak at the United Nations in November 1974. This change in the attitude of the United Nations constituted an acknowledgment of the national rights of the Palestinians, who in Resolution 242 were referred to only as "refugees." At the peak of Arab political influence, with oil prices skyrocketing, the UN General Assembly passed a resolution in 1975 labeling Zionism as racism.

The crushing defeat of the regular Arab armies in 1967 convinced the

Palestinians that they should take charge of the struggle against Israel. Drawing an analogy with other armed revolutionary movements, particularly the Vietcong and their victory over the Americans in Vietnam, they decided that an escalation in guerrilla-style warfare would be the best way to achieve their objectives.[155] But unlike other movements, the Palestinians lacked a base within their scene of operation, and had to rely on permission from Arab countries to use their lands as staging points. In the occupied territories, where the PLO needed the collaboration of the local residents, the Israeli authorities monitored Palestinian activities and imposed harsh measures against those who tried to organize underground cells. At times, the whole population suffered from collective punishment. To protest the continued Israeli military occupation, the Palestinians often engaged in civil disobedience, mostly in the form of strikes.

From the outset, the Israeli attitude toward increased Palestinian activism was negative. The PLO's involvement in indiscriminate killing of civilians hardened the Israeli position, both in the government and the Israeli public. Israel viewed the PLO as a terrorist organization dedicated to the destruction of Jews by methods comparable to those of the Nazis. To increase internal security, Israel reacted to attacks against its population by implementing strict counterterrorism measures. Roadblocks and handbag searches became a way of life, while the country tried to maintain an atmosphere of normalcy. The appearance of peace was important for the survival of the tourist industry, the primary source of foreign currency.

In Jordan the PLO had conflicts with the government. Shortly after the war, guerrilla attacks on Israel from Jordan intensified, causing Israeli reprisals and dragging the Jordanian army into clashes with the Israelis. The growth of the PLO into a state within a state undermined the authority of Jordan's king and endangered the stability in a country that had a majority Palestinian population. The conflict with the Jordanian government took on an ideological character as well. In the words of Prime Minister Wasfi al-Tall: "Under the influence of communism, the PLO was no longer a movement of liberation."[156] King Hussein saw the PLO's use of a Jordanian airstrip to blow up three hijacked airliners in September 1970 as an example of the PLO's attempt to challenge his authority, which would lead to chaos in Jordan and ultimately bring down his regime. The following day he ordered his army to crush the Palestinian guerrilla movement. In the ensuing battles, in which the Jordanians heavily bombarded refugee camps, thousands were reported killed.[157] A Syrian invasion of Jordan to help the guerrillas was halted after Israel, with U.S. backing, warned Syria not to intervene.

Events in Jordan were considered a major setback for the Palestinian groups. The crackdown eliminated small factions and left mainly the groups of George Habash, Nayif Hawatma, and Ahmad Jibril, in addition to Arafat's Fatah. Bickering among themselves, the surviving factions soon faced additional attacks from the Jordanian army, eventually leading to their expulsion from the major cities. In July 1971, while King Hussein was on his way to meet with other Arab leaders to discuss a possible modus vivendi with the Palestinians, his forces made their final onslaught, putting an end to the guerrillas as a viable force in Jordan.

After the closure of their bases, Palestinian guerrilla factions moved from Jordan to Lebanon. Using the Palestinian refugee camps as their power base, they established training camps and built a strong military infrastructure. From bases in southern Lebanon they expanded their control over a large area on Israel's northern border, which came to be known as Fatahland. Lebanon soon became the center of operations and headquarters for the PLO, undermining the Lebanese government's authority in the south. During the 1970s the PLO initiated military activities from Lebanon and later expanded its operations beyond the Middle East, attacking targets in Europe and hijacking airplanes. Among their most notorious acts was the murder of 25 passengers, mainly North American Christian pilgrims, at Lod airport in Israel in May 1972.[158] In September of the same year, during the Olympic Games in Munich, the eleven-member Israeli team was kidnapped and killed. Several passenger airplanes were hijacked and a Swissair airliner was destroyed in a mid-air explosion in 1970. In June 1976, an Arab-German team hijacked an Air France plane to Entebbe in Uganda. As negotiations with hijackers failed, an Israeli commando unit flew over 2,000 miles to rescue the 104 passengers.[159] According to John Laffin, over 300 attacks were carried out by Palestinians in 26 countries outside Israel between 1968 and 1980, killing 813 people and wounding 1,013 others.[160]

Inside Israel the population lived under the shadow of terrorism, particularly in Jerusalem, as bombs went off in the streets, on buses, and in other public places, inflicting casualties by the dozens. In the 1970s, attacks on Israeli towns from southern Lebanon increased in intensity and in frequency. Rocket shelling became part of life in the settlement towns at the border, causing many residents, mostly immigrants from North Africa, to flee for safety. Border infiltrations became more and more daring, often resulting in indiscriminate civilian deaths. In April 1974, eighteen residents of the town of Kiryat Shmona, including women and children, were killed by members of Ahmad Jibril's faction. A month later, eighteen children and four adults were murdered at a school in Ma'alot on the Lebanese border. In March 1978, eleven infiltrators came from Lebanon in rubber boats and seized Tel Aviv's main highway to Haifa, killing 37 civilians.

The Israeli public reacted with outrage. Israel held the Lebanese government responsible for the attacks, although it was well-known that it had no control over the situation. From 1975 on, Lebanon was engaged in a civil war, with Christian and Muslim militias battling each other, causing heavy damage to the capital city of Beirut. At the same time, Israel conducted massive retaliatory air strikes inside Lebanon, only adding to the destruction, and hitting PLO targets situated among noncombatants. Due to the difficulty in pinpointing the bombing, most of the victims of the air raids were civilians. To protect the northern border, Israel mobilized and trained Lebanese Christian units to serve as a buffer against Palestinian incursions.

In April 1981, the Syrians attacked the Christian forces of Phalangist leader Bashir Jumayel, situated in the mountainous area close to Israel. In response to his plea for help, Prime Minister Begin ordered the air force to bomb Syrian positions to relieve the pressure on the Christians. The Israelis shot down two Syrian helicopters in their attack. Syria reacted by moving antiaircraft missiles to the Bekaa Valley in east Lebanon, increasing the danger of a wider Syrian-Israeli confrontation. In July 1981, the PLO opened a barrage of Russian Katyusha rockets and long-range cannons on the entire Israeli population within range. After ten days of gun duels that forced Israeli civilians to remain in shelters, the government launched a fierce bombing of PLO targets in Beirut and throughout Lebanon. Although a shaky, U.S.-mediated cease-fire was arranged, it became clear for the first time since 1948 that Israel was at war with the Palestinians. Unlike prior limited engagements, the Israelis now faced a military force possessing heavy weapons, organized not as a guerrilla band but as an army. Israeli leaders, deciding that limited attacks on PLO bases across the Lebanese border, such as the one in 1978, were insufficient, ordered an invasion.

Intending to seize and destroy PLO installations and stockpiles, Israeli forces entered Lebanon on June 6, 1982. According to Defense Minister Ariel Sharon, the "mopping-up" operation was to cover a depth of 25 miles. Israel's ultimate goal was to put an end, once and for all, to the PLO presence in Lebanon, and to open the way for a peace treaty between the two countries. But the battles did not go according to plan. The PLO had more weapons than previously known, and the Palestinians were tough to beat. In fierce battles, the Israelis suffered heavy casualties, until they finally pushed the PLO all the way to Beirut and put the city under siege. In a final assault on the Palestinians, the Israeli army bombed and shelled Beirut constantly, causing massive damage to the area and numerous casualties. On August 12, after eleven hours of aerial bombardment, U.S. President Ronald Reagan called Menachem Begin and demanded an end to the destruction. It took additional international pressure to end the assault on the city. American mediator Philip Habib made arrangements to allow the beleaguered Arafat and his estimated 8,000 remaining fighters to leave Beirut.[161]

Although the Syrians were not the primary target, Israel decided to launch an offensive against Syrian missile sites and push their forces back, away from the Israeli border. In the battles that followed, 86 Syrian planes were shot down.[162] For the Israeli soldiers, these engagements with the Syrians only added to the already high cost of the war.

Israel seemingly had achieved the objectives of her operation, with the PLO having lost its stronghold and moved its headquarters to faraway Tunisia. The Syrians lost their missile bases, and Sharon came back from Beirut with a peace agreement signed by the Lebanese president-elect, Bashir Jumayel. But a few days later Jumayel was assassinated by Muslim rivals, ending hopes for peace with Lebanon. At that point, the Israelis decided to enter West Beirut. To avenge Jumayel's death, Christian militia entered the Palestinian refugee camps of Sabra and Shatila on September 17, slaughtering hundreds of men, women, and children. The massacre shocked the international community, as well as the Israeli public. Under condemnations and mounting public pressure, the Israeli government appointed a commission of inquiry, which concluded that the Israelis were partly to blame because they allowed the Christians into the camps without supervision. The commission recommended the transfer of Sharon from his post as minister of defense.

The war in Lebanon, named "Operation Peace for Galilee," was costly to Israel. What was supposed to be a limited operation caused more casualties than the Six-Day War. Moreover, Israeli forces now had to be kept in the quagmire of Lebanon, suffering even more losses. Mounting public dissatisfaction and the establishment of a Labor-Likud joint coalition brought about the withdrawal of Israeli forces in 1984. By then, Menachem Begin had lost interest in the premiership and had resigned for health reasons.

Israel expected that the evacuation of the PLO from Lebanon would calm the unrest among the Palestinians in the occupied territories. But events in Lebanon, which the Palestinians did not consider a defeat, left them with unchanged attitudes toward living under Israeli occupation. A majority continued to view the PLO as the sole representative leader of the Palestinians, and no alternative emerged from the territories. The predicament of the Palestinians under occupation and their frustration with the political stalemate erupted into an uprising, or *intifada*, in 1987. What began as protest demonstrations in the Gaza area developed into riots, stone-throwing, and firebomb assaults on Israeli soldiers. Israel committed a sizable force to put down the riots, and in almost daily encounters hundreds of Palestinians, including many children, have been killed by army fire. In the most serious incident, the police killed seventeen Arabs during a demonstration on the Temple Mount (al-Haram al-Sharif) in Jerusalem in October 1990. The incident provoked a strong condemnation of Israel

by the United Nations. Although the intifada has not achieved a change
in Israeli policy toward withdrawal, it has attracted international attention
and increased pressure on Israel. It also reminded the country of the existence of a demarcation line between Israel and the territories. After several
cases in which Jewish citizens were stabbed to death in the streets of Jerusalem and elsewhere, Israel temporarily barred Arab workers from crossing that line into the country.[163] The uprising has affected Jerusalem in
particular, as fewer Israelis and tourists visit the Arab sector, bringing
business at the once-bustling Old City bazaar to a near standstill.

The current conflict between the Israelis and the Palestinians centers
around the disputed territories captured in 1967, namely the West Bank
and the Gaza Strip. In exchange for peace, Israel initially declared her
willingness to return the land, except for Jerusalem, with border adjustments. But with the passage of time and the lack of progress toward settlement, the willingness to return the land has diminished. Israel first argued that some territorial depth was needed for security, hence the "Allon
Plan," which proposed an Israeli withdrawal coupled with the retention
of settlements along the Jordan Valley for security. Then a historical attachment began to develop toward the West Bank, which led to reviving
its biblical names of Judea and Samaria. In particular, the Zionist religious
group Gush Emunim has managed to pressure the government into allowing its members to settle on Palestinian land and expand their presence on
the West Bank. Since the late 1970s more and more settlements have been
spreading in the territories, encouraged by the ascent of the nationalist
Likud Party to power. The resignation of Begin transferred the premiership to Yitzhak Shamir, who is committed to the idea of "Greater Israel."
In addition, the decline of the Likud in the post-Begin era has necessitated
an alliance with coalition partners from the extreme right, bringing more
pressure on the government to hold on to the territories. Although polls
have shown that the majority of Israelis favor the return of most of the
land taken in 1967, the government, in its present composition, is unlikely
to make major concessions.

Historically, aside from the issue of land, the conflict between Israelis
and Palestinians has also been caused by the refusal of each side to recognize the other as a nation. The Israelis find a contradiction between the
claim, on the one hand, that the Arabs are a single, unified nation, and the
demand, on the other, that a separate Palestinian national identity be recognized. The result is a lack of distinction between Palestinians and other
Arabs and the common argument that the Arabs already have many states
and do not need one more. On the other side of the conflict, the Palestinians, as well as other Arabs, dispute the validity of Jewish nationalism. This
challenge to the fundamentals of Zionism is embedded in the Palestinian
Covenant, which spells out the principles of the Palestinian national move-

ment: "Judaism being a divine religion is not an independent nationality. Nor do Jews constitute a single nation with an identity of its own: they are citizens of the states to which they belong."[164] This view ignores the strong historical link between nationalism and religion in Judaism, and overlooks the fact that from its inception the Jewish faith was tied to that disputed piece of land. King Hussein's statement that "Israel was a religious invention" represents, therefore, a misunderstanding of the essence of Israel's being.[165] Zionism has been in existence since the first Jews were forced into the Babylonian exile in biblical times, and was kept alive through the centuries by faith and prayers. In fact, Arab nationalism itself is not devoid of religion, because all Arab nations maintain a strong Islamic character.[166] This link between nationalism and religion was emphatically stated by King Hussein himself, who is not a religious fanatic: "First and foremost, we hold that we are Arabs and that Arab nationalism makes sense only within its religious framework, meaning Islam."[167]

From the perspective of national identity, the mutual denial of existence is at the core of the Israeli-Palestinian conflict. To put it simply, the Arabs see the Israelis only as Jews, while the Israelis see the Palestinians only as Arabs.

From these misconceptions comes the claim that the other side has no national rights. The Arab argument that Jewish-Israeli nationalism is only fiction ignores the fact that the Israelis are no longer first-generation immigrants. They have a strong sense of nationalism, which they have defended and died for in several wars. The Jews of Israel are Israelis, who communicate in their own language and are distinctly different from the Jews of other countries. It is absurd to suggest that a hundred years of social evolution, through which a Jewish national group has developed within Palestine, can be reversed.[168] Israeli society's trend toward integration, which has led to the gradual obliteration of differences of origin, is similar to the process that has shaped American society. That similarity was noticed, from his own perspective, by Yahya Hammuda, who preceded Arafat as head of the PLO. In an interview in 1969 he declared: "America isn't a nation at all. It's one enormous gang! . . . They have no moral sense. It's a mixture of people of different national origins, just like Israel!"[169] On the other hand, the rejection of Palestinian nationalism by Israelis has been equally faulty. While denied self-determination for several decades, the Palestinians have maintained a national identity tied to the land. The statement attributed to Golda Meir that Palestinians "do not exist" is difficult to accept in today's situation.

Excluding fringe groups of extremists, the policy of the PLO in the conflict has changed, and no longer demands that Israel be dismantled or destroyed by armed struggle. In 1988, the organization announced its acceptance of Resolution 242, implying recognition of Israel's existence in exchange for complete withdrawal. Since then Arafat has been proposing a Palestinian state alongside Israel. Although fear, distrust, and suspicion toward the ultimate intentions of the Palestinians are still prevalent among the Israelis, the door has been opened for negotiating a peaceful solution. The Madrid conference in November 1991 may prove to be the beginning of the process toward peace.

Notes

1. Wasif ʿAbboushi states that the Arabs of Palestine regarded themselves as Syrians, and that wealthy residents of Beirut, the majority of whom were Christians, owned large portions of the land. He concludes that "Palestine was a British invention." ʿAbboushi, *Filastin Qabla al-Diyaʾ* (London, 1985), 9. Contrary to this statement is the comment that "One of the strangest contradictions in history is that Palestine has been dropped from the map of the world." Edward Said and Ibrahim Abu Lughod, *Al-Waqiʾ al-Filastini* (Cairo, 1986), 7.

2. *Tsion* (Zion) is one of the names which appear interchangeably in the Bible both for Jerusalem and for the Holy Land. Throughout Jewish history the land was more commonly referred to as *Eretz Yisrael* (Land of Israel), and this name remained in use after the establishment of Israel, primarily as a historical name. It has been revived, however, since the emergence of the "Greater Israel" movement in the aftermath of the 1967 war, and is currently used in the nationalist camp synonymously with "Israel."

3. It was discovered later that the evidence presented at the trial was fabricated by Dreyfus' fellow officers. After his innocence was proven, his military rank and decorations were reinstated. The strong condemnation of the trial in Emile Zola's "J' Accuse!," an open letter to the French president, was instrumental in overturning the verdict.

4. Despite the title, it is obvious that Herzl did not mean the state to be Jewish in the religious sense. In fact, he spoke clearly about the need to contain religious interference: "We shall therefore prevent any theocratic tendencies from coming to the fore on the part of our priesthood. We shall keep our priests within the confines of their temples . . . Army and priesthood must not interfere in the administration of the State." Theodor Herzl, *The Jewish State,* translated by Sylvie D'Avigdor (London, 1972), 71.

5. *Ibid,* 30. Other locations for settling Jews, one of which was Uganda, were considered at various times. But Palestine soon became Herzl's choice, and in his utopian novel *Altneuland,* published in 1902, he elaborated on his vision of the shining future of that land. It should be noted that apart from Messianic Zionism, the idea of the return of the Jews to the Holy Land had been expressed long before Herzl. It was proposed by Napoleon in 1799, by British philanthropist Montefiore in 1839, by Frenchman Laharanne in 1848, and in the Zionistic novels *Tancred* by Benjamin Disraeli and *Daniel Deronda* by George Eliot. To Herzl, the boundaries of the state were an open question. When asked by Germany's Reich Chancellor

Hohenlohe if the Jewish territory would extend as far as Beirut in the north, his reply was: "We ask for that which we need. The more immigrants, the greater the area. The land will naturally be purchased from its present owners." Alex Bein, *Theodore Herzl* (Philadelphia, 1962), 288.

6. Recorded in Herzl's diary on September 3, 1897, and quoted in *The Jewish State*, 4.

7. When Herzl died of pneumonia at the age of 44, in the midst of a quarrel with the Russian Zionists, his political Zionism seemed a failure. It recovered only when the leadership passed into the hands of those who advocated slow but steady progress on the ground in Palestine rather than the pursuit of quick diplomatic achievements.

8. In return for financial assistance to liquidate Turkey's debt, Sultan Abdul-Hamid agreed to allow Jewish refugees to settle in his provinces as Ottoman subjects, except in Palestine. After lengthy negotiations, Herzl returned from Istanbul empty-handed. Arab authors praise the sultan's hostility to Zionism, saying, among other things, that Herzl had to wait five years to see him. Abdul-Aziz 'Awad, *Muqaddima fiTarikh Filastin* (Beirut, 1983), 51–61.

9. The baron was the chief financier of the first wave of immigrants that came to Palestine from Russia, following the pogroms of 1881. He built the first colonies which established the wine industry and invested over $50 million in various settlement projects through PJCA (Palestine Jewish Colonization Association).

10. For a discussion of this issue, see Nadav Safran, *Israel, the Embattled Ally* (Cambridge, Mass., 1981), 20–23.

11. The chief rival of the Zionist movement in Russia and Poland was the Bund, the General Jewish Workers' Organization, which was ideologically and pragmatically opposed to Zionism. It argued that Jewish energy and resources should be spent on the working class rather than be wasted on unrealistic dreams. Ibid., 21.

12. Those two organizations were the most active among the forerunners of Zionism. Hovevei Zion (Lovers of Zion) consisted of several groups that appeared in various locations in eastern and central Europe in the late 1870s, calling for the establishment of a Jewish government in Palestine. A central office for the movement was established in Odessa in 1884 by Leo Pinsker. Bilu (Hebrew acronym for "House of Jacob, let us go," from a verse in Isaiah) was founded in Kharkov in 1881 and sent the first immigrants to Palestine, laying the foundation for Jewish agriculture in the land.

13. In addition to receiving large donations from the rich, the Zionists set up an elaborate system of collecting money through the establishment of Keren Kayemet (Jewish National Fund), which distributed donation cans in many countries.

14. That number declined to 56,000 in 1918, as approximately 10,000 Jews perished from hunger and disease, and thousands of others left the country. Alex Bein, *Entziklopedya Ivrit,* Vol 6 (Jerusalem, 1957), 517. 'Abboushi estimates the Jewish population in 1918 to be 58,000 (27). It is generally difficult to establish population figures based on reliable statistics. Jewish sources tend to inflate the number of Jews who arrived or resided in Palestine, while Arab sources attempt to minimize the Jewish presence on the land.

15. Among those who came in this wave between 1905 and 1914 were some of

the founders of the state of Israel, including David Ben-Gurion, the first prime minister.

16. Muhammad Muslih, *The Origins of Palestinian Nationalism* (New York, 1988), 71.

17. Some Zionist leaders reacted to Arab attacks with surprise, because they were led to believe that there was no serious Arab opposition and that incidents of violence were provoked by a few instigators. Arthur Ruppin, one of the founders of Brit Shalom (Alliance of Peace), which called for conciliation with the Arabs, complained that the impression created by the Zionists was that Palestine was an uninhabited land.

18. The Balfour Declaration in full reads as follows: "His Majesty's Government view with favour the establishment in Palestine of a national home for the Jewish people, and will use their best endeavours to facilitate the achievement of this object, it being clearly understood that nothing shall be done which may prejudice the civil and religious rights of existing non-Jewish communities in Palestine, or the rights and political status enjoyed by Jews in any other country."

19. Walter Laqueur and Barry Rubin, *The Israel-Arab Reader: A Documentary History of the Middle East*, rev. ed. (New York, 1985), 35.

20. Najib Azuri, *Yaqzat al-Umma al-Arabiyya* (Beirut, 1978), 41.

21. Laqueur and Rubin, *The Israel-Arab Reader*, 16.

22. The most active newspaper in opposing Zionism was *al-Karmil*, which was founded in Haifa in 1908 by Najib Nassar. In a book titled *al Sahyuniyya*, published in 1911, Nassar labeled Zionism a "racist movement aiming at the colonization of Palestine." Rashid Khalidi, "The Role of the Press in the Early Arab Reaction to Zionism," *Peuples Méditerranées* (July–September 1982).

23. In response to the failure of the Arab conference in Paris in 1913 to confront the Zionist problem, Najib Nassar called on Palestinians to take matters into their own hands and put forth a Palestinian identity. 'Awad, *Muqaddima fi Tarikh Filastin*, 36–37.

24. Haqqi Bey al-Azm, a political activist, wrote in an article in *al-Ahram* that the Jews would help Syria with their capital and skill. An organization named al-Lamarkaziyya, founded in 1913 by Syrians, called for a dialogue with the Zionists. Muslih, *The Origins of Palestinian Nationalism*, 86.

25. Both the English version in Laqueur and Rubin, and the Arabic version in Ali Sultan's *Tarikh Suriyya* (Damascus, 1987), 427–428, indicate that Faisal accepted the plan for a Jewish national home. Article III of the agreement states that "all such measures shall be adopted as will afford the fullest guarantees for carrying into effect the British Government's Declaration of the 2nd of November, 1917," a reference to the Balfour Declaration. That refutes the claim by Muslih that "the agreement permitted Jewish immigration into Palestine without supporting the idea of a Jewish national home" (p. 121). Similar denials are common in Arab historical literature, perhaps due to the embarrassment in Faisal's acceptance of the Zionist agenda in Palestine. It is true, though, that a note in Faisal's own handwriting, stating that his consent was contingent upon the fulfillment of British promises to the Arabs, was attached to the agreement.

26. Laqueur and Rubin, *The Israel-Arab Reader*, 19.

27. A meeting between Weizmann and "paramount sheiks and other leaders of Transjordan" took place in Jerusalem to "entertain the principle of Arab-Jewish cooperation," as reported in the *Palestine Post* (Jerusalem, April 10, 1933).

28. Herbert Samuel, who was a Jew, was accused by the Arabs of being a Zionist, although he tried to maintain a balance between the antagonists ('Abboushi, *Filastin Qabla*, 35), and in the 1930s he spoke against the establishment of a Jewish state (Ibid, 219). In trying to promote Arab leadership, he appointed, in 1921, Haj Amin al-Husseini, who was competing against his rivals in the Nashashibi clan, as mufti of Jerusalem.

29. The attack on Tel-Hai in the upper Galilee resulted in the death of Joseph Trumpeldor, one of the influential Jewish settlers. But the most serious incident occurred in Jerusalem, when Arabs who had gathered in the city for the Nabi Musa celebration attacked Jewish residents. The riots lasted three days and caused the death of six Jews and the wounding of 200, with an unspecified number of Arab casualties. Jewish defenders, among them Vladimir Ze'ev Jabotinsky, a strong proponent of a Jewish military force, were arrested and sentenced to prison. Following an inquiry, the British government decided to abolish military rule and establish a civilian administration.

30. In testimony before the Anglo-American Inquiry Commission in 1946, Ihud leaders Judah Magnes and Martin Buber declared that because Palestine was "not just an Arab land or just a Jewish land," the historical rights of the Jews and the natural rights of the Arabs require the formation of a bi-national state where "the two nations will have equal freedom and independence, equal participation in government." A transcript of the testimonies appears in *Arab-Jewish Unity* (Westport, Conn., 1976). Ironically, Judah Magnes, who was president of the Hebrew University, was murdered in 1947 in an Arab attack on a convoy of doctors and nurses near Mount Scopus in Jerusalem.

31. Israeli sources estimate Arab immigration to Palestine, encouraged by favorable employment conditions, to be around 100,000 during the period of the British Mandate.

32. A common reference to the Jewish community in pre-state Palestine.

33. The military contribution of the kibbutz movement was evident in the formation of the Palmach, the crack commando unit of the Hagana, from its ranks.

34. There was also help from individual volunteers, some non-Jews, from other countries. One of those supporters was Orde Wingate, a captain in the British army, who became a believer in the Zionist cause and helped the Hagana develop a combat strategy.

35. Prominent American Jewish figures, such as Louis Brandeis, Felix Frankfurter, and Bernard Baruch, were instrumental in winning the support of successive American administrations. The following quotation attributed to Baruch, who was not a declared Zionist, illustrates the Jewish political influence in the Truman era: "The Administration will sell all seven Arab states if it is a question of retaining the support of New York alone; never mind the rest of the country." Zvi Ganin, *Truman, American Jewry, and Israel* (New York, 1979), 101.

36. Muslih, *Muqaddima fi*, 26–27.

37. During his tenure as the chief leader of the Palestinian Arabs, al-Husseini

followed a militant, religious-nationalistic policy, calling for the destruction of the British and Zionist "infidels." His views brought him to Berlin in 1937, where he met with Hitler and proclaimed his support for Nazism. Barred from Jordanian-controlled Jerusalem and the West Bank because of his animosity toward the ruling Hashemite family, he spent his last years in exile.

38. 'Abboushi, *Filastin Qabla*, 120–121.

39. The Revisionist movement, which evolved as the main opposition to the Labor camp, demanded the establishment of a state with a Jewish majority in the entire pre-mandate territory, including Transjordan. The claim over the land east of the Jordan River was maintained by Menachem Begin's Herut party long after the state of Israel came into being.

40. The total number of Jews killed was 133, with 339 wounded. Arab losses were counted as 87 dead and 91 wounded.

41. As the unrest in Palestine intensified, an increasing number of Arab irregulars poured into the country from neighboring states. The establishment of the Committee for the Salvation of Palestine, under the leadership of Qawuqji, facilitated the recruitment of hundreds of volunteers to fight on the side of the Palestinian Arabs. Isma'il al-Tubasi, *Kifah al-Sha'b al-Filastini* (Amman, 1977), 47.

42. Armed attacks were accompanied by acts of civil disobedience. A resolution to refuse to pay taxes unless Arab demands were met was adopted by organizers of the Arab strike under the leadership of Amin al-Husseini. *The Palestine Post* (May 8, 1936).

43. In addition to 91 deaths and 369 injuries, the Jews suffered heavy damage to property and agricultural production. Arab losses, although unknown in actual numbers, were equally heavy.

44. *The Palestine Post* (November 26, 1936).

45. al-Tubasi, *Kifah al-Sha'b*, 51–52.

46. The plan presented an unbalanced picture so far as land and population were concerned. Compared to a few Jews who would end up within the boundaries of the Arab state, owning less than one percent of the land, 54,000 Arabs would reside in the Jewish state, holding twice as much land. 'Abboushi, *Filastin Qabla*, 208.

47. al-Tubasi, *Kifah al-Sha'b*, 54–56.

48. In a speech before Parliament on November 24, 1938, Colonial Secretary Malcolm MacDonald acknowledged Jewish contribution to the development of Palestine by "turning sand dunes into orchards," but argued that the feelings of the Arabs should also be taken into account. *Parliamentary Debates, Commons,* 1938–1939, Vol. 341.

49. Under the headline "Tel Aviv Outlawed," *The Palestine Post* reported on March 3, 1947, that half the Jewish population of Palestine was under martial law. The government had previously dispatched 20,000 soldiers and police to Tel Aviv to search for terrorists.

50. In November 1944, Lord Moyne, the former British colonial secretary, was assassinated in Cairo. The two perpetrators, members of the Stern band, were convicted and executed. The murder drew sharp condemnations from Jewish leaders, and widened the rift between the Hagana and right-wing groups. One of the most notorious acts of the Irgun was carried out in 1946, when they blew up

an entire wing of the King David Hotel in Jerusalem, which served as the head-quarters of the British police. Ninety-one people, including some Arabs and Jews, were killed in the explosion. The leadership of the Yishuv strongly denounced the act as a "dastardly crime perpetrated by the gang of desperadoes." *The Palestine Post* (July 23, 1946).

51. The Nazi threat compelled the authorities to reexamine their attitude to-ward the Hagana. Not only did they seek the aid of Jewish forces to put down the Arab rebellion, they also mobilized and trained a brigade of Jewish volunteers who fought in Europe against the Germans. There was even some cooperation with the outlawed Irgun, which was allowed to send a unit to Iraq to help in crushing the pro-Nazi coup of Rashid Ali al-Kailani in 1941.

52. Laqueur and Rubin, *The Israel-Arab Reader*, 546.

53. In the words of parliament member Mayhew, Bevin was "passionately and unshakeably anti-Zionist." Christopher Mayhew, *Publish It Not* (London, 1975), 17.

54. Laqueur and Rubin, 88.

55. In a meeting initiated by King Farouq of Egypt in May 1946, Arab gov-ernments declared that the Palestine issue was not solely the concern of the Pales-tinian Arabs, but a pan-Arab problem. That commitment was strengthened in a meeting of the Arab League a month later, when a resolution was adopted that rejected "any form of partition in principle" and pledged military assistance to the Arabs of Palestine. al-Tubasi, *Kifah al-Sha'b*, 83.

56. Bevin's opposition to Jewish immigration was expressed in a speech he made in February 1947: "Why should an external agency, largely financed from America, determine how many people should come into Palestine, and interfere with the economy of the Arabs, who have been there for 2,000 years?" Howard Sachar, *History of Israel* (New York, 1976), 273.

57. For an extensive discussion of the activities of both the pro-Zionist and the oil lobbies during the Truman administration, see Michael J. Cohen, *Truman and Israel* (Berkeley, Calif., 1990).

58. al-Tubasi, *Kifah al-Sha'b*, 87.

59. The refugee ship *Exodus* became the cause célèbre of the Jewish struggle for free immigration. Seized outside the territorial waters of Palestine, the ship was forcefully boarded by British troops, who killed three refugees and wounded a hundred. They towed the ship to Haifa. Contrary to the common policy of send-ing illegal immigrants to detention camps in Cyprus, Bevin decided to make an example of the *Exodus* passengers by returning them to Europe. That decision backfired, as the world watched the plight of the refugees who were being physi-cally forced into German internment camps after a three-month ordeal at sea. What appeared as British brutality and Jewish suffering made a strong impact on world public opinion, no less than on the members of UNSCOP. When a subcommittee was dispatched to refugee camps in Europe, it found a quarter of a million Jews demanding immediate entry to Palestine. *The Palestine Post* (July 30, 1947).

60. Based on the historical argument that the Jews were driven out of the land after the destruction of their commonwealth, Ben-Gurion, Shertok, and Weizmann pleaded the case for a Jewish state, with its boundaries to be negotiated. Magnes, on the other hand, proposed the establishment of a bi-national state. *UN Document A/364*, Add. 3, pp. 1–64.

61. al-Husseini was arrested in Germany during the sweep of the Allies in the spring of 1945. He was detained in Paris but managed to escape to Egypt. From Cairo he controlled Arab Palestinian politics through his followers after eliminating the opposition. It was his uncompromising stance that dictated the boycott and thus denied the Palestinian Arabs the opportunity to present their case before UNSCOP. As a result, the UN files contain only 29 pages of Arab testimony before the committee, compared to 237 pages reflecting the Jewish viewpoints. 'Abboushi, *Filastin Qabla*, 357.

62. In its meeting in Lebanon in September 1947, the Arab League officially assumed responsibility for the Palestine question. After a military assessment of the situation, it was decided to deploy forces along the borders of Palestine in anticipation of a showdown. The League also decided to arm and train the Palestinian Arabs under a unified Arab command. al-Tubasi, *Kifah al-Sha'b*, 94–96.

63. The vote of the Communist countries in favor of self-determination for the Jews, perhaps out of a desire to deprive Britain of an important strategic position, marked a departure from the traditional anti-Zionist policy of the Soviet bloc.

64. The UNSCOP report contained population figures based on the British estimates of December 1946. Accordingly, of the total number of 1,845,000 inhabitants, 498,000 Jews and 407,000 Arabs would be residing in the Jewish state, while the Arab state would have 725,000 Arabs and 10,000 Jews. The population of Jerusalem would consist of 100,000 Jews and 105,000 Arabs and others. 'Abboushi, *Filastin Qabla*, 368.

65. al-Tubasi, *Kifah al-Sha'b*, 93.

66. *Henderson Papers*, Box 11, 11-20-77, in Cohen, *Truman and Israel*, 90.

67. Cohen, *Truman and Israel*, 155.

68. Truman's hesitations were also attributed to the assessment of his military advisers that a Jewish state could not defend itself against an Arab invasion. Ibid., 158, 213.

69. *The Palestine Post* (October 14, 1947).

70. *UN Document A/364*, Add. 3, p. 32.

71. General Assembly Resolution 181 (II), November 29, 1947. According to the plan, Jerusalem and Bethlehem were to become an international zone, administered by a United Nations high commissioner, who would also supervise the holy sites within the boundaries of the Arab and Jewish states. The residents of the two cities would register as citizens of the state of their choice.

72. The archives of Ben-Gurion's party, Mapai, reveal that until the last minute there was plenty of skepticism about the ability of the Yishuv to survive a coordinated attack by regular Arab armies. It was recently found that speeches by those who argued against declaring statehood and later became cabinet ministers had mysteriously disappeared from the protocols.

73. Noah Lucas, *The Modern History of Israel* (New York, 1975), 272; Simha Flapan, *The Birth of Israel* (New York, 1987), 44; *Statistical Abstracts* (Jerusalem: Israel Bureau of Statistics, 1987), 33.

74. In his last speech before the national council, two days before he declared Israel's independence, Ben-Gurion expressed his belief that the Jews would win, albeit with heavy losses, if left face-to-face with only the Arabs of Palestine. But he

warned of a possible disaster if there was a blockade while help for the Arabs continued to flow from across the borders. In that case, "the Jews would survive only by a great miracle." David Ben-Gurion, *Behilahem Yisrael* (Tel Aviv, 1952), 106.

75. Weizmann, Ben-Gurion's rival, was later elected by the Knesset, Israel's parliament, as president of the state, a position that is merely ceremonial.

76. al-Tubasi, *Kifah al-Sha'b*, 105.

77. It seems that the British did not always stand by and allow Arab forces to invade at will. When the village of Kfar Szold in the upper Galilee was attacked in January 1948 by a Syrian-backed battalion, the British sent forces to help the Jewish settlers repel the attack. Chaim Herzog, *The Arab-Israeli Wars* (New York, 1982), 24.

78. Ibid., 19–20.

79. The rapid attacks by the Arabs following the UN resolution created the impression among their leaders that they had the initiative and that the Jews were about to surrender. al-Tubasi, *Kifah al-Sha'b*, 104.

80. In his memoirs, al-Tal claims credit for the Arab victory. He states that he was sent to Gush Etzion by Sir John Glubb, the British commander of the Jordanian Legion, to oversee the battle personally, due to the incompetence of the commander in charge. He adds that 500 Jews were killed and 350 were taken prisoner. Abdullah al-Tal, *Karithat Filastin* (Cairo, 1959), 31–34.

81. al-Tubasi, 108.

82. Ibid., 113.

83. Abdullah al-Tal, who was in charge of the Jordanian assault, justifies the destruction of the Jewish quarter by claiming that had he not destroyed the homes, he would have lost half his men. He adds that "the systematic demolition inflicted merciless terror in the hearts of the Jews, killing both fighters and civilians." al-Tal, *Karithat Filastin*, 112.

84. Ignoring an agreement it had with the government, the Irgun attempted to retain some of its forces and brought in the supply ship, *Altalena*, in violation of the terms of the cease-fire. To prevent the Irgun from undermining the authority of the state, Ben-Gurion ordered the shelling of the ship when it was beached at Tel Aviv. Sixteen Irgun members were killed as the ship blew up, and scores of its passengers were arrested. Hebrew daily *Ma'ariv* (Tel Aviv, June 23, 1948).

85. It is common belief among Arabs that the cease-fire saved Israel from defeat, and enabled Britain to "cheat and deceive to create a Jewish entity in the heart of the Arab countries." al-Tubasi, 116–117. Calling it a "major crime," Abdullah al-Tal, Jordan's chief commander in Jerusalem, condemns his government for pressuring its Arab allies to accept the cease-fire when the war was not going well for the Jews, by "making shameful threats that will remain a stain of dishonor on Jordan." Referring to an Israeli air raid on the capital, Amman, he pokes fun at King Abdullah, saying that "the Jews succeeded because the king feared for his life and his palace facing a single commercial airplane." al-Tal, *Karithat Filastin*, 202. Indeed, there were reports that Ben-Gurion desperately wanted an immediate cease-fire due to the deterioration of Israel's military position. See Sydney D. Bailey, *Four Arab-Israeli Wars* (New York, 1990), 25. Ben-Gurion himself, however, painted a different picture in his address to the nation the day before the cease-fire

went into effect. After speaking of Israel's victories and capture of land beyond the boundaries of the partition plan, he declared: "New Jerusalem is almost entirely in our hands, and our might has increased in the air, on land, and in the sea." On that occasion he accused Britain of assisting the Arabs "both openly and secretly." Ben-Gurion, *Bihilahem Yisrael*, 126–127.

86. Israel also accepted volunteers from abroad, whose number reached about 5,000. That brought the total strength of the Israeli army in manpower to about 90,000 by the end of 1948.

87. The Arab governments initially informed Bernadotte that they would not prolong the cease-fire. Under pressure from the Arab masses, who were inflamed by official propaganda of imminent victory, Arab rulers ignored the obvious conclusion that the Israelis were gaining more territory with every day of continued fighting. As the call for a cease-fire was finally heeded, causing the Arab public to feel it had been misled, mass demonstrations broke out in several Arab capitals. al-Tubasi, *Kifah al-Sha'b*, 123.

88. In a statement before the state's Provisional Council, Ben-Gurion condemned the murder as "a despicable crime committed by a gang of terrorist murderers . . . not only against the sanctity of human life, but against the highest institution of our time, the United Nations." Ben-Gurion, *Bihilahem Yisrael*, 251.

89. One of the Egyptian officers who were trapped in that pocket was Gamal Abdul-Nasser, who later organized the coup against King Farouq and subsequently became president of Egypt.

90. Security Council Resolution 73 (S/1376, II), August 11, 1949.

91. On the day of the third anniversary of the vote on the partition plan, the number of immigrants reached 500,000. *Ma'ariv* (November 29, 1950).

92. al-Tubasi, *Kifah al-Sha'b*, 128. Despite the king's efforts, none of the Arab countries recognized the union.

93. al-Tal claims in his memoirs that there was even some military coordination with the Jews. In one case, he charges that the Jordanian Legion had betrayed the Egyptian army by abandoning a joint battle near Jerusalem, leaving the Egyptians no choice but to retreat. al-Tal, *Karithat Filastin*, 266–267. Regarding another case, the Israeli takeover of Eilat, he accuses the king of stupidity in dealing with the Jews. Ibid., 483.

94. Some of that dialogue took the form of face-to-face conversations, such as the one between the king and Golda Meir. But the contact was mostly through friendly correspondence, part of which appears in al-Tal's memoirs. As reports about the talks with Israel began to leak, several Arab countries threatened to sever ties with Jordan. Sachar, *History of Israel*, 451.

95. In an interview with an American reporter, Abdullah called for a peace treaty between Israel and Jordan and blamed the problems between the two countries on "outside interference." *Ma'ariv* (November 18, 1948).

96. Shortly before his death, Abdullah dissolved the parliament because of growing opposition within it to ties with Britain and the armistice agreement with Israel. The assassin was a Palestinian with ties to a violent pro-mufti gang. *The Jerusalem Post* (July 22, 1951).

97. Claiming that Israel was only an "alleged" state, the Arab leaders took a

long time to acknowledge defeat and assume some responsibility for it. In a speech on December 13, 1953, President Nasser of Egypt complained that the Arabs had not done much: "We were saying at our meetings and in our speeches that we were going to throw the Jews into the sea, but after the speeches each of us went home." Gamal Abdul-Nasser, *Filastin,* a collection of speeches (Cairo, nd.), 10.

98. See Sachar, *History of Israel,* 331–335.

99. A case in point was the massacre at Deir Yassin, near Jerusalem, committed by members of the Irgun and Stern, who claimed they were fired upon by snipers. On April 9, 1948, the Irgun and Stern attacked the village that was strategically located on the highway to Tel Aviv. Between 200 and 250 villagers were killed, causing a shock that reverberated around the world. The Arabs retaliated by murdering 77 Jews, mostly doctors and nurses, who were on their way to Hadassah Hospital in Jerusalem. The Deir Yassin incident created panic among the Arabs throughout the country. Many Arabs, fearing a Jewish retaliation for the killing of Jews, fled before the advancing Israelis, while others were driven out. See Flapan, *The Birth of Israel,* 81–118. There are, however, some contradictory statements in Flapan's account. Although he states that "these tactics (the systematic ousting of the Arab population) were not part of a deliberate Zionist plan . . . Official Jewish decision making bodies . . . neither discussed nor approved a design for expulsion" (p. 87), on the other hand, he claims that the Jewish army, under the leadership of Ben-Gurion, "planned and executed the expulsion" (p. 89).

100. In a speech before the Israeli parliament on June 15, 1949, Foreign Minister Shertock stated that Jewish immigrants were filling the "geographical and economic" vacuum that was created by the Arab exodus, thus facilitating their absorption. Moshe Sharett, *Besha'ar Ha'umot* (Tel Aviv, 1966), 370.

101. While admitting that the Palestinian refugees had suffered a human tragedy, which he blamed on the Arab leadership, Shertock presented several arguments against their return. First, by agreeing to the partition plan, Israel had accepted in good faith an Arab community that would have constituted 40 percent of the population, but the war turned those Arabs into a security risk, so that "allowing them to return without peace with the neighboring countries would be an act of suicide." Second, the presence of a large Arab population would create enormous economic problems and change the character of the state. Third, the refugees would find themselves in a situation much different from the one that existed before they left, thus creating the potential for continuous unrest with which the state could not cope while absorbing a large number of Jewish immigrants. Sharett, Ibid., 370–372.

102. General Assembly Resolution 194 (III), Article 11, December 11, 1948.

103. A total of 56 military coups occurred or were attempted in the Arab countries from 1951 to 1970. Khaldoon Hasan al-Naqib, *al-Majalla* [Arabic weekly] (London, August 28, 1991), 12.

104. The idea of an alliance between Israel and Western imperialism is a dominant theme in Arab literature. See Ali Muhammad Ali and Ibrahim al-Hamsani, *Isra'l Qa'da 'Udwaniyya,* Ch. 1, "Israel a tool of neo-colonialism," (Cairo, nd.), 9–21. Putting the conflict with Israel in an East-West context, Nasser declared in a speech in the Soviet Union in April 1958 that "Imperialism has established Israel in

the heart of the Arab world in order to threaten the Arabs and force them to ask the imperialist bloc for protection." Gamal Abdul-Nasser, *Filastin*, 30.

105. The decision to finance and construct the Aswan Dam and the arms deal between Egypt and Czechoslovakia were the first major inroads made by the Soviet Union to gain influence in the region.

106. In a meeting with British Foreign Secretary Selwyn Lloyd, Nasser reportedly said that he would negotiate peace with Israel, but only on the basis of the 1947 partition plan. He added, however, that he first needed to achieve Arab unity. *Ma'ariv* (March 2, 1956). But such conciliatory remarks were quite rare. In his fiery speeches, Nasser left no doubt in the minds of the Arabs that he sought the eradication of Israel, whose establishment he called a "crime." Toward that end, he declared in a speech in December 1960: "We shall obtain the nuclear bomb at any price." Nasser, *Filastin*, 85.

107. Nasser also succeeded in isolating Israel internationally. Due to his efforts, an Israeli delegation was not invited to attend the first conference of developing countries in Bandung, Indonesia, in April 1955. A unanimous decision of the 29 participating nations supported the Palestinian Arabs.

108. The claim that Israel was a Western threat to all Arabs was a cornerstone of Nasser's political philosophy. Addressing an audience in Syria in May 1958, he repeated his theme that "Israel constitutes a bridgehead for imperialist aggression against the Arab world. Its establishment was intended to crush Arab nationalism into pieces." Nasser, *Filastin*, 31.

109. Egypt was adamant in refusing to allow shipping to and from Israel. In a speech in February 1960, Nasser said: "Yesterday there were statements by the old woman of Tel Aviv [a reference to Foreign Minister Golda Meir] saying that Israel would not remain silent . . . I hereby say to her and to Ben-Gurion her master that Israeli ships will never pass through the canal." Nasser, Ibid., 55.

110. As the Anglo-French military preparations shifted into high gear, France became Israel's main ally, pouring heavy artillery, tanks, and jet fighters into the country.

111. It was reported that in the face of the deteriorating situation in the Middle East there were suggestions in NATO to use Israeli territory for military movements, in return for security guarantees against Egypt. *Ma'ariv* (July 15, 1958).

112. Nasser's agents were believed to have been behind the August 1960 assassination of Jordanian Prime Minister Khaza' al-Majali in an explosion at a cabinet session, which also killed ten ministers. King Hussein narrowly escaped death when he did not arrive at the meeting on time. After evading a Syrian jet fighter that tried to shoot him down while he was piloting his airplane, the king relayed to the Israelis a plan to invade Syria. Herzog, 145–146.

113. The union between the two countries did not last long. In 1961 the Syrians revolted and reestablished their independence from Egypt.

114. King Hussein objected to guerrilla attacks on Israel through Jordanian territory, and accused the Syrians of using Jordan as a launching pad, thus exposing the kingdom to Israeli reprisals. Hussein of Jordan, *My "War" With Israel* (New York, 1969), 27.

115. To prevent an Israeli-Syrian war over water resources, in 1964 President

Lyndon B. Johnson signed an agreement for a joint nuclear desalination program with Israel, which included a plan to construct a power station in Eilat. The project was never carried out, however.

116. Herzog, *The Arab-Israeli Wars,* 148; Dean Rusk, *As I Saw It* (New York, 1990), 384.

117. Initially, the belligerent statements from Cairo were not taken seriously in Israel, on the advice of American officials. Israeli observers believed that Egypt's actions were merely "a psychological gesture" toward Syria. *Ma'ariv* (May 16, 1967).

118. Herzog, *The Arab-Israeli Wars,* 149.

119. Dean Rusk recalls that Nasser later told American officials, who were "both upset and alarmed" at the secretary-general's action, that once the UN forces were withdrawn, he could not allow Israeli ships to pass through the Straits of Tiran, in the absence of a buffer force. Despite that excuse, Rusk expresses his opinion that the closure of the straits "played a major role in provoking the June 1967 war." Rusk, *As I Saw It,* 384–385.

120. *The Jerusalem Post* (May 24, 1967).

121. According to Eban, de Gaulle's attitude was expressed in his repeated warning during their conversation: "*Ne faites pas la guerre*" (Do not make war). Abba Eban, *An Autobiography* (New York, 1977), 341–343.

122. Rusk, *As I Saw It,* 385.

123. Herzog, *The Arab-Israeli Wars,* 149.

124. Shuqeiri had been persona non grata in Jordan. His declaration "To liberate Tel Aviv we must first free Amman" typifies his animosity toward the king. Hussein, who scornfully called him "a millionaire refugee," blamed him for harming the Arab cause by declaring his intention to "throw the Jews into the sea." Hussein, *My "War" with Israel,* 14.

125. There are conflicting reports regarding President Johnson's position. According to a former CIA official, W. C. Eveland, the president, while refraining from giving the Israelis a clear signal to strike, informed them that "the United States would not intervene to stop an attack on Egypt." W. C. Eveland, *Ropes of Sand, America's Failure in the Middle East* (New York, 1980), 324. Dean Rusk, on the other hand, denies that Israel was given the go-ahead: "On May 26 Abba Eban came to Washington, where President Johnson and I urged restraint upon him in the strongest terms. LBJ also told him that Israel would not be alone unless it acted alone." Rusk, *As I Saw It,* 386. But after saying "we were shocked and angry as hell, when the Israelis launched their surprise offensive," Rusk does justify Israel's action: "But in all fairness to Israel, considering the major Arab mobilization, the movement of sizable Egyptian forces into the Sinai . . . the movement of Iraqi and Egyptian forces into Jordan . . . if the Israelis had waited for the Arabs to strike first, their situation would have been very grim . . . if there ever was a justification for preventive action, the Six-Day War might have been the case for it." Ibid., 387. Eban's account of his May 26 conversation with Johnson indicates that the president left the decision in the hands of the Israeli government: "If your cabinet [Israel's] decides to do anything immediately and to do it on their own, that is for them." Eban, *An Autobiography,* 357.

126. King Hussein maintained that the Arabs indeed lacked the time they needed: "To get back to my May 30 trip to Egypt . . . our position seemed less perilous because we have revived our system of military coordination with Nasser . . . if only we could have had a little more time!" Hussein, *My "War" with Israel*, 50.

127. *Ma'ariv* (June 5, 1967).

128. In the first hours, nineteen Egyptian air bases were attacked, destroying 309 of a total of 340 military aircraft. Herzog, *The Arab-Israeli Wars*, 152–153.

129. Hussein, *My "War" with Israel*, 35–36. The same explanations for joining the war were given by Wasfi al-Tall, Jordan's prime minister: "We were prodded into joining the others in the 1967 war not by the fear of public opinion or a desire to be in on the spoils, but by our honor, which demanded that we observe our mutual defense agreements." Ibid., 127. Because of his conflict with the Palestinians, Wasfi al-Tall was assassinated in Cairo in November 1971.

130. Rusk, *As I Saw It*, 387.

131. In that conversation, monitored by the Israelis and broadcast on their radio, Nasser and Hussein agreed to fabricate a claim that American and British aircraft were participating in the bombing of Egypt. The transcript of the conversation was published in Hussein's book, 82–83. Blaming the United States for Israel's victory, Nasser decided to sever diplomatic relations with Washington. Other Arab countries soon followed suit.

132. Contrary to their obligation under the armistice agreement of 1949, the Jordanians denied the Jews access to the Wailing Wall during their reign over Jerusalem.

133. By dragging their feet and attaching conditions unacceptable to the Israelis, the Arabs and the Russians delayed a cease-fire decision at the United Nations, thus giving Israel time to widen her conquests. In Rusk's words: "Arab leaders and their Soviet friends badly served the Arab cause by complicating and thereby delaying an immediate cease-fire." Rusk, 387.

134. Arab casualties, believed to be in the many thousands, were not made public, except for Jordan's reported 6,094 dead of missing. Hussein, *My "War" with Israel*, 88. Israel lost 764 soldiers in the war. Herzog, *The Arab-Israeli Wars*, 183.

135. *Ma'ariv* (June 13, 1967).

136. In an article published in the *Jerusalem Post* on October 12, 1991, reporter Moshe Zak writes that Hussein responded to Dayan's call via Washington. In the secret talks that followed between the Jordanian king, Golda Meir, and Dayan, Hussein refused to accept border changes or Israeli settlements on the West Bank.

137. The Soviets, who were unhappy with the defeat of their clients and the poor performance of their weapons, may have contributed to the refusal of the Arabs to change course. Fearful of losing their credibility and influence in the region, they dispatched a military delegation headed by Soviet President Nikolai Podgorny to Egypt and Syria to start an immediate reconstruction of their armies.

138. *The Jerusalem Post* (June 6, 1967).

139. Despite those decisions, Hussein formulated with Nasser a common "Arab position." Based on a total Israeli withdrawal and the right of the refugees

to return to their homes, the two would agree to recognition of Israel's right to live in peace and to an end to the state of belligerency. The Jordanian king blamed Arab extremists for stalling the plan. Hussein, *My "War" with Israel,* 117–119.

140. The wording of the clause that applies to Israeli withdrawal has been the subject of controversy. While the original English text refers to "Withdrawal of Israeli armed forces *from territories* occupied in the recent conflict," the French version contains the phrase *"Retrait des forces armées Israéliennes* des territtoires *occupés lors de récent conflit."* The Israelis have argued that because the English version, based on the British draft, does not say *"the* territories," Israel is not obliged to withdraw from all captured land. It is the general consensus, though, that the resolution meant a total withdrawal. The following is the English version:

> 1. Affirms that the fulfillment of Charter principles requires the establishment of a just and lasting peace in the Middle East which should include the application of both the following principles:
>
> (i) Withdrawal of Israeli armed forces from territories occupied in the recent conflict;
>
> (ii) Termination of all claims or states of belligerency and respect for and acknowledgement of the sovereignty, territorial integrity, and political independence of every State in the area and their right to live in peace within secure and recognized boundaries free from threats or acts of force;
>
> 2. Affirms further the necessity
>
> (a) For guaranteeing freedom of navigation through international waterways in the area;
>
> (b) For achieving a just settlement of the refugee problem;
>
> (c) For guaranteeing the territorial inviolability and political independence of every State in the area through measures including the establishment of demilitarized zones;
>
> 3. Requests the Secretary-General to designate a Special Representatiave to proceed to the Middle East to establish and maintain contacts with the States concerned in order to promote agreement and assist efforts to achieve a peaceful and accepted settlement in accordance with the provisions and principles in this resolution;
>
> 4. Requests the Secretary-General to report to the Security Council on the progress of the efforts of the Special Representative as soon as possible.

141. Subject to interpretations, the resolution was accepted by Egypt, Israel, and Jordan immediately, by Syria in 1973, and by the PLO in 1988.

142. It was indeed a problem for Israel to bear the losses of the war of attrition, as the casualty rate escalated. Low public morale and pressure on the government were behind Dayan's suggestion in 1971 to withdraw to about twenty miles from the canal and allow its reopening. President Anwar Sadat of Egypt was interested, but he attached conditions that were rejected by Israel.

143. Nasser's declaration before a mass demonstration in Cairo that "what had been taken by force can only be returned by force" was seen by Israel as a proof of his belligerent policy.

144. The acceptance of the cease-fire by Nasser came as a surprise. According to former U.S. Secretary of State Henry Kissinger, Nasser may have feared an Israeli invasion with American involvement. Henry Kissinger, *White House Years* (New York, 1979), 582.

145. The American arms sales to Israel had increased substantially over the years. After the embargo that was imposed when Israel fought the 1948 war, President John F. Kennedy changed U.S. policy when he agreed to sell Israel Hawk antiaircraft missiles. President Johnson raised both the quality and the quantity of the weapons by supplying Israel with American tanks through Germany, followed by shipments of Skyhawk and Phantom jets. From the 1973 war on, the United States gave the Israelis whatever sophisticated weapons they said they needed, although Israel had become considerably self-sufficient.

146. Israel's radio was silent on that day, so that no mobilization codes could be transmitted until it went back on the air when the Arab offensive became known.

147. Bailey, *Four Arab-Israeli Wars,* 307.

148. Sachar, *History of Israel,* 750−751.

149. In the first 24 hours of the Syrian offensive, an entire Israeli brigade was wiped out. Herzog, *The Arab-Israeli Wars,* 288.

150. Although the war was trumpeted as a victory in Egypt, investigations were conducted there as well. The *Sunday Times of London* reported that several Egyptian officers were executed for disregarding warnings of an impending Israeli crossing of the Suez Canal.

151. Using oil as a political weapon was always an option, but had not been previously practiced. Nasser spoke about Arab oil as early as 1953: "We have the only weapon that we can deny them, the weapon of oil . . . we can destroy the West." Nasser, *Filastin,* 11−12.

152. The common notion that Israel was an agent of imperialism was inscribed in the Palestinian National Covenant ("*al-Mithaq al-watani al-filastini*"), Article 22: "Israel is a political movement organically associated with international imperialism." Y. Harkabi, *The Palestinian Covenant and its Meaning* (London, 1979), 88.

153. Factionalism among the Palestinians was acknowledged in the Palestinian National Covenant, Article 8, which stated that "the conflicts among the Palestinian national forces are secondary," compared with the struggle against Israel. Ibid., 58.

154. For details on those factions and their strength, see William B. Quandt, in *The Politics of Palestinian Nationalism* (Berkeley, 1974) 66.

155. On the basis of shared revolutionary ideology, the PLO formed alliances with terrorist groups in Europe, Japan, and South America. Communist countries, which sponsored that type of organization, provided weapons and training facilities.

156. Hussein, *My "War" with Israel,* 23.

157. According to a Fatah spokesman, 9,000 guerillas were killed and tens of thousands of Palestinians were injured. *Ma'ariv* (September 22, 1970). Arafat said later that 900 of his people had died and that the civilian casualty figure stood at 20,000. The events of that month gave birth to the notorious "Black September" group.

158. The attack was perpetrated by three members of the Japanese Red Star terrorist group. It was the first known cooperation between Palestinians and foreign groups.

159. Four passengers and all hijackers were killed in the rescue mission. Ugandan President Idi Amin, who supported the hijacking, lost an unspecified number of his troops.

160. John Laffin, *The PLO Connections* (London, 1983), 98–99.

161. It was the U.S. government who persuaded Arafat to leave and guaranteed his safe exit: "it seems to have been the utter failure of Arab efforts during July to change the U.S. position . . . which brought the PLO to decide that there was little point in holding out further." Rashid Khalidi, *Under Siege: PLO Decisionmaking During the 1982 War* (New York, 1986), 92.

162. Herzog, *The Arab-Israeli Wars,* 347–348.

163. Approximately 150,000 Arabs from the territories are employed in the Israeli sector and depend on free access to their jobs for their livelihood.

164. The Palestinian Covenant, Article 20, based on the translation of Leila S. Kadi in Harkabi, *The Palestinian Covenant,*, 78.

165. Hussein, *My "War" with Israel,* 17.

166. The only exception is Lebanon, which has been struggling to survive as a nation. It is the only Arab country without Islamic dominance, but is still torn by religious factionalism.

167. Hussein, 24.

168. The PLO previously demanded that Jews who immigrated to Palestine after 1917 should go back to their countries of origin. This is supported by Article 6 of the Palestinian Covenant: "The Jews who had normally resided in Palestine until the beginning of the Zionist invasion shall be considered Palestinians." Harkabi, *The Palestinian Covenant,* 43. But later statements by the movement's leaders have retracted that condition. Quandt, *The Politics of Palestinian Nationalism,* 101–104.

169. Hussein, *My "War" with Israel,* 134.

History of the Israeli-Palestinian Conflict

Muhammad Y. Muslih's academic degrees include an associate degree in arts from Bir Zeit College in 1970, an M.A. degree in political science from the American University of Beirut in 1972, and a Ph.D. in political science from Columbia University in 1985. He is currently assistant professor of political science and Middle Eastern studies and director of the International Relations Program at C.W. Post College, Long Island University. He is the author of several books and articles, including *The Middle East after the Gulf War* with Augustus Richard Norton, to be published by the Foreign Policy Association (in press) and *Palestinian Political Thought since 1948*, Westview Press (forthcoming).

THE ROOT CAUSE of the Palestine problem lies in two political decisions made by Europeans living far from Palestine. Both decisions were deliberate acts of will and were made without consulting the indigenous people of Palestine. The first of these decisions was made in 1897, when a Jewish political movement of European provenance, known as the World Zionist Organization, met in Basel, Switzerland and resolved to establish a Jewish state in Palestine. At the time, Palestine was under Ottoman sovereignty; approximately 95 percent of the population was Arab, and 99 percent of the land was owned by the local Arab population.

The second political decision was made in London and was articulated in the Balfour Declaration of 2 November 1917. The declaration was in the form of a letter addressed to Lord Rothschild from British Foreign Secretary Arthur James Balfour. With this letter, which suppressed and undermined the rights of the Palestinian Arabs, the Zionist program became official British policy backed by the full weight of the British Empire.

The defeat of the Ottoman state at the end of World War I made the implementation of the Zionist program possible. Palestine fell to the British just as Transjordan and Iraq did. Britain's occupation was consecrated by the League of Nations under a trusteeship system known as the Mandate. To facilitate the fulfillment of the Zionist program, the British government incorporated the Balfour Declaration into the instrument of the Mandate. France agreed to the provisions of the Mandate in exchange for

British acquiescence to French control over Lebanon and Syria. The Palestinian Arabs were neither consulted nor taken into consideration, despite the fact that the principle of self-determination was enshrined in Article 22 of the Covenant of the League of Nations.

Under the British Mandate, the territory of Palestine covered a total area of approximately 10,400 square miles, approximately the size of the state of Vermont. At the time of the Balfour Declaration, there were approximately 900,000 people living in Palestine; generally accepted figures recognize the total population as being 570,000 Muslims, 70,000 Christians, and 60,000 Jews. Transjordan, although part of the Palestine Mandate, was excised from the scope of the Balfour Declaration. Repeated Zionist attempts to include Transjordan in their political scheme were rebuffed by the British, who wanted to give the appearance that the MacMahon promises made to Arabs in 1915 were being honored.

From the very beginning, the Palestinians were at a disadvantage vis-à-vis the Zionists. The Zionist movement was strategically allied with and politically, materially, and morally supported by an empire at the peak of its power and global influence. Moreover in terms of organization and political skills, the Palestinians were no match for the Zionists, who, being part of Western society, understood the inner workings of that society and knew how to influence its centers of power. From a position of great strength and organization the Zionists proceeded to push their program forward. The Palestinians, by contrast, struggled from a position of weakness to stand their ground in the face of the enormous odds against them. The result was a protracted struggle between two unequal forces. Each side's strategy reflected its vision, its political style, and the nature of its alliances.

The Zionist Strategy

Up to the end of the Mandate period in 1948, three basic and interrelated goals were paramount on the Zionist movement's political agenda. The first was to change the demographic balance in favor of the local Jewish community, which constituted less than 7 percent of the total population of Palestine at the time of the Basel program.[1] Logistically, this would be achieved by flooding Palestine with Zionist immigrants from Europe and elsewhere, despite stiff opposition on the part of the indigenous Palestinian population.

The second goal was to drastically increase the tiny portion of land possessed by the Jews, which was put at 2.04 percent in 1919, through land purchases and the acquisition of monopolistic concessions from the British authorities in Palestine, as well as through the forceful dispossession and displacement of the local Arab Christian and Muslim Palestinians.

The third, and perhaps most important, goal was to strike an alliance with a dominant external power that would commit itself to the Zionist agenda, thus legitimizing it and giving it military and legal protection in Palestine.

Running parallel with these goals was a persistent and carefully orchestrated campaign of propaganda, political manipulation, and military planning. The focal point of the campaign was to delegitimize Palestinian nationhood by persistently negating the existence of the Palestinians as a separate and identifiable people. This effort assumed a most extreme form in the slogan: "Land without people, for a people without land." To the architects of Zionism this qualitative and continuous denial of the existence of the Palestinians appeared necessary not only to sidetrack the human rights of the local people, but also to hide from the world their destruction of an indigenous community. Doubtless, still another reason for the denial was the Zionist leaders' insistence on bypassing negotiations with Palestinian leaders. From the beginning, Zionist policy makers were willing to negotiate strategic issues with Arab rulers, but not with Palestinian leaders. It was as if the Palestinians constituted a political vacuum, and their fate therefore was to be determined by outside actors.

Another aspect of the campaign was based on a plan to reduce Palestinian opposition to the Zionist undertaking. According to a secret Zionist memorandum, dated 5 May 1920, this involved, *inter alia*, the cooptation of Palestinian notables; the "destruction" of the connections between Palestinian groups and other Arab groups in Syria and Transjordan; the purchase of unfriendly Arab papers; and "the separation between Christians and Muslims."[2] So, rather than seeking a modus vivendi with the Palestinian Arabs, based on hiring Arab officials in the fields of Jewish commerce, industry, and agriculture, key Zionist leaders, including Chaim Weizmann, opted for a policy of "buying" support and sowing discord among the Palestinian Arabs.

A third essential component of this multifaceted Zionist campaign was a determination to use *force majeure* if the Palestinian Arabs did not acquiesce voluntarily to their diminished status in Palestine. As David Ben-Gurion admitted in 1937, Zionist military strength had to be built up in order to coerce the Palestinian Arabs into accepting the Zionist program because, as he conceded, "we [Zionists] are the aggressors and they [the Palestinians] defend themselves."[3]

At the heart of the Zionist strategy was one non-negotiable political goal: the establishment of a self-contained, "mono-religious" Jewish state on Palestinian soil entirely separate from and, if circumstances permitted, in the place of the Palestinian Arab community. There is no question that this strategy led to the creation of a Jewish nation in Palestine, which was a uniquely constructive endeavor as far as Jewish interests were concerned. For the Palestinians, the forcible transformation of Palestine into a Jewish state despite opposition led to the destruction of Palestine as a politico-cultural community.

This was indeed the bitter harvest reaped by the Palestinians after forty-one years of British colonial rule in Palestine. The British sponsorship of Zionism enabled the Zionist movement to translate what appeared to be a utopian plan into reality. Despite the ups and downs in the British-Zionist relationship, the British government never withdrew its strategic support for the dominant political goal of Zionism. Under British sponsorship, the Zionists were able to engineer one of the best political deals of the century.

By the end of World War II, the ratio of the Jewish population increased through mass immigration from 9.7 percent in 1919 to 35.1 percent in 1946. At the same time, the ratio of Palestinian land owned by the Jews rose from 2.04 percent in 1919 to 7.0 percent in 1946.[4]

While Jewish immigration resulted in the rapid reduction of the indigenous Palestinian Arab population from an overwhelming majority to a much smaller and dwindling community, Jewish land acquisitions led to the displacement of Arab farmers and the deterioration of large tracts of Palestine's agricultural land. The destructive impact of land transfers was well documented as early as 1930 by Sir John Hope Simpson, a British civil servant who was sent by the British government to Palestine to study the effect of Zionist colonization on the existing population.

Simpson's conclusions can be summarized as follows: (1) land acquired by the Jewish National Fund became extraterritorialized, which meant that the Arabs could gain no advantage from it "either now or at any time in the future"; (2) Arabs were completely excluded from the land purchased by Jews, since the Jewish National Fund requested all Jewish settlers to have Jewish workers only; (3) the displacement of Arab farmers, coupled with the exclusion of Arab labor from the Jewish agricultural enterprises, created serious and widespread unemployment among the Arabs.[5] More detailed analyses of the unique impact of the Zionist enterprise on the Palestinians can be found in the works of Howard Lamar and Leonard Thompson.

The Palestine civil war (November 1947 to 15 May 1948) and the regular war (15 May 1948 to spring 1949) provided the Zionist movement with the opportunity to complete the process of creating a Jewish state. The two wars ended with the establishment of Israel on roughly 77 percent of the total land area of Palestine. As for the remaining 23 percent of the country not conquered by Israel in 1948, the West Bank, including East Jerusalem, was merged with Jordan, and the Gaza Strip was administratively incorporated by Egypt.

In the course of creating Israel, the Palestinian community was virtually destroyed. Approximately 780,000 Palestinians became refugees as a result of Israel's establishment in 1948. Some Palestinians fled as a result of the panic produced by Zionist military and psychological warfare, while others were driven out by force.[6] Moreover, 418 Arab villages were destroyed and/or depopulated. Nothing remains of them but decayed churches, mosques, shrines, and, above all, memories in the minds of their dispossessed owners.[7] According to one estimate, all-inclusive Palestinian *wealth* losses in 1948 add up to $147 billion when converted into 1984 prices. Of course, this does not include the value of the lost homeland and the lost lives, all of which cannot to be assessed in monetary terms.[8]

Once established, Israel became the institutional embodiment of political Zionist strategy. At the center of Israel's efforts to realize that strategy was a plan to consolidate its seizure of 77 percent of Palestine. Operationally, the plan had four aspects. The first pertained to Israel's absorption of a massive influx of Jewish immigrants, or the policy of the "in-gathering of the exiles." By 1952, Israel's Jewish population more than doubled, rising from 680,000 in 1949 to about 1,405,000 in 1952.

A second aspect of Israel's consolidation was the dispossession and de-institutionalization of the remaining Palestinian community in what became Israel following the Palestine war. In addition to the 418 destroyed Arab villages mentioned previously, the major Palestinian towns or mixed townships were Judaized, with their Arab assets transferred to Jewish hands. Inside Israel, Palestinians lived under an Israeli military government for nearly eighteen years. Much of their land was confiscated, and education, employment, and agricultural and rural development were severely disrupted. In a word, the institutional foundations of Palestinian Arab society were largely destroyed.[9]

A third component of Israel's plan was the so-called concept of security. From Israel's perspective, its security entailed three things: (a) a decisive military superiority vis-à-vis any combination of Arab forces; (b) a policy of massive and disproportionate retaliation for any Arab infiltration; and (c) a blitzkrieg based on the doctrine of carrying the battle to enemy territory. This security doctrine was as much a result of Israel's feeling of besiegement in a hostile environment as it was the product of a desire to justify its behavior toward the Palestinians and its Arab neighbors. Israeli practices such as the confiscation of Arab land, administrative detention, and deportations were all justified in the name of "security." In the words of one observer,

> They take our land. Why? For security reasons! They take our jobs. Why? For security reasons! And when we ask them how it happens that we, our lands and our jobs threaten the security of the state—they do not tell us. Why not? For security reasons![10]

The fourth aspect of Israel's plan of action represented a continuation of the pre-1948 Zionist policy of securing the support of a foreign power. With the demise of British power after World War II, the Zionists shifted their focus to Washington. Ever since then, the United States, which is the major modern superpower, has put its full political, moral, and material weight behind Israel. By its actions and inactions, the United States government has enabled Israel not only to consolidate its presence, but also to expand and to undermine the legitimate interests of the Palestinians. To paraphrase an observation made by a Palestinian, the cumulative impact of American policies has rendered the United States a decisive part not only of the Israeli-Palestinian problem but also of its solution.[11]

Israel's seizure of the remaining 23 percent of Palestine was made possible by the June 1967 war. Jamal Abd al-Nasir's shortsighted decision to close the straits of Tiran, as well as the mistakes of the radical Ba'athist regime in Damascus, gave Israel's generals the pretext to launch that war, fully confident that they would defeat the Arab forces and expand Israel territorially, particularly in the West Bank.[12] Israel's ability to decisively defeat the Egyptians and Syrians, even if they were to fire first, was recognized by the administration of President Lyndon Johnson. This has been well documented in William Quandt's analysis of U.S.-Israeli relations during this period.[13] By the end of the war the Arab armies of Egypt, Syria, and Jordan were swiftly destroyed in a humiliating defeat. Israel captured the West Bank, including East Jerusalem, the Gaza Strip, and the Golan Heights.

As far as the West Bank and Gaza were concerned, what had been exclusively Arab territory, with about 0.5 percent of Jewish land ownership just prior to the June war, was rapidly colonized, annexed, or incorporated de facto in Israel. Following are some of the highlights:

• Until now, Israel has confiscated about 55 percent of the land of the West Bank and about 45 percent of the land of Gaza.

• In 1980, after Judaizing East Jerusalem and doubling its surface area, Israel enacted through its Knesset the "Basic Law" which formally annexed the city and declared it the eternal capital of Israel. In response, the UN Security Council passed Resolutions 476 (1980), which deplored Israel's Judaization measures, and 478 (1980), which called upon those states that had established diplomatic missions in Jerusalem to withdraw such missions from the Holy City.

• All known Palestinian water reserves in the occupied territories are being used by Israel. As a result, the area of irrigated Arab land fell from 27 percent in 1967 to 3.7 percent.

• There are now about 215,000 Jewish settlers living in occupied Arab land, with 120,000 living in East Jerusalem and the rest living outside the expanded area of the city. Settlers irrigate 70 percent of their farmland from Arab water reserves. Many Israelis have swimming pools at a time when Arab neighborhoods are experiencing water shortages.

• According to official Israeli statistics, 99.65 percent of Jewish areas are settled by Jews.

• About 250,000 Soviet Jews (excluding one million more expected in the very near future) are already waiting to immigrate to Israel, thus accelerating the process of what the late Moshe Dayan called "creating new facts on the ground."[14]

• Since 1967, Israel has deported to Jordan or Lebanon an entire generation of local Palestinian leaders, including members of municipal councils, educators, doctors, engineers, and other professionals. The purpose was simple: to eliminate the prospects for developing self-governing institutions for the Palestinians.[15]

The Israeli government continues its attempts to delegitimize the Palestinian people not just by denying their national rights, but also by refusing to respect and meet with their designated representatives. Hence Israel's total rejection of negotiating with the Palestine Liberation Organization, and its insistence on limited autonomy confined to the Palestinians living in the occupied territories and not to their land.

Palestinian Responses

The Palestinian reaction to Zionist colonization can be broken down into three stages: the state of saving Palestine, the stage of liberating Palestine, and the state of sharing Palestine. In all three stages, the Palestinians were strategically on the defensive, determined to protect themselves from the threat of Zionism. Moreover, nationalism with its emphasis on political self-determination was at the very center of the political and intellectual life of the beleaguered Palestinian community. The strategy adopted in each stage grew out of an identifiable structure of politics as well as out of the political climate of the times.

THE STAGE OF SAVING PALESTINE, 1917–1948

In this stage, Palestinian nationalism and its modus operandi were tailored to the unique nature of the threat posed by the British-Zionist alliance, as well as to the political style and social class of the Palestinian leadership. Viewing Zionism as a political movement that strove to negate and annul the political rights of the Palestinians in their own homeland, the Palestinian nationalist elite attempted to balance delegitimation with counter-delegitimation, seeking in the process to justify Arab political rights in Palestine.

The Palestinian nationalist ideology revolved around three basic arguments. First, security, much more than ideology, was the fountainhead of the Palestinian nationalist elite's thinking. To them, the Zionist movement, under British protection, aimed at dispossessing and displacing the Palestinians. Therefore, accepting Zionism was tantamount to committing political suicide. Neither natural law nor religious law, they believed, justified the attempt to solve the problems of Jewish dispersion and virulent anti-Semitism in Europe at the expense of another politically conscious people already established in a national home of their own.

Second, the Palestinians stressed their right to national self-determination. From their perspective, this right had three pillars: (a) the uninterrupted presence of the Palestinian Arabs in the country long before the Muslim conquest of A.D. 637; (b) the demographic and land-holding balances, which were overwhelmingly in favor of the Palestinians, who viewed it as a travesty of justice to make a small Jewish minority, which possessed a very tiny fraction of the land, predominate over the vast majority of Christian and Muslim Arabs who basically owned the country; and (c) Allied pronouncements at the end of World War I, together with paragraph 4 of Article 22 of the Covenant of the League of Nations, which entitle Palestinians to political independence and the freedom to determine the future of their country.

Third, the Palestinian nationalist elites argued that the Jews had no political rights in Palestine, even though they had spiritual connections with the country. After a lapse of two thousand years, the European leadership of the Zionist movement had no right to assign to contemporary Jews, who were scattered all over the world, political rights in Palestine that overrode those of the indigenous Palestinian population.[16]

The methods used to promote the goals of Palestinian nationalism mirrored the political style of the social class from which the Palestinian leadership was drawn. In this stage, the Palestinian leadership hailed from influential urban notable families who derived their influence from their education, administrative experience in late Ottoman times, and, in most cases, land ownership. Whether dominant Palestinian politicians descended from the Husayni, Khalidi, Nashashibi, or other upper-class families, they all shared a similar political style.

Imbued as they were with the Ottoman tradition of civic politesse (*talattuf madani*) and unrestrained respect for authority, Palestinian politicians tended to act in a timid and legalistic manner.[17] In an attempt to protect the rights of their constituency,[18] petitions were used as the principal political instrument to register their concerns with the British authorities. In short, nationalism in the hands of the Palestinian leadership was not a revolutionary ideology intent on using armed struggle or overturning the existing local power relations, but rather was oriented toward maintaining the status quo.

For two decades, al-Hajj Amin al-Husayni, the leader of the Palestinian nationalist movement during the Mandate years, followed a dual policy of cooperation with the British colonial authorities and nonviolent opposition to the Zionist movement. After all, Amin was an officer of the British government and his family had a long tradition of guaranteeing local stability for the Muslim Ottoman state.

Even when Amin became active during and after the general strike of 1936, he was forced to do so by virtue of the events themselves rather than by his own initiation. As Amin's biographer indicates, Palestinian public pressure on Amin led to the strike, and the end of British confidence in him served to radicalize Amin and to convince him that revolutionary armed struggle was the method that would protect Palestinian national existence.[19]

Even after his exile to Lebanon, Amin managed to lead the Palestinian armed revolt of 1937–1939. The cost of the revolt to Palestinians was staggering. Of the total population of 960,000, more than 3,000 Palestinians were reported killed, 110 were hanged by the British, and 6,000 were jailed for security offenses in 1939 alone.[20]

After the defeat at the hands of the British, the revolt was followed by persistent Palestinian opposition to Zionists and their British sponsors. The opposition culminated in the Palestinian civil war, which concluded not only with the establishment of Israel but also with the virtual destruction of the Palestinian Arab community. The belated and ineffective intervention of the Arab armies after mid-May 1948, as a response to the great pressure put on politicians by Arab public opinion, simply postponed the inevitable. Had it not been for the Arab intervention, the Jewish forces would have seized all of historic Palestine in 1948.

To some Western observers, the catastrophe that befell the Palestinians was their own doing. Despite the myths and semi-myths surrounding this argument, the following observations can be made.

First, throughout British colonial rule over Palestine, the balance of power was decisively in favor of the Zionists. The British embraced Zionism. They armed the Jews and disarmed the Arabs. Manipulation and force exerted by the Zionists through their powerful British sponsor enabled them to build the institutional foundations of the Jewish state.

Second, the upshot of British policy was the emergence in Palestine of a Jewish military force that enjoyed overwhelming superiority over the Palestinians and the regular Arab armies from the standpoint of its combined organization, military planning, logistical support, political independence, and weaponry.[21] This ultimately decided the fate of Palestine in 1947 and 1948.

Third, with the exception of the 1939 White Paper, British offers made to the Palestinians were impossible to accept morally, politically, and materially. Proposals for a legislative council in 1922 were unacceptable to the Palestinians because the proposed institution rested on the Balfour Declaration. At the same time, its Arab members would be outnumbered by the combined votes of the Jewish representatives and the government officials. The 1937 partition scheme was also anathema to the Palestinian leadership. While the scheme offered the Palestinian Arabs a state united with Transjordan under Emir Abdullah, it gave Palestine's strategic and religious region, including Jerusalem, to the British and offered the Jews a state in the Galilee and much of the coastal plain, the most fertile land in Palestine. The 1947 UN partition plan was not much better. It called for increased Zionist land ownership, from 7 to 55 percent of Palestine, but asked Palestinians to give up 45 percent of what they possessed and expected one-third of them to live as a minority under Jewish rule. In the words of one observer, ". . . if to the Zionists partition was more than half a loaf, to the Palestinians it was less than half a baby."[22]

One could argue, with the benefit of hindsight, that the Palestinian leadership should have realized its severe limitations vis-à-vis the British-Zionist alliance. They should have also realized that the alliance was irreversible, and should have tried to overcome, on the basis of that, the stubborn psychological barriers to yielding on matters of national survival.

Fourth, neither Palestinian society nor the political style of its leadership was a match for the Jewish community and its leadership. While the Jewish population was organized, highly mobilizable, and politically well integrated, the Palestinians were disorganized, stratified vertically, and poorly prepared to coordinate their activities on the national level. Meanwhile, the political style of the Palestinian leadership was not equal to the realpolitik of the Zionists and their British sponsors. Being themselves products of Western, industrialized societies, the Jewish leaders were highly efficient and well versed in the art of strategic planning. In terms of their level of political development, neighboring Arab societies were no better than the Palestinians. But ultimately, they assumed independence. Unfortunately for the Palestinians, the realization of the political goals of Zionism entailed the annulment of their peoplehood. The Zionists wished that, and the British supported that wish. The Palestinians were too weak and too inept to face the overwhelming challenge. And thus, the Zionist wish was fulfilled.

THE STAGE OF LIBERATING PALESTINE, 1948–1969

While 1948 marked the complete destruction of the Palestinian Arab community, the two decades that ensued marked the initiation of a process of rebuilding the uprooted and dispersed community in preparation for the ultimate goal of liberating Palestine. Forced to become refugees in neighboring Arab states and elsewhere, the Palestinians faced problems that varied from country to country—problems which were mainly a function of the state of politics of the host countries they were living in.

In Jordan, which annexed the West Bank in 1950, the Palestinians were integrated and were granted Jordanian citizenship, but their freedom to develop their own political institutions was sharply curtailed by the Hashemite monarchy. To a large degree, the same applies to Syria. Palestinians were integrated into the areas of employment and education, but were effectively barred from engaging in political activity that was not directly controlled by the Syrian regime. In Lebanon, where there was a large Palestinian refugee population, Palestinians were prohibited from working without a permit. In general, many of them were exploited in the unskilled labor market. Until 1969, the year in which the Lebanese state began to weaken, Palestinians were politically suppressed by the Lebanese security forces.

The small Palestinian community in Egypt was given employment opportunities and was allowed to organize politically, as long as its active members adopted a political line that was compatible with that of the Egyptian government. Palestinians who lived in Kuwait at this stage were integrated into Kuwait's economy and bureaucracy. They were also allowed to form unions and political organizations as long as their activities did not threaten the security of the Kuwaiti regime.[23]

Attempts aimed at liberating Palestine took two forms: one was focused on pan-Arabism, while the other was focused on a more strict Palestinian perspective. The first enjoyed the support of the overwhelming majority of Palestinians in the diaspora. At the time, the popularity of the Arab nationalist sentiment was widespread in the Arab world. Until the defeat of the frontline Arab states in June 1967, most Palestinians were committed first and foremost to Arab unity, believing that a united Arab nation was the road to the liberation of Palestine. The other, a minority trend lacking widespread popular support, mistrusted the Arab regimes and rejected their custodianship over the Palestinian cause. Among its principal advocates were the founders of Fatah, which later became the mainstream Palestinian movement, as well as the activists working within the framework of the General Union of Palestine Students (GUPS) founded in 1959, the General Union of Palestine Workers (GUPW) established in 1963, the General Union of Palestinian Women (GUPWom) created in 1965, and other unions or societies designed to address the changing needs of the dispersed Palestinian communities. These institutions were heirs to a rich pre-1948 Palestinian tradition of establishing political parties and societies dedicated to the national cause as well as to social concerns.

Despite differences in approach, the Palestinians were unanimous in their dedication to one central goal: the total liberation of Palestine. This was clearly reflected in the Palestine national (*qawmi*) charter of June 1964. A special committee (*lajnat al-mithaq*) formed by the Palestine National Council (PNC) drafted the charter. Since the creation of the Palestine

Liberation Organization (PLO) under Arab auspices in 1964, the PNC has acted as a Palestinian parliament-in-exile. The concept of total liberation appears sixteen times in the twenty-nine articles of the charter. Total liberation, of course, meant the dismantling of Israel as a political entity. This forced those drafting the charter to address the question of the future of the Jews in a liberated Palestine. Being themselves unsure about how to handle this important matter, they provided a vague answer. Article 7 of the 1964 charter stipulated that the "Jews who are of Palestinian origin will be considered Palestinians if they are willing to live loyally and peacefully in Palestine."[24]

Closely associated with total liberation was the concept of return. Writing fifteen years after the destruction and exile of the Palestinian community, the late Palestinian historian Abd al-Latif Tibawi analyzed the intensity of the Palestinian emotion concerning the return. The sentiment of return, he noted, has a comprehensive hold on the Palestinians:

> It [return] embraces not only those adults, men and women and their children who are now homeless, but also children of refugees born in exile. All are being thoroughly and systematically instructed in the mystique of "the return" in schools and through all the modern media of communication.[25]

The visions of liberation and return reflected the psychological and emotional forces that motivated the Palestinians: the deep sense of injustice, the pain of exile, the powerful attachment to all of Palestine, and a deeply ingrained historical belief in the justice of the Palestinian cause. It was against this background that the Palestinians rejected permanent resettlement (*tawteen*) in neighboring Arab countries, thus forcing the United Nations Relief and Works Agency (UNRWA) to drop its plans for integrating Palestinian refugees into the host Arab countries, and to focus instead upon relief, health, and educational activities. For the Palestinians, life outside their homeland meant that they would remain a people condemned to eternal suffering, a people without credentials, without the means of self-defense, and without any freedom to determine their own fate.

To achieve the two intertwined goals of liberation and return, politically active Palestinians proposed two courses of action. Each course mirrored the social class and political ties of its advocates. In this stage, the PLO was largely an organization of traditional Palestinian notables. Its leader, Ahmad al-Shuqayri, an upper-class Palestinian and a protege of Nasir, subscribed to the theory of collective Arab action through the regular armies of the Arab states. As it was structured at the time, not only did the PLO owe its existence to the Arab regimes that created it, but it was also under the control of those regimes. Its trademark, therefore, was inaction and bombastic verbal outbidding. Revolutionary armed struggle was not an option that appealed to the PLO's conservative leaders.

On the other hand, Fatah—the major underground Palestinian movement during the period under survey—stressed the principles of armed struggle or guerrilla warfare, self-reliance, and Palestinian political independence. Three factors motivated the founders of Fatah to move in this direction: (a) a young, dynamic, and cohesive leadership that was not tied to any Arab regime; (b) Fatah's ability to utilize inter-Arab quarrels to its advantage, as was evidenced in the support it received from Syria for its raids against Israel in 1965–1967; and (c) Israel's unclear program and the impending completion of its project for the diversion of the Jordan River waters. Through its military arm, al-Asifa (the Storm), Fatah launched commando operations against Israel. Although the raids were primarily of symbolic significance, the strategy behind them was to provoke Israel in the hope of engaging the frontline Arab states in a decisive war of liberation before Israel became a nuclear power.[26]

Fatah's vision of nationalism and armed struggle clashed with that of status quo–oriented Arab regimes that had no plan to liberate Palestine and no intention of risking a military confrontation with Israel. Theirs was a world of fiery speeches and verbal outbidding. With the exception of Syria, the Arab governments therefore clamped down on al-Asifa. Equally fettering was the fact that most Palestinians and other Arabs continued to regard combined, traditional military action under the leadership of Nasir as the key to the liberation of Palestine.

THE STAGE OF SHARING PALESTINE, 1969–1991

The June 1967 defeat was a major watershed in the history of the Arabs in general and the Palestinians in particular. The old style of Arab politics, based on oratory and metaphysical dreams, gave way to a more cautious and pragmatic approach. Arab nationalism was on the retreat. By virtue of its close association with discredited Arab regimes, the traditional leadership of the PLO was pushed aside by a younger generation of Palestinian activists. These were the leaders of the commando organizations that took control of Palestinian politics.

Yasir Arafat, the leader of centrist Fatah, George Habash, the head of the leftist Popular Front for the Liberation of Palestine (PFLP), Nayif Hawatma, the leader of the leftist Democratic Front for the Liberation of Palestine (DFLP), and a few others, who led Palestinian commando organizations, became the leaders of the PLO. The PLO enjoyed the support of the overwhelming majority of the Palestinians. Within the framework of Palestinian politics, Arafat had a long lead in his primacy.

Two points ought to be emphasized here. First, in order to understand the character, style, and organization of Palestinian nationalist politics during this stage, it is necessary to place the PLO squarely in the context of the Palestinian diaspora. Being a national movement whose adherents lived primarily in exile, the PLO had to articulate the wishes of the diaspora Palestinians, who constituted a large portion of the Palestinian people as a whole. Diaspora Palestinians had their homes and roots in the three-quarters of Palestine that was captured by the Jewish forces in 1948. Thus, they felt they had little to gain from a settlement that did not guarantee their return. Second, the PLO is not a monolithic organization. Indeed, we find in it a significant degree of pluralism and political bargaining embodied in the quasi-parliament, the PNC, and in the unfettered debates that take place among its constituent units. In view of this, PLO decisions, especially the PNC resolutions, are the product of lengthy debate and hard-won consensus.

As far as Palestinian thinking about the conflict with Israel is concerned, this stage can be divided into three phases.

These phases are:

• The "secular democratic state" phase, from 1969 through 1973. In this phase the PLO continued to stress the importance of armed struggle and reject the partition of Palestine. However, it placed new emphasis on the specifically Palestinian (rather than Arab) character of the country and held out the hope that Palestine could be shared by all citizens, whether Jewish, Christian, or Muslim, on the basis of nonsectarian principles (democracy, equality, and mutual respect). Although Zionist institutions would be dismantled, Jewish Palestinians would have the same rights as other citizens, regardless of the date of their arrival in Palestine. The concept of a nonsectarian, democratic state was the Palestinian answer to the challenge of dealing with the Jewish population that was already in Palestine. A burgeoning tendency to employ diplomatic as well as military means to achieve these goals appeared.

• The "two-state solution" phase, which began in 1974 and culminated in the acceptance of a Palestinian state alongside Israel, not as a transitional stage but as a *point final*. The strategy during much of this phase has been to concentrate on diplomatic efforts at the expense of military efforts, to contact moderate Israeli groups and individuals directly, to insist on PLO participation in a Middle East peace conference, and to affirm the PLO's readiness to open a direct dialogue with the Israeli government. This phase culminated in the PLO's acceptance of Resolution 242 in 1988.

• The "provisional arrangements" phase, which began after the second Gulf War and culminated in the participation of a non-PLO Palestinian delegation from the occupied territories in the U.S.-Soviet-sponsored peace conference within the framework of a joint Jordanian-Palestinian delegation. The strategy during this phase has been to adopt a more flexible approach, particularly on issues of procedure, in order to adapt to the new realities that emerged after the recent Gulf War and to heal the rift between the anti–Saddam Hussein Arab coalition partners and the PLO leadership that adopted a pro-Iraqi stand during the Gulf events of 1990–1991. As reflected in the twentieth PNC program of September 1991, the new concepts adopted in this phase are the acceptance of a regional rather than international peace conference, the relaxation of the Palestinian insistence on a direct and equal role for the PLO, and, finally, the endorsement of the concept of *marhaliyya,* that is, Palestinian self-government over people, land, and natural resources in the occupied territories pending agreement on the final status of the territories.[27]

This 180-degree shift in the thinking of the Palestinians with regard to the conflict with Israel took place against a backdrop of Arab failure to help the Palestinian cause, an Arab readiness to live in peace with an Israel contained within its pre-1967 borders, a quiescent international community, and a balance of suffering that has been overwhelmingly in favor of the Palestinians. Above all, the change took place against the background of the *intifada* (uprising). The outbreak of the intifada in December 1987 catapulted the priorities of the West Bank and Gaza Palestinians to the top of the PLO agenda.

Being the daily victims of Israeli occupation, they have made compromise, not absolute justice, the foundation of their thinking. Most are willing to pay the painful price for ending Israel's occupation.

The weakening of the PLO after the Gulf War accelerated this process. Organizationally speaking, a new system of Palestinian politics is emerging. In all likelihood, this system will neither be based on the old formula of total PLO dominance nor exclusively derived from the expanding role of Palestinian activists in the occupied territories. The new system will rather rest on interaction between the emerging leadership of the Palestinians living under Israeli occupation and the PLO leadership in Tunis.

Conclusion

At the root of the Arab-Israeli conflict is the Palestine problem. In their response to the realization of the Zionist dream, the Palestinians have been on the defensive, though they have sometimes resorted to nonconventional methods of violence. Throughout the history of the conflict, the balance of power was decisively in favor of the Zionist movement, and later Israel. Without British protection, the Zionists would not have succeeded in establishing a Jewish state in Palestine. Similarly, without American support and largesse, Israel would not have been able to expand and consolidate.

We may disagree with the choices made by Palestinian leaders over the years. However, we must understand the reasons for their choices, the odds they fought against, and the range of alternatives that were open to them. They felt that they were asked by others, outside their country and outside their region, to yield on fundamental issues of security and national survival. So during the mandate years the Palestinians rejected the transformation of their ancestral homeland into a state for alien Jewish settlers. For nearly two decades and a half after the 1948 Nakba (Catastrophe), they also refused to accept the reality of Israel.

But, as we have seen, the Palestinians changed their attitude toward Israel in a real and fundamental way. The Arab states have also done so, as has been amply manifested in successive Arab summit resolutions, from the late seventies down to the present. Today, a dominant concept in Arab political discourse is "political flexibility" (*al-muruna al-siyasiyya*). Arab governments have indicated privately and publicly, in Arabic and in English, that should Israel allow the Palestinians to exercise their internationally recognized right to national self-determination, and withdraw from occupied Arab land on all fronts, they would be willing to live in peace with the Jewish state. Through their highest policy-making bodies, the Palestinians have consistently expressed their willingness to accept a state on a mere 23 percent of their historical soil. To accommodate Israeli wishes, they have recently declared themselves ready to accept a self-governing regime as an interim arrangement.

The instrumentalities most appropriate to the solution of the Israeli-Palestinian and Arab-Israeli conflicts are already in place, in the form of the regional peace conference recently launched in Madrid under American and Soviet auspices. The conference is based on long-standing Israeli conditions: direct bilateral face-to-face interstate negotiations; UN Security Council Resolution 242; non-PLO participation; and a joint Jordanian-Palestinian delegation, with the Palestinian component drawn from the occupied territories minus East Jerusalem.

The old story of Arab intransigence and rejectionism is now a fairy tale. With Egypt neutralized and Iraq bombed back to the pre-industrial age, Israel has reached a new pinnacle of military superiority in the Middle East. Moreover, the Palestinians and the Arab states have succumbed to Israeli demands. What they will not do is forsake their honor, or endorse the Likud government's wish to see the Palestinians legislate themselves out of existence. Certain Israeli individuals and groups, notably the Peace Now movement, appreciate the change and its strategic significance. They see in it a great advantage for Israel's security, assuming the Israeli government reciprocates in kind.

Will the Israeli government oblige, or will it continue to dogmatically adhere to an archaeological ideology whose central ingredients are refusal to yield any occupied Arab land and the total denial of Palestinian national rights? Ultimately, the answer to that will be largely determined by how far the U.S. government is willing to go in order to convince Israel that there can be no peace without territorial compromise and, above all, without setting the Palestinians free in less than a quarter of their ancestral homeland. The convincing must be immediate, consistent, and unmistakable. Failing that, the alarming pace of expansion through settlement within the framework of Minister Ariel Sharon's "Seven Star Plan,"[28] will dash what remains of the hope for peace in the Land of Peace.

Notes

1. Justin McCarthy, *The Population of Palestine: Population Statistics of the Late Ottoman Period and the Mandate* (New York: Columbia University Press/IPS Series, 1990).

2. Central Zionist Archives, Record Group Z4, File #2800II, 5 May 1920.

3. As quoted in Simha Flapan, *Zionism and the Palestinians* (London: Croom Helm, 1979), p. 141.

4. John Chapple, "Jewish Land Settlement in Palestine," as reproduced in Walid Khalidi, ed., *From Haven to Conquest: Readings in Zionism and the Palestine Problem until 1948* (Beirut: Institute for Palestine Studies [IPS], 1971), pp. 841–843.

5. Great Britain, *Palestine: Report on Immigration, Land Settlement and Development*, Sir John Hope Simpson, 1930 Cmd. 3686 (London: His Majesty's Stationery Office, 1930), pp. 52–56.

6. For explanations of the 1948 Palestinian exodus, see Benny Morris, *The Birth of the Palestinian Refugee Problem, 1947–1949* (Cambridge: Cambridge University Press, 1988), and the same author's *1948 and After: Israel and the Palestinians* (Oxford: Oxford University Press, 1990). See also debate on the exodus involving Norman Finkelstein, Nur Masalha, and Benny Morris in *Journal of Palestine Studies (JPS)*, Autumn 1991, pp. 66–115.

7. Walid Khalidi, ed. *All That Remains: The Palestinian Villages Occupied and Depopulated by Israel in 1948* (Washington, D.C.: IPS, 1991).

8. Sami Hadawi, *Palestinian Rights & Losses in 1948: A Comprehensive Study* (London: Saqi Books, 1988), pp. 183–189.

9. Sabri Jiryis, *The Arabs in Israel* (New York and London: Monthly Review Press, 1976); Maxime Rodinson, *Israel and the Arabs* (New York: Random House, 1968); Tom Segev, *1949: The First Israelis* (New York: The Free Press, 1986). Segev, a leading Israeli journalist, bases his book on declassified Israeli documents and personal diaries.

10. Walter Schwarz, *The Arabs in Israel* (London, 1959), p. 15, as quoted in Jiryis, *The Arabs*, p.7

11. Walid Khalidi, "The Palestine Problem: An Overview," *JPS* 21, no. 1 (Autumn 1991): 16.

12. Ezer Weizman, *On Eagles' Wings* (London: Weidenfeld and Nicolson, 1976), pp. 219ff.; Abba Eban, *Abba Eban: An Autobiography* (London: Weidenfeld and Nicolson, 1977), pp. 352–359.

13. William B. Quandt, *Decades of Decisions: American Policy toward the Arab-Israeli Conflict, 1967–76* (Berkeley and London: University of California Press, 1977), pp. 49–50.

14. Peace Now, "Government Investment in the Settlements in the Occupied Territories" (Jerusalem, May 1991); Nadav Shragai, *Ha'Aretz*, 28 January 1991; Al-Haq, "Urban Planning in the West Bank under Military Occupation: Summer Report" (Ramallah, West Bank, June 1991).

15. Ann Lesch, "Israeli Deportation of Palestinians from the West Bank and Gaza, 1967–1978," Parts I and II, *JPS* 8, no. 2 (Winter 1979): 101–131, and *JPS* 8, no. 3 (Spring 1979): 81–113.

16. Muhammad Muslih, *The Origins of Palestinian Nationalism* (New York: Columbia University Press/IPS Series, 1988), pp. 191–211; Yehoshua Porath, *The Emergence of the Palestinian-Arab National Movement, 1918–1929* (London: Frank Cass, 1974), pp. 39–45.

17. Jamal al-Husayni, "al-Mudhakkirat" (Diaries), unpublished manuscript in my possession.

18. Muslih, *Origins*, pp. 217–220; Porath, *Emergence*, pp. 305–307; Ann M. Lesch, *Arab Politics in Palestine, 1917–1939: The Frustration of a Nationalist Movement* (Ithaca and London: Cornell University Press, 1979), pp. 17–20.

19. Philip Mattar, *The Mufti of Jerusalem: Al-Hajj Amin al-Husayni and the Palestinian Nationalist Movement* (New York: Columbia University Press, 1988), pp. 119–125.

20. Cited in ibid, p. 122.

21. See Khalidi, *From Haven to Conquest*, Appendices VIII, IX-A, and IX-B, pp. 858–871.

22. Khalidi, "The Palestine Problem," p.8.

23. For details, see Laurie A. Brand, *Palestinians in the Arab World: Institution Building and the Search for State* (New York: Columbia University Press, 1988).

24. See analysis of 1964 charter in M. Muslih, *Palestinian Political Thought since 1948* (Westview Press, forthcoming).

25. A. L. Tibawi, "Visions of the Return: The Palestinian Arab Refugees in Arabic Poetry and Art," *Middle East Journal* 17, no. 5 (Autumn 1963): 508.

26. Helena Cobban, *The Palestinian Liberation Organization: People, Power and Politics* (New York: Cambridge University Press, 1984).

27. For details, see M. Muslih, *Toward Coexistence: An Analysis of the Resolutions of the Palestine National Council* (Washington, D.C.: IPS, 1990), and the same author's article, "Political Trends among the Palestinians after the Gulf War," *Current History*, January 1992.

28. This is a plan aimed at setting the foundations for the de facto annexation of the West Bank and Gaza by using the "sandwich" method of settlements.

New History, New Politics:
A Revisionist Historical View

Joel Beinin has been engaged in the politics and history of the Palestinian-Israeli conflict since he spent six months milking cows on a *kibbutz* in Israel after graduating from high school in New Jersey. After receiving his A.B. from Princeton, he returned to live in Israel from 1970 to 1972, working as a cowboy and a translator and completing a year of graduate study at the Hebrew University. He received his Ph.D. from the University of Michigan. He has also lived, studied Arabic, and conducted research in Egypt. He has been a member of the Editorial Committee of *Middle East Report* since 1981 and has taught Middle East history at Stanford University since 1983. His most recent book is *Was the Red Flag Flying There? Marxist Politics and the Arab-Israeli Conflict in Egypt and Israel, 1948–1965.*

DURING THE last decade, much of the conventional wisdom about the history of Israel and the Palestinian-Israeli conflict and many of the assumptions upon which it was based have been revised. Younger Israeli scholars have been in the forefront of this reassessment, relying heavily on recently declassified documents and driven by normal skepticism about the accomplishments of their elders and disappointment over the kind of society Israel has become. The earliest accounts of Israel's history were often written by journalists, political figures, and other contemporaries of the founding generation who shared its ethos. Their close personal ties to the subjects of their work gave them privileged access to information that lent their narratives authority and authenticity. The work of the Israeli "new historians" is characterized by profuse documentation supplied from the many Israeli public and private archives and a willingness to examine critically the foundation myths of their society. Because their narratives have challenged the previously dominant version of Israeli history, they have been subjected to sharp criticism (Teveth 1989 and 1990, and in part, Oren 1989). Although the critics have scored some points on matters of detail and interpretation, there has not been an effective refutation of the major arguments advanced by the revisionists.

This essay has benefitted from perceptive comments by Zachary Lockman.

The main themes of the new historians are: (1) the origins of the Palestinian refugee question; (2) the nature of the 1948−1949 war; (3) relations between Israel and King 'Abd Allah (Abdullah) of Jordan; (4) possibilities for Arab-Israeli peace in the period from 1949 to 1956; (5) relations between the first Zionist settlers and the indigenous Arab inhabitants of Palestine; and (6) the status and treatment of Palestinian-Arab citizens of Israel.

The Palestinian Refugee Problem

Benny Morris's work on the origins of the Palestinian refugee problem (1988 a, b) has received more attention than any other single writing of the new historians because it addresses the very heart of the Palestinian-Israeli conflict: Who has the right to the land and how did those who currently occupy it come to be there? The official Israeli argument has been that the Zionists never intended to dispossess the Palestinian-Arabs or drive them off their lands. The refugees left the country during the course of the 1948−1949 war in response to orders of Arab political and military leaders, who promised them that they would return behind victorious armies. The common Palestiniain view has been that the Zionist authorities intentionally drove the Palestinians out of the country during the course of the war in order to create as large a Jewish majority as possible and to seize their lands for use by Jewish settlers, and that this was a natural extension of the Zionist settlement project.

Morris argues that neither of these contentions is correct. No evidence exists that there was a general call by Arab leaders to abandon the land, although in certain circumstances local military commanders gave such orders; there is no "smoking gun" indicating a premeditated Israeli plan to expel Palestinians. But Morris does describe numerous cases of outright expulsion of Palestinians, several wartime atrocities that frightened Palestinians into leaving their villages, a widely held sentiment among Israeli military commanders and political leaders that it would be a "good thing" if as many Palestinians as possible left the country, a decision as early as mid-June 1948 not to permit those who had left to return, and determined efforts by some figures close to the government to encourage expulsions and seizure of Palestinian agricultural land by Jewish *kibbutzim* and other farmers. Thus, although there was no plan, there was a complex mix of actions, inactions, and attitudes that encouraged the Palestinian exodus.

One of Morris's most important pieces of evidence is an Israeli military intelligence report stating that by June 1, 1948, 391,000 refugees (out of an eventual total of about 725,000) had left the country: 55 percent in response to hostile Haganah/Israel Defense Force military operations; 15 percent in response to military actions by the dissident Zionist forces (the ETZEL, commanded by Menachem Begin, and LEHI, commanded by a triumvirate including Yitzhak Shamir, the current Israeli prime minister); 2 percent because of direct expulsion; 2 percent in response to Zionist psychological intimidation; 1 percent because of fear of retaliation after an Arab attack on Jews; 5 percent because of orders by Arab authorities; and the remainder for various reasons (Morris 1986). The document asserts that Arab authorities made great efforts to stop the flight. This report probably underestimates the extent of expulsions, which in any case increased significantly in the second phase of the fighting soon after it was composed—from July 9 to 18, 1948, during which Israeli forces conquered Lydda and Ramle and then expelled some 50,000 civilians. Morris discovered a copy of this document in a private archive; the original has not been declassified by the Israel State Archives. After he published his findings, Israeli security officials ordered the directors of the archives in which Morris found the document to remove it from public access—an indication of its perceived significance.

The 1948–1949 War

The Israeli role in the Palestinian exodus is only one aspect of the dispute surrounding the conduct of the 1948–1949 war. The massacre at Deir Yassin (on April 9, 1948, in which some 254 civilians were killed) has been considered an exceptional breach of Israeli military conduct attributable to the virulent anti-Arab sentiment of a small minority, the ETZEL, as opposed to the pre-state Haganah and its successor, the Israel Defense Forces, whose actions were governed by the dictum of "purity of arms." But Morris and Tom Segev (1986) describe several instances of atrocities committed by the Labor Zionist-led military forces (at Duwayma, Eilabun, and Sa'sa, for example).

Israeli politicians have often pictured their country as a tiny David which is surrounded by a monolithic Arab Goliath but which has miraculously prevailed. Studies of the military history of the 1948–1949 war by Meir Pail (1979) and Uri Milstein (1989) corroborate Morris's characterization and indicate that the Jewish forces had essentially defeated the poorly organized and inadequately armed local Palestinian armed resistance before the invasion of the neighboring Arab states on May 15, 1948. According to Chaim Herzog (1985), Jewish armed forces outnumbered the combined invading forces (45,000 to 36,000), although at the start of the invasion, two-thirds of the Jewish forces were reservists, and even the front-line units were not fully armed. But Israel began to acquire large quantities of weapons from the Soviet bloc in April. At the end of the first phase of the war (May 15 to June 10) Israel was on the offensive; and by the last phase, its combat forces had adequate arms and outnumbered the

Arabs. Superior communications, logistics, and planning throughout the war meant that at the moment of engagement Israeli forces usually had the advantage.

'Abd Allah and the Zionists

Avi Shlaim (1988 and 1990) relates the history of the collaborative relationship of King 'Abd Allah of Jordan and the Zionist leadership from 1921 to 1951, which culminated in a tacit agreement to allow 'Abd Allah to occupy and annex the territories of British Mandate Palestine designated as an Arab state by the 1947 UN partition plan. These territories ultimately became known as the West Bank. The story of this arrangement, and the meetings between 'Abd Allah and Golda Meir and other Zionist leaders undertaken to avert a Jordanian-Israeli clash altogether, have been known since the late 1950s, but Shlaim's rendition is the most fully documented and comprehensive.

Shlaim also reveals that 'Abd Allah had received subventions from the Zionist authorities since the 1930s because they hoped to win his agreement to establishing a Jewish state. 'Abd Allah's Hashemite family, originally from the Arabian Peninsula, was not indigenous to the country; hence, the Zionist leadership hoped he might agree to compromise with them on terms that would be unacceptable to Palestinian nationalists. Indeed, 'Abd Allah's younger brother, Faisal, reached such an agreement with Chaim Weizmann in 1919, accepting the principles of the Balfour Declaration; that accord became void when the British reneged on their promise to recognize an independent Arab state in geographical Syria, Mesopotamia, and the Arabian Peninsula.

Peace Offers, the Jewish Settlers, and Israel's Palestinians

When Anwar Sadat of Egypt signed a peace treaty with Israel in 1979, he was widely acclaimed as the first Arab leader willing to make peace with that country. But there were many previous Arab peace offers: a Syrian proposal in 1949; a draft Jordanian-Israeli treaty in 1950 (aborted by the assassination of 'Abd Allah in 1951); and extensive secret contacts between Israel and Egypt in the 1950s, including discussion of a possible face-to-face meeting between Israeli Prime Minister Moshe Sharett and Egyptian President Gamal Abdel-Nasser (Jackson 1983, Shlaim 1983 and 1986, Touval 1982). Israel rejected these offers and often pursued a provocative military policy ("activism") based on Prime Minister Ben-Gurion's belief that it could achieve the best settlement by demonstrating overwhelming military supremacy (Shlaim 1983, Ya'ari 1975). It is not that the Arab states have always refused to make peace with Israel, whereas Israel has always desired peace. The real question in the relationship has not been war or peace, but "peace on what terms?", although this does not mean that peace was therefore any easier to achieve.

Amos Elon (1981) articulated the classic liberal Israeli view that the first Jewish settlers in Palestine were barely aware of the Arabs' existence; and if in their idealist zeal they ignored the presence of others, their guilt for displacing them is to some degree mitigated. Neville Mandel's (1976) discussion of Arab-Jewish relations in late–Ottoman Empire Palestine should have preempted Elon's myopic narrative. But it is decisively refuted by Gershon Shafir's (1989) account of the struggle over the land and labor markets on the frontier of Zionist settlement from 1882 to 1914. Shafir argues that Israel is "not completely different from some of the other European overseas societies that were also shaped in the process of settlement and conflict with already existing societies" (p. xi; his comparison is with the United States, South Africa, Australia, Algeria, Kenya, and the Eastern Marches of Prussia). He concludes that the dominance of Labor Zionism in the pre-state period was due to its successful resolution of the contradiction between Jewish capitalist and nationalist objectives by creating a split labor market and establishing Jewish exclusivity (although never total) where this was possible—in a part, rather than the whole, of Palestine. Thus, the Zionist project was shaped by the confrontation between Jewish settlers and the indigenous inhabitants of the land. Rashid Khalidi (1988) extends this argument, demonstrating that Palestinian opposition to Zionist settlement was expressed in clear political terms even before the outbreak of World War I.

One revisionist theme established well before the emergence of the new historical school is the status of Israel's Palestinian-Arab citizens. Some of the new historians who have addressed this are Segev (1986) and Kamen (1987–1988). One of those Arab citizens, Sabri Jiryis (1969), compiled a comprehensive critique of the Israeli military government, confiscation of lands, discriminatory treatment, de facto segregation, and legal and administrative practices that made Arabs second-class citizens in Israel. Ian Lustick (1980) confirmed and expanded Jiryis's basic argument; and Charles Kamen demonstrated the detailed development of Israeli policies designed to control the Arab minority and efface its national identity from the first days of the Jewish state.

The overall effect of this new history has been to assign considerably more responsibility to Israel for the continuation and exacerbation of the conflict than has previously been common in Israel and the West. Some of the scholars engaged in this project have explicitly acknowledged this aspect of their work; and Benny Morris (1988a, 102) has suggested that establishing a more balanced account of the history of the Palestinian-Israeli conflict "may . . . in some obscure way serve the purposes of peace and reconciliation."

References

Elon, Amos. 1981. *The Israelis: Founders and Sons.* Harmondsworth: Penguin.

Herzog, Chaim. *The Arab-Israeli Wars: War and Peace in the Middle East from the War of Independence to Lebanon.* London: Arms and Armour Press.

Jackson, Elmore. 1983. *Middle East Mission: The Story of a Major Bid for Peace in the Time of Nasser and Ben-Gurion.* New York: Norton.

Jiryis, Sabri. 1969. *The Arabs in Israel.* Beirut: Institute for Palestine Studies.

Kamen, Charles. 1987, 1988. "After the Catastrophe: The Arabs in Israel, 1948–1951." *Middle Eastern Studies* 23(4) and 24(1).

Khalidi, Rashid. 1988. "Palestinian Peasant Resistance to Zionism." In *Blaming the Victims: Spurious Scholarship and the Palestinian Question,* Edward W. Said and Christopher Hitchens, eds. London: Verso.

Lustick, Ian. 1980. *Arabs in the Jewish State: Israel's Control of a National Minority.* Austin: University of Texas Press.

Mandel, Neville J. 1976. *The Arabs and Zionism before World War I.* Berkeley: University of California Press.

Milstein, Uri. 1989. *The War of Independence* (in Hebrew), 3 vols. Tel Aviv: Zmorah, Bitan.

Morris, Benny. 1986. "The Causes and Character of the Arab Exodus from Palestine: The Israel Defense Forces Intelligence Branch Analysis of June 1948." *Middle Eastern Studies* 22(1).

———. 1988a. *The Birth of the Palestinian Refugee Problem, 1947–1949.* Cambridge: Cambridge University Press.

———. 1988b. "The New Historiography: Israel Confronts Its Past." *Tikkun* 3 (6, November–December).

Oren, Michael. 1989. "Out of the Battleground." *Radical History Review* (45).

Pail, Meir. 1979. *From the Haganah to the Israel Defense Forces* (in Hebrew). Tel Aviv: Zmorah, Bitan, Modan.

Segev, Tom. 1986. *1949: The First Israelis.* New York: The Free Press.

Shafir, Gershon. 1989. *Land, Labour and the Origins of the Israeli-Palestinian Conflict, 1882–1914.* Cambridge: Cambridge University Press.

Shlaim, Avi. 1983. "Conflicting Approaches to Israel's Relations with the Arabs: Ben-Gurion and Sharett, 1953–1956." *Middle East Journal* 37(2).

———. 1986. "Husni Za'im and the Plan to Resettle the Palestinian Refugees in Syria." *Journal of Palestine Studies* 15(4).

———. 1988. *Collusion across the Jordan: King Abdullah, the Zionist Movement and the Partition of Palestine.* New York: Columbia University Press.

———. 1990. *The Politics of Partition: King Abdullah, the Zionist Movement and Palestine, 1921–1951,* abridged and rev. New York: Columbia University Press.

Teveth, Shabtai. 1989. "Charging Israel with Original Sin." *Commentary* (September).

————. 1990. "The Palestine Arab Refugee Problem and Its Origins." *Middle Eastern Studies* 26(2).

Ya'ari, Ehud. 1975. *Egypt and the Fedayeen, 1953–1956* (in Hebrew). Giv'at Haviva: Institute for Asian and African Studies.

Other Sources

Flapan, Simha. 1987. *The Birth of Israel: Myths and Realities*. New York: Pantheon.

Lockman, Zachary. 1989. "Original Sin." In *Intifada: The Palestinian Uprising against Israeli Occupation*, Zachary Lockman and Joel Beinin, eds. Boston: South End Press.

Moughrabi, Fouad. 1989. "Redefining the Past." *Radical History Review* (45).

Pappé, Ilan. 1988. *Britain and the Arab-Israeli Conflict, 1948–1951*. New York: St. Martin's Press.

Touval, Saadi. 1982. *The Peace Brokers: Mediators in the Arab-Israeli Conflict, 1948–1979*. Princeton: Princeton University Press.

Chronology

1850	Palestinian Arabs and a small minority of Jewish people resident in the province of the Ottoman Empire known as Palestine
1896	Theodore Herzl: the "Jewish State"
1897	First Zionist Congress meets in Basel, Switzerland.
1898	Kaiser Wilhelm II of Germany visits Jerusalem.
1905	Program of the Arab Fatherland: first open demand for the secession of Arab lands from the Ottoman Empire
1908–1909	Young Turk Revolution in Istanbul
1911–1913	Ottomans fight a series of wars in the Balkans.
1914	**Outbreak of World War I**
1915	The McMahon letter: negotiations between British high commissioner in Cairo and sherif of Mecca
1916, May	The Sykes-Picot agreement on partition of the Ottoman Empire signed in London by British and French representatives.
1916, Nov.	Arab uprising in the Hijaz against the Turks, with British assistance
1917, Nov.	Balfour Declaration: British pledge to establish a national home for the Jews in Palestine.
1917, Nov.	British troops occupy Jerusalem.
1919	The Faisal-Weizmann Agreement and Faisal-Frankfurter Letters
1919	Versailles Conference of post-war settlement
1919	Recommendations of the King-Crane commission concerning mandatory power for Palestine
1920, Apr.	San Remo Conference: Palestine designated as one of the mandated territories.
1920, Apr.	Anti-Zionist riots in Jerusalem
1921	Anti-Zionist riots in Jaffa after clashes during May Day demonstrations between different sections of the Jewish labor movement
1922	The British Mandate established.
1922	The Churchill White Paper calls for limitation on number of Jewish immigrants.

1929	Wall Street crash; beginning of world trade recession
1929	"Wailing Wall" riots in Jerusalem
1931	British White Paper calls for restrictions on Jewish immigration into Palestine.
1931	The MacDonald letter (dubbed the Black Paper by the Palestinians) reaffirms Britain's commitment to the National Home Policy.
1933	Hitler comes to power in Germany.
1933	Anti-British riots in Jaffa and Jerusalem
1936	Arab general strike and rebellion
1936	Royal commission (Peel Commission) designated to investigate strike is partially boycotted by Arab leadership.
1937	Peel Commission recommends partition of Palestine into Jewish and Arab states. Strong opposition from Arabs.
1937	Second phase of Arab rebellion
1938	British Statement of Policy against partition
1939	Roundtable conference on Palestine held in London.
1939	White Paper issued that recommends restricting Jewish immigration and land buying.
1939	Statement by the Jewish Agency in response to White Paper
1939	**Outbreak of World War II**
1942	The Biltmore Declaration is issued by the Jewish Agency, which demands unlimited Jewish immigration into Palestine and the establishment of a Jewish commonwealth there.
1945, Aug.	World Zionist Congress demands that Palestine be opened to 1 million Jews.
1945, Oct.	Egypt, Iraq, Syria, and Lebanon warn United States that creation of Jewish state in Palestine will lead to war.
1946	Anglo-American commission visits Palestine, recommends continuation of British mandate.
1946, Jul.	Irgun, a Jewish terrorist organization, blows up King David Hotel in Jerusalem.
1946, Sep.	London conference, Arabs propose Palestinian state, Jews boycott conference. Both Jews and Arabs favor British withdrawal from Palestine.
1946, Dec.	Zionist Congress demands Jewish state. Weizmann removed from leadership.
1947	London conference on the future of Palestine to consider British proposals for its division into Jewish and Arab provinces under a British high commissioner. No representatives of Palestinian Arabs or Zionists attend.

1947, Feb.	Arabs and Jews reject British proposal for division of Palestine into Arab and Jewish zones administered as trusteeship territory.
1947, Feb.	British refer Palestine question to the United Nations.
1947, May	United Nations appoints special committee on Palestine.
1947, May	Arab summit meeting calls for halt to Jewish immigration and independence of Palestine.
1947, Jul.	"Exodus" Jews denied entry into Palestine.
1947, Jul.	Irgun hangs two British sergeants.
1947, Sep.	Britain announces intention to withdraw from Palestine.
1947, Nov.	UN General Assembly issues resolution on partition of Palestine. Palestine to be divided into Jewish and Arab states. Jerusalem to be under UN trusteeship administration. Plan is approved by Jews but rejected by Arabs. Anti-American riots occur in Arab capitals.
1948, Jan.	Units of Arab Liberation Army enter Palestine from Syria.
1948, Apr.	Massacre of Arabs at Deir Yassin
1948, Apr.	Hadassah medical convoy massacred by Arab irregulars in East Jerusalem.
1948, May	End of British Mandate in Palestine. Israel proclaims independence. United States extends de facto recognition. Beginning of 1948–1949 Arab-Israeli war.
1948, May	Soviet Union recognizes Israel.
1948, Sep.	Bernadotte, UN representative to Palestine, murdered by Jewish terrorists.
1948	The Arab National Movement founded in Lebanon.
1949	UN resolution on the internationalization of Jerusalem issued.
1949, Feb.–Jul.	U.S. mediator arranges armistice agreements between Israel and Egypt, Lebanon, Jordan, and Syria, respectively. The Arab states still refuse to recognize Israel's right to exist.
1955, Aug.	Dulles announces new principles for Arab-Israeli peace efforts.
1956, Mar.	Secret U.S. negotiations between Egypt and Israel fail.
1956, Oct.	As part of a secret agreement with Britain and France, Israel attacks Egypt in the Sinai.
1956, Nov.	Israeli-Arab war ends due to American pressure on Britain, France, and Israel.
1957	Eisenhower doctrine to deter communism in the Middle East unveiled.
1962	Palestine refugee problem arises; Joseph Johnson mission to resolve problem fails.

1963	Manifesto of the United Arab Republic issued.
1963	Arab Summit Conference occurs.
1963	Palestine Liberation Organization constitution drafted.
1964	Palestine Liberation Organization created.
1967, Jun.	Six-Day War. Israel occupies the Sinai as far as the Suez Canal, the Golan Heights, East Jerusalem, the West Bank, and Gaza Strip.
1967, Nov.	UN Resolution 242 issued—outline for Middle East settlement.
1970, Sep.	Jordanian civil war involves Syrians and Palestinians.
1973, Oct.	Arab-Israeli conflict: Syria and Egypt attack Israel.
1973, Oct.	Security Council Resolution 338 calling for cease-fire issued.
1975	Egyptian-Israeli accord on Sinai signed.
1975	Lebanese civil war begins.
1976	Land Day strike occurs in Israel.
1977	Arab League Summit held in Tripoli, Libya.
1977, Mar.–Jul.	President Carter meets separately with Mideast leaders; plans are made to convene a Geneva conference for a comprehensive Middle East settlement.
1978	Camp David summit between the United States, Egypt, and Israel produces accords on the Palestinian question and Egyptian-Israeli peace.
1979	Egypt-Israel Peace Treaty signed.
1979	Talks between the United States, Egypt, and Israel on Palestinian autonomy on the West Bank and Gaza Strip begin.
1980	European Council issues Venice Declaration stating what must be done for comprehensive solution of Arab-Israeli conflict.
1981	Jewish settlements on the West Bank begin.
1981	United States suspends the new strategic cooperation agreement with Israel after the Likud government applies Israeli law to the Golan Heights.
1982	Twelfth Arab Summit Conference held in Fez, Morocco.
1982	Israel invades southern Lebanon and West Beirut.
1982	President Reagan announces a new U.S. plan for Mideast peace calling for "self-government by the Palestinians of the West Bank and Gaza in association with Jordan."
1983	The Kahan Commission Report issued concerning Sabra and Shatila massacres.
1984	Incomplete unilateral Israeli withdrawal from Lebanon
1987, Dec.	Intifada—the Palestinian uprising begins.

1990	Iraq invades Kuwait.
1991, Jan.	US takes military action against Iraq.
1991	Negotiations for an Arab-Israeli peace conference in process

Compiled by Roberta Micallef from the following sources

Sara Graham-Brown. *Palestinians and Their Society: A Photographic Essay* (London; New York: Quartet Books, 1980).

Walter Laqueur and Barry Rubin, eds. *Israel-Arab Reader: A Documentary History of the Middle East*, rev. ed. (New York: Penguin, 1984).

Wm. Roger Louis and Robert Stookey, eds. *The End of the Palestine Mandate* (Austin: University of Texas Press, 1986).

Itamar Rabinovitch and Jehuda Reinharz, eds. *Israel in the Middle East: Documents and Readings on Society, Politics, and Foreign Relations, 1948–Present* (New York: Oxford University Press, 1984).

Steven L. Spiegel. *The Other Arab-Israeli Conflict: Making America's Middle East Policy from Truman to Reagan* (Chicago: University of Chicago Press, 1985).

Various issues of *Middle East Report* and the *Middle East Journal*.

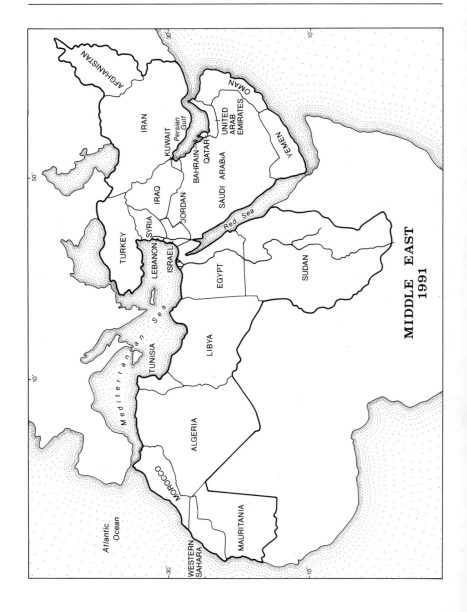

MIDDLE EAST
1991

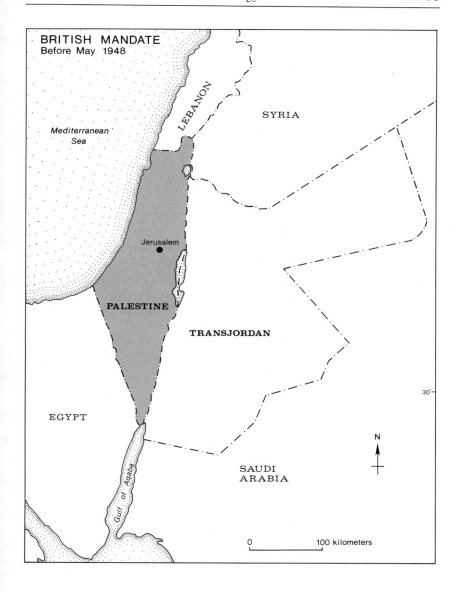

BRITISH MANDATE
Before May 1948

Mediterranean
Sea

LEBANON

SYRIA

Jerusalem

PALESTINE

TRANSJORDAN

30°

EGYPT

Gulf of Aqaba

SAUDI
ARABIA

N

0   100 kilometers

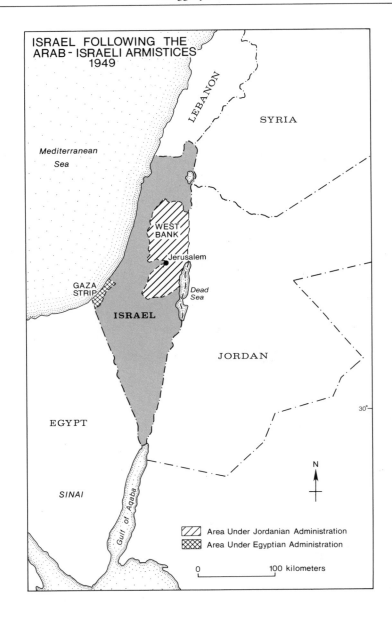

ISRAEL FOLLOWING THE
ARAB - ISRAELI ARMISTICES
1949

LEBANON

SYRIA

Mediterranean
Sea

WEST
BANK

Jerusalem

GAZA
STRIP

Dead
Sea

ISRAEL

JORDAN

EGYPT

30°

N

SINAI

Gulf of Aqaba

▨ Area Under Jordanian Administration
▧ Area Under Egyptian Administration

0   100 kilometers

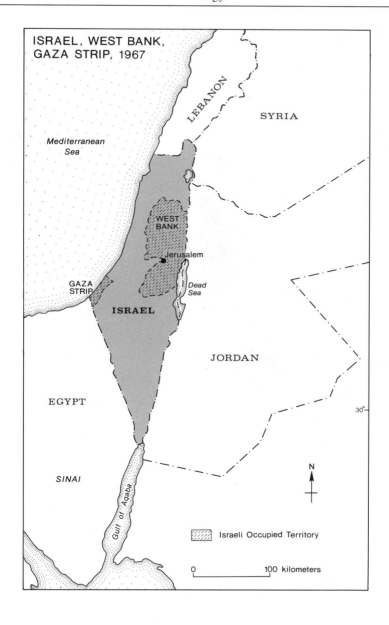

ISRAEL, WEST BANK, GAZA STRIP, 1967

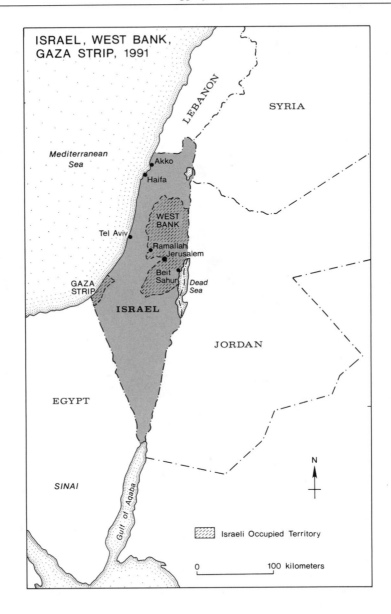

ISRAEL, WEST BANK,
GAZA STRIP, 1991

LEBANON

SYRIA

Mediterranean
Sea

Akko
Haifa

WEST
BANK

Tel Aviv

Ramallah
Jerusalem

Beit
Sahur   Dead
         Sea

GAZA
STRIP

ISRAEL

JORDAN

EGYPT

N

SINAI

Gulf of Aqaba

Israeli Occupied Territory

0   100 kilometers

PART II. THE VIEW FROM OUTSIDE

EDWARD F. SHERMAN

Applications of Dispute-Resolution Processes in the Israeli-Palestinian Conflict

Edward F. Sherman is Edward Clark Centennial Professor of Law at the University of Texas School of Law. He is co-author of casebooks on alternative dispute resolution, complex litigation, civil procedure, and military law. He has extensive experience as a mediator and an arbitrator. Sherman has taught dispute-resolution and negotiation courses at the University of Texas and the University of London and has co-authored materials published by the National Institute for Dispute Resolution for teaching alternative dispute resolution to practicing lawyers.

ANY MEANINGFUL resolution of the Israeli-Palestinian conflict must include a process for encouraging dialogue and cooperation between the two peoples. Increased interdependence between Israelis and Palestinians seems the likely result of a political settlement, and, if it is to work, the historical, cultural, and societal antagonisms must be ameliorated. In the past there has been an endless circle of hostility. Territorial occupation and closed political structures have fostered separation and group injustices that have fueled hostility on an individual level, which, in turn, has reinforced the continuation of the territorial and political arrangements. A negotiated political solution can only go partway in breaking that cycle. Hostility at individual and community levels must be addressed if political accommodations are to succeed.

Modern methods of conflict resolution offer a way to confront and ultimately to lessen the antagonism between the Israelis and Palestinians. A wide variety of creative and flexible forms of mediation have come into being in the last few decades. These processes vary considerably as to the methods for bringing the disputants together, the techniques used to encourage communication and problem solving, and the inducements and pressures used to achieve a solution. They have in common, however, the use of intermediaries to facilitate communication and reliance on the empowering effect of a process that encourages the disputants to recognize, confront, and, finally, resolve their disputes among themselves.

Informal methods of conflict resolution through the use of interme-diaries have long existed in civilized societies. Humans have a natural in-stinct to seek the approval and guidance of others in settling their differ-ences, and the use of intermediaries to facilitate communication between disputants predates the creation of formal law.[1] In the last several decades, creative approaches to the use of intermediaries have been developed for internal disputes in many countries and for conflicts between nations in the international community. Some have worked and some have not, but there is a growing body of principles that suggests that conflicts can be resolved if there is both sufficient willingness to try and careful attention to an appropriate methodology for enhancing communication and prob-lem solving.

The Israeli-Palestinian conflict presents special problems for resolu-tion through a cooperative mediation process. Dispute-resolution tech-niques that have been developed to address such disputes as discord between neighbors, marital breakups, and even social-class conflict rely on certain shared cultural values. Cross-cultural conflict, exacerbated by intense nationalist, racial, and religious differences, leaves less room for discovering common values and interests.[2] But the intermediary process ultimately depends on the goodwill and humanity of individuals, and cross-cultural mediation, although difficult, is still capable of promoting greater understanding and cooperation.

Disputants as the Voluntary Creators of the Solution

Voluntariness is at the heart of the modern mediation process. The strength of mediation is that it permits the parties to achieve their own resolution of a dispute without being bound to a formal, and possibly inflexible, legal solution.[3] Research supports the conclusion that disputing parties will be more satisfied, and thus more likely to abide by an agree-ment, if it is of their own creation. For example, a study of small-claims disputes in Maine found a higher compliance rate with settlements that resulted from mediation than from a court-ordered judgment.[4] This con-clusion is not surprising if the result is a mutually acceptable solution to the dispute and the parties feel a sense of obligation to comply with its terms. The trick is to bring disputing parties to a state of mind in which this result is achievable.

Advocates of mediation view it as an "empowering" process by which the parties are given, by the very nature of the process, the power to con-front each other on both a moral and personal level.[5] This is a heady con-cept, and one might well be skeptical of the ability of the process to break through the existing pattern of relationships between the parties to move them to view the dispute from a different perspective. But mediation advocates believe that the very act of participating in a mediation, accompanied by the mediator's demand for a commitment to participate in good faith and the mediator's assistance in identifying shared values, can alter the existing dynamic between the parties. By forcing the parties to hear each other's justifications and to confront each other's feelings, mediation seeks to empower the less-powerful party to invoke shared community standards to support his or her position. The ultimate objective is to bring the parties to a mutual acceptance of standards of fairness and broad equity that might not be possible in a formal legal proceeding.

Despite the philosophical preference that mediation be undertaken voluntarily by the parties, participation must sometimes be encouraged, indeed, even pressured or coerced. Parties are sometimes required to go to mediation in the United States, as when mediation is a prerequisite for being allowed to go to trial, for prosecuting a criminal complaint, or for receiving some government benefit such as continuing to stay in a low-income housing project, avoiding expulsion from school, or obtaining enforcement of zoning, land use, or other regulations.[6] Experience suggests that even such coerced participation may still be beneficial in bringing the parties into a process where cooperation may ultimately arise.[7] In many mediations, at least one party is a reluctant participant because of pressure from persons who carry influence with him or her—for example, a counselor or member of the clergy, family members or friends, or even the opposing party. This does not mean, of course, that the resulting mediation is not voluntary, but it signifies that the degree of cooperativeness may vary considerably from party to party. It should also be remembered that coerced participation is not coerced agreement; no party to mediation can be forced to enter an agreement.

Appreciating that pressured or coerced mediation can still be efficacious is important to resolving conflicts such as that between the Israelis and Palestinians. Where one side, like the Israelis, holds effective political power, it is not likely that it will willingly enter a mediation process that seeks to empower its adversaries. In the same manner, peer pressures have long kept Palestinians from accepting the possibility of accommodations short of the official goals of the Palestinian movement, such as the creation of an independent state. But participation in a mediatory process can be encouraged by pressure of various kinds—legal, political, moral, or by force of public opinion. As demonstrated by the pressures from the United States and other nations that led to the talks that began in November 1991 between the Israelis, Palestinians, and neighboring Arab states, such effort will only be successful if it offers a face-saving justification that would allow both sides to retreat from an intractable position.

The international community can play a considerable role in pressuring and wheedling the parties into a mediation process. Important as that role was in achieving the high-level negotiations begun in November 1991, international pressure is also needed to encourage the internal reconciliation that is necessary to effectuate an ultimate political settlement. On the individual and community level, the willingness of some Israelis and Palestinians to seek peaceful resolutions, as shown by the moving film, *The Struggle for Peace: Israelis and Palestinians,*[8] demonstrates the power of the moral force that can be brought to bear in favor of participation in mediatory processes. That moral force could be enhanced by legal mechanisms, such as by mandating through law or agreement a "meet and consider" process for discussion, creating on-going procedures and processes to be carried out by an international force or the United Nations, threatening economic or other forms of sanctions from outside (as with South Africa), or using boycotts and other external pressures.

The Process of Assisted Dialogue and Problem Solving

Mediation takes many different forms, depending on the culture and setting. A mediator is essentially a facilitator of communication between the parties, assisting them to engage in a dialogue directed toward the objective of mutual resolution of their dispute. A mediator is thus different from a decision-maker—whether in the form of a chief, a priest, a judge, or an arbitrator—who resolves a dispute through fiat. A mediator may be chosen for special qualities or status—for example, the "prestige-mediators" of the Singapore Chinese, the "big man" in the Ifugao tribe, or the Iranian "bazaar mediators."[9] On the other hand, a mediator may be simply a friend or neighbor, acting, for example, under the rules of the Society of Friends, which have long required that disputes be discussed before common friends.[10] A mediator may have particular expertise in the subject matter, as in labor mediation and certain kinds of international dispute mediation.[11] On the other hand, a mediator may only be a disinterested person skilled at facilitating communication, as in mediations conducted in "community dispute resolution centers" now operating throughout the United States.[12]

The mediator's role varies with the circumstances. The roles may include being a facilitator of communication, encourager of problem solving, generator of possible solutions, arranger of processes to inform and enlighten the disputants, impresario of a structured dialogue, or shuttle-diplomat, who uses control of the information flow to focus on areas of agreement without the dangers of face-to-face confrontation by the parties involved.

The degree of activism, or directiveness, of the mediator depends on the situation. A mediator who is known, trusted, and respected by the parties may play a more directive role because his or her opinion is likely to be important to the parties. The techniques, however, are essentially the same, whatever the degree of mediator activism: The mediator will seek to make the parties hear and confront the grievances and views of the other side and, if possible, to recognize the different perspective of the other side and then to discover common values and goals that can be met through a realistic resolution.

In recent years, new techniques for discovering mutually acceptable solutions have arisen, such as having the parties participate in simulations, make formal evaluations of their positions, perform trial runs of their presentations, and even play computer-assisted games to generate a range of alternatives.

An example of creative mediation techniques is the settlement negotiation conducted by a court-ordered special master in a 1985 American lawsuit involving rights to tribal treaty waters of the Great Lakes.[13] The plaintiffs were three Indian tribes and the United States, and the defendant was the state of Michigan, which represented various competing interests for use of the waters, such as commercial fishing, tourism, and sport. The special master convened at a resort a mediation conference attended by representatives of the various parties.

It had become apparent that disagreements among the expert witnesses in biology for each side would constitute a major portion of the evidence at trial. The biologists were therefore asked to cooperate in developing a joint computer model of the five critical variables that they had identified. The representatives were then asked to participate in a computer-assisted scorable game that would mimic the actual dispute. They were required to identify each party's interests and rank their priorities, select all feasible elements of any water-allocation plan, and determine the various systems that could be used to organize those interests and elements. The structure of the game was based on the theory of *differences orientation,* as described by the special master, Francis McGovern:

> The negotiation theory applied to the game was so-called differences orientation. For example, each party might value the same portion of Lake Michigan differently. The tribes living in the northern Michigan peninsula would probably prefer unlimited access to waters close to their homes. In contrast, the sports fishers generally lived in southern Michigan and would value the southern waters more highly. Differences orientation was particularly valuable here because of the economic and cultural disparities among the parties: What appeared in the litigation context to be a major problem of fundamental value differences was actually an asset in developing a mutually acceptable allocation plan.[14]

The primary purpose of the game was "as an educational tool, not just to provide specific answers, but to teach the parties how to negotiate."[15] Negotiations over the model revealed that the biologists were generally in agreement; thus, the differences really lay with the perceived interests of the parties. After three days of negotiations the parties reached a settlement. This high-tech procedure was able to accomplish with great speed and efficiency a course of analysis that a more ordinary mediation might also pursue—getting the parties to identify the competing interests and priorities, to brainstorm the variety of combinations for resolving the dispute, and to come to a negotiating stance in which trade-offs can ultimately be achieved.

Reality-Testing of Perceptions and Positions

A key aspect of the mediation process is to force the parties to confront the realities of their firmly held perceptions and positions. Mediators may reality-test with parties at various stages in the mediation. Coming to an awareness of error in one's perceptions or weakness in one's positions may derive from open sessions in which the opposing party presents its arguments and point of view or from private sessions with one party (called a caucus) in which the party can discuss frankly and in confidence its doubts, ultimate interests, and bottom lines.[16] One mediator described his approach: "My strategy is to try to get the recalcitrant person to see the other's view. If the other person doesn't do it, I do it in caucus myself. It usually works to point out how the other person sees things—that usually produces an agreement."[17]

Reality-testing seeks to get parties with an exaggerated view of the wrong done them, or of the strength of their position, to come to a more realistic understanding of the dispute. Reality-testing is also often necessary when the parties have stereotyped attitudes about the other side. The Israeli-Palestinian conflict is awash with stereotypical thinking. David K. Shipler, in his book, *Arab and Jew: Wounded Spirits in a Promised Land,* describes "the interlocking stereotypes that Jews and Arabs use to categorize and explain each other": The Arabs are hostile, violent, craven, undisciplined, mercurial, fanatical, and careless of life; the Jews are heartless, power-mad, cowardly, self-absorbed, and willing to use any tactics to achieve their objective.[18]

Stereotypes are not necessarily overcome by personal contact. What is necessary is a new outlook, a willingness to see things from the other's point of view, a form of contact that opens the understanding rather than quickly reinforcing prejudices. Initiatives to bring Israelis and Palestinians together for dialogue are a means of undermining stereotypes. Legacy International, based in Alexandria, Virginia, has a program for bringing together seventeen- to twenty-seven-year-old Israeli Jews, Israeli Arabs, and West Bank Palestinians to receive training in intercultural methods of cooperation and dialogue exchange.[19] Another not-for-profit organization,

Interns for Peace, places young Jewish and Arab volunteers in neighboring Jewish and Arab towns for a year or two and holds four-day workshops to address their prejudices and seek understanding.[20]

Mediated dialogues hold special promise for reducing stereotypical thinking because the process itself is directed at overcoming perceptual barriers. As will be discussed shortly,[21] a wide variety of mediated dialogues at various levels are available and should be pursued in conjunction with a political settlement.

Search for Mutually Beneficial Solutions

Mediation is "fundamentally a process of assisted negotiation."[22] Thus, negotiation strategy is central to what goes on in mediation. A considerable amount of research and analysis in the last several decades has resulted in a specialized discipline referred to as negotiation theory.[23] Like other behavioral sciences, there are no universally accepted principles, and a great deal must be left to interpretation and individual preference. Negotiation theory, however, suggests what factors contribute to, or detract from, success in negotiation and to settlement possibilities, and therefore provides important insights for the use of mediation.

Two general styles of negotiation can be identified. The first, often called *distributive bargaining,* arises when there are no opportunities for joint gain for both parties, and when any potential solution that results in an increase in benefit for one party will result in a concomitant decrease for the other. This is also referred to as a *zero sum* situation, where whatever is given to one must be taken from the other.[24] Lawsuits for money damages often seem to fall into this category, although a perceptive mediator may be able to discover other non-zero sum interests that can be satisfied through a creative settlement, for example, use of a "structured settlement" that provides a plaintiff with the security of an income stream in the future through an annuity at much less cost to the defendant insurance company.[25] Disputes over territory, such as that involved in the Israeli-Palestinian conflict, would also appear to pose a zero sum situation, although the existence of interests apart from the strictly territorial question suggests that the conflict cannot be so easily characterized in this fashion.

In contrast to a distributive or zero sum negotiation is the *integrative* bargaining situation, in which a solution is possible that provides benefits for both sides. The solution may not provide exactly equal benefits; indeed, the merits of a particular conflict may not justify equality of benefits. But a mediator attuned to the principles of integrative bargaining seeks to discover a breadth of interests on both sides that can go into the equation for a mutually acceptable settlement.

Roger Fisher and William Ury, in their book, *Getting to Yes,* popularized a version of integrative bargaining that they call "principled negotiation."[26] Basic to this approach is a philosophical attitude that seeks to identify interests, not positions, and to find solutions that expand, rather than divide, the available benefits or resources. This often requires a shift away from strictly rights-based or power-based analyses and solutions. This approach has increasingly been used in public policy disputes in the United States involving such matters as environmental concerns, land-use regulation, and racial disharmony.[27]

A simple example will indicate the interest-based, or integrative, approach. A mediation takes place between two neighbors concerning one's complaints about the other's barking dog.[28] If the issue is characterized as "the howling dog," the opposing positions of the parties will line up quickly, with a possibly endless debate over how much the dog barks. Each side is likely to be defensive and rigid about his or her perception of that question. On the other hand, if the mediator is able to get the parties to focus on their interests—for example, the owner's need for the dog for protection, and the neighbor's need for quiet time at certain hours—they may be put upon a more fruitful path toward a mutually acceptable solution. When does the neighbor need quiet time? Can the dog be taken in during that time? Would the owner be willing to take the dog to obedience school in exchange for the neighbor accepting a certain amount of barking in the interests of their joint protection? Could the neighbor get to know the dog and thus make the dog less likely to bark when the neighbor is at home? Could both parties enjoy the benefit of protection by sharing the dog at certain times? And on and on. Mediation is not a search for blame but for interests that can be satisfied by mutual solutions.

Fisher and Ury provide another example of the interest-based, as opposed to position-based, approach to negotiation. Two men are quarrelling over a window in the library. One wants it shut, the other, open. Their wrangling brings the librarian into the room. "She asks one why he wants the window open: 'To get some fresh air.' She asks the other other why he wants it closed: 'To avoid the draft.' After thinking a minute, she opens wide a window in the next room, bringing in fresh air without a draft."[29]

Notice that the solution was not a compromise; a compromise would have been to leave the window half-open, resulting in neither party being satisfied. Instead, the librarian found a resolution based on the interests of the parties, which turned out not to be in opposition. Such a facile solution, of course, is not always possible, but the approach of focusing on interests and seeking to find mutually acceptable solutions that satisfy those interests is at the heart of the success that mediation can have.

The Israeli-Palestinian conflict involves vastly more complicated issues and poses much more intractable barriers to agreement. But at heart, the structured negotiation that we call mediation, whether in a simple or a complex dispute, involves such central aspirations as identifying the parties' true interests, coming to a realization of the opposing point of view, appreciating common values, reality-testing as to the strength of one's perceptions and position, and searching for solutions that provide some kind of mutual benefit.

More complex negotiation models reveal a broader range of considerations suited to disputes such as the Israeli-Palestinian one. Frank Edmead of the Center for the Analysis of Conflict at the University of London devised a model with special relevance to reality-testing of disputants in political and international conflicts.[30] He concluded that a mediation's degree of success depends on a variety of factors and how they are handled in the mediation, including the expectations of the parties as to their ability to attain the objective they seek, the resources they have invested to attain the objective, their ability to obtain additional resources, and the economic and psychological repercussions of a decision to cut one's losses and alter one's objective. A party's resources include anything under his or her control that may be used to achieve the desired objective, such as natural resources, money, goods or services, efforts at disruption, resort to force, or expenditure of time. The value a party places upon an objective depends upon a complex set of influences, including expectations for success, the costs (both past and future) of achieving the objective, the mindset over having expended past resources, and the perception of the available alternatives.

The Israeli-Palestinian conflict reflects many of the factors in Edmead's model. The parties have a long and fiercely held commitment to their positions and their objectives. Enormous resources have been expended in the cause on both sides, with each side inevitably willing to up the ante in response to a perceived threat from the other. The values the parties place on their objectives derive from a complex range of factors. Edmead views the territories occupied by Israel in the 1967 war as having originally been regarded by the Israelis as bargaining resources (that is, "land for peace"), but having changed over time into an objective in itself. This made territorial compromise much more difficult, requiring a reassessment of the balance of factors required for settlement. Finally, neither side has generally been willing, at least until the November 1991 negotiation initiative, to consider seriously the possibility of cutting losses or of alternatives beyond their committed positions.

Edmead's model, with its insights on the effects of cost/benefit and risk considerations on parties' adherence to objectives, is particularly useful in analyzing the stakes in high-level political negotiations between the Israelis and Palestinians. But it also has relevance to the lower-level conflicts and antagonisms that exist alongside the overriding political question of territory. Individuals on both sides have made similar commitments to that of their government or movement, eschewing compromise, expending ever-greater resources in hopes of breaking the deadlock (for example, support for the *intifada* on one side or for harsh occupation policies on the other), and remaining unwilling to consider cutting losses and shifting objectives. A third-party mediatory process could provide an opportunity for the parties to take a more realistic look at costs, benefits, risks factors, and alternatives in determining whether, and to what extent, they are willing to accept a modification of their objectives.

Correcting Power Imbalances in Mediation

Power imbalances, or at least potential power imbalances, arise in every mediation. They may arise out of personality features: One party may be more forceful, articulate, smarter, tougher, have been dominant in the prior relationship between the parties, or be more willing to take the risk of going to court. They may arise out of strategic considerations: One party may have superior information, better access to legal advice, or a better ability to find favorable witnesses or evidence. They may arise out of the inherent strength of one's case or out of a more sympathetic or stronger legal position.

Not all power imbalances are real. The sources of the parties' powers may be different, and because the comparative strengths are difficult to assess, one party may not fully appreciate that it has countervailing powers of its own.[31] Mediators often deal with such situations by trying to enhance the perception of equal power. Techniques include encouraging each party to list its bases of power and to identify the costs and benefits to each from exercising that power. Another method is to shift the focus from power relationships to interests by concentrating on how the parties' needs can be satisfied.[32] The openness of the mediation process allows the mediator to remind the parties that they have agreed to certain process values, such as respect for the other party and a commitment not to intimidate.

In any kind of negotiation with Israelis, the relative weakness of the Palestinians has been obvious. The Palestinians traditionally relied on such power bases as the increasingly dubious threat of military action by Arab states and the self-defeating conduct of domestic and international terrorism. With the intifada, they sought a new source of power through noncooperation and internal disruption as a means of marshaling world public opinion. This strategy had some success, but the Palestinians continued to be plagued by an inability to present their position in a way that was appealing not merely to Arabs but to Westerners as well. The civil rights movement in the United States and the anti-apartheid movement in South

Africa experienced similar difficulties in trying to preserve the zeal and integrity of the movement while making its cause and objectives palatable to outsiders.

Perhaps the most significant development arising out of the advent of the summit talks in November 1991 was a new awareness by Palestinians of the public relations aspects of the negotiations and a willingness to package their claims in a fashion more agreeable to world public opinion. Despite the setback the Palestinians experienced from supporting the losing side in the Gulf War, "paradoxically, from their weakness, the Palestinians emerged stronger than before, determined to be viewed as reasonable negotiators who have a point to make and who are not about to have their legitimate aspirations held hostage to old patterns of diatribe or to the nay-saying antics of anti-Israel rejectionists like Syria."[33]

A similar change in attitude by Palestinians would lessen the power imbalance concern in lower-level negotiations with Israelis concerning greater autonomy and independence at local and regional levels. Mediation relies heavily upon faith in rationality, the value of dialogue, the putting aside of threats, and the search for mutual advantage. Palestinians seem less attuned culturally to this dynamic than Israelis, but with some training and help they can develop skills for using the process to advantage. Training in dispute-resolution techniques in schools and other institutions can lead to changes in attitudes towards the utility of peaceful bargaining with an adversary, and in the style and methodology of bargaining. In recognition of this fact, the Conflict Clinic at George Mason University in Fairfax, Virginia, brought together a group of Lebanese Christians and Muslims for training in negotiation problem-solving techniques, with the expectation that they would apply these skills in their institutions and communities. Similar initiatives on a wider scale could help to change attitudes and approaches of both Israelis and Palestinians toward the utility of mediatory processes.

Levels for Applying Dispute Resolution in the Israeli-Palestinian Conflict

There are a number of levels on which dispute resolution could be brought to bear on the Israeli-Palestinian conflict. The basic principles of conflict resolution are applicable at each level, although their application may involve vastly different approaches and processes.

INDIVIDUAL CONFLICT

At the lowest level, dispute resolution might be used to focus on distrust and misunderstandings between individual Israelis and Palestinians in their daily lives. Israel and the West Bank are small areas, and personal contact between Israelis and Palestinians is impossible to avoid. Personal contact could be a source of greater empathy and understanding, or instead, it could simply reinforce hostility and stereotypes. Relationships in public areas, markets, neighborhoods, workplaces, and schools are appropriate subjects for dispute resolution, which can lead to a lessening of the aggravations that arise from interpersonal conflict. The objective of dispute resolution on the personal level would be to sensitize both groups to the concerns of the other and to attempt to discover commonalities that may still survive fixed, opposing positions on larger issues.

Dispute-resolution centers in the United States have had considerable success at the level of interpersonal conflict. Neighborhood Justice Centers sprang up in the 1960s in response to a new concern for empowering people to resolve their own problems. That movement expanded to embrace mediation and related services in storefronts, churches, schools, and courthouses, and, in recent years, to formal dispute-resolution centers, often publicly funded, offering assistance in such disputes as those between families, neighbors, landlords and tenants, and consumers and sellers.[34] Most of these disputes would never have gone to court because of cost and inappropriateness for judicial resolution. Interpersonal disputes between Israelis and Palestinians similarly are the subject of official neglect. They do not normally fall within the formal legal processes unless they escalate into lawbreaking, and the traditional helping auspices of religious and community groups have generally been unavailable because of the unwillingness of either group to go outside its own religion and culture for intermediaries. Thus, an important component of dealing with interpersonal conflict would be the development of alternative intermediary sources for bringing the disputants together.

GROUP CONFLICT

The second level at which dispute resolution might be applied to the Israeli-Palestinian conflict concerns disputes between groups. These disputes are more difficult to resolve because accommodations must be acceptable to groups as a whole. Sources of conflict at the group level include clashing nationalistic aspirations, cultural and religious differences, political and social injustices, and territorial disagreements. Such conflicts are less likely to be resolved by a mediatory process if there is no resolution of the underlying political issues. But the fact that an ultimate political solution is problematic in the short term does not mean that certain intragroup conflicts cannot be usefully addressed by dispute resolution. For example, such discrete issues as the grievances of Palestinians over class-based discrimination in private employment or in the provision of public services may be susceptible to dispute resolution with the appropriate persons responsible (that is, employers concerning private employment, and civil servants concerning public services).

Often of critical importance to resolving group conflict is the willingness of some individuals within each opposing group to undertake a dialogue and seek to resolve limited problems. This was critical in the civil rights movement in the United States and in the anti-apartheid movement in South Africa.

The experience in the United States of dispute resolution with intragroup conflict provides an interesting example. The civil rights movements of the 1950s and 1960s and the race antagonism and violence of the 1960s and 1970s led to greater attempts to resolve group conflicts through dispute resolution. A Community Relations Service was established in the 1960s as a division of the Department of Justice to provide mediation for community conflict, especially involving racial incidents and law enforcement.[35] A number of municipal police forces, civic groups, and government agencies also created "task forces," "response groups," and "civilian review panels" to use mediation and conciliation investigation techniques to try to diffuse racially violent situations. There were some successes, especially in providing racial minorities with a sense that there was a place to go to have grievances looked into. Unfortunately, however, once the sense of crisis had passed, such remedies became less effective.

In contemplating dispute resolution for intergroup conflict, it is important to recognize that basic cultural and religious divisions do not necessarily mean that there are no common interests. Individuals are usually members of a number of groups, some of which cut across their cultural and religious identifications. They may be members of neighborhoods, buyers of goods, tenants, employees, and users of parks and public services, and they may have common interests that transcend their religious and cultural status as to such matters as combatting pollution, crime, and neighborhood decay. Dispute resolution has been applied with some success in the United States in environmental disputes, as new groups come together to confront government agencies, corporations, or institutions.

A new sense of common interests must be developed by Israelis and Palestinians. Old antagonisms over full autonomy and territory may still remain, but a sense of joint concern over those matters that affect them equally can arise out of dialogue. They all share concerns, for example, about a safe and healthy environment, traffic and congestion, economic viability, and protection from random violence. These are matters that can and should be worked on jointly, and opportunities for dialogue, both mediated and not, are important for developing a new sense of shared interests.

A change in official Israeli attitudes concerning the propriety of organizing and group discussion to accomplish social objectives must also occur. The occupation mentality that views all forms of Palestinian organizing and group efforts at presenting grievances as treasonous discourages efforts at dialogue. David Shipler tells of how Nakhle Shakar, an Arab who worked as a civil engineer for the city of Tel Aviv, assembled some neighbors to promote the preservation of Arab Jaffa and was repeatedly summoned for interrogation by the authorities.[36] A respect for discussion, perhaps heated but peaceful, is necessary for both sides, and mediated dialogue is particularly well suited to that objective.

TRANSNATIONAL CONFLICT

A third level at which dispute resolution could be used is the transnational or international sphere. The Israeli-Palestinian dispute is much more than an internal Israeli problem because it involves the holding of territory obtained through armed conflict. The dispute continues to attract the concern and interest of many nations, and both parties have appealed to outside groups and nations for support.

Dispute resolution at the international level rests on more formal and fixed practices than the process of individual and group conflict resolution already discussed. There is a body of recognized international diplomacy that would allow, upon acceptance by the nation involved, for outside intervention through mediation or conciliation. Mediation is undertaken upon the consent of the disputing parties, with the mediator as simply a facilitator of discussion. The role of U.S. President Jimmy Carter in accomplishing the Camp David accords between Israel and Egypt in 1978 is a well-known example.[37] Conciliation is a slightly different process. It involves a fact-finding role, usually by an international commission, but also essentially requires some form of consent. Both involve the basic techniques of mediation previously discussed.

The summit-level talks begun in November 1991 represent the classic model of transnational or international dispute adjudication. The parties were brought together by pressure exerted by other countries and the international community. The negotiations that took place involved a variety of intermediaries whose good offices were critical to the process. No resolution of the Israeli-Palestinian dispute would be possible without such summit negotiations. But they can only deal with the large political issues; implementation must be left to lower levels of negotiation and diplomacy.

Systems Design for Dispute Resolution

Systems design involves creating processes and procedures to be invoked at different stages of relations or operations that might ultimately result in conflict. Its purpose is to institutionalize procedures for conflict avoidance, control, and resolution. Once the stage of conflict is reached, a design might provide for obtaining an initial analysis of the conflict's systemic causes and their connections to the relationship of the disputants, eliciting metaphors for conflict from the culture or organization that can be used to reshape attitudes toward the conflict, invoking at various stages a variety of dispute-resolution mechanisms, and creating on-going structures for continued dialogue.[38]

A systems design could be centered in a community, an ad hoc organization, a governmental body, an independent mediatory source, or an international body like the United Nations.[39] At the lowest level, in the neighborhood or community, it could provide for initial resort to discussion, consultation, and, finally, mediation as disputes arise. At a group level, it could mean that certain groups and organizations will incorporate similar processes into all aspects of their operations. And finally, at the international level, UN or transnational agencies could use their auspices to encourage mediatory responses to crises.

It is often important to create a systematic means of monitoring continuing relations and guaranteeing partial agreement. This might involve creating a personnel structure to assure communication, techniques for continuing dialogue, and ceding of limited authority to a third party or parties. Such a third party might be a community group, an ad hoc group formed by the disputants, an independent conflict-resolution organization, an international, not-for-profit organization like the the Red Cross, a bi-national organization, or an international organization like the United Nations.

Conclusion

The promise offered by expanded resort to dispute-resolution techniques in the Israeli-Palestinian conflict is a slender reed. Its virtue is a coherent set of process standards that invoke universal human values and principles of individual autonomy in resolving disputes. A great deal more can be done in this arena.

Notes

1. See Northrop, "The Mediational Approval Theory of Law in American Legal Realism," *Virginia Law Review* 44 (1958): 347; P.H. Gulliver, *Disputes and Negotiations: A Cross-Cultural Perspective* (New York: Academic Press, 1979).
    2. See Janosik, "Rethinking the Culture-Negotiation Link," *Negotiation Journal* 3 (1987): 385.
    3. Fuller, "Mediation—Its Forms and Functions," *Southern California Law Review* 44 (1971): 305, 308, 325–326; Stulberg and Montgomery, "Design Requirements for Mediator Development Programs," *Hofstra Law Review* 15 (1987): 499, 504.
    4. See McEwen and Maiman, "Mediation in Small Claims Court: Achieving Compliance through Consent," *Law and Society Review* 18 (1984): 11. See also Vid-

mar, "An Assessment of Mediation in a Small Claims Court," *Journal of Social Issues* 41 (1985): 127; McEwen and Maiman, "The Relative Significance of Disputing Forum and Dispute Characteristics for Outcome and Compliance," *Law and Society Review* 20 (1986): 439; Vidmar, "Assessing the Effects of Case Characteristics and Settlement Forum on Dispute Outcomes and Compliance," *Law and Society Review* 21 (1987): 155.

    5. See C. Moore, *The Mediation Process: Practical Strategies for Resolving Conflict* (San Francisco: Jossey-Bass, 1986).

    6. See N. Rogers and R. Salem, *A Student's Guide to Resolving Conflicts without Litigation* (New York: Matthew Bender & Co., 1984), 10; J. Murray, A. Rau, and E. Sherman, *Processes of Dispute Resolution: The Role of Lawyers* (New York: Foundation Press, Inc., 1989), 279–281.

    7. See Pearson and Thoennes, "Divorce Mediation: An Overview of Research Results," *Columbia Journal of Law & Social Problems* 19 (1985): 451; Wall & Schiller, "Judicial Involvement in Pre-Trial Settlement: A Judge is Not a Bump on a Log," *American Journal of Trial Advocacy* 6 (1982): 27.

    8. E. Fernea and S. Talley, *The Struggle for Peace: Israelis and Palestinians* (1991). Film.

    9. P. H. Gulliver, *Disputes and Negotiations,* 214.

    10. *Rules of Discipline of the Yearly Meeting* (New Bedford, Mass., 1809), 3.

    11. See D. Kolb, *The Mediators* (Boston: MIT Press, 1983); R. Fisher and W. Ury, *International Mediation: A Working Guide* (Boston: Harvard Negotiation Project Publication, 1978).

    12. See Shonholtz, "Neighborhood Justice Systems: Work, Structure, and Guiding Principles," *Mediation Quarterly* 5 (1984): 3.

    13. This account is based on F. McGovern, "Toward a Functional Approach for Managing Complex Litigation," *University of Chicago Law Review* 58 (1986): 440.

    14. Ibid., 464. See also Susskind, "Scorable Games: A Better Way to Teach Negotiation?" *Negotiation Journal* 1 (1985): 205.

    15. F. McGovern, "Toward a Functional Approach," 465.

    16. See Moore, "The Caucus: Private Meetings That Promote Settlement," *Mediation Quarterly* 16 (1987): 87.

    17. Silbey and Merry, "Mediator Settlement Strategies," *Law and Policy* 8 (1986): 19.

    18. D. Shipler, *Arab and Jew: Wounded Spirits in a Promised Land* (New York: Times Books, 1986), 181–264.

    19. *Friends of Legacy,* December 1989, p. 3.

    20. D. Shipler, *Arab and Jew: Wounded Spirits in a Promised Land,* teacher's guide (New York: Times Books, 1989), 12–13.

    21. See the sections "Individual Conflict" and "Group Conflict," in this chapter.

    22.   Marcel, "Why We Teach Law Students to Mediate," *Journal of Dispute Resolution* 77 (1987).

    23. See, e.g., T. Schelling, "An Essay on Bargaining," *American Economic Review* 46 (1956): 281; T. Schelling, *The Strategy of Conflict* (Boston: Harvard University Press, 1960, 1980); Eisenberg, "Private Ordering through Negotiation Dispute-Settlement and Rulemaking," *Harvard Law Review* 89 (1976): 637; O. Bartos, *Process and Outcome of Negotiations* (New York: Columbia University

Press, 1974); H. Raiffa, *The Art and Science of Negotiation* (Boston: Harvard University Press, 1985).

24. See J. Murray et al., *supra* note 6, 76–82; G. Williams, *Legal Negotiation and Settlement* (St. Paul, Minn.: West Publishing Co., 1983).

25. See Zitter, "Annotation: Propriety and Effect of Structured Settlements Where Damages Are Paid in Installments over a Period of Time, and Attorneys' Fees Arrangements in Relation Thereto," *American Law Review* 31 (1989): 95; Souk, "Settlement Negotiations: Structured Settlements," in *Personal Injury Defense Reporter* 18-1, M. Dombroff, ed. (New York: Bender, 1987).

26. See R. Fisher & W. Ury, *Getting to Yes: Negotiating Agreement without Giving In,* rev. ed. (New York: Viking Penguin, 1991), 41–57. See also White, "The Pros and Cons of 'Getting to Yes,'" *Journal of Legal Education* 34 (1984): 115; R. Fisher, "Beyond Yes," *Negotiation Journal* 1 (1985): 67; R. Fisher and S. Brown, *Getting Together: Building a Relationship That Gets to Yes* (New York: Viking Penguin, 1988); W. Ury, *Getting Past No: Negotiating with Difficult People* (New York: Bantam Books, 1991).

27. See Curtis, "Private Agreements in Residential Development Disputes," *Mediation Quarterly* 8 (1991): 225; Susskind & Ozawa, "Mediated Negotiation in the Public Sector: Objectives, Procedures and the Difficulties of Measuring Success" (Boston: Harvard Law School Negotiation Project, 1984).

28. This example is taken in part from Shaw, "Divorce Mediation: Some Keys to the Process," *Mediation Quarterly* 9 (1985): 27.

29. Fisher & Ury, *supra* note 26, 41.

30. F. Edmead, *Analysis and Prediction in International Mediation* (London: UNITAR [United Nations Institute for Training and Research], 1971).

31. See Moore, *supra* note 5.

32. See Moore, *supra* note 5, 281–282; Davis & Salem, "Dealing with Power Imbalances in the Mediation of Interpersonal Disputes," *Mediation Quarterly* 6 (1984): 17, 21.

33. Haberman, "Palestinians, in Talks, Reflect a New Reality," *The New York Times* (Nov. 10, 1991): 4E, col. 1.

34. See Singer, "The Quiet Revolution in Dispute Settlement," *Mediation Quarterly* 7 (1989): 105.

35. See Singer and Schechter (Center for Community Justice), "Mediating Civil Rights: The Age Discrimination Act," *National Institute for Dispute Resolution Reports* 4 (1986): 20.

36. Shipler, *supra* note 18, 432.

37. See J. Carter, *Keeping Faith: Memoirs of a President* (New York: Bantam, 1983).

38. See Cloke, "Conflict Resolution Systems Design, the United Nations, and the New World Order" *Mediation Quarterly* 8 (1991): 343; W. Ury, J. Brett, & S. Goldberg, *Getting Disputes Resolved: Designing Systems to Cut the Costs of Conflict* (San Francisco: Jossey-Bass, 1989).

39. See R. Fisher and W. Ury, *International Mediation: A Working Guide.*

Culture and Negotiation [1]

Robert A. Rubinstein is an associate research medical anthropologist in the Francis I. Proctor Foundation at the University of California, San Francisco. He is a co-chair of the Commission of the Study of Peace of the International Union of Anthropological and Ethnological Sciences. He received his Ph.D. in anthropology from the State University of New York at Binghamton. He also holds a master's degree in public health from the University of Illinois at Chicago. He has conducted research in Mexico, Belize, Egypt, and in the United States. He is currently conducting research on "Cultural Aspects of Multilateral Peacekeeping." His study focuses especially on the work and development of the UN Truce Supervision Organization. Dr. Rubinstein is editor of *Fieldwork: The Correspondence of Robert Redfield and Sol Tax,* and a co-editor with Mary LeCron Foster of *The Social Dynamics of Peace and Conflict: Culture in International Security,* and of *Peace and War: Cross-Cultural Perspectives.*

NEGOTIATION is a set of communicative processes through which individuals or groups try to resolve disagreements that exist among them. Nearly every human communicative interaction involves negotiation. Sometimes the negotiation process is explicit. At other times it is taken for granted, taking place without the participants recognizing that they are involved in negotiations at all. Whether explicit or not, negotiation is a shared process that occurs within a social and cultural matrix that shapes both how problems are defined and what solutions are conceivable.

In general, negotiators seek to resolve disagreements, which may involve eliminating the source of controversy. Resolution may also result from reframing items under discussion so that disagreement no longer exists, or if disagreement persists, those involved no longer consider it meaningful. In any event, negotiators work within the boundaries of their cultural expectations and symbols to make judgments about the status of their efforts.

When negotiators come from a common background, many fundamental aspects of the negotiation process are part of their shared tacit knowledge—such as whether a proposal should be made with blunt straightforwardness or with artful indirection. When negotiation involves actors with sensibilities, understandings, and expectations grounded in different cultural backgrounds, additional complexities are involved. In such instances, structures of understanding and patterns of behavior and communication that might otherwise be effective, and thus taken for granted, may produce paradoxical results—unintended insult or confusion where clarity is intended, for example.

In this chapter I sketch some of the ways in which culture provides the context for negotiation and peacemaking, and indicate how matters of culture and communication impinge on negotiations between Arabs and Israelis.[2] The literature about negotiation and conflict resolution is large. It is not my intention to survey that literature here. Rather, I merely wish to illustrate how symbolic repertoires and cultural traditions shape, and are in turn shaped by, negotiations.

Studying Negotiation

Communicating with others in order to arrive at a resolution of differences is the essence of negotiation. It "is a basic means of getting what you want from others. It is a back-and-forth communication designed to reach an agreement when you and the other side have some interests that are shared and others that are opposed" (Fisher and Ury 1991, xi). Like many other social processes that are ubiquitous parts of social life, negotiation ranges from mundane, taken-for-granted activities to institutionalized, formal, or highly elaborated social forms.

The process and patterns of various kinds of negotiations have been studied in some depth. In general, such studies have had two very different emphases. First, institutionalized forms of negotiation—such as labor-management bargaining or arms control negotiations—have been subjected to considerable analysis. These analyses have tended to study negotiation through one or more of three general strategies: (1) through laboratory experiments; (2) in terms of abstract mathematical decision and game theory models; or (3) through the qualitative analysis of memoirs of participants in particularly important negotiations, such as the Cuban missile crisis (Janis 1983) or the Camp David negotiations (Raiffa 1982). Especially when laboratory analyses and mathematical modeling have been used, this approach to the study of institutionalized negotiation has sought to describe its formal characteristics.

Second, a less-frequent approach examines the implicit negotiations of daily life. The aim of these studies is to understand how agreement is derived through the interaction of individuals. Anselm Strauss (1978), for instance, argues that all social orders are, to some degree, negotiated orders. To understand the forms that negotiation takes, researchers focus on how the larger social context in which individuals interact affects how

people in particular societies actually negotiate (in a broad sense) the resolution of differences.

Much of this study of mundane negotiation is found embedded in
anthropological descriptions of conflict resolution in particular societies.
Greenhouse (1986, 54–58), for example, describes how the resolution of
meaningful differences among people in a small American town depends
upon a calm, negative attitude toward conflict. In contrast, in Egyptian
popular culture, one form of negotiation involves a ritual pantomime—a
dowsha—in which sham gestures of violence are used to focus attention
on a dispute and to attract the attention and legitimate the intervention of
third parties to resolve the dispute and re-establish harmony (Rugh 1982,
xvi). By explaining episodes of mundane negotiation, these studies help
reveal the cultural and symbolic components that contribute to successful
negotiations in a particular society.

Lessons from Formal Negotiations

The study of institutionalized negotiation has been a long-standing
concern among students of international affairs (e.g., Ikle 1964; Schellenberg 1982), and provides considerable insight into the formal aspects of
negotiation. By examining how groups and individuals resolve disputes in
controlled settings, studies of institutionalized negotiation have explained
the structural stages of achieving agreement and the formal properties of
decision making in bargaining situations. The resulting literature mainly
develops two lines of thinking. The first describes past and possible negotiations (those held in laboratory settings), often as instances of "*n*-player
games," and analyzes how decisions conform to a notion of rational decision making (see, e.g., Raiffa 1982). The second, related literature describes
how we can improve prospects for negotiations, for example, by creating
win/win situations or by developing a variety of confidence-building
mechanisms. This line of work has resulted in several guidebooks that describe how to negotiate successfully and fairly (e.g., Fisher and Ury 1991).
Both approaches provide useful starting points for thinking about negotiation and peacemaking.

This general school of thought can be traced to the 1940s, when it
began with the analysis of two-player, single-choice games. It rapidly developed, however, into a field in which sophisticated analyses are made of
ongoing, multiple-player negotiations. According to these studies, a number of structural features are critical to the success of negotiation, including: (1) the number of negotiating parties involved; (2) the degree of consensus that exists within each negotiating group; (3) whether the
negotiation is ongoing or one-time only; (4) the number and relationship
of issues being considered; (5) to what other issues the negotiations are

linked; (6) whether discussions are held in public or private; and (7) how agreements reached through the negotiation will be enforced (Raiffa 1982, 11–19).

Each of these seven structural aspects of negotiations introduces its own complexity into a bargaining setting. Each of these kinds of structural conditions is present in the possibilities for Palestinian-Israeli negotiations, and is treated in-depth by other contributors to this volume (see, e.g., the essays by Norton and Vitalis). In order to illustrate the substantial impact of such structural conditions, consider only the question of intragroup consensus and its relation to the issue of public versus private debate.

Neither Israeli nor Palestinian parties to negotiations can be taken to be single actors. Each represents a diverse constituency and contains internal divisions within any negotiating team.

Variation among Palestinians in their perceptions of the land of Palestine and the possibilities for satisfactory settlement runs along geographic and religious-ideological identifications (Lesch and Tessler 1989; Grossman 1988). Among Palestinians living in the occupied territories of the West Bank and Gaza Strip, Arabs living within Israel, and Palestinians living in Jordan, there exist differences in perception of the nature of the "problem" and possible solutions to it. Raja Shehadeh, who chose to remain in the West Bank as a *samid*—one who resists Israeli occupation by leading a life of principled noncooperation and nonacquiescence to Israeli authority—described how his perceptions of political action and of his attachments to the land differed markedly from those of his cousin residing in Jordan (1982, 7–11), and how he felt almost alienated from Arabs in Acre (1982, 20–23). In addition, there are ideological loyalties that crosscut and confuse this variation: the scorn of the freedom fighter and political prisoner for the *samidin* is keenly felt, as is the frustration of the samidin with romanticization of the conflict by Palestinians living abroad (Shehadeh 1982, 23–26, 56–58).

The Israeli community is similarly varied in opinion and perception, depending upon religious-ideological and geographic factors. Views on the nature and possible resolution of the "problem" of the occupied territories are shaped by political affiliations, religious commitment, and personal experience, among other factors. For example, Benvenisti (1989) describes the range of these variations and Shavit (1991) describes the variety of reactions to military service in a Gaza Strip internment camp. The divisions internal to Israeli society are evident in the variety of political parties—religious and ideologically based—and social movements, such as Peace Now and Gush Emunim (the latter of which seeks to develop Jewish settlements in the West Bank).

Under such circumstances, presenting a united front in negotiations is an extremely difficult task for each. Privately and in public, both must negotiate among themselves in order to arrive at bargaining positions that can be put forward, and considerable intragroup negotiation is needed in order to arrive at responses to proposals made by their interlocutors. These intragroup negotiations, moreover, may themselves be explicit or tacit, conducted in public or private. And negotiators must continually touch base with their constituencies. All of these tasks are difficult, and failure in either group's internal negotiations may render the possibilities and potentials for intergroup negotiations moot (Fahmy 1983; Maksoud 1985; Eban 1985; Grossman 1988; Friedman 1989; Schiff and Ya'ari 1990; PASSIA 1991; Alternative Information Centre nd).

In addition to identifying the structural characteristics of negotiations, some analysis explains the role of different negotiation techniques within negotiation settings. Ikle (1968, 117–118) for instance, describes the techniques of threat and commitment. In the former, one of the negotiating parties asserts its intention to cause the other party loss of some valued asset should that other party not comply. Threat, of course, may be credible or bluff. Commitment, on the other hand, imposes constraints on the party making it. By making a commitment, a negotiating party makes it difficult for itself to renege on a position it has advanced. Because the party imposes such limitations on itself, the act of commitment is a move to convince the other negotiating parties of the sincerity of the position advanced.

The "guides to better negotiations" genre of this line of analysis seeks to transform the information derived from analytic studies of negotiation into practical and straightforward advice for better negotiation practice (Karrass 1970; Coffin 1976; Fisher and Ury 1991). Some of the books in this genre offer useful suggestions about how to conduct negotiations. *Getting to Yes: Negotiating Agreement without Giving In*, by Roger Fisher and William Ury, is among the most influential of such books.

Fisher and Ury develop a negotiation method they call "principled negotiation" or "negotiation on the merits," which is concerned with meta-negotiation. Each negotiation move is to be made with the awareness that it "helps structure the rules of the game you are playing" (1991, 10). They contrast this with the more usual account of negotiation—"positional bargaining," which focuses on a give-and-take about positions. In this form of bargaining, negotiators define and defend positions that become their own raison d'être, often overshadowing the parties' underlying interests.

The method of principled negotiation depends upon four general strategies for insuring good negotiations. Although each of the four is discussed at length in their book, Fisher and Ury summarize them by saying, "Separate the people from the problem. Focus on interests, not positions. Generate a variety of possibilities before deciding what to do.

Insist that results be based on some objective standard" (1991, 11). These principles form the core of the method of principled negotiation (and usefully embody enough of its essence to be released in their book on a credit-card-sized card for easy reference).

The method of principled negotiation is intended to have very practical results: to produce wise agreements, efficiently, and with those involved parting on amicable terms. Fisher and Ury (1991, 14) say, "in contrast to positional bargaining, the principled negotiation method of focusing on basic interests, mutually satisfying options, and fair standards typically results in a *wise* agreement. The method permits you to reach a gradual consensus with a joint decision *efficiently* without all the transactional costs of digging into positions only to have to dig yourself out of them. And separating the people from the problem allows you to deal directly and empathetically with the other negotiator as a human being, thus making possible an *amicable* agreement."

The method of principled negotiation has been put to very good use. Its directives are admirable and productive, especially in the situation where negotiators share tacit understandings of the nature and purpose of negotiation in general. Like other methods of understanding negotiation, however, the application of the method of principled negotiation encounters a unique set of obstacles when applied in cross-cultural contexts.

Culture and Negotiation

Once a method of understanding or action is developed that is said to be universally applicable, it is easy to become overly sanguine about the possibilities for using it to solve previously intractable problems. This happens especially easily in the context of international and intercommunal disputes (Rubinstein 1988a; Rubinstein and Foster 1988).

An example of the complexities involved in real international disputes is the Camp David negotiations between Egypt and Israel. After a long and difficult process of negotiation, Egypt and Israel signed the Camp David peace accords in September of 1978 and a peace treaty in March of 1979. It is widely acknowledged, however, that the successful conclusion of this accord did not result in an equally successful peace. Israeli and Egyptian accounts and interpretations of the course of their post-accord relations varied widely, and each side finds that its expectations have gone unmet (Lesch and Tessler 1989; Fahmy 1983; Cohen 1990). For these reasons, the peace between the two countries thus has been described as a "cold peace."

I share with Fisher and Ury (1991, 4) the view that a good negotiation method "should produce a wise agreement if agreement is possible. It should be efficient. And it should improve or at least not damage the relationship between the parties." By this measure, negotiations between Egypt and Israel over the Camp David accords must be judged as wanting. Resolutions have been achieved, but with each subsequent negotiation the relationship between the two countries appears to deteriorate (see Cohen 1990).

I suspect that Fisher and Ury's criteria for judging a method of negotiation appeals to me because I share with them a (North American) culturally defined, tacit understanding of what negotiation is all about. Negotiators whose tacit cultural knowledge leads them to see efficiency and the improvement of interpersonal relations as mutually exclusive (see, e.g., Cohen 1990) may not view these criteria so warmly. More obviously, the search for objective standards for use in resolving disputes may produce wildly varying responses: What one person takes to be neutral objectivity is not infrequently taken by another to be biased in the extreme (Rubinstein 1989, 52–56). In the Egyptian-Israeli case, for instance, the record seems to indicate that each side would view its conduct in negotiations as principled. Yet, each views the other as having dealt with them in bad faith (Fahmy 1983; Cohen 1990).

Dealing with long-standing problems in cross-cultural negotiations introduces a variety of pitfalls that guides to negotiation technique and structural models of the negotiating process are unable to overcome. In order to deal successfully with the problems presented by cross-cultural negotiation, an understanding of culture as a dynamic, symbolically based system through which people construct and enact meaning (Kertzer 1988) is necessary. One of the most salient, symbolically based aspects of the Israeli-Palestinian issue is the way in which the devotion to the land of Israel/Palestine has become invested with multiple meanings and emotions. Both Palestinian and Israeli interlocutors bring to their discussions a *symbolic* understanding that frames their discourse. The Palestinian concept of "the perserving" (samid) and the Israeli conception of a special homeland (*moledet*) exert powerful emotional and cognitive influences on those who hold them (Shehada 1982; Benvenisti 1989).

Successful cross-cultural negotiation depends, therefore, upon integrating the results of formal studies of negotiation with contextual information about the role of culture in mundane negotiation. The following section of this chapter considers the importance of intracultural variability and the role of symbols in political discourse.

Culture and Internal Variability

In part because negotiating cross-culturally introduces new dimensions of difficulty, interest in the formal aspects of negotiations has been supplemented by attempts to characterize national negotiating and decisionmaking styles. The literature resulting from these efforts seeks to specify how national cultures affect negotiations in order to advise diplomats about what to expect in their negotiations with different countries. This work treats culture as though it is stable, and discovers patterns by collecting the impressions of one's own diplomatic and military personnel of "what it was like to deal with *them*," or by gathering impressions from the personnel of a third country. Interviews with Polish personnel are used in this manner to reveal the cultural basis of Soviet negotiation strategies (Checinski 1981). Similarly, Middle Eastern negotiation styles are stereotyped as deriving from the haggling behavior sometimes observed in bazaars (Binnendijk 1987).

Relying on stereotyped characterizations of cultural negotiating styles is misguided because doing so assumes that cultures are homogeneous and stable, and that once described, the patterns stay intact. The characterization of patterns of behavior, belief, and interaction as cultural is not inherently a misguided activity. Such characterizations can be useful if they are strictly anchored in specific circumstances. Rather, it is always misguided and unhelpful to treat such characterizations as stable and unchanging in any significant degree. To do so is to commit what I call the "fallacy of detachable cultural descriptions."

Anthropological work shows that there are cultural norms and preferences such as social harmony or directedness, but not all individuals from a particular society hold or behave according to a single set of norms. And, of course, such norms are constantly affected by social, political, economic, and other events and contradictions within the society. Thus, cultural styles are not stable in this way, even if they are well described in relation to a particular problem or situation. This is because societies always contain within them a variety of styles, some of which will be in direct tension with each other.

Ismail Fahmy, former Egyptian minister of foreign affairs and deputy premier, recalls that "It takes time to learn to deal with the Soviets and understand their tactics. For example, the Russian negotiator never answers 'da,' (yes) at the outset. The answer is always 'niet.' Often the first 'niet' means 'da,' but at other times 'niet' is 'niet.' The problem is to learn to tell the difference. Once I learned, I enjoyed tremendously negotiating with the Soviets. It was always tough, but they could be outmanoeuvered once their tactics were understood" (Fahmy 1983, 124).

Yet, during the period that Minister Fahmy was dealing with the Soviets, their interests in the region shifted many times, as did the constraints on their actions. As even the record of missed opportunities and misunderstandings reported in his own memoirs shows, Fahmy's view that once understood, Soviet negotiators could henceforth be handled with aplomb was, in fact, chimerical.

Beeman (1986, 1989) and Bateson (1988), for example, describe how U.S. assumptions about Iranian political styles proved inaccurate precisely because they failed to be aware of cultural heterogeneity. Bateson and her colleagues (see Bateson 1988) isolated two distinct political styles in Iran—the opportunistic and the absolute forms of political discourse. At the time of the Iranian revolution, public rhetoric and public policy changed in ways that baffled U.S. analysts. Yet, Beeman and Bateson argue, when viewed within the context that contrasting themes generally coexist in any culture, these events are more understandable. As Bateson (1988, 39) puts it, "Iranian public policy and public rhetoric, both domestically and internationally, went through an apparent radical change at the time of the revolution into a style that appeared totally different and therefore unpredictable, but we would argue that the two styles—and more significantly the tendency to think of them as alternatives facing individuals and societies—were and still are both implicit in Iranian culture."

Understanding that opposing styles exist in any society, and being aware of which styles are ascendant in a particular situation, requires that the analyst be aware of the different contexts in which negotiators frame their work, and further requires that he or she understands how the give-and-take of social process in these situations keeps the cultural matrix within which actions are situated in constant flux. Indeed, "the truth of the matter is that people have mixed feelings and confused opinions, and are subject to contradictory expectations and outcomes, in every sphere of experience" (Levine 1985, 8–9).

Paying exclusive attention to memoirs of formal negotiations, or to laboratory simulations of formal negotiations, or to mathematical modeling of decision making during formal negotiations can all be misleading. Studies that rest on analyses of these kinds direct attention toward a limited number of characteristics of negotiations and away from other, less easily explained or measured, but equally critical, aspects of the negotiation process (Rubinstein 1989).

Culture, Symbols, and Negotiation

The elements of negotiating competence in one culture may insure failure in negotiation in another. This is because meta-communicative rules of negotiation are culturally specific. Egyptian communicative competence incorporates a high value on maintaining face agreement and a smooth and harmonious social order. Often, as a result, negotiations are structured in a way that is cyclical in structure, incorporating within them a large amount of repetition. Once a point is put forward, in a relatively indirect way, it is discussed until a sense of closure appears imminent. At this stage, the discussion might return to consider the point anew. Again closure is approached and again discussion is reopened. This next episode of discussion may be briefer than its predecessor; this process continues until all have gotten a chance to speak fully to the point and consensus is presumed. Each of these episodes of discussion may be quite animated, and important information is conveyed in an indirect fashion. All of this might well strike a Western observer as wasteful of time and energy. This pattern of negotiation is not efficient in reaching a conclusion—but it is efficient for maintaining social harmony.[3]

The rules of communicative competence characterizing Israeli negotiation are very different. There, according to Cohen (1990), little care is taken to sugarcoat positions that may be unpalatable to an interlocutor. Rather, the value is on direct, forthright, "clear" communication. Thus, negotiating positions tend to be put forward directly and little attention is paid to the human side of the social transaction. On the other hand, when every word is listened to, analyzed, and taken seriously, as by Israeli negotiators, the effect of artful ambiguity and hyperbole, often employed by Egyptian negotiators, rankles and insults just as deeply as blunt disregard for social niceties.

Communication, of course, is more than just the content of message. Language, like all symbols, is essentially ambiguous. There is nothing novel in observing that the same words, spoken in different ways or in different contexts, may convey a range of different meanings. Indeed, Cohen (1990) shows that Israeli and Egyptian interlocutors repeatedly misunderstood one another, and took insult from their interaction, precisely because their meta-communicative expectations were not consistent one with the other.

Among many examples that Cohen offers, his description of then Egyptian Acting Foreign Minister Boutros-Ghali's first meeting with then Israeli Foreign Minister Moshe Dayan is instructive. Cohen (1990, 57–58) observes:

> Within hours of President Sadat's historic arrival in Israel, on the evening of 19 November 1977, with nerves at a high pitch of anticipation, Israeli diplomacy made its first tactless and maladroit overture. . . . Without trying to soften the blow in any way, Dayan brusquely informed Boutros-Ghali, with astonishing insensitivity, that since there was no chance of Jordan or the Palestinians' joining in the negotiations—as Sadat hoped at that point, anxious to avoid isolation in the Arab world—'Egypt had to be ready to sign a peace treaty with us [Israel] even if she were not joined by others.'
> Boutros-Ghali was profoundly shocked by Dayan's ill-timed proposal of a separate peace, as was Sadat when it was reported to him. At issue was not the idea itself, which was based on an objective analysis of the situation. . . . It was the unsubtle directness of the approach that was utterly repellent to

the Egyptian minister. This first conversation with an Israeli leader rankled in Boutros-Ghali's mind for years afterward.

The value placed on directness is not the only communicative expectation over which Egyptians (and other Arabs) and their Israeli counterparts part company. Israeli negotiators often appeared to be immediately concerned with working out the details of an agreement. In contrast, Arab diplomats have tended to seek frameworks for solution, leaving aside the details. For the Israeli actor, attention to the precise wording of an agreement is considered an expression of good faith. In contrast, for the Egyptian negotiator, good faith is displayed by agreement to a broad conceptual framework; details are left to be worked out at a future time (see Fahmy 1983, 285–308; Carter 1982, 342).

In his book *Culture and Conflict in Egyptian-Israeli Relations: A Dialogue of the Deaf*, Raymond Cohen traces these and other obstacles to negotiations between the Israelis and the Egyptians, and other Arabs. These obstacles all belong outside of the structural character of formal negotiations. Indeed, both the Israeli and the Egyptian negotiators understand and seek to adhere to the structural features of negotiations as these are understood by the international diplomatic community. The stumbling blocks that remain are the result of conflicting meta-communicative expectations.

Conclusion

Expectations about what is proper and good are cultural and they are encoded in a society's symbolic forms. Most importantly, symbols are ambiguous in that they refer to several meanings—often they are not given precise definition—and they invoke emotional response. As Cohen (1979, 89; see also Kertzer 1988) notes, cultural symbols have great political impact because they allow political relationships to be "objectified, developed, maintained, expressed, or camouflaged by means of symbolic forms and patterns of symbolic action." Such symbolic forms include the repetitive, ritual organization of negotiations (Rubinstein 1988b), the public rhetoric of political leaders (Cohen 1990, 45–48), and the literature of resistance (Lesch and Tessler 1989, 125–139), among other things. Because symbolic forms have both an ambiguous cognitive component and a strong emotional loading, they are powerful factors in structuring political perceptions.

The cultural factors that affect negotiation, like the meta-communicative expectations, are encoded in symbols. These cultural factors structure the way that negotiators respond to their interlocutors; they affect the perception of what is fair, what is objective, and how to begin and end discussions. The technical understanding of the negotiation process and the guides for good negotiating technique contribute to clarifying and strengthening negotiations. But, especially when disagreement is emotionally laden and rich in symbolic elements—as are discussions among Palestinians and Is-raelis—it is necessary to add a dynamic understanding of the role of culture to increase the possibilities of a successful outcome.

Notes

1. Preparation of this paper was supported in part by a grant from the Ploughshares Fund, which I gratefully acknowledge. I thank Martha Diase, Mary LeCron Foster, Sandra D. Lane, and Emma Playfair for comments on a draft of this paper.

2. Because discussions among residents of the region are sometimes referred to as taking place between Arab and Israeli, it is easy to suppose that all Arabs share a single culture and set of meta-communicative rules. It is important to rec-ognize that just as differences exist between and within the Palestinian and Israeli communities, there are cultural and meta-communicative differences among Pales-tinians and other Arabs.

3. Descriptions of Egyptian communicative styles derive from my own work and from Cohen (1990). The analysis of Israeli negotiating styles presented in this section is based primarily on Cohen (1990).

References

Alternative Information Centre. nd. *Three Years of Intifada: News from within from December 1987 to the Gulf Crisis.* Jerusalem: Alternative Information Centre.

Bateson, Mary Catherine. 1988. "Compromise and the Rhetoric of Good and Evil." In *The Social Dynamics of Peace and Conflict: Culture in International Affairs,* R. A. Rubinstein and M. L. Foster, eds., 35–46. Boulder: Westview Press.

Beeman, William O. 1986. "Conflict and Belief in American Foreign Policy." In *Peace and War: Cross-Cultural Perspectives,* M. L. Foster and R. A. Rubinstein, eds., 333–342. New Brunswick, N.J.: Transaction Books.

Beeman, William O. 1989. "Anthropology and the Myths of American Foreign Policy." In *The Anthropology of War and Peace: Perspectives on the Nuclear Age,* P. R. Turner and D. Pitt, eds., 49–65. Granby, Mass.: Bergin and Garvey.

Benvenisti, Meron. 1989. *Conflicts and Contradictions.* New York: Eshel Books.

Binnendijk, Hans, ed. 1987. *National Negotiating Styles.* Washington, D.C.: U.S. Department of State.

Carter, Jimmy. 1982. *Keeping Faith: Memoirs of a President.* New York: Bantam.

Checinski, M. 1981. *A Comparison of the Polish and Soviet Armaments Decisionmaking Systems.* Santa Monica: RAND Corporation.

Coffin, R. A. 1976. *Negotiator: A Manual for Winners.* New York: Everyday Hand-book Service.

Cohen, Abner. 1979. "Political Symbolism." *Annual Review of Anthropology* 8: 87–113.

Cohen, Raymond. 1990. *Culture and Conflict in Egyptian-Israeli Relations.* Bloomington: Indiana University Press.

Eban, Abba. 1985. "Multilateral Diplomacy in the Arab-Israeli Conflict." In *Multilateral Negotiation and Mediation: Instruments and Methods,* A. Lall, ed., 40–48. New York: Pergamon Press.

Fahmy, Ismail. 1983. *Negotiating for Peace in the Middle East.* London: Croom Helm.

Fisher, Roger, and William Ury. 1991. *Getting to Yes: Negotiating Agreement without Giving In.* Rev. ed. Boston: Houghton Mifflin.

Friedman, Thomas. 1989. *From Beirut to Jerusalem.* New York: Farrar Straus Giroux.

Greenhouse, Carol. 1986. "Fighting for Peace." In *Peace and War: Cross-Cultural Perspectives,* M. L. Foster and R. A. Rubinstein, eds., 49–60. New Brunswick, N.J.: Transaction Books.

Grossman, David. 1988. *The Yellow Wind.* London: Jonathan Cape.

Ikle, Fred. 1964. *How Nations Negotiate.* New York: Harper.

———. 1968. "Negotiation: A Definition." In *International Encyclopedia of the Social Sciences,* D. Shills, ed., 116–119. New York: The Free Press/Macmillan.

Janis, Irving. 1983. *Groupthink: Psychological Studies of Policy Decisions and Fiascoes.* 2d ed. Boston: Houghton Mifflin.

Karrass, C. L. 1970. *The Negotiating Game: How to Get What You Want.* New York: Crowell.

Kertzer, David. 1988. *Ritual, Politics, and Power.* New Haven: Yale University Press.

Lesch, Ann, and Mark Tessler. 1989. *Israel, Egypt, and the Palestinians: From Camp David to the Intifada.* Bloomington: Indiana University Press.

Levine, Donald N. 1985. *The Flight from Ambiguity: Essays in Social and Cultural Theory.* Chicago: University of Chicago Press.

Maksoud, Clovis. 1985. "Arab League Negotiations." In *Multilateral Negotiation and Mediation: Instruments and Methods,* A. Lall, ed., 32–39. New York: Pergamon Press.

PASSIA (Palestinian Academic Society for the Study of International Affairs). 1991. *Palestinian Assessments of the Gulf War and Its Aftermath.* East Jerusalem: PASSIA Publications.

Raiffa, Howard. 1982. *The Art and Science of Negotiation.* Cambridge, Mass.: Harvard University Press.

Rubinstein, Robert A. 1988a. "Cultural Analysis and International Security." *Alternatives* 13(4): 529–542.

———. 1988b. "Ritual Process and Images of the Other in Arms Control Negotiations." *Human Peace* 6(2): 3–7.

———. 1989. "Culture, International Affairs and Peacekeeping: Confusing Process and Pattern." *Cultural Dynamics* 2(1):41–61.

Rubinstein, Robert A., and Mary LeCron Foster, eds. 1988. *The Social Dynamics of Peace and Conflict: Culture in International Security.* Boulder, Colo.: Westview Press.

Rugh, Andrea. 1982. "Foreword." In *Khul-Khaal: Five Egyptian Women Tell Their Stories,* by Nayra Atiya, vii–xxii. Syracuse: Syracuse University Press.

Schellenberg, James. 1982. *The Science of Conflict.* Oxford: Oxford University Press.

Schiff, Ze'ev, and Ehud Ya'ari. 1990. *Intifada: The Palestinian Uprising—Israel's Third Front.* New York: Simon and Schuster.

Shavit, Ari. 1991. "On Gaza Beach." *The New York Review of Books.* 38(13): 3–5.

Shehadeh, Raja. 1982. *The Third Way: A Journal of Life in the West Bank.* London: Quartet Books.

Strauss, Anselm. 1978. *Negotiations.* San Francisco: Jossey-Bass.

Peacekeepers for a Changing World

Christian Harleman has been involved in peacekeeping operations since his graduation from the Swedish Military Academy in 1963. He holds a degree in international relations and humanitarian law from Stockholm University. In 1984, he was in charge of the UN Department of the Swedish Army Headquarters, and in 1985 became the Commanding Officer of the Swedish UN Training Center. He has been the chief coordinator of Swedish Emergency Relief to Mali and a consultant to various relief organizations in Africa and South America. From 1990 to October 1991, he was the director of peacekeeping programs at the International Peace Academy. Presently, Col. Harleman is the director of a pilot program for peacekeeping and peacemaking at the United Nations Institute for Training and Research. The institute will coordinate the establishment of peacekeeping training centers for the United Nations and teach the basic elements of peacekeeping to diplomats and military leaders stationed at the permanent missions of the United Nations.

Background

The effort to build effective machinery for peacekeeping has followed a long and difficult path. The United Nations first established a peacekeeping force in 1956 when the Security Council was deadlocked over the Suez Canal War. This impasse provided an opportunity for the UN General Assembly to take action under a "uniting for peace" resolution. However, the General Assembly's exercise of responsibility in the field of peacekeeping became a controversial issue and a subject for long and intensive discussions between the superpowers.

Later peacekeeping operations (PKOs) were established by the Security Council under Chapter VI, Article 40 of the UN Charter, which enables the council to "call on the parties concerned to comply with such provisional measures as it deems necessary or desirable . . . without prejudice to the rights, claims or position of the parties concerned." A legal basis may also be found in Chapter V, Article 29, which authorizes the Security Council to establish subsidiary organs necessary for the performance of its functions.

From 1956 to 1985, thirteen PKOs were established. The major troop contributors were the Nordic countries (except Iceland), Austria, Canada, and Ireland. These countries held neutral views of the conflicts, which made them acceptable to the disputants. The countries were willing to contribute to the UN because part of their foreign policy included providing means to maintain international peace and security. They therefore welcomed the opportunity to strengthen UN peacekeeping machinery as an instrument for avoiding conflicts. These countries were suitable also because of their availability in terms of material and personnel. By 1987, approximately four hundred and fifty thousand men and women had participated in a UN peacekeeping operation; more than 25 percent of the peacekeepers came from the traditional UN troop-contributing countries previously mentioned.

During these early years, the participating countries—particularly the Nordics—gained considerable experience as part of the UN peacekeeping efforts and an increasing understanding that the demands and the complexity of these operations would grow. The experiences of the peacekeepers in the Congo, Gaza, and Cyprus, as well as in other theaters, indicated a need for better education and training, matters to which the UN gave little or no guidance. At this time, neither international education nor training in peacekeeping existed and diplomatic and military policymakers were largely unaware of the difficulties of implementing such an operation.

To meet the need for training, the International Peacekeeping Academy was established in 1970. It offered training and research for officials and others likely to be involved in peace efforts. As PKOs were, and are, more political than military in nature, it was essential to provide diplomats and military officers with an understanding of how and when to authorize and utilize UN peacekeeping machinery. In addition, the Nordic countries organized training centers for their own peacekeeping standby forces. These centers offered a variety of courses and began research activities in peacekeeping.

The Current Situation

For the third time in this century, the political map of Europe has been redrawn. The military blocs dominated by the two superpowers have ceased to exist. In time, the lessening of tensions between the superpowers will provide the basis for a better world. However, these international changes have brought other kinds of conflicts to the surface. Under the previous threat of mass destruction and the blanket of strategic and ideological aspirations, little room existed for regional or local ambitions. As the situation has changed, ethnic, economic, and political conflicts have become more frequent. Border disputes, largely silenced since World War II, have again become an issue.

In light of these ethnic conflicts, it is even more important that the world community assume an increasing responsibility concerning international peace and security. As the harmony between the two superpowers has affected the United Nations, prospects for peace have become more positive than ever. The mutual distrust in the Security Council has diminished considerably and the attitude among the Western powers toward the Soviet Union has radically changed.

In this new period of unity since 1987, the Security Council has established five new PKOs in Afghanistan, Iran/Iraq, Angola, Namibia, and Central America. It seems obvious that present world political leaders are currently more favorable to the United Nations and its peace machinery. For example, never before have so many countries contributed to peacekeeping efforts as in the past few years.

Implications of Peacekeeping

Peacekeeping is not just a military operation to prevent and/or terminate hostilities between belligerents; it also involves negotiation and mediation as diplomatic tools to be used before establishment of a peacekeeping force and later in finding a peaceful resolution to the conflict. It may be helpful to analyze a few recent peacekeeping missions that illustrate these points.

NAMIBIA

The operation in Namibia was not a traditional peacekeeping effort in that it was partly designed to supervise an election process. Many UN member states were involved, with up to eight thousand men and women from more than 110 countries. Of these, forty-five hundred were military personnel and the rest, civilians. Of the twenty-three troop-contributing countries, seven were well-experienced in peacekeeping, six had some experience, and the rest had little or none.

From the training point of view, the picture was rather simple. The political situation was understandable. The idea of Namibia's independence had been well known for more than ten years, and Resolution 435 and the UN's responsibility to advocate and implement it were also well known. In 1988, when South Africa decided to participate in and govern Namibia's transition to independence, the political picture became even more clear.

The United Nations Transition Assistance Group (UNTAG) could rely on a thin but well-functioning infrastructure, which was very important for a UN operation of this magnitude. The South African administration was accustomed to governing Namibia and conducted its responsibilities in an efficient manner. Security was a minor problem, and environmental factors turned out to be less problematic than assumed.

Even if the basic political and operational structure was easily understandable, problems existed that could have been avoided. UNTAG found difficulties in the multidivisional task it had to fulfill in dealing with the military, police, and political, logistical, and administrative matters. There were also the usual questions regarding the impartiality of UNTAG or any outside organization, as well as the expectations of the Namibian population.

The UN Secretariat understood the importance of well-prepared personnel and consequently organized week-long training sessions for the professional staff before they were dispatched to the mission area. Some troop-contributing countries also carried out an extensive training program before their units went to Namibia and UNTAG, but some countries conducted no training. When UN personnel arrived in July to participate in the registration process, local citizens briefed them about the current situation and their tasks. Comprehensive training was also developed for the election supervisors, who arrived a week before the election.

Personnel preparations were emphasized and those personnel were well placed, particularly where UN staff was concerned. Training for other staff members was not so complete. The civilian police, consisting of fifteen hundred police monitors, were trained in a variety of subjects. Many of them, however, had no knowledge of the United Nations in general and UNTAG in particular. This became critical in the initial period, when local police monitors were assigned to sensitive liaison and monitoring tasks.

Another problem concerned the confusion over roles between components. The election supervisors came from many different backgrounds, and a large number had only vague ideas about their duties. Training of the election supervisors by UNTAG was not particularly well organized, but fortunately, executive responsibility for the electoral process rested upon the South African administration, which carried out its duties in a professional and commendable way.

The UNTAG operation became an unquestioned success. The problems that did exist were generally of an organizational and logistic nature. However, it would be a mistake to assume that future operations could be carried out as well in a more challenging situation. How different the outcome would have been, for example, if

1. the infrastructure had been nonexistent (as in Cambodia);
2. support from (or capacity of) the administrative authorities had been weak; or
3. the political and/or security situation had been similar to that in Lebanon.

Before the next operation, therefore, the lessons from Namibia with regard to training should be critically analyzed in detail. It seems clear that for the future, in similar operations the United Nations has to abandon an ad hoc approach in favor of a more institutional familiarity with administrative procedures, logistic processes, election laws, etc.

CHAD

The operation in Chad can be scrutinized from the political angle. Due to ethnic and religious differences between the Christians of the Saras-dominated south and the Muslim population of the north, the country had never really been unified. A revolt in 1965 led to civil war and a general crisis in Chad, although it was not until 1977 that the Organization of African Unity (OAU) decided to address itself to the question. As the OAU did not achieve any progress, in 1979 Nigeria initiated and chaired a conference with the attendance of, among others, the five Chadian factions. After weeks of negotiation, a peace agreement was signed that went into effect on March 23, with the following provisions:

1. cease-fire in Chad and the establishment of a peacekeeping force;
2. creation of a monitoring commission;
3. establishment of a transitional government;
4. demilitarization of the capital city, N'Djamena;
5. amnesty of political prisoners; and
6. dissolution of political organization.

Thus, Nigeria had taken upon itself a peacemaking and peacekeeping responsibility. However, not all Chadians fully accepted Nigeria's role and after deteriorating relations between Chad and Nigeria, Nigeria's peacekeeping troops withdrew in June 1979. It was quite clear that any further peacekeeping efforts must be under an OAU umbrella, but offers of troops were not matched with offers of funds. Realizing this, the OAU sought UN support in providing finances and logistics. The UN hesitated for two reasons. First, in the Congo it had learned the pitfalls of trying to keep the peace without a sustained commitment from the parties. Second, there were important procedural questions about financial support for a politically delicate operation over which the United Nations had no effective control.

After Libyan intervention in Chad in 1980, followed by extensive political discussions and a subsequent Libyan withdrawal, the OAU again agreed in 1981 to raise a peacekeeping force of about five thousand military personnel from six countries. This time, France offered to help to pay part of the costs. This peacekeeping effort also failed, partially because the African countries resisted French involvement, and the force was withdrawn in June of 1982.

These peacekeeping efforts only resulted in frustration. Their failure was partly due to a fundamental lack of two things—an institutional framework and an operational capability. First, the OAU was not formulated as an alliance, but more as an organization to coordinate common interests, without any provisions for enforcement action. It had no machinery for, and no training in peacekeeping. Additionally, the OAU had limited political resources and was further weakened by ideological differences among the member states.

Second, the mandate for peaceful negotiations was unclear and written in such loose terms that it became unrealistic, which affected the operational procedures. The organizational capacity was limited because its main components, financial and administrative resources, were missing. Without these elements, a successful operation could not be mounted, even if political and institutional frameworks had existed.

The last constraint was Chad, itself. The peacekeepers found themselves caught in the internal difficulties of the country, and as various components of the OAU force were never introduced to the concept of impartiality in peacekeeping, they further aggravated the situation.

In the end, the situation became even more complex. The country was bankrupt, the population was starving, and the capital was without water and electricity. The OAU had no choice but to withdraw the force, leaving the situation unresolved.

THE INTER-AMERICAN SYSTEM

Peacekeeping within the inter-American system has been carried out a number of times. So far, two types of operations have occurred: (a) regional peacekeeping actions in accordance with international law, and (b) primarily political actions, which have included peace observing, verification, joint border patrols, technical missions, etc. Only one traditional peacekeeping operation, in the Dominican Republic from 1965–1966, has occurred. The United States initiated and controlled the Inter-American Peace Force engaged in this operation. In the following example, I will indicate how the system was used and what lessons were learned.

A political crisis in 1965 in the Dominican Republic resulted in civil strife, with considerable repercussions. The existing government, a junta, was overthrown by a group of young officers and civilians who wanted to restore power to the previous president. The situation resulted in heavy fighting between the two groups and in order to "protect" U.S. citizens, U.S. forces landed in the Dominican Republic on April 25, 1965. The United States formally reported this to the Organization of American States (OAS) and the United Nations on the following day. Because of the cold war between the two major powers—the United States and the Soviet Union—action through the UN Security Council was impossible.

The only remaining institutional mechanism for peaceful settlement was the OAS. Mainly as a result of U.S. diplomacy in the regional organization, the following decisions were made:

1. establish a cease-fire;
2. create a commission for promotion of peace;
3. exercise the good offices of the OAS Secretary General;
4. establish a peacekeeping force (troops);
5. create a special fund to meet operational and emergency costs; and
6. form an ad hoc committee to contribute later to the formation of a provisional government.

The peacekeeping force (approximately fourteen thousand members) was established on May 6, 1965, and consisted mainly of troops from the United States (twelve thousand), Brazil (fifteen hundred), and five other nations (five hundred). Their mandate included, among other things: to restore normal conditions, maintain security, uphold the inviolability of human rights, and create a favorable climate for the functioning of democratic institutions. Although the theoretical objectives were well expressed in the mandate, the political will required to enforce that resolution did not exist. On May 24, 1966, the OAS passed another resolution ordering the force to withdraw from the Dominican Republic.

A number of lessons can be learned from the OAS's first peacekeeping attempt. The OAS undoubtedly has the institutional mechanism to handle conflicts within the region, but not necessarily the knowledge and understanding of how to use it most effectively. The successful management of a conflict, when employing peacekeeping forces, requires, among other things, finding the right balance between political and operational considerations and expressing political impartiality in the diplomatic arena and in the composition of the force. With 80 percent of the force consisting of U.S. troops and with a unilateral intervention by the United States at the beginning of the crisis, it is no wonder that later attempts to establish PKOs in the region have been viewed with great suspicion. The peacekeeping force's mandate was rather weak, and because the OAS was unwilling to express its mandating authority, too much power was given to a force commander who was not always impartial.

International support for an end to the conflict was achieved under the UN Security Council, which decided first to call for a cease-fire and then to send a representative of the secretary general to report on the situation. Regional efforts to settle the dispute consequently came under the legal structure of the international system, and the UN presence in the Dominican Republic contributed finally to a peaceful settlement. This was a first step, however halting, in OAS-UN collaboration to settle conflicts.

IRAN-IRAQ

Through Resolution 619 of August 9, 1988, the UN Security Council decided to establish an observer mission along the border between Iran and Iraq. Even if there had been some indications in the spring regarding a possible breakthrough in the Iran-Iraq negotiations to resolve their war, the resolution came suddenly and surprised the predesignated contributors of peacekeeping troops. Among the "traditional" peacekeeping countries, necessary preparations had already been completed, due to well-established organizing units with previous peacekeeping experience. Selected officers were on standby. Equipment, uniforms, sleeping bags, medical kits, maps, gas masks, UN flags, etc., had been readied and a four-day training program was prepared. These officers were ready to carry out their operational tasks as soon as they arrived at their mission.

Other countries' contingents were not as effectively organized. Some observers did not clearly understand the meaning and mandate of the mission. Their knowledge of supervisory techniques was slight, but even worse, they did not understand the need for impartiality. Three hundred and fifty observers from twenty-five countries arrived in the area and had to immediately proceed to the border and carry out part of the UN resolution. Of these twenty-five countries, no more than 50 percent had substantial UN peacekeeping experience, and the confusion and misunderstandings that occurred in the beginning were to be expected. The two host countries, Iran and Iraq, were ignorant of UN operations. This was particularly true of the Iranians. Conditions were more satisfactory on the Iraqi side, because the Egyptian Army provided them with knowledge and experience based on previous operations.

Undoubtedly, the initial peacekeeping phase is far more critical than the following stages, as demonstrated in the examples of Namibia and Iran-Iraq. A peacekeeper, irrespective of rank, will enter a new environment where he or she knows little about the language, people, political background, ethnic and social patterns, or operational procedures. These peacekeepers are far away from their home countries, with little or no communication among themselves or with the outside world, and in a climate that may be depressing. The peacekeeper will gradually adapt to the new situation, begin to understand it, and, after a couple of months, be prepared to meet the challenges. Training, therefore, should focus mostly on the problems that occur in the first phase of an operation.

Peacekeeping in the Middle East

The Arab-Israeli conflict has been on the international agenda for four decades. Since 1947, four full-fledged wars have stricken the region known as the Middle East and five peacekeeping operations have been established. Most recently, tensions escalated into the previously mentioned war between Iran and Iraq and an invasion of Kuwait by Iraq, which resulted in intervention by several Middle East countries and the United States and Great Britain, among others.

Much has been said about the necessity of working out adequate security arrangements to prevent recurrence of fighting and to ensure lasting peace and stability in the Middle East. Ideally, such arrangements should be worked out in a conference involving all states in the regions, including Israel. These arrangements would cover: (a) the resolution of all pending disputes; (b) nonaggression pacts; and (c) reduction and control of armament levels in all the region's countries.

Until such a conference could be arranged, it will be possible to attempt only limited security arrangements among the Arab and Muslim countries. However, UN peacekeeping could be maintained as part of those arrangements until the related conflicts are resolved. A key issue of such a security arrangement would be to find and establish a reasonable military balance among the countries.

A verification system for arsenals and military units should be established. Used in conjunction with the commitment of regional governments to disarm, this system would ensure compliance with regulations concerning arms and security. The system would consist of various groups of international professionals with different backgrounds and opinions about the roots of the Middle East conflict. These groups would be trained to execute the verification process in such a way as to earn the confidence of the involved parties.

Such an information or training program would have a considerable impact on the task of verification and would certainly serve as a peace-building instrument. Training, therefore, should be seen not only as a preparation activity but also as an instrument to explore the peace-building process, to end hostilities, and to serve as a catalyst for new roles for the military establishment. This is of utmost importance to future peacekeepers.

The Future

In the past, the UN has been hampered in its efforts to advocate international peace and security. Now there is new hope. The harmonizing climate between East and West has again raised the question of activating the Military Staff Committee of the UN, but the international climate outside and inside the United Nations is not favorable to such a solution. Most countries are not prepared to accept a new political/military hegemony of the five permanent members. Lessons from the past indicate that peacekeeping operations must be approached systematically. One possibility might be that peacekeeping operations involving large military components be handled regionally under the UN umbrella. The United Nations would give observer missions a variety of tasks, such as monitoring a cease-fire, supervising peacekeeping troops, and verifying disarmament and other activities. Disarmament under international control has been discussed for decades. Although many governments have supported the idea, very little has been done so far. The new political climate has fundamentally changed the prospects and it seems more possible to approach the question and try to establish an integrated, unilateral verification instrument within the framework of the United Nations. It seems clear that the future will bring dramatic changes: the United Nations will have an expanding role in planning, implementing, and conducting PKOs, which will be more multidimensional and will include more civilians.

PART III. THE VIEW FROM INSIDE

Making a Film about Mideast Peacemakers

Steve Talley first visited Israel in 1971 as a student volunteer with a Princeton-Duke archaeological expedition to Khirbet Shema in the Galilee. After studying early Christianity and ancient Near Eastern religions at Princeton (B.A., 1973) and Harvard Divinity School, he began working in television in 1976. In 1987 he produced *My Enemy is My Friend,* a documentary on attempts at dialogue between Arabs and Jews living in Los Angeles. Besides films made in Israel and the West Bank, his international producing and directing experience includes work in Vietnam, Indonesia, Japan, Korea, and Mexico. He has also written a novel, *The Secret,* in collaboration with Adrian Malone. His television programs have won three Emmys and many other awards.

> *Every time I make a film, I live a whole lifetime.*
> —Robert Altman

MORE THAN ONCE during the making of *The Struggle for Peace: Israelis and Palestinians,* I found myself secretly envying my professional brethren who make pornographic films. They know exactly what their subject is and what scenes communicate it best. The task of turning the historical and political complexities of the Israeli-Palestinian conflict into a comprehensible, engaging film cannot be approached with such certitude. In fact, more than most other subjects I've filmed, "peace in the Middle East" illustrates the tensions (not to say contradictions) inherent in the very idea of an "educational" film.

Film is a kind of highly organized, rational dreaming, a dream-like experience structured by a rational discipline for the sake of effective communication. Film is more akin to music than to any other art form. The experience of watching a film is much more like listening to music than attending a lecture, or even a play. A film's power, and even meaning, derive as much from its rhythms, pacing, and the emotions it evokes as from its words. What holds a film viewer's attention is not only what someone in a film says (be it the narrator or an interview subject) but also how it is said, what is seen while it is said, what else is heard while it is said, and the speed at which sight, sound, and word pass by, especially in relation to the rest of the film. A person in a film may be saying the truest thing in the world, but if it is said in a long, rambling, complex manner, and if the only accompanying image is that of the person saying it, most viewers will not listen for very long. A good film must be concise and simple. It cannot demand much of viewers' intellects if it hasn't already engaged their emotions with sight, action, and sound. Unlike a reader, a film viewer can't turn back the page and re-read something he or she didn't understand or skipped over the first time. A film viewer can't ask speakers to repeat what they just said. A film has to communicate successfully the first time or it won't communicate at all.

What film does supremely well (better than any other medium) is to show what people *do*. It allows viewers to participate indirectly in some unfamiliar activity, to walk a mile in someone else's moccasins, giving them a vicarious experience, which, hopefully, will make them think about something in a new way, as if they had lived through a bit of it themselves.

It follows, therefore, that the best subjects for films are ones that can be told through simple, straightforward, engaging action. But educational films, and "journalistic" documentaries, usually deal with complicated and abstract subject matter, whether that subject matter is overtly academic, like a telecourse, or an "important issue" that is indeed important but utterly lacking in visuals or action. Making subjects like these work on film is not easy. (I once had to make a ninety-minute television program explaining to Californians why their auto insurance rates were so high. I hired a comedian.) And what could be less simple and straightforward than the contemporary Middle East? Although there is certainly plenty of "action" in a region so torn by war and unrest, the historical and political context of that action, without which it cannot be properly understood, is labyrinthine. Take, for example, the history of international and United Nations initiatives to settle the Arab-Israeli conflict: there were nine of them between 1967 and 1989. Then there are the roots of the conflict: although it is easy enough to say that Israelis and Palestinians both claim the same land, explaining the historical bases of these claims, and the political and military history of the twentieth-century conflict they engendered, is at least one whole film in itself.

Fortunately, enough films have been made (and books written) about the background of the conflict so that Elizabeth Fernea and I felt we could focus our film elsewhere—on the nonviolent, grass-roots efforts of ordinary Israelis and Palestinians to promote peace. We believed that these efforts, which were not well known in the United States, and had not received the same attention as international diplomatic initiatives, could be a kind of advance guard, similar to the "Freedom Riders" and lunch-counter integrators of the early civil rights movement in America. We thought such efforts might someday inspire a greater popular demand for peace while the peacemaking efforts of governments (with the notable exception of the Camp David accords) failed. Moreover, the struggles of ordinary people—literally the human face of Mideast conflict resolution—seemed a better subject for a film, more personal and action-oriented, than maps and interviews with politicians and diplomats.

But personalizing the peace process did not free us from the Mideast maze. We were immediately confronted with the question of what, in the Middle East, defines peace, or more specifically, how many definitions of peace there are. If we said our film was about "peace in the Middle East," whose definition did we mean? To a left-wing Israeli, peace means an end to the military occupation of the West Bank and the Gaza Strip, acceptance by Israel of an independent Palestinian state in those areas, and the peaceful coexistence of Israelis and Palestinians as political equals. To a right-wing Israeli (and to Israel's Likud government), peace means simply the absence of war between Israel and its Arab neighbors, and the cessation of Palestinian terrorist activity against Israelis, achieved through Israeli military might without any territorial or other concessions to anyone on Israel's part. To a moderate Palestinian, peace means something similar to what it does to liberal Israelis: the establishment in the occupied territories of an independent Palestinian state whose capital would be East Jerusalem and which would peacefully coexist with Israel. To a radical or Muslim fundamentalist Palestinian, peace means the aftermath of a successful war that has driven the last Israeli into the Mediterranean and established a single Palestinian state, perhaps an Islamic republic, from Akko (Acre) to Beersheba, from Jerusalem to Tel Aviv.

Obviously, our definition of peace coincided with those of liberal Israelis and moderate Palestinians, because each of those groups sought a peace based not on one side defeating the other (the historical solution in the Middle East) but on mutuality and compromise. But because we chose this definition didn't mean that the others were "wrong"—especially as their adherents (like the government of Israel and the Islamic Jihad) have considerable influence over events in the region. Moreover, the uncompromising stance on both sides had unignorable historical arguments. An Israeli whose parents have been shipped off to Auschwitz, and whose children have been killed by Arab soldiers or terrorists, can make a case for distrusting opponents and trusting only in superior strength. A Palestinian whose parents' land has been confiscated, and whose children have been shot down in the streets for throwing rocks, can make a case for wanting justice and, indeed, revenge.

In a different medium, such as a book, the equal presentation of several different points of view on a single subject is not a significant problem. In a film, it's a nightmare. The film becomes either an endless series of long and complicated statements to the camera—"talking heads," as they're known in the trade—or a choppy, unsatisfying assembly of brief sequences that tell the viewer too little about too many things, and not enough about anything. To be good, a film must limit itself to one, or at most two, points of view, for all the reasons previously discussed. There's a limit to the amount of information a film can successfully convey, and if that information is complicated, it must be doled out in small, easily digestible amounts over the length of the film, which limits the amount of content even further. Again, film is an experience of something, not an analysis of it, and certainly not an inventory of opinions.

On the other hand, any film about peace in the Middle East that presents only one point of view opens itself to quite legitimate questions about its political bias. To respond by saying that the rules of good filmmaking forced the choice of only one viewpoint isn't enough, especially when your film has been designed (and funded) not only for broadcast but also for use in classrooms. If the film is going to introduce hundreds of students to the Israeli-Palestinian conflict, it had better give them at least a hint that there's more than one interpretation of that conflict.

Faced with this problem, it became painfully clear to us why many films on our subject had fallen prey to the Scylla of talking-head complexity or the Charybdis of biased oversimplification. How do you develop one point of view and present other points of view at the same time? How do you make a "personal" film, which looks at the conflict through the eyes and the actions of ordinary people trying to end it, and at the same time present enough of the "big picture"—the historical and political context—so that the film is more than just a vehicle for passionate personal opinions?

As we groped for a solution to the problem of defining peace, another problem confronted us: How do you define "peacemaking"? Even if you decide to define peace the way liberal Israelis and moderate Palestinians do, as the peaceful coexistence of two independent states, you cannot simply present like-minded Israelis and Palestinians working toward that goal. If you do, you will seriously mislead your audience about the vastly different circumstances under which Israelis and Palestinians live and pursue any goal, peaceful or otherwise.

Within its pre-1967 borders (known as the Green Line), Israel is a Western-style democracy. It protects freedom of speech and of the press about as well as other democracies. Israelis who wish to protest their government's military occupation of the West Bank and Gaza Strip are as free to do so as Americans were free to protest the war in Vietnam or the lack of civil rights. They may, of course, be attacked by others who disagree with them, as frequently happened to American war and civil rights protesters; and they may find that the laws that in theory protect them are sometimes ignored by a hostile "establishment," but in essence they have a right to do what they do. Like America, Israel is a contentious society, but also like America, it strives, at least within its own borders, to be an ethical one. (At every pro-peace demonstration we filmed in Israel, police were present and intervened when necessary to protect the demonstrators from attacks by their opponents. On the other hand, in previous years police have turned on demonstrators, as they did in 1989 at the peace march around the walls of Jerusalem.) Therefore, in Israel peacemaking means working against the policies of the national leadership, at considerable personal risk (one of the first Israeli peace activists was murdered by a right-wing Israeli, using a grenade), but with the confidence that dissent is a citizen's inalienable, if hazardous, right in a democracy.

In fact, some cynics maintain that the Israeli peace movement is really just an internal argument over what constitutes ethical Jewish behavior, without any real compassion for the plight of Palestinians. Most Israeli peace activists would, of course, deny this. But one of our principal film interviewees carefully distinguished between demonstrating against the occupation as an "Israeli cause" (which was her reason) and opposing it as a "Palestinian cause."

For Palestinians, peacemaking is something very different. First of all, Palestinians do not live in a democracy. They live under Israeli military occupation, which denies them the right of dissent or even of assembly. If they defy this occupation in any way, they can be (and have been) detained, imprisoned, or even killed. The price for taking a stand against the policies of the Israeli government—or the rules of resistance set by the various Palestinian factions leading the *intifada*—may be the ultimate one. But greater risk is not the only difference between Palestinian and Israeli peacemakers. Israelis promoting a two-state solution are working against their national status quo; Palestinians pursuing that goal are in step with the policies of their own leadership, the Palestine Liberation Organization (PLO). In Israel, peacemaking is a defiant, antiestablishment act; among all but the most radical Palestinians (who reject any compromise with Israel), it is part of the common struggle for national independence. This must be understood in order to fathom certain seemingly paradoxical statements Palestinians make in the film about their search for peace— most notably those by the Beit Sahur agronomist Jad Isaac, who says, "I believe that the intifada itself is a peace message. It's the way the Palestinians decided to send their message of peace to the Israelis and the world." To viewers familiar with television news images of street battles between Palestinian youths and Israeli soldiers, and with the frequent stabbings of Israelis and murders by Palestinians of other Palestinians suspected of collaborating with Israel, the assertion that "the intifada is a peace message" must seem strange indeed, unless it is understood from the point of view of Palestinian experience, and not equated with Israeli peacemaking, which takes place in a society somewhat similar to that of the United States. If one understands that Palestinian peacemaking is not separate from the Palestinian national struggle (although Palestinian peacemakers may favor less-violent methods of struggle) and that underneath the violent surface of the intifada is a wide network of nonviolent, less well known civil disobedience, statements such as Jad's begin to make sense. But unless our film provided that background, our viewers would erroneously equate Palestinian peacemaking with Israeli efforts because they shared a similar goal, only to be brought up short by assertions such as Jad's.

Confronted with these fundamental problems of definition, we conceived our film as a counterpoint of microcosm and macrocosm, an interweaving of personal stories and historical-political context. The original treatment called for segments profiling individual peacemakers or peacemaking groups that would be connected by shorter segments that, relying heavily on archival footage, would summarize for the viewer the principal issues and historical facts behind the actions of the various peacemakers and their opponents. In this way, the film would give at least an overview of the necessary background and still present peacemaking as a personal, vital experience.

As anyone who's ever made a film knows, original concepts tend to be modified, by choice and by necessity, and ours was no exception. In the end, we put most of the historical and political background into an extended opening that preceded our peacemakers' stories, and made the connecting segments into very brief introductions of the personal stories. Although there were many reasons for doing this, two are worth mentioning because they further illustrate the peculiar difficulties we encountered in designing a film on peace in the Middle East.

One reason was a question we posed to ourselves as we sat down to edit: "Who goes first?"—meaning, whose story gets told first in the film? In the treatment, we had looked at peacemaking first from the Israeli side, and then from the Palestinian side, so as to make it perfectly clear that, as previously discussed, like-minded individuals on both sides of the conflict pursue the same goal under very different circumstances and, to some extent, for different reasons. But politics intruded, as it does in any portrayal of events in the Middle East. Questions were raised about the "bias" of putting one side "first" and the other "second." As a general rule, political considerations should be as resolutely ignored in designing a film as they should be in designing an airplane or a bridge. At best, political considerations contribute nothing; at worst, they result in serious structural flaws. However, political passions run so hot on both sides of the Israeli-Palestinian conflict that we felt we had to do everything we could to prevent our film from being dismissed, rightly or wrongly, as biased. In the end, we adopted an "Israeli-Palestinian-Israeli-Palestinian" structure, with pains taken to explain, in the film's opening and its transitions, the different circumstances of each. This structure actually turned out to have certain storytelling advantages, although it allowed less exploration of the different worlds of Israeli and Palestinian peacemakers and the internal disputes within each. (Of course, viewers who were so inclined dismissed the film as "pro-Israeli" or "pro-Palestinian" anyway.)

A second reason for structural changes in the film was the Gulf War. This regional crisis threw off our production schedule by several weeks and caused us no little anxiety. Would our film still have any relevance in the "new order" of the postwar Middle East? Would grass-roots peacemaking mean anything if political leaders capitalized on the extraordinary American-Arab-Israeli cooperation that occurred during the war to launch a successful peace initiative? Would the widespread Palestinian support for Iraqi leader Saddam Hussein bring an end to the Israeli peace movement?

Assuming that the depth and complexity of the Arab-Israeli conflict would make its sudden resolution unlikely, even under the most euphoric circumstances, we flew to Israel as the war ended and contacted the peace activists we had met when researching the film the year before. We discovered, of course, that they still were hard at work; and as the weeks went by, and U.S. Secretary of State James Baker made his rounds of Middle Eastern capitals, it became apparent that, despite postwar hopes, an Arab-Israeli settlement was not imminent. We added a new section to our treatment, in which our Israeli and Palestinian peace activists discussed the war and the Palestinian support for Saddam with us and with each other, and began filming.

We immediately discovered that the Arab-Israeli conflict presents not only film conception but also film production with unique "challenges" (problems). Although between Elizabeth Fernea and myself, we had plenty of international filming experience and considerable knowledge of Israel and the Arab world, neither of us knew much about the peculiarities of crossing the Green Line on a regular basis, especially with a camera. Some of these problems were the ones we had anticipated—such as having to cancel a shooting day in the West Bank because a killing or a demonstration, or the fear of one, had caused the Israeli army to impose a curfew and close the roads. But others surprised us and, despite the aggravation they caused, also amused us (at least in retrospect).

It turned out, for example, that much of one's success in filming (or doing anything else) in the occupied territories depended on having the right combination of vehicle, driver, license plate, and dashboard decoration. We knew that Israeli license plates were yellow, and West Bank license plates were blue—this difference enables the Israeli army to immediately distinguish between Israeli citizens and Palestinians from the territories at checkpoints. It also, of course, enables young Palestinians inside the territories to immediately decide which cars to stone or set on fire. To drive a yellow-plated car through the territories is to invite Palestinian wrath, especially if the car is an Israeli rent-a-car (all of which have telltale green-and-white-striped license plate frames). On the other hand, to drive a blue-plated car through the territories is to invite inspection by the Israeli army, especially at a checkpoint where you attempt to return to Israel. Inside the Green Line, in Israel, you cannot be legally prevented from filming anything except military installations. But across the Green Line, the only law is that of military occupation, and if soldiers see or suspect you of filming, they can simply explain that you are in a "closed military area" and order you to leave. So the potential for problems with someone exists, no matter what license plate is on your vehicle.

After several misadventures with various cars (including a Hertz van that someone tried to immolate in East Jerusalem), we discovered that a professional taxi, clearly marked as such, was the best way to traverse the Green Line—as long as the taxi had Israeli yellow license plates (so the Israeli army wouldn't stop it), a Palestinian driver (so Palestinians wouldn't stone it), and one more crucial detail: a *kaffieyeh* (a Palestinian traditional headdress, similar to the headcloths worn by all Arab men) spread across the dashboard.

In the occupied territories, the kaffieyeh was a signal to restive stone-throwers that the occupants of your vehicle, despite its yellow plates, were Palestinians or Palestinian sympathizers. The trick, of course, was to remember to take it off the dashboard when approaching an Israeli checkpoint, or if the army suddenly came into sight. Because one can encounter a checkpoint or a patrol around any bend of any road in the territories, this sometimes resulted in some rather hectic action at the dashboard as successive curves were rounded and a checkpoint, then young Palestinians, then another checkpoint, then more young Palestinians, etc., came into view!

Having solved the vehicle–driver–license-plate challenge, we encountered the problem of Palestinian time. Because of the delay caused by the Gulf War, we began our filming—originally scheduled for February of 1991—in mid-March, just before the annual Muslim month of fasting, Ramadan. Not long after Ramadan begins on March 30, Israel switches, as the United States does in the spring, to daylight saving time (DST). However, Palestinians in East Jerusalem and the occupied territories do not do this, because setting their clocks ahead would delay sundown by an hour, and during Ramadan Muslims must wait until sundown to break their daily fast. (I suspect the Palestinians also see in this an annual opportunity to defy the Israelis.) Until Ramadan ends, and Palestinians also switch to DST, businesses situated next to one another in East Jerusalem are frequently in different time zones, one hour apart. This meant that our Israeli locations in West Jerusalem were on DST, while our East Jerusalem Palestinian locations were not. Our hotel, located in East Jerusalem, had switched to DST, but our appointments one block away had not. Remembering to clarify, over and over again, whether an interview you had just scheduled for one o'clock was at one o'clock Palestinian time or one o'clock Israeli time, and remembering when calculating travel time between locations that you gained or lost an hour every time you crossed the Green Line, caused a considerable amount of anxiety, lest carefully timed schedules suddenly fell apart. And then, as soon as we had finally learned to factor Palestinian time into our scheduling, Ramadan ended, and we had to unlearn. This was not as easy as it sounds. One night in mid-April, in our hotel bar, I ran into two American friends, longtime East Jerusalem residents who worked for a refugee relief organization. They were killing time after work before going to an important social occasion hosted by Palestinians—and scheduled, therefore, on Palestinian time. After spending an hour in the bar, checking their watches, they suddenly remembered to their horror that Ramadan had ended that day—and they were an hour late for their party!

Less humorous was the problem of respecting the safety of our Palestinian subjects while trying to make the best possible film. When we visited the West Bank in January 1990 to research our film, towns such as Beit Sahur and Ramallah were swarming with Israeli soldiers intent on suppressing the intifada. Whole neighborhoods had been confiscated and turned into military camps. As we sipped coffee and chatted with middle-class Palestinians, we saw heavily armed Israeli patrols prowling the streets outside. But one year later, when we returned to film in the same areas, the Israeli military was eerily invisible. I say "invisible" instead of "absent" because our Palestinian friends assured us that, having understood that their presence in the streets inflamed the intifada, the Israeli troops now hid themselves on rooftops, where they could see Palestinians without being seen. This led to an uncomfortable feeling for us (and especially Palestinians with us) that every time we took our camera outside we were being watched by soldiers we couldn't see. If the soldiers chose, they could stop the filming and order us out of the territories, which would be annoying for us but nothing compared to what the Israeli military could do to Palestinians it apprehended talking to us, most of whom had already been detained or imprisoned for their nonviolent resistance to Israeli authority. (One of our Palestinian friends, who had spent six months in an Israeli prison, told us that during the Gulf War the Israeli military tried to jail his eight-year-old daughter for visiting a friend next door after dark—technically a violation of the curfew imposed on the territories during and after the war.)

This put us in a dilemma that anyone who has ever worked in television news can appreciate: If we pointed our camera at anything and anyone we wanted, simply because it was a good shot, we could get in very little trouble ourselves—and ultimately escape to Israel and the United States—but could put our Palestinian friends in a great deal of difficulty. This meant respecting their wishes and not pointing the camera in directions that made them nervous, even if we saw nothing obviously threatening. For a television journalist, this dilemma is very real, because the more thick-skinned in the news-gathering profession take the position that the story is more important than what may or may not happen to those who help you get it. More than once during our filming I was grateful not to be working for a thick-skinned executive producer.

In particular, I was grateful on a hot afternoon when we were in the occupied territories interviewing a Palestinian man on his rooftop. This man had already been arrested and detained by the Israeli authorities for participating in a dialogue group with Israeli peace activists. As the interview proceeded, we heard in the distance, getting closer, a familiar, laboring thuk-thuk sound. Turning, we saw an enormous Israeli army helicopter circling over the town. From the roof, the ominous helicopter hovering over the quiet, sunbaked village was a striking image of domination. I decided to tell our film crew to stop the interview, reposition the camera, and film the helicopter. But as I started to do so, our Palestinian interviewee asked us to hide the camera with our bodies until the helicopter left, because if the soldiers in the chopper saw him talking to a foreign film crew, he would be arrested again. He added that the previous year an army helicopter had spied him giving a television interview and had dropped tear gas on his home. We hid the camera with our bodies. A few moments later, the helicopter flew away, with me looking wistfully after it.

As we drove through the occupied territories on our last day of filming, heading back to Jerusalem and America, I felt that regardless of all the difficulties we had encountered, we had accomplished much of what we had set out to do. But as we approached the Ramallah checkpoint, my warm feeling of accomplishment evaporated. Our taxi, despite its yellow license plate and the absence of a kaffieyeh on its dashboard, was ordered to stop by the Israeli soldiers on duty.

A burly Israeli soldier approached my side of the car and motioned for me to roll down my window. All of us tried nonchalantly to cover our cans of exposed film with jackets and elbows. "No one takes film from me . . ." muttered our Israeli camera assistant.

Without speaking, the soldier gestured for my passport. He studied it for what seemed like a decade. Finally he looked at me.

"You're from Los Angeles?" he asked.

"That's right," I replied.

The soldier grunted and resumed studying my passport. After another decade he looked at me again.

"Tell me," he said. "Do you know how many Californians it takes to change a light bulb?"

I thought, Pretend you've never heard this.

"Why, no, I don't."

The soldier laughed. "Ten—one to change it and nine to have the experience!"

Still laughing, he returned my passport and waved us on.

"Have a nice day," I said as we left.

Viewing the finished film, I think we at least partially succeeded in coping with the potential pitfalls of making films about the Arab-Israeli conflict—from historical complexity to the Gulf War to having the wrong license plates. I think we captured at least a little of the vision and passion of the remarkable Israelis and Palestinians we set out to profile, whose peacemaking efforts have received very little media coverage in the United States. Whether or not I am justified in these conclusions is for the viewer to decide. Watching the film, I had the same thought I always have when a project is complete: One loves all of one's children, in spite of their faults. Anyone who has ever made a film will know what I mean.

Women in Black gather in Terra Santa square in Jerusalem to protest against Israeli occupation of the West Bank and Gaza Strip. They stand together every Friday from 1 to 2 p.m. Reaction to their three-year silent vigil is strong enough that Israel has assigned police to protect them.

The message of Women in Black is simply to stop the Israeli occupation of the West Bank and Gaza Strip. This woman holds her sign in Haifa.

Jad Isaac is here seen working in his backyard garden in Beit Sahur on the West Bank near Jerusalem. He is one of the leaders of the Palestinian nonviolent resistance movement against Israeli occupation of the West Bank and Gaza Strip.

Peace Now, the largest and oldest peace movement in Israel, demonstrates regularly throughout the country and often discusses its platform with passersby.

Young men and women members of the Israeli army officers' group, *Yesh G'vul,* prepare for a demonstration against the occupation. Yesh G'vul usually means "there is a limit" in Hebrew; its members refuse on principle to serve in the West Bank and on the Gaza Strip.

The dialogue group in Beit Sahur, near Bethlehem on the West
Bank, consists of Israelis and Palestinians who have been meeting, person to person, for many years, to discuss peace.

Students at the Friends School, in Ramallah on the West Bank, take part in a special program of peace education.

The film crew in Jerusalem includes, left to right, David Ben-
chetrit, assistant camera; Ziad Darwish, camera; Steve Talley,
director.

The film crew, pictured here in Akko, includes Martha Diase,
production assistant; Elizabeth Fernea, producer; and Yaron
Shemer, production manager.

Diana Ruston, sound recorder for the film, works for a clear
"take" of the sound of the sea.

Profiles of Israelis and Palestinians Concerned with Peace

Martha Diase, a young scholar of Middle Eastern society, is currently doing research in Cairo on Egyptian media as part of her Ph.D. in communications theory from the University of Texas at Austin. She holds B.A. and M.A. degrees from Texas, where she wrote her M.A. thesis on the peace movement in Israel. Of Palestinian descent, she worked as a member of the crew for the documentary film, *The Struggle for Peace: Israelis and Palestinians*.

Introduction

The biographical essays on the following pages were compiled from interviews conducted with Israeli and Palestinian peace activists in March and early April 1991, during the filming of the documentary *The Struggle for Peace: Israelis and Palestinians*. These profiles provide additional details about the lives, hopes, and beliefs of the activists who appear in the film—individuals from widely differing backgrounds, most of whom share the common characteristic of having worked for a peaceful solution to the Israeli-Palestinian conflict.

While conducting the interviews for these essays, I was primarily interested in learning about the backgrounds of the various individuals and about what elements or events in their lives led them to become peace activists. Thus, in addition to questions about family background, occupation, and education, each also addressed the following questions:

1. Was there ever a period in your life when you did not support a peaceful settlement between Israelis and Palestinians?
2. What happened to change your position?
3. What peace organizations have you worked with?
4. Do you believe that the activities of the peace movement have positive results?
5. Have you faced any difficulties as a result of your political work?
6. What is your vision of an ideal peace settlement between Israelis and Palestinians? and

7. Is there anything else you would like to say to people abroad about the situation here?

Many moving stories were told in response to these questions, including Jalal Qumsiyah's history of the "transferred" cows and Hanoch Livneh's recounting of one night's events during his service in the occupied Gaza Strip in 1973. Many of the stories were also inspiring. Veronika Cohen, for example, continues to work for peace despite physical threats; Ghassan Andoni, despite imprisonment; and David and Carmela Ovadia, despite economic hardship.

Almost without exception, the essays that follow end by requesting the American people to learn more about the conflict and about the major role they play in perpetuating it. Almost all the individuals request that Americans begin to hold the billions of dollars of aid sent annually to Israel conditional upon Israeli moves toward peace, emphasizing that this is in the interest of both Israelis and Palestinians. Finally, all call for a two-state solution to the conflict, with many believing that a future confederation of Israel, Palestine, and other neighboring states is not only desirable, but possible.

I would like to thank Elizabeth Fernea for conducting the interview with Radwan Abu Ayyash. I would also like to thank Yaron Shemer for translating during the interviews with David and Carmela Ovadia. Finally, I would like to thank all the persons profiled in the following pages. I wish them peace, justice, and security.

"Once people take a stand for justice, they are really promoting peace."

NAIM ATEEK

Born in Beisan, 1937
B.A. in chemistry from Hardin Simmons
    University, Abilene, Texas
M. A. from Church Divinity School of the Pacific,
    Berkeley, California
D.D. from the San Franciso Theological
    Seminary, Berkeley, California
Canon at St. George's Cathedral, Jerusalem

DURING 1948, Naim Ateek's family was forcibly expelled by Jewish forces from Beisan, located about forty kilometers south of the Sea of Galilee. They relocated in the large Palestinian city of Nazareth in the Galilee. Educated in the United States, Ateek is author of the book *Justice, and Only Justice: A Palestinian Theology of Liberation.*

Ateek says that when he was younger, before going to school in the United States, he was not supportive of a peace settlement between Israelis and Palestinians. "I entertained the idea that the only way to solve the problem was to get back the whole of Palestine, and have a Palestinian state where Jews, Christians, and Moslems could all live. But after I began my studies in the States, I started to think about a peacefully negotiated settlement. I was trying to look at the conflict from a perspective of faith and arriving at the conclusion that I could not accept a military solution. That doesn't mean that as a human being I never fluctuated. Sometimes, one feels that the only language that the Israelis understand is the language of power, strength, and force. You feel this especially when you observe the acceleration in violence. You feel that a negotiated settlement is far away, and that force might bring a quicker way of achieving a settlement. But I've never really wavered. From my perspective of faith, I've always known in the depth of my heart that the only satisfying settlement would be one that is peacefully negotiated."

In promoting a peaceful resolution of the conflict, Ateek has spoken internationally to a wide variety of groups. He also promotes peace through his writings. He believes the work of individuals for peace has had positive results: "Otherwise I would have given up a long time ago. Even if one's contribution is insignificant, you have the satisfaction of feeling that you are helping the process of peace. I have no way of measuring the success of the peace movement here, but I have been encouraged when I have spoken to groups that there is a positive response. The people that have been affected have gone on to make their own contribution to the peace process."

Ateek hopes "for a first step, the establishment of a Palestinian state on Palestinian soil, alongside the state of Israel. For me, it can be the result of a process of different stages, but definitely the establishment of a Palestinian state has to be at the end of that process. The establishment of that state must also be the beginning of another process, a process that would make Israel, Palestine, as well as possibly other states in the region, become much more interdependent. In my vision for peace, I talk about a federation of states. Ultimately, my vision would be the confederation of four states—Lebanon, Israel, Palestine, and Jordan—with Jerusalem as the federal capital, where we would all feel that we're interdependent upon each other and all benefit from the widening base of the economy. This confederation could eventually develop into a federation. I am convinced this is the best way to bring justice and peace to all the peoples of the area."

Ateek encourages the international community to help solve the Israeli-Palestinian conflict. "I hope all people become motivated to solve problems on the basis of morality and justice, rather than on the basis of national or personal interests. If people are motivated by a sense of justice and morality, we will achieve a just solution. But if people are motivated primarily by selfishness or national interests, many problems are going to remain unresolved. So, it's an encouragement to all people, especially the people of the United States, to take a stand for justice. Once people take a stand for justice, they are really promoting peace."

". . . I looked upon the Palestinian land as my baby, and who would think of partitioning their baby? But nowadays, I recognize that people are more precious than land . . ."

GHASSAN ANDONI

Born in Beit Sahur
M.A. in physics from Reading University,
    England
Professor of physics, Bir Zeit University
Wife: Selwa Andoni
Son: Majd

ANDONI DESCRIBES his part within the peace movement as working toward getting both "Israelis and Palestinians at the grass-roots level to recognize a compromised reality." A solution to the conflict should "be based on justice, or at least on international legitimacy, on the 1947 resolution, or the 1967 resolution, but in the end, a two-state solution.

"A serious problem that prevented me from supporting negotiations with the Israelis at first was that I looked upon the Palestinian land as my baby, and who would think of partitioning their baby? But nowadays, I recognize that people are more precious than land, and therefore I think in different terms. Also, before going abroad to study, my experience with Israelis had only been with soldiers, settlers, and officials inside the occupied territories. I was often imprisoned, beginning in 1972, when I was a kid in secondary school. I perceived Israelis as not really a people, but as a group of gangsters here only for a single objective: to oppress the Palestinians and to confiscate their land. Therefore, I thought it was impossible to talk, to negotiate, with gangsters. Later, I began to think, well, there are some gangsters, but there are also people who are worried about their families like we are, who want to just make a living like we do, who want to live in peace, like us. My first positive contact with an Israeli was in 1979, when I had a Jewish lawyer at a military court . . . I was amazed that this Israeli woman was defending me and was more politically active regarding Palestinian rights than I was at that time.

"So, I wanted to know more about this society, but I couldn't do that before the *intifada* started. We had been suffering from serious psychological problems, which are the feeling of being powerless and the loss of dignity. After the intifada, I felt that not only I, but Palestinians as a whole, had regained their dignity. We started feeling more powerful, so now we think that it's time to have a dialogue, that now we can deal with the Israelis on an equal basis."

Andoni helped to organize and participate in the dialogue groups between Israelis and Palestinians held in Beit Sahur. The success of such dialogue, he notes, is that "Palestinians have now opened a way to Israeli and international public opinion through our activities. For the first time, I've started seeing people, Israelis and others, looking at Palestinians as human beings, as individuals. We have for a long time been dealt with as a package deal, as a group of terrorists, because we have never had the chance to deal with individuals. We have the good, the bad, the ugly, the radical, the moderate. If we can manage to get people, Israelis and others, to understand that the Palestinians are a nation of people with different points of view, different class positions, all of the characteristics of other peoples, I think we will achieve a step forward."

He describes part of the price he has had to pay for participating in the dialogue group. "People like us are a constant target of the Israeli authorities. Since the intifada began, I have been imprisoned four times. I was also continuously harassed, but this brought me and our activities more popular support. I was never charged with anything, but after my release from Ansar this last time, the authorities issued a press release accusing me of being the mastermind of the tax revolt in Beit Sahur." [The tax revolt started in Beit Sahur in December 1989, under the well-known theme of "no taxation without representation." Palestinians in the occupied territories are subject to Israeli military authority, and although taxed, have no representation within the system that taxes them.] "I think the American people can save us part of this suffering by applying pressure on the Israeli government. If not, suffering will continue here for a long time, and America is responsible for at least part of this suffering and bloodshed."

"If I can get peace for my son, who is going to be in the army in a few years, . . . I'm ready . . . to give up even Jerusalem that I love so much."

MOSHE AMIRAV

Born in the USSR, 1945
B.A. in political science and Jewish history from
    Hebrew University, Jerusalem
M.A. from New York University
Member of Jerusalem City Council
Served as general secretary of the Shinui (Liberal)
    party in Israel, 1990
Wife: Anna Hoffman
Son: Iri

Aᴍɪʀᴀᴠ was an educator, instructor, and leader in the Beitar youth movement, which is part of the right wing in Israel. "I was a very enthusiastic Zionist, very active in what I called at that time 'patriotism'." In the army, Amirav was part of the elite paratrooper corps. Later, he became an active member of the conservative Likud party, and many considered him to be Yitzhak Shamir's right-hand man, until he was expelled from the party in 1988 because of his reformist views.

The war in Lebanon became a primary factor behind his reevaluation of political positions. During that war, he says, "I was in the war with a good friend. We had spent so many wars together, this friend of mine and I. The first was when we were eighteen. Now we were forty and we were once again together because of war. We'd both lost many friends in all these wars. In the middle of the war, my friend's son came to him wearing a uniform. This shocked me, and I asked myself if this has to be our destiny, to have fathers and sons in the same war. Suddenly I started to think about the possibilities of changing this situation, about how we could achieve peace."

Amirav began to examine Palestinian views, and "the minute I started to ask who are the Palestinians, what do they want, what is their pain, I started to find out things I had never thought about because they were the other side, they were the enemy, they were trying to kill me. Through this voyage into the views of the other side, I found out they were human." Subsequently, he began to meet with Palestinian leaders. In 1987, he had a meeting with Faisal al-Husseini, a meeting he describes as "symbolic." "We met as enemies, but now we are good friends. He had cherished the idea of a greater Palestine, and I had cherished the idea of a greater Israel. Through our talks I found out not only about Palestinian political positions, but that people can change. I saw that Faisal al-Husseini and other Palestinians I now consider my friends were ready to change, ready to give up ideas about Jaffa and the Galilee, places that, for them, was Palestine. So I said, 'OK, if you are ready to do that, I'm ready to give up Bethlehem, the Judea mountains, and Samaria that, for me, was Israel.'

"I was ready to give up my ideas and change because I think that in this conflict neither side can get everything. If I can get peace for my son, who is going to be in the army in a few years, if I can get peace for this suffering people, I'm ready to give up the historic land of Israel, give up even Jerusalem that I love so much. For me, Jerusalem was more than a mere symbol. I named my son Iri, 'my city,' after Jerusalem. I feel, however, that I'm ready to give up Jerusalem, too, in order to have peace in this city."

He argues for the need to look at the Palestinian-Israeli conflict, and indeed any conflict, from the views of both sides. "Even in a conflict between me and my wife, if I look only through my eyes, I will never understand her. If I try and look through her eyes, however, I might, it's not definite, but I might understand her. There is another thing with the Palestinians that reminds me of my wife. Israelis and Palestinians are living together like a married couple here in the Middle East. We will not be able to divorce each other for the next one thousand years. They are here, we are here."

Because of these positions, however, he says, "I'm considered an extremist here in Israel. When you change politics in Israel, you don't just leave a political party—in Israel, a political party is like a home. You go to members' bar mitzvahs, marriages, you go out to picnics with ministers in the government. Now I'm attacking their policies. It's very difficult. Some just can't understand it and have stopped all contacts with me and with my wife. They just say 'We don't know you anymore.'"

"Talking to the other side makes both sides more realistic, more eager to solve the problem . . ."

KHALIL MAHSHI

Born in Jerusalem, 1951
Attended American University, Beirut, and
    London University, England
Director of the Friends' School in Ramallah
Children: Saji, Lour

KHALIL MAHSHI has long been involved in activities aimed at attaining a peaceful resolution to the Israeli-Palestinian problem. An advocate of dialogue between Israelis and Palestinians, he argues that "talking to the other side makes both sides more realistic, more eager to solve the problem, and, hopefully, more interested in making concessions. My interest in solving the Palestinian problem leads me to want to understand the other side of the conflict, the Israeli side." He speaks of the numerous problems of being a peace activist. "There are difficulties from both sides. Sometimes you are misunderstood by the Israeli groups and sometimes you're misinterpreted by your own people. There is also the problem of how your position is reported in the media. Sometimes the media, basically the Israeli media, play a negative role, reporting that alternative Palestinian leaders are emerging, which is not the case. I'm just a human being who is interested in peace talks. And sometimes, they don't even talk about leaders but just about potential alternative Palestinian representatives and therefore you can become discredited with your own people." Another difficulty he faced was subtle threatening by the Israeli secret police. "At the beginning of the *intifada,* the Israelis were taken by surprise by the uprising, and they thought that there was a new leadership other than the PLO. At that time, I was called upon by many Israeli groups to appear and talk, to explain what the intifada was about. I was harassed and vaguely warned by the secret police that I should become more quiet. When you're warned to not be active but you're not told exactly what activity the warning was about, it's very scary. So I wasn't sure what they were worried about and they wouldn't say . . . but they kept warning me."

Despite these difficulties, and despite feelings of futility about whether work for peace has had any effect at the governmental level, Mahshi argues that such work "has its own rewards. First of all, you grow as a Palestinian. You mature, you become more realistic, which is really very important. And then you build new frontiers; you become more internationalist as opposed to nationally chauvinistic. This is again at a personal level. Via an exchange of ideas, you help both sides become more realistic and more sensitive to the needs and views of the opposing position. It's much more positive than if nobody talks to each other."

Like many of the other activists interviewed, Mahshi hopes that a two-state solution will be achieved in the short term, but that the long term will see close cooperation between Israel, Palestine, and other states in the region. "I hope that in the era of peace, we will think in new ways as well . . . [where] we will have economic and other cooperation between the countries of the region, which will help the region survive in a more competitive world. This is my hope. Each state with defined boundaries, but also eventually with good neighborly relations and cooperation."

". . . The only thing that will bring us peace is . . . pressure from the outside and a lessening of fears and hatreds."

HILLEL BARDIN

Born in Haifa, Palestine, 1935
Father immigrated to Palestine from Russia
Mother immigrated to Palestine from the United
    States
Studied at Columbia College and at the
    University of Pennsylvania
Computer programmer at Hebrew University,
    Jerusalem
Wife: Anita Bardin
Children: Ariel, Noam, and Daphna

Bardin believes that the "most practical" solution to the Israeli-Palestinian conflict is the creation of a Palestinian state alongside the Israeli state, with eventual "open borders, tourism, and economic cooperation between them."

He has participated in joint Israeli-Palestinian activities for many years. Before the *intifada,* he was involved in attempting to secure piped water for the Arab village of Obedia. He also served on a committee of people from his Jewish neighborhood in Talpiot, together with people from the neighboring Arab village of Sur Bahir, to try to prevent the villagers' farm-lands from being taken away from them. Since the intifada, he has been active in dialogue groups in Jericho, Beit Sahur, Ramallah, Deheisha and 'Aideh refugee camps, Jebel Mukkabir, and other locations. He was also instrumental in the creation of the joint Palestinian-Israeli runners' group, Runners for Peace.

Bardin describes what made him become involved in the political work for peace: "It just seemed like a natural thing to support peace activities between Israelis and Palestinians. Among Israelis, there are two groups of people who are not supportive of peace. One are people who don't rec-ognize the rights of the Palestinians and want all of the land, all of the resources, and feel that the Jews are the only ones that have rights here. The other group distrusts the Palestinians and are afraid that peace would lead to disaster. I'm in the third group, which believes that it's worth it to try for peace."

Working for peace, however, has not been without personal costs, he says. "I went to prison as a result of my peace activities. I served twice in the Israeli army during the intifada, the second time in Ramallah, and I went to prison for talking to Palestinians. I was sentenced to two weeks, but I was only kept for six days."

Despite his commitment to peace, Bardin believes that although "all these activities have had positive results, we're no closer to a peaceful so-lution." Some positive results that he feels have been achieved: "we've learned a lot from each other, and I think both sides have gained a lot of trust in each other." Nevertheless, he continues, "I think that the only thing that will bring us peace is a combination of pressure from the outside, which is essentially U.S. pressure, and a lessening of fears and hatreds of Israelis towards Arabs. I think without both of these, we're not going to achieve peace. If the United States is not committed to forcing Israel into territorial concessions, I think we'll manage to hold on to all of the land. There will be more wars, continued fighting, and in the end, the Palestinians will have nothing. What I've been working on is trying to help people overcome their fears of each other and their hatred of each other by meeting each other, having activities together. We need an awful lot more of this to be successful, but even if we succeed in this, without pressure from outside countries to force us to make concessions, we will continue to take more and more land and the Palestinians will wind up with nothing."

"The message was that as an Israeli you can sleep in the house of a Palestinian and be safe if you come as a guest and not as an occupier."

VERONIKA COHEN

Born in Hungary, 1944
Family fled from Hungary to Austria and then to
    Baltimore, Maryland
Immigrated to Israel in 1979
Ph.D. in music from the University of Illinois
Teaches music at Rubin Academy, Jerusalem
Children: Becky, Jonathan

COHEN EXPLAINS her dedication to working with the peace movement as being due to "an orientation in life that justice is of primary importance." She works in affiliation with the Israeli religious peace movement, Oz ve Shalom-Netivot Shalom and participates in the activities of Peace Now and Women in Black. She says, "At the beginning of the *intifada,* some of us started a group called 'Israelis by Choice,' immigrants to Israel, new and old, who were opposed to the occupation, and who felt that we didn't come here to displace the people that lived here, but to live with them. I participated in a daily vigil for nine months, standing for two hours on a street corner each day trying to engage passing Israelis to talk about the occupation. Then I became involved with A Committee for Beita, trying to make sure that the villagers were compensated for homes destroyed by the Israeli army, that there was some semblance of justice for prisoners, that the houses would be rebuilt, etc. Others worked to make places habitable so that the people whose homes had been blown up would at least have roofs over their heads.

"Also, there is a village not too far from here where a massacre took place, the village of Nahalin. It is really a horrible story of the Israeli authorities not letting ambulances in and injured Palestinians out, and there was a dispute about how many were injured. We went in to verify that about one hundred people were injured rather than the ten the authorities claimed. We try to publicize that facts are different from what the authorities say.

"I've been involved with the dialogue group in Beit Sahur for the last three years. The week before Christmas 1988 a group of about fifty Israelis went to Beit Sahur, and they were received by about five hundred of the people of the town at the church. The idea was to come as visitors, not occupiers. The message was hatred of Arabs against Jews is a hatred of the occupied against occupiers. When you come as a visitor, you are welcome. Then we had another activity. Twenty-five families with children spent Friday and Saturday at Beit Sahur. Each family was the guest of a Palestinian family. Again the message was that one can sleep in the house of a Palestinian and be safe if you come as a guest and not as an occupier. We also did a 'prayer for peace.' We tried to help them find a situation where they [the Palestinians] could have a nonviolent demonstration and not have it broken up by the army. The 'prayer for peace' in Beit Sahur drew about three thousand people. But the army kept the press out, so it was not reported to the world."

Cohen says she has faced dangerous situations as a result of her work for peace. "Five of us women, demonstrating against settlers hiking through Palestinian villages, were standing at a kind of junction near Beita and a settler came and tried to run us down. It was like one of those grade B films—the driver cut through a parking lot and came right at us. Fortunately, a journalist was taking pictures, and I think he [the driver] finally realized he was being photographed and left. He was brought to trial, but we never found whether he was actually charged or imprisoned or what. And then there are the threatening phone calls and people telling us that they'll settle accounts with us, and so on."

Like many other activists involved in working toward the resolution of this conflict, Cohen argues that "Americans should educate themselves about this situation so that when their government makes decisions about this area, they will be aware of what the implications are. It's dishonest for Americans to say that they are not involved in the conflict here. They're financing what's happening in this part of the world, so they are involved in our internal matters. We only hope they will use their considerable power to stop settlements and force Israel, or encourage Israel, to move for peace."

"A nation occupying another nation can never be free or at peace, no matter what sort of military power, military strength they have."

JAD ISAAC

Born in Beit Sahur, 1947
M.S. degree from Rutgers University, New Jersey
Ph.D. from the University of East Anglia, Great
    Britain
Biologist and current director of the Applied
    Research Institute
Wife: Ghada Andoni Isaac
Children: Firas, Fadi, Dima, Usama

A FAMILY TREE in Jad Isaac's living room traces his ancestors in Beit Sahur back to 1635, but, he says, "I tend to believe that they were here as shepherds when the angels came to announce that Christ was born. Our ancestors can claim to be the first Christians, and I am proud of that." Isaac has long been involved in peace activities aimed at the creation of "two independent, secure states for two people: a Palestinian state that is secure and independent, and a secure and independent Israeli state." Since the *intifada*, he has joined the dialogue group in Beit Sahur. He describes the positive effects such groups have: "The dialogue has had positive results on the personal level. Those who are in conflict tend to forget the concerns of the other side. I learned about the concerns and fears of Israelis and I hope that I conveyed some of the concerns and the fears of the Palestinians. At the wider societal or political levels, I'm not sure whether dialogue groups have any effect."

Another activity that Isaac became involved in during the intifada was that of encouraging Palestinian self-reliance through gardening. "I started gardening as my hobby. During the intifada, the hobby gained importance. People were looking to find a way to reduce their dependence upon Israeli goods. Many curfews and strike days caused people to have a lot of time on their hands. People began knocking on my door, asking for my advice about growing edible things because I have a greenhouse and I worked at the university laboratory as a biologist. Eventually, with the help of a friend at Jericho, we started a center to sell seeds and plants, and soon we expanded the center to include selling livestock, chickens, goats, sheep, etc., and so we provided people with food, selling things at cost. Two months after we started the center, however, the Israeli forces started harassing us with interrogations and arrests. Finally, I was put in jail for six months. Last December I was issued a card which bars me from leaving the Bethlehem and Hebron area, so I'm really in a big cage. I haven't been to Jerusalem since that day."

Isaac encourages the American people to learn more about the conflict. "Americans should try to look beyond what is being told them by their media. I don't blame the American people. If I were in their position, I would have the same feelings toward the Palestinians. If you look at the way we are portrayed in the media, I would not support the Palestinians. But I hope that the American people will begin to ask questions and demand that the whole picture is presented, not just one side. We have been demonized. . . . The Palestinians have been subjected to much oppression and humiliation for the past hundreds of years, one occupation after another. But we have never felt as threatened by the other occupations as we have by this one because this occupation tries to uproot us from the land. Even though some of the Israeli politicians advocate it, they are finding it morally difficult to do a forced physical transfer of all the people here. So they force us off the land by other measures, withholding our water, confiscating our lands, imprisoning us without charges, destroying our economy. The United States is not simply supporting Israel's existence, it is supporting Israeli expansion and aggression against the Palestinians. It is in the interests of Israel that Palestinian human and national rights are respected. A nation occupying another nation can never be free or at peace, no matter what sort of military power, military strength they have. They should come to the negotiating table and exchange land for peace. Without negotiation, Israeli practices will drive the Palestinians to become more extreme, more desperate, and once a person is desperate, he does anything because he has nothing more to lose."

"The government has come up with all kinds of ideas. . . .
The only idea the government doesn't come up with is to negotiate peace."

MIKE LEVIN

Born in London, 1942
Hometown, Jerusalem
Director of road safety in municipalities
        throughout Israel
Wife: Tovah Levin

L EVIN IS AN active member of Yesh G'vul (There Is a Limit), soldiers who opposed service in Lebanon and the occupied territories, and
has participated in the dialogue group in Beit Sahur. His parents, who
came to Palestine from Russia in the 1920s, were active in the Revisionist
party, founded by Vladimir Jabotinsky; later to become the Herut party,
founded by Menachem Begin after the establishment of the state of Israel.
As a young boy, he belonged to the Beitar youth movement, an "extreme-
right youth party in Israel, with quite a military orientation. Also founded
by Jabotinsky, it was based on the belief of a greater Israel," he says.

"It was a political house because both my mother and my father were
very involved in the party. But at the same time, because both my parents
were what I might call atheists, I was never educated that the Jews were
better than everyone else. No 'chosen people.' My mother hated that
phrase.

"I had been educated at home along two lines, one very nationalistic,
the other very liberal and democratic. After the war [1967], we in Israel
had to choose between being nationalistic or being democratic, because
by occupying and oppressing almost two million Palestinians, the country
cannot be democratic or liberal. You either had to give up extreme nationalism or your democratic principles." Whereas Levin chose to give up his
"extreme nationalism," the majority of Israelis did not. He says, "I think
other Israelis don't care that there is oppression in the occupied territories
because we are losing our sensitivity. About twenty years ago we used to
say that a Jew cannot be a fascist. Today the situation is different. They
don't regard themselves as fascist, but they talk like fascists, they think like
fascists, and they behave like fascists, some of them." Levin dates his participation in the peace movement to the time shortly after Rabbi Meir
Kahane was elected to the Knesset. [Kahane was a right-wing leader who
advocated, among other things, the "transfer" of Arabs from Israel and the
occupied territories.] Levin served once during the 1982 Lebanon war, but
when called a second time, he refused.

Levin believes that a withdrawal from the occupied territories is in
Israel's interests: "I think that other societies under these circumstances
would act the same as Israel is doing. That's why we have to change the

circumstances. It's difficult to blame soldiers who shoot Palestinians in the camps after the Palestinians attack them, throw stones, try to kill them, etc. Anyone would lose his temper. We shouldn't blame the individual; we should blame our government for creating the situation and for doing nothing to change it. The government has come up with all kinds of ideas. . . . The only idea the government doesn't come up with is to negotiate peace. Our government is a rejectionist government, rejecting every step toward peace."

Although Levin is not optimistic that the Israeli government will turn toward peace, he says, "Maybe I'm optimistic that public opinion in a way will change, and we will develop a strong alternative to the government." If this does not happen, however, he believes that "people will come to understand the hard way; I hope it will not be too hard. There will be other wars, and people will eventually come to understand."

Levin believes that "America should pressure Israel by making the aid that it gives to Israel conditional; not stop the aid, but put conditions on it. I would like people who support Israel to know that their task is to work to move the Israeli government toward negotiations with the PLO, as well as the Arab countries, and to be ready to give the territories back because this is in Israel's interests. I'm not crazy about the PLO but whatever leadership the Palestinians choose is who should represent them. I'm sure the Palestinians are not enthusiastic about dealing with [Yitzak] Shamir, but they cannot tell us who should represent us. Both terrorists—Shamir and [Yasir] Arafat—should deal with each other. Shamir was also a big terrorist in Israeli history, and [Menachem] Begin, too. They committed terrorist acts against the British and the Arabs for the establishment of Israel. It's funny how ex-terrorists cannot understand present-day terrorists. People should write to the Israeli embassy, write to their own government, and support any of the peace organizations here in this country. Both sides need to deal with their extremists, and on both sides there are many extremists."

"Those who think they are supporting Israel by giving unconditional aid are only supporting the next war in this region."

HANOCH LIVNEH

Born in Ramle, Israel, 1952
Parents are Polish survivors of Holocaust who
    immigrated to Israel in 1949
Graduate of the department of sociology at
    University of Tel Aviv
Investment banker
Wife: Omra Livneh
Children: Adi, sixteen; and Noa, fourteen

After serving in the Israeli army during the war in Lebanon, Livneh refused to return there when his unit was called to serve a second time. The week he was called up to serve again, Israeli newspapers were carrying a story about an army general who had been punished for shooting a Palestinian in the back with a hunting gun while the general was in a helicopter. As punishment, the general was dismissed from the army. Livneh recalls asking his commander if he felt that being dismissed from the army was punishment enough. When the commander answered "yes," Livneh decided to refuse service. After being released from jail, he joined Yesh G'vul (There Is a Limit), an organization of soldiers opposed to service in the war in Lebanon and to service in the occupied territories.

Since then, Livneh has spent another period of two weeks in prison, this time for refusing to serve in the occupied territories. The events of a night in 1971, when he was an eighteen-year-old soldier, underlie his refusal to serve in the territories today. One rainy, cold December night, Livneh, another private, and their sergeant were conducting a 1 a.m. to 5 a.m. patrol of the town of Khan Yunis in the Gaza Strip. "Our sergeant had a brilliant idea—why not choose a house at random and search it for three or four hours before returning to camp? So he chose a house and banged on the door. An old woman, around eighty years old, answered with a frightened look. He pushed her aside and entered the house. It was a one-room house, with ten to twelve people sleeping on the floor." General bedlam ensued, with "people crying, begging, shouting. The sergeant broke a chair, poured out rice and sugar on the floor." As Livneh watched the scene, he noticed that the only calm person in the room was a young child about three years old. The child stood by his mother and stared at Livneh. "I think that he was in kind of a shock. I couldn't stand his look, so I went outside and stood in the rain until the search was completed. No ammunition or arms were found, and I imagine that now, after twenty more years of such humiliating experiences, the child that stared at me is fighting in the *intifada*." Livneh criticizes the other young private who stayed inside the house, in comfort, quietly watching the oppressive scene: "He symbolizes for me the silent majority of Israelis, staying inside, not getting wet, and becoming a criminal."

Livneh believes that the peace movement and organizations such as Yesh G'vul have had an impact on Israeli society. He cites a 1985 study at the University of Tel Aviv which showed that among seventeen to eighteen year olds throughout Israel, only 17 percent could understand the position taken by those who refuse to serve in the occupied territories. By 1989, however, the percentage of those in the same age group who said that they could understand was 54 percent.

Livneh believes that the only solution to the conflict is a two-state solution, achieved by Israeli government negotiation with the PLO. In order to achieve this, however, pressure from both internal and external sources must be brought to bear on the Israeli government. He calls upon the United States to exert financial pressure upon Israel in order to achieve peace. "U.S. support for Israel is unique in the world—we receive $3.5 billion each year, without conditions! This shouldn't continue because the Israeli government is using half this money for constructing settlements in the occupied territories. If people abroad want a strong, safe, secure Israel, they should also want peace, and the only road to peace is by stopping the occupation. Those who think they are supporting Israel by giving unconditional aid are only supporting the next war in this region. The Palestinians will fight until they have something to lose—a state of their own."

"Despite all the tension produced by the Gulf War, we must remain strong in our commitment to peace."

FAIRUZ NAGAMI

Born in Haifa, Israel, 1961
Parents are Palestinian Muslims, from Haifa and
  Acre (Akko)
Mother: Leila Nagami
Attended the College of Dental Hygiene in Ain
  Karem
Employed as a dental hygienist
Active in Women in Black

Fairuz describes some of her experiences growing up as an Arab within Israel: "I grew up in a mixed [Arab-Jewish] neighborhood. There were times when we had peaceful coexistence and it was wonderful, but there were also times when it was very painful to live here. Until now, I haven't forgotten times when I used to be walking home from school and young Jewish kids would throw stones and trash at us, saying 'dirty Arabs.'"

She describes how the relationship between Arabs and Jews inside of Israel changed regularly according to the external political situation. "During periods of war it was especially terrible. During the Lebanon war, I had to stop going to classes because I was the only Arab in the class and there were always political arguments. I just used to walk out. There was so much tension between me and the other students that I didn't feel I could invite my parents to the graduation ceremony. . . . During all the time that I was in college, I never had a Jewish friend to go out to dinner with, to go to the movies with. I would try and they would try, but it never worked out. It's hard. You'd be eating with someone from the same plate, and an hour later they would be cursing you or your people. It was hard because the people they were killing in Lebanon could have been my relatives. They used to tell me that if we want equality in Israel, we have to support the army and fight in it. How can I fight against my uncles and cousins? Today, I've learned to avoid these conversations, to ignore provocations, in order not to lose my job. But sometimes it's so hard to ignore them that you don't want to leave home."

Despite, or perhaps because of, such difficulties, Fairuz says that "I have to believe in peace. I have a lot of strength and the will to change the point of view of those around me, and this helps me to continue working for peace. I want real peace, and the *intifada* has provided a foundation for it to be negotiated. Despite all the tension produced by the Gulf War, we must remain strong in our commitment to peace." She believes that the peace movement has influenced the Israeli public in a "very positive" way. "It was slow, but we have made an impression. We know this because more and more people are joining us at demonstrations. It has also had great impact on the relationship between Jewish and Palestinian women in Israel."

She argues that real peace entails "the full recognition of the rights of the Palestinian people for self-determination, and recognition of the PLO as their sole legitimate representative. Two states must exist in this land—Israel and Palestine—and there must be international recognition for the rights of each nation. . . . The world should not deny the Palestinians their rights, and pressure should be put on Israel to exchange land for peace. The American government, especially, has the ability to pressure Israel to negotiate a real peace settlement. . . . I wish Americans would come and see the conditions that Palestinians live under."

"After all these wars, all this destruction, all this killing, we need all the governments in the area to make peace so that our children can grow up without hatred and violence."

LEILA NAGAMI

Born in Acre (Akko), 1942
Director of the Acre Women's Union

L EILA NAGAMI was born in the countryside near Acre, on the coast
of Palestine, where her parents and grandparents were also born. During
the 1948 war, her family fled to the city, and Leila and her family lost all of
their land and property in the area to the Israeli forces. Leila has been
director of the Acre Women's Union for the past seventeen years.

Active in Women in Black, Leila describes some of the circumstances
that led to her involvement in peace activities: "At first, Jews lived in together with the Arabs in old Acre. But soon it was prohibited for Arabs
to renew their homes or to buy new ones in the area, so quickly the majority of people in old Acre became Jews. I moved to another mixed neighborhood, and while living there I started to work in peace activities between Arabs and Jews. I started to think that Palestine had gone through
so many troubles, through so many wars, that maybe there could be a way
to live together with the Jews without wars, without our children being
killed.

"I respect and support the peace movement because its goals are reconciliation, life, and peace. I participate in Women in Black because it's an
expression of hope as well as of pain. I have also participated in a lot of
activities of other groups, including things like the demonstrations of
Peace Now, and activities of any organizations that call for a Palestinian
state, or more precisely, for a two-state solution. I hope that someday there
will be a real peace settlement. The world has offered us so many peace
processes in the last twenty years, but how many of them have been realized? After all these wars, all this destruction, all this killing, we need all
the governments in the area to make peace so that our children can grow
up without hatred and violence."

Leila notes that the difficulties she has faced as a peace activist have
come from both inside and outside the home. In addition to an outside
"security" threat, she tells of how there were those in her family who felt
that women should not be involved in public activities, that they should
be at home taking care of the family. "The freedom of women was very
limited, but fortunately it has started to change," she says.

Leila calls upon the women of the world to join in working with
Israeli and Palestinian women who are struggling to achieve peace. She

argues that women's voices in the peace movement should be stronger because "women are the ones who give birth to and raise children; their sons and husbands die in war." Finally, she says, "I would like to tell the Americans, especially American women, about my shock that America, a democratic, technological superpower, went and completely demolished a third-world country [Iraq]. Why such total destruction? I would also like to ask that they look into how the Palestinians have been forced to live these past forty-four years."

*"A lot of Jews think that you shouldn't criticize Israel publicly, but this is
ridiculous. . . . only by criticizing oneself does one get any better."*

HANNAH SAFRAN

Born in Haifa, 1950
Father immigrated to Palestine from the Ukraine
    in 1924
Mother immigrated to Palestine from Latvia in
    1929
Children: Daniel, ten; Naomi, six
Coordinator of women's center in Haifa, Isha
    L'Isha (Woman to Woman)

SAFRAN DESCRIBES the evolution in her political thinking that led to becoming a peace activist. "For a long time I was brought up to believe that Palestinians did not exist—the Arabs, yes, somewhere, but there were no Palestinians. You know Golda Meir used to say 'There is no such thing as a Palestinian.' Even today there are people who would say the same. This is the way we were brought up, the way we are taught in school. We are told that there were no others here when we came. Even though in Haifa until 1948, half of the population was Arab and half of the population was Jewish, they don't really mention it [the Arab population], it's not spoken about. I used to live in a neighborhood where ten minutes from us there was an Arab school and an Arab community but we never knew about them. And this is not unusual, it's a common thing in Israel." However, at the same time, "I was brought up in a household and also within a youth movement [Hashomer Hatzair] with left-wing tendencies. My family was critical of many of the [Israeli] government's policies.

"Later, in 1967, when I was seventeen, it was obvious to me that we had conquered places that didn't belong to us, and that for peace we would have to give these lands back. Since Israel did not annex the territories right away, and even Jerusalem was not annexed until very recently, it shows that even some of the leaders of the time saw that this would be an asset to negotiate peace. . . . But there is another reason why Israel did not annex the territories immediately—if we have a democratic state where each individual gets a vote, then we won't have a Jewish state anymore. Now we are in the twenty-fourth year of the occupation of these areas, and for twenty-four years we have the Palestinians there who have never been allowed to vote for any form of government. They are denied the basic rights of any democracy and this is only the beginning. Now they are in conditions of having nowhere to work and little to eat."

Safran is active in Women in Black and in the Women and Peace coalition. She says, "These are organizations of women voicing their anger and opposition to the government's policies, by announcing to the public 'I don't agree.' These groups also see that women's problems in society are unique and horrifying. Only yesterday we were discussing the fact that since the [Gulf] war, every week, one woman was murdered by her husband in Israel. Not only does this violence take place, but when these men go to court, they get only seven years in prison or so, which is very little. A feeling that many women have is that their blood is 'permitted,' that it's acceptable to kill women. When we stand as Women in Black, people abuse us for being women, not for our politics or our slogans. . . . 'Why don't you go prepare the Shabbat?' 'Why don't you go to the kitchen?' 'I'll rape you', etc. The reason why we care for peace so much comes from our understanding of our own situation in society. If we want for ourselves self-determination, equal rights, how can we deny it to the other? For Israelis, 'the other' is the Palestinians."

Safran insists that the work done by the peace movement is necessary, whether or not its effects on the government and the public can be detected: "It's very difficult to judge whether these activities have any tangible results . . . [but] I cannot work otherwise. I just can't go on without speaking out against what I don't believe is right. I feel that every society is in need of a conscience, so we serve as a conscience though we cannot make a judgment about whether it's politically effective. It's like the conscience of an individual—you don't really know what is the value of the relationship between your own conscience and your body, but you know that you need it. You would not like to live without it. So in this way, our work is successful. Israel has a moral conscience, and we keep on making it difficult for people who do not want to know to not know. But in reality we do very little."

Safran works for a two-state solution because "at this particular place and time in history, the Palestinians need a national identity. This is a small country and it's unfortunate that there are two peoples here, but we cannot deny it, and the solution is to divide it. Many times I quote the Bible, the story of Solomon, where there are two women arguing over a child. Each woman says, 'The child is mine.' Solomon tells them that they have to divide the child. You know, in Palestinian reasoning about the history of the conflict, they ask 'Why did the Jews choose in 1947 to partition Palestine?' They say the Jews are like the mother who agreed to the partition of the baby in Solomon's story—she agreed because she was not the real mother. They did not agree because they were the real mother. Maybe they are right . . . but not completely."

Safran notes with astonishment that many overseas supporters of Israel think that any criticism of Israel is anti-Semitic. "When we criticize Israel sometimes, especially when we go abroad, people say that we're anti-Semitic! A lot of Jews think that you shouldn't criticize Israel publicly, but this is ridiculous. Israel, like any other place, will benefit from full criticism, because only by criticizing one's self does one get any better." She requests that American Jews learn more about the conflict and use their influence to persuade the Israeli government to negotiate peace. "To the

Jews in America: if you support Israel, don't support her blindly! You should find out what you are supporting. Do you support your own children without giving them your views or guidance? Jews in America should learn more about Israel and speak from their own consciences, not from what they hear the government of the day announcing. And to the American people, after the Gulf War, I would like to say that I wish the American people would learn more about peace and try to work for peace around the world whenever possible."

". . . there is a misconception that for there to be a peaceful solution, Israelis and Palestinians have to love each other . . . You don't need to be buddies with somebody in order to say 'I need to make peace with you.'"

REGINA SANDLER-PHILLIPS

Born in New York City, 1959
B.A. in women's studies; M.A. in social work and
    M.A. in public health
Works with the Women's Center in Haifa Isha
    L'Isha (Woman to Woman)
Active in Arab-Jewish peace and coexistence
    groups
Community social worker, Haifa

Rᴇɢɪɴᴀ sᴀɴᴅʟᴇʀ-ᴘʜɪʟʟɪᴘs describes herself has having grown up in a traditional American Jewish household, where support for Israel "was something that you took for granted." The evolution in her thinking that prompted her to work for Israeli-Palestinian peace since the late 1970s was stimulated by her struggle to clarify her identity as a woman and a Jew. "Working out what it means to be a Jew is something that has preoccupied me from an early age," she says. "What was the Holocaust about, and what does it mean to be a Jew in the post-Holocaust age? I don't have a Zionist background and I don't identify as a Zionist for all kinds of reasons. I basically do not think that Israel is the answer to the Jewish question. I think that it's the continuation of the question, that it's another level of working out Jewish existence but now in a place where Jews are the majority in power. What do we do with that power? I have a sense of justice that needs to be pursued, and I try to follow its implications.

"I came to Israel in 1989 to work for social change and to dedicate part of my life to living the paradoxes of life here. It was very important to me during the Gulf War, for example, to be seated in a room with a gas mask on and missiles falling all around, and to ask myself 'Am I still in the same place politically?' My answer is 'yes.'"

One of Sandler-Phillips' major activities is working with Women in Black: "I feel that first and foremost we are out there to express our opposition to the continuing state of war and hatred. We're also pricking the conscience of the public. I think there is a misconception here that for there to be a peaceful solution, Israelis and Palestinians have to love each other, personally as well as ideologically. There are many circumstances that distort relations here between Arabs and Jews, institutional and structural influences of the society that have their expression at the interpersonal level. But all the personal disappointments don't alter the basic fact of what needs to be worked toward. You don't need to be buddies with somebody in order to say 'I need to make peace with you.'

"Some family members and friends in the United States are extremely ambivalent about what I do, even though they support me. I've also faced difficulties in the neighborhood where I live, Hadar, where every once in a while someone will curse me, or spit on me, or threaten me because they've seen me in Women in Black."

She says, "There are a lot of emotional reasons why American Jews cannot come face-to-face with the reality of what goes on in the Middle East. I sometimes think that Israel is the adult American Jew's version of Santa Claus and the Easter bunny put together—that there's a vision of Israel as this perfect place where Jews are free and everybody lives on *kibbutzim* and runs around eating oranges and everything is fine except when some nasty Arab throws a bomb and spoils it all. That's a very simplistic version of the picture presented of Israel until recently in general American Jewish discourse. Even for those who are able to admit that there are problems, it's very difficult to come to a practical confrontation of those problems in a way that generates real change. I would like American Jews to take a lot more responsibility for the support that they give to Israel. Let it be informed and not blind support. People should not feel that because they do not live in Israel they have no right to speak out. For me, the same Jews who are called upon to give material, financial, and moral support to the state of Israel, also have a right and a duty to speak out about where that support is going and whether it is helping or hurting the people involved."

"Here [in Israel] the American Constitution is considered a radical leftist document . . ."

GIDEON SPIRO

Born in Berlin, Germany, 1935
Immigrated with his family to British-occupied
    Palestine in 1939
B.A. in political science and diploma in tourist
    and hotel administration
Freelance journalist living in Jerusalem
Children: Hagar, Adam

"THERE WAS A TIME when I was not so concerned about whether Israelis and Palestinians reached a peace settlement," says Gideon Spiro. "Of course, during my army days between 1954–1957 it was still early in Israel's history and we were all still in a very patriotic phase. I was for the survival and the flourishing of the state of Israel. I was a paratrooper, part of the elite troops. I wanted to be a pioneer in our army, in the forefront of the fighting. In the 1956 war, the Sinai campaign, I received a medal for participating in the Mitla Pass jump."

Between 1956 and 1982, Spiro came to feel a need to choose between nationalist ideals and "the principles of equality and human dignity" that he had learned from his parents, who "were steeped in classical values of European liberalism." He explains, "In the 1967 war, I participated in the occupation of East Jerusalem, and found myself for the first time confronting a civilian population as a soldier, which caused me much discomfort. I had hoped that this would only be for a short period, a transitional period. No one thought in 1967 that the newly occupied territories would become a permanent part of our society . . . For over half of our country's history, we have been an occupying power. As the occupation increasingly became a permanent part of our society, my liberal side became more and more dominant. I found myself becoming more active in various activities against the occupation, activities for Palestinian human rights, and against the oppressive measures of the Israeli army. More and more we came to adopt a colonial mentality; racism developed and grew."

Spiro was also one of the founders of Yesh G'vul (There Is a Limit), a movement of soldiers who, at first, refused to serve in the army during the Lebanon war, and today, refuse to serve in the occupied territories. "In Israel, everyone who is against the occupation is automatically a leftist. Here, the American Constitution is considered a radical leftist document, and the Universal Declaration of Human Rights is ultra-leftist—it is almost a dangerous document, the enemy of Israel, as perceived by many here. Our whole political map has moved so much to the right that to raise the flag of human rights here makes one automatically a dangerous leftist. It reminds me a little bit of the McCarthy period in the United States."

Spiro believes that when he lost his government position due to his political activities, the Israeli government purposely made an example of him, in order to subdue other would-be public dissenters to its policy: "I was the only Israeli who was ever taken to court for public criticism of government policy while being a state employee. While working in the Ministry of Education during the war in Lebanon, I wrote many news-paper articles and letters calling upon everyone who has a human con-science and who is committed to human rights to refuse to serve in the war. The state prosecutor decided to sue me for being in violation of an obscure law which forbids government employees to criticize the govern-ment of Israel. In Israel, we don't have human rights principles that are guaranteed in the law. . . . In the end, I lost the case. The punishment was severe—I was dismissed from my position. I was also disqualified from holding any government position for five years, and my pension rights were cut as well. This means that my children, too, will suffer. It was clear that this was a vendetta because of my political views, not because of the severity of the crime. Of course, if I compare my situation with that of the Palestinians, I am still very lucky—no one is demolishing my home or sealing it; I'm not under administrative arrest. But it can happen in the future; it's all part of the Israeli law system. Everything we are doing in the occupied territories can eventually be transferred into Israel itself. . . . We know of cases here where people were murdered during torture. The Israeli court system sentenced two Israeli interrogators from the Israeli secret service who murdered a Palestinian—this Palestinian was not judged to be guilty of anything, by the way, he was only suspected of being guilty—to prison terms of a *few months*, not even what a regular criminal with an ordinary offence would receive. The legal court system, too, has adopted this double standard: if you kill a Jew the sentence is always more severe than if you kill an Arab. The whole system in Israel has adapted itself to the occupation. This ugly Israel is frightening me. Little by little, the dictatorial norms we apply there will be applied to us also; they will swallow us."

Spiro believes that the only way to reverse this course of events is the creation of a Palestinian state in the occupied territories: "The Palestinians were mistaken forty years ago when they refused to accept the partitioning of Palestine, but they have since accepted reality—they don't need to love it. Now Israel is the refuser. It's a combination of biblical beliefs with contemporary security considerations, a very dangerous mixture. It's fuel for fascism, the mixing of religion with nationalism."

Discouraged by the lack of impact those in the peace movement are having upon Israeli society, Spiro nevertheless insists that the work is nec-essary: "Over the years that I've been involved in peace activities, the right wing has become stronger, and the racists have become stronger—racist parties are today present in the government. So it's discouraging on the one hand. On the other hand, I don't do these things because somebody guaranteed me that they would bear immediate fruit. I do them because they should be done."

He calls upon Americans and Europeans to recognize their role in the conflict, and the role they could play in a peaceful solution. He says, "I feel sure that without all the monetary support of the external world, things would change here. Part of the reason that Israel has been able to hold on to the occupied territories is that the outside world sends so much aid to Israel. . . . In outside aid we get more than $5 billion a year! This has enabled us to develop a huge military machine that we would not have been able to afford on our own. This aid has also enabled us to have little sense of freedom. With all of our social problems, all of our unemployment, still the Israelis are living closer to European standards of living than to third-world levels, all because the world is assisting us. If only the world would be sincere in its desire to see this problem solved, it would say to Israel 'If you want to continue the occupation, do it on your own account. We are not going to finance it.' Then I believe every Israeli would be interested in peace."

"Every single Palestinian individual hopes for liberty and independence. This is what the intifada *was started for . . . We are ready, fully, to sacrifice everything."*

JALAL QUMSIYAH

Born in Beit Sahur, 1943
Grandfather and father were mayors of Beit
    Sahur
His wife, Asma, teaches at the government school
    in Beit Sahur
Children: Jiries, Jane, Issa, and Elias

Qumsiyah was a teacher at a government school in Beit Sahur until 1982, before participating in a teachers' strike. The teachers were attempting to establish a teachers' union for better pay, better school facilities, and more teaching materials. "In Israel," Qumsiyah notes, "there is a teachers' union where teachers have their rights; here we do not. We were lacking so many things in our laboratories, libraries, visual aids, etc. The teachers would go to school just with a blackboard and chalk and that's it. There was nothing else. In addition, the average salary of a teacher in the West Bank was one-third the average Israeli teacher's salary." All 140 teachers were arrested, and Israeli authorities ordered their dismissal. None of the conditions for which they were striking were met.

After his dismissal, Qumsiyah worked with the Palestinian self-reliance movement. He tells a funny but poignant story about the efforts of people in Beit Sahur to establish a dairy farm: "We were sure it was impossible to get a license for a new cooperative project such as a dairy farm under the martial law of the occupation. Others have applied many times for similar local projects, but in vain. Yet, we took the risk and went to an Israeli *kibbutz*, bought eighteen cows, and brought them to a special place very near town. Well, we started taking care of these cows, but a month later the authorities discovered them and it seemed that they thought a dairy farm was a very dangerous thing. The military governor, the Shin Bet people [the Israeli secret police], the civil administration officers, and a lot of soldiers went to the farm, surrounded it, and they took photos of each cow, with identification numbers. Then they gave us a military order to close the farm within twenty-four hours or else the military governor would order the place to be bulldozed. They said that the cows were a security threat. I asked the military governor myself, 'Just please explain to me, I can't understand it, why this is so dangerous for you? How can eighteen cows be so dangerous for the state of Israel?' He said that I didn't need to understand; that they understood well enough what's dangerous for Israel and what's not. So, there was no explanation. We had no other alternative but to go late at night and move the cows secretly. So when the military governor went the next morning to the farm and didn't find any cows, he got very angry—it seemed like he had lost eighteen terrorists. So he did something very strange—at least for our area, it was the first time such a wide search campaign was organized. People say hundreds of soldiers participated, even with helicopters, looking for the cows, those terrorists. The soldiers carried photos of the cows, showed them to people, and asked them 'Have you seen these cows?' It was amazing. Sometimes we wonder why they didn't put up 'Wanted Dead or Alive' posters for them. After ten days of searching, they located the cows. They found them with a butcher, and a butcher has a license to buy cows in order to slaughter them afterwards. He told them 'I have bought these cows, here are the papers. I'm going to slaughter them later for the meat.' The military governor was very pleased; the problem was solved. So they waited a week before coming back to check whether the butcher had indeed killed the cows. They found them still there, though, and indeed, there were then twenty-three cows instead of eighteen because all of them had been pregnant when we bought them and five had delivered. They didn't know what to do. Then they started harassing the butcher's family, so we soon decided that it was time to move the cows again. Once again, we moved them at night, this time away from Beit Sahur. It was a transfer. And I'm afraid that this is what is going to happen to the people of Beit Sahur, also, because what has been going on here since the beginning of the occupation is a slow transfer of people. But I can tell you something, the cows are still hidden somewhere and they are still providing the children of Beit Sahur with the milk of the *intifada*."

Since the beginning of the intifada, Qumsiyah has also been active in the dialogue group that meets in Beit Sahur. He says, "An Israeli suggested the [dialogue] idea to us, and we welcomed it. We were excited because it was the first time such a thing happened in our area. We started learning about each other. We didn't think of solving any problems or reaching any agreements—we were not politicians, just ordinary people. But the interesting thing is that I, myself, learned a lot of things about Israelis and Jews that I didn't know before, and I have noticed that they have started to understand how much we suffer under the occupation, what our motives are, and they have started to change a lot of their ideas. So we encouraged each other, and we've been doing this for three years now. We hope we will continue."

Like other male Palestinian participants in the dialogue group, Qumsiyah served time in prison. He is not sure, however, whether it was his involvement with the dairy farm or the dialogue group that was behind his arrest. "I waited all the time I was under arrest for someone to come and interrogate me or charge me, but they didn't," he says. "They didn't explain anything. They just came and took me from my house at night and sent me to jail without any questioning. No one ever told me what I was accused of."

"On the other hand, when I was released from prison, I found my friend, Hillel Burdin, an Israeli peace activist, waiting on the desert road to take me back home in his car. He worked hard with two Israeli Knesset members to get me released, and that's something I'll never forget."

Qumsiyah asks Americans to learn more about the conflict. "We have learned a lot about Americans. I wish they would do the same about us. Please, learn something about us! Read something about us. Hear from us. Palestinian people have been suffering for a long time. At least try to understand why these people perceive themselves as suffering all the time. . . . Every single Palestinian individual hopes for liberty, independence, and peace. This is what the intifada was started for, and I believe strongly, as I know my people very well, that we are still determined to reach this goal. We are ready, fully, to sacrifice everything. We have sacrificed a lot already—thousands of martyrs, tens of thousands of wounded and handicapped young people, hundreds of thousands detained, hundreds of homes demolished, many people expelled. But I can tell you for sure that the Palestinian people are ready to sacrifice even more until we reach our goal: liberty and independence."

"Why did the army try to stop us from meeting? What does our government have to hide? What are they afraid the Palestinians will tell us . . . ?"

DAVID AND CARMELA OVADIA

David Ovadia
Born in Jaffa, Israel, 1951
Son of Iranian immigrants
Electrical technician in Tel Aviv
Member of Yesh G'vul

Carmela Ovadia
Born in Baghdad, Iraq, 1951
Free-lance artist
Children: Sharon, Yamit, and Mor

"Before the Yom Kippur war [1973]," says David, "I was a right-
ist. It's part of the mentality here in Israel, especially among people who
have origins in the Middle East. Over the years, reflecting on that war, I
began to change. I was an ambulance driver in that war, and I transported
many who were injured or dead. I started to ask myself why so many had
to die. Humanity shouldn't do this. Our government always talks about
peace, but I think that no one here really wants peace. They only want to
speak about peace. When they see that peace is a possibility, they do something to postpone it. The Likud and all the other right-wing parties always
declare what we won't do—we won't give up land, we won't do this, and
we won't do that. What do we offer? If we wanted to solve the problem,
if we wanted peace, we would think about how we can solve the problem
and offer some compromise solutions. For forty years, we have been the
best army in the area, and we always have war. We've won all the wars
we've entered into and nothing has changed, we always face another war.
So this is the time to understand that forty years of war is enough."

Carmela agrees with David's statements that the Israeli government
does not want peace: "Once we were part of a group of Israelis that tried
to visit Beit Sahur to participate in a dialogue group there. The army
stopped our bus, though, and didn't let us enter Beit Sahur. They also
prevented the people of the village from coming out to talk to us. So the
women of our group decided to enter the village through a back route. I
was touched by how the Palestinian women came out and greeted us with
hugs and kisses despite what our government is doing to them. Why did
the army try to stop us from meeting? What does our government have to
hide? What are they afraid the Palestinians will tell us, or that we will tell
them? This bothers me. They want to stop people from trying to make
peace."

The couple faces social and financial problems. David states, "I have a
lot of difficulty every day because everyone around me, in my family and
at work, is against me politically." When David went to jail for refusing to
serve in the occupied territories, checks bounced, and Carmela had to seek
money for food from friends and relatives. She could not even buy the
entry ticket to visit David in prison. Now the family plans ahead and saves

a little each week to prepare for the next time David will be imprisoned for refusing to serve.

Both Carmela and David advocate negotiations between the Israeli government and the PLO. "We must talk to the PLO. We can't choose our enemy. The PLO is our enemy, the people who kill, the people who hijack. I don't like them, but this is our enemy. If you want to solve a problem, you must talk with your enemy, not just with the people you want to talk to. But here in Israel, if you speak to Palestinians who support the PLO, you go to jail, because it's against the law. First of all, we must talk to them. Second, we must give up more than what the government wants to give up for peace. The government thinks that we have time, and power, so everything is all right. A few Israelis die here and there, but we are controlling the situation. In fact, we are not controlling anything. We must talk. We must give up land. What is land that we're sacrificing so many lives for?"

"It is very important that the Palestinians be given the opportunity for self-determination. . . . I see no reason why we cannot get over the difficulties between us."

NAOMI RAZ

Born in New York City, 1952
Immigrated to Israel in 1970
Member of Kibbutz Shamrat
Nursery school teacher
Active in Women in Black and Peace Now

Naomi Raz describes her interest in a peaceful resolution of the Palestinian-Israeli conflict as growing out of the environment of her youth. "I was always interested in peace with the Palestinians. From the age of ten, I belonged to a Zionist youth organization called Hashomer Hatzair. This youth movement was aligned with the political party of Mapam. The movement recognized the fact that there were two peoples living in this area, and two peoples that claimed the same land, so they advanced the solution of a bi-national state. Until the United Nations partition plan, it was a recognized fact that Palestinians were a people we would have to live with."

She says that peace activities have had positive results: "I think some of our demonstrations, like the one in Akko (Acre), created ties between Jews and Arabs in the area. We met through the demonstration, and now we continue to speak with and to see each other, and we plan further joint activities. These activities have also politicized people in the *kibbutz*—it brought up the issue that we *can* take steps to do something. A lot of people who never used to do anything began to come out to these demonstrations once a week, so that was a good thing also."

The major difficulty that Raz has faced as a peace activist is that of being threatened with bodily harm. She says, "There is often a feeling of physical threat. At the very beginning of our demonstration in Akko, there was a lot of violence directed against us. At first, there was only a little, but as time went on, a group of thugs, I don't know where they came from, tried to run over us. I had to jump back quickly from the car. It was a critical moment for me. . . . There have also been times when stones were thrown at us."

Raz describes the positive effect that support from abroad has on the peace movement in Israel. Every December, a conference of Women for Peace is held in Jerusalem. Last December, she says, "American delegates came, and it really felt good that there were people there from overseas to support us. People abroad need to know that there is an Israeli peace camp that is working very hard against tremendous difficulties. It would help if they sent money to the peace groups. It would also be really nice if the Jews in America didn't feel so defensive about the existence of the state of

Israel that they blindly support any of the government's policies. They should try to understand rationally what is going on and not give support just because it is the state of Israel."

She also argues that "it is very important that the Palestinians be given the opportunity for self-determination. What they want is to establish a state of their own, and I think we have to move in that direction. But also in much broader terms, for the whole area, I would like to see a situation that resembles the European Economic Community—economic and political contacts in the whole region. I see no reason why we cannot get over the difficulties between us. It could be a very powerful organization."

"Ideally, I would like to see no borders between the states of Palestine and Israel, with everyone living freely, with security and dignity."

ELIAS RISHMAWI

Born to Palestinian Christian parents, 1948
Graduated from School of Pharmacy, Alexandria,
     Egypt, 1971
Pharmacist in Beit Sahur
Runs a medical supply distribution center in the
     occupied territories
Wife: Iman
Children: John, Adham, Suzan

Rishmawi hopes for "a just, durable, peaceful settlement." Ideologically, the Palestinians wanted back all of Palestine, and the Israelis wanted the "land of Israel." He says, "While I respect their needs and desires for a homeland, and security, I also need these things. The Palestinians' right to a state and self-determination has long been unrespected, while their existence as a nation has always been threatened. . . . Ideally, I would like to see no borders between the states of Palestine and Israel, with everyone living freely, with security and dignity."

Rishmawi was one of the first Palestinians to join the dialogue group with Israelis in Beit Sahur, perhaps the only such group that, as of April 1991, had survived the Gulf War. He enthusiastically describes some of the other activities Palestinians and Israelis have conducted together in Beit Sahur. "We have held together some wonderful events, like the prayer for peace after the taxation raid conducted by the Israeli occupation authority against Beit Sahur. And the weekend where 25 Jewish families spent it and celebrated Shabat in Beit Sahur, under the slogan of 'Let's break bread, not bones,' a response to the policy of the Israeli defense minister, Yitzhak Rabin." He tells of his own beliefs and of the changes in the political environment that contributed to his participation in the dialogue groups and the joint Palestinian-Israeli peace activities. "I am in favor of a peaceful solution to the conflict here, but peace can never be made between a master and a slave. (This is how the Israeli occupation authority deals with us.) Besides, there is something in human psychology, which is that you cannot consider a human being as sufficient unless he or she is able to maintain dignity. Without dignity, they are not free. Palestinians in the diaspora have practiced some kind of resistance, but from Palestinians inside the occupied terrorities there has been minimal resistance against the occupation before the *intifada*. Thus, we couldn't consider ourselves as free human beings. We hadn't regained any of the dignity and pride that we'd lost as Palestinians in 1948. With the intifada, we broke a barrier of fear. We are no longer cowering, for we stood up to the strongest army in the Middle East, and the fourth strongest army in the world! After breaking this fear barrier, I can tell you, with full confidence, that we have gained back our lost dignity and pride. This made it the right time to talk about peace."

He believes that the dialogue groups have had positive results on the personal level. "We meet as human beings, to break the stereotypes. We both have learned to see each other as people, as human beings, with the good, the bad, the ugly, the sad, etc. Once you identify your enemy as a human being, you start to perceive that person differently, although we don't agree on everything."

However, like other Palestinians participating in Israeli-Palestinian dialogue, Rishmawi has had to pay a price. He says, "I have been arrested, and all the male members of the [dialogue] group have been arrested more than once. No one told us why we were arrested, but there are hints that it was because of these kinds of activities. The director of the center was arrested several times. He was also summoned many times to the military headquarters in Bethlehem and questioned about the center and the dialogue activities. He was informed that what he might see as being good might not be seen in the same way by the authorities."

Rishmawi, a Christian Palestinian, asks people abroad, and especially the Americans, to learn more about the conflict. Shaking his head, he laments, "Many Americans, many Europeans, don't even know there are Christians in this part of the world where Christianity was born!" He continues, "The American administration is acting and interfering in every place on the earth without any regard to what the native people want. The only goal is their own interest."

Rishmawi is also one of the leading figures in the tax struggle in the occupied territories. He says, "In the occupied territories, taxes are to be collected according to the principles of the Hague Convention IV of 1907. Any violation of the restrictions mentioned in articles 43 and 48 of the Hague Convention deprives the occupant of the legal basis for tax collection. We are trying to move within this context, which is based on international law and legitimacy. I am challenging the legality of the taxation system in the occupied territories through the trial raised against me and others in the military court of Ramallah."

"You can't force people to have a union, even a marriage of convenience, when they don't want it themselves."

SALIM TAMARI

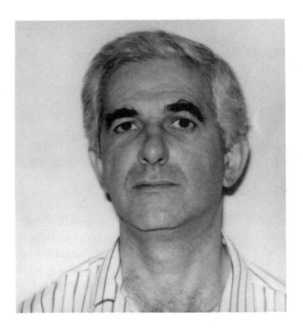

Born in the city of Jaffa on the coast of Palestine, 1945
Ph.D. from Manchester University, England
Professor of sociology at Bir Zeit University on the West Bank
Editor of the journal *Afaq/Horizons*

Early in the 1970s, Salim Tamari identified with Palestinians on the left who held internationalist ideals and who worked with like-minded Israelis, "seeking, if not a common future (one state with equal rights for both Jews and Arabs), then at least a solution agreeable to both peoples." Eventually, however, he abandoned the hope for a single democratic state for both Jews and Arabs. "I think the same thing that encouraged Soviet Premier [Andrei] Gromyko to vote at the UN for the creation of two states in the area in 1947 influenced my turning to a two-state solution: that the nature of the conflict, the hardened attitudes on both sides, and the new Jewish-Hebrew nationalism in Palestine made it imperative to seek a new solution which corresponds to people's new consciousness," he explains. "You can't force people to have a union, even a marriage of convenience, when they don't want it themselves."

Tamari has long participated in dialogue with Israelis. He believes that the peace movement, including the dialogue efforts, has had some positive repercussions: "The results of dialogue have been less positive than anticipated at the beginning. We thought we were moving people to an equitable solution, but this did not happen. But having said that, some positive developments were that committees of solidarity were established and pressure was exerted to lessen the restrictions on Palestinians, which sometimes worked, sometimes didn't. In the long term, these groups were able to implant a vision of a two-state solution which, ultimately, in 1988, became the official policy of the PLO, and entered the platform of some Israeli parties, left of center; and this, I think, is a considerable achievement."

Although Tamari has not personally faced difficulties as a result of his political work for peace, he suffers along with most Palestinians "from the massive restrictions on our freedom, freedom of movement, economic restrictions and hardship, curfews, censorship, restrictions on travel, etc." He notes that although he has not been imprisoned, many other Palestinian peace activists have been because of their work. "For example, one of the leading advocates of dialogue with Israelis today, Dr. Mahmoud Aker, a renowned urologist, has been incarcerated for over a month and half now," he says. "He has not been charged, has been subject to sleep deprivation, has been put in solitary confinement and subjected to an immense amount of interrogation and torture and is still in jail . . . and he has not been charged with anything at all! He has no previous prison record. But of course, such suffering is not comparable to that of the thousands of Palestinians who have been shot, imprisoned, or deported."

Tamari argues that the American public can and should make their government pressure Israel to give up the territories it occupied during the 1967 war. "The Americans are not neutral observers, they are very much a part of the conflict via the immense military and economic aid they give to Israel. We are not saying that the Americans should drop Israel, because there are historical affinities between America and Israel, and they perceive Israel to have a strategic role in the Middle East. But Americans certainly do not have much credibility in the rest of the Middle East, where they are seen as a big boy with a stick. The Americans should restrict the use of their military and civilian aid to Israel; it should not be used to oppress the Palestinian people or to establish settlements in the occupied territories."

"It came to me naturally, even during the 1950s, when I was in high school. From studying the history of the Jewish people, the conclusion I came to was that we should not do to other people what other nations did to us. This seemed to me so natural, so obvious."

DAPHNA LEVY

Born in Palestine
Mother immigrated to Palestine from Poland in
   the 1930s
Father immigrated to Palestine from United
   States in the 1920s
Children: Itamar, Jonathan

Daphna levy is a translator of literature from English into Hebrew. She is active in Women in Black and Peace Now. Levy has long supported negotiations between Israelis and Palestinians. "It came to me very naturally, even during the 1950s, when I was in high school. From studying the history of the Jewish people, the conclusion I came to was that we should not do to other people what the Germans or the European nations did to us. This seemed to me so natural, so obvious. I don't know why other people don't see it. It's a very simple, very basic philosophy: 'Don't do to your neighbor what you don't want them to do to you.'"

Levy believes peace can only be achieved if Israel withdraws from the occupied territories. "I don't have a very specific vision of a just settlement, but there has to be an Israeli withdrawal from the occupied territories, and if it's a Palestinian state, let it be a Palestinian state," she says. "I'm not a Palestinian patriot, but if that's what they want, what is necessary for peace, I'm willing to accept it."

Toward such an end, she is dedicated to working with the peace movement, despite her doubts about whether such work is effective. "I'm afraid that it doesn't have any effect, but it's the least that I can do. I don't want to lose hope."

*"We need our state, to live in peace, to let our children live
as other children do."*

GHADA ANDONI ISAAC

Born in Beit Sahur, 1953
Formerly a school teacher
Husband: Jad Isaac
Children: Firas, Fadi, Rima, and Usama

AFTER THE *intifada* started and the Israelis closed Palestinian schools, Andoni and other Palestinians in neighborhoods throughout the occupied territories organized popular schools. "In every neighborhood we gathered together and decided to teach our children in our homes," she says. "In my house, we teach students science; in other homes, they are taught English, math, Arabic, and so on. Everything is conducted in a very secret way because it's illegal for us to teach our children in our homes. So the children hide the books under their clothes and I'm always preparing my house to look as if there is a party so that if soldiers invade our house we can say that we're having a party."

Since the beginning of the intifada, Isaac has been active in a variety of activities that aim toward a two-state solution. "I've been active in the self-sufficiency gardening movement, in demonstrations which were held every Sunday after the mass, leading from the church through the streets of Beit Sahur. I've also participated in the dialogue groups, and many other activities. I started to go to the dialogue groups because I wanted people to know about our problems, about our situation. There are dialogue groups where foreigners, Americans and Europeans, are present. These, I felt, were very effective. Too many people overseas do not know about our problems here and about what kinds of fears we have. After talking to them, I can feel that they understand a lot more. Of course, talking to the Israelis is also useful. We really don't know them and they don't know us. So I think dialogue makes us know each other and maybe later on we can live together in peace."

She speaks of the difficulties faced by those who have participated in the dialogue group, difficulties that are a result of their participation: "The men in the dialogue group were put in prison for six months. The Israeli government didn't say why, but we know. Once people from the Israeli peace movement came here to see my husband after he was released from prison. Soldiers surrounded the house and ordered the peace group to leave. On other occasions, when the military heard of some planned activity, they tried to stop it."

Isaac insists on the necessity of the creation of a Palestinian state. She says, "We need our state, to live in peace, to let our children live as other children do. Our children don't have anything. There are no parks, no cinemas, nothing. Nobody takes care of us and we are forbidden to organize anything for ourselves. We don't even have a single library here. That's why we want independence and to live in peace. I would like Americans to know that our children aren't allowed to go to school by the Israeli government. Since the beginning of the intifada [December 1987] our children's schools have only been open a total of one hundred days. I also would like them to know that we have so many wounded, so many handicapped, so many people imprisoned without charge. We need our independence."

"We as Jews should know what it means to stand by silent when atrocities are being committed. Haven't we learned anything? We've learned that we can't be silent."

ANAT HOFFMAN

Born in Jerusalem, 1955
B.A. from the University of California at
    Los Angeles
M.A. from Bar Ilan University, Ramat Gan
Husband: Michael
Children: Tanya, Ariel

As a teenager, Anat Hoffman was a national swimming champion. After her military service, she attended the University of California at Los Angeles, where she received a bachelor's degree in psychology. She went on to get a master's degree in Israel and afterwards worked for the Jewish Agency for several years. An active member of Kol ha Neshama Reform Synagogue, Hoffman is an advocate for social justice in Israel. Her husband lectures in psychology at Bar Ilan University.

An active member of Women in Black, Hoffman advocates an end to the occupation of the West Bank and Gaza Strip and a two-state solution: one for Palestinians and one for Israelis.

Hoffman has been politically active for many years. She was first attracted to non-Orthodox Judaism while at UCLA; she was drawn by the combination of spirituality and social justice that the Reform movement offered. This commitment to the principles of social justice, she says, guided her career in public life. She began as a consumer advocate on a Jerusalem newspaper, and eventually she developed and continues to coordinate a consumer complaints bureau, now under the auspices of the Reform movement. In 1989, Hoffman was elected to the Jerusalem City Council as a member of the Ratz Party (Citizens Rights Movement).

Her interest in social justice prompted Hoffman to become involved in political work for peace. Hoffman said she joined Women in Black because she felt that as a Jew she could not stand by inactive while atrocities were being committed. Hoffman stands every Friday from 1 p.m. to 2 p.m. at a busy intersection in Jerusalem to protest the occupation of the West Bank and Gaza Strip. Others struggling for peace in different forms have said that "while all these activities have positive results, we're no closer to a peaceful solution." But, points out Hoffman, the presence of an elected city council member in the ranks of those struggling for peace shows that the movement is no longer a fringe one.

"Jerusalem is like a rose. Everybody has the right to smell this rose. Nobody has the right to pick it for himself."

RADWAN ABU AYYASH

Born in the Ashtar refugee camp, 1950
Parents were refugees from Deir Yassin
School teacher and a journalist
President of the Arab Journalists Association,
    1985–1991

Radwan abu ayyash was born in the Askar refugee camp on the West Bank, near Nablus. His parents came from Jamasin, a Palestinian village once located near today's Tel Aviv. Abu Ayyash says, "I don't have any registration recording the year I was born, it's just according to my father's memory. The family had fled to this area near Nablus and was living in a tent. It was June of the year in which there was a big snow. Our tent had been swept away by the snowstorm, and my parents thought that I would die, but I didn't."

Abu Ayyash was a member of a large family—eight children and two parents—all living in a one-room dwelling. After finishing secondary school, he was a schoolteacher for six years before becoming a journalist, and then an editor, of the newspaper *El Shaab* (*The People*). Later, he became editor of the weekly political magazine *El Auda* (*The Return*), and is currently director of the Arab Media Center in Jerusalem. From 1985 to 1991, he was president of the Arab Journalists' Association. He is one of the founders of the Palestinian Journalists' Association, which recently earned the highest prize of the International Federation of Journalists for activities contributing to peace issues. He is also a published poet.

Abu Ayyash describes the life of a Palestinian in the occupied territories: "To be a Palestinian under occupation is to struggle under very difficult circumstances. You are in a state of war, you are in a state of oppression . . . I cannot close my door at night without thinking that a group of soldiers might knock down the door, dash into my bedroom, and take me away."

Although Abu Ayyash believes that the Israeli peace movement has good intentions, he would like to see efforts directed toward more concrete ends. "I don't want Peace Now to come and demonstrate because I was in prison," he says. "I want them to have a political program that would prevent jailing anyone without a trial."

Abu Ayyash advocates "two states for two peoples." Palestinians, he says, need a state where they can be free and that will allow the two peoples to live side by side with mutual respect. Israel's security would not be compromised by the presence of a Palestinian state. He adds, "Peaceful resolution will not come easily, but we have to search for a dream, we have to think of a dream, and we have to live for a dream. A human without a dream is like a piece of stone without a soul."

"I don't believe that weakness or compromise on the side of Israel will produce goodwill on the other side."

MOSHE SHAMIR

Born in Safed, 1921
Raised in Tel Aviv
Member of the Knesset for the Likud and Tehiya
    parties
Novelist, writer

SHAMIR WAS A member of *Kibbutz* Mishmar Haemek from 1941 to 1947 and in 1944 joined the Palmach. He was the founding editor of a number of magazines and also served as editor of the underground weekly of the Haganah and later the official weekly of the Israeli Defense Forces. Since the publication of his first novel in 1948, Moshe Shamir, with an output of fifty volumes of fiction, drama, essays, and journalistic pieces, has become the literary spokesman for Israel's *sabra* (native-born) generation. In 1988 he was awarded the Israel Prize for Literature.

After the Six-Day War, Shamir became increasingly active in politics, identifying himself with the Greater Israel movement of the right wing. From 1977 until 1981, he served as a member of the Knesset for the Likud and Tehiya parties. Like many Israelis, Shamir believes the only way to peace is through Israeli strength.

He believes that Israelis have a claim to all of the land: "Historically, there is no doubt that from ancient times this is the cradle of Jewish civilization, of Jewish belief, of Jewish culture, the culture that became part and parcel of humanity's greatest and most important values." Shamir does not believe that the Palestinians are really interested in the two-state solution within the framework of the land west of the Jordan River. He says, "I believe that what the Palestinians truly have in their heart is to take all of what is now Israel and not be satisfied with the small areas they are now claiming."

Shamir is in favor of the settlements in the occupied territories, which he sees as being essential for Israel's security. He feels that those who see the Jewish settlements as obstacles to peace are blind to the realities of the area. He believes that Israel must always negotiate from a point of strength.

Israeli and Palestinian Women's Peace Movements

Roberta Micallef is a graduate student in comparative literature at the University of Texas at Austin. She received a B.A. in political science from Oberlin College in May 1987, and an M.A. in Middle Eastern studies from the University of Texas in May 1990. Her research interests are gender and ethnicity in Middle Eastern literatures.

WOMEN'S PEACE MOVEMENTS have emerged around the world in the latter half of the twentieth century, ranging from the Mothers of the Disappeared in Argentina to the women's movements in Holland and Germany. These movements are so different from earlier political activist groups in format, approach, and composition that they might be called "a new beginning" in women's political organization. In Israel and the occupied territories, a number of Israeli and Palestinian women's groups have emerged to protest the occupation of the West Bank and Gaza Strip. These organizations are examples of this new trend.

In the Occupied Territories

Shortly after the outbreak of the *intifada,* or uprising, in 1987, the major women's organizations and charitable associations in the West Bank and Gaza Strip issued a leaflet that they signed as the "Palestinian Women in the Territories." The leaflets asked Palestinian women to participate in "Popular Committees" that would organize to deal with school closings, take care of the wounded, establish home economies, and organize boycotts.[1]

The popular committees replaced the traditional structures and institutions, such as schools, which Israel had closed down. These committees appeared in each community, and in 1991 continued to deal with a number of local issues, including health, agriculture, community work, education, and legal aid. Women were the driving force behind the Popular Committees and they continue to share leadership roles along with the men.[2]

Indeed, after the intifada began, food cooperatives became essential, not only as an alternative source of income and food supply to what was lost because of extended curfews and boycotts, but also to reinforce the

Palestinian boycott of Israeli products. Women operated these cooperatives. Women were also active in the Popular Committees that dealt with
health-care services. Due to the problems in getting the sick and injured
to hospitals under the curfew, women put together mobile medical units.
They gathered crucial medical information, such as blood types, well in
advance. Specialized medical relief committees, in which women were
prominent, blood-typed neighborhoods and issued personal identification
cards.[3]

Of the Popular Committees, the education committees became the
ones in which women were most active. As Ghada Andoni Isaac, a Palestinian secondary schoolteacher, related in an interview, "When the intifada
started, the army closed schools and universities as a collective punishment. Our children were in the streets. And here you find ten to fifteen
teachers in each neighborhood. So we had a meeting and decided that we
were going to teach our children inside our homes. The results were excellent, so good that the authorities decided to threaten to close these
home schools as well."[4]

Perhaps the most dramatic testimony to the increased political activism of Palestinian women is the rise in the number of demonstrations by
women and the resulting number of casualties. Through March 8, 1988,
women's demonstrations in the occupied territories averaged 115 per week,
and sixteen women from different locations had been killed.[5]

In Israel

Israeli women had been involved in extraparliamentary activity before
the intifada. For example, at least half of the activists in movements such
as Peace Now were women. According to Dr. Naomi Chazan, the more
"left" one looked, the more women were involved. In "mixed" movements
of men and women, the women played an active role in the daily organizational life of the groups, but a less active one in decision making.[6]

Is this what compelled women to start their own organizations? Quite
a few Israeli women peace activists seem to believe so. Rachel Ostrowitz,
the editor of *Noga*, an Israeli feminist journal, said in an article in *Jewish
Women's Call for Peace*, ". . . hundreds of women in the Israeli women's
peace movements were forced by men to take separate action. Women in
the mixed peace groups were not allowed to take leadership roles, were
never chosen as spokespersons for the group, were never invited to conferences to take part in dialogue and discussion. Women became marginal
in their own organizations, forced to deal with trivial matters rather than
decision making. Women felt that within the framework of 'mixed organizations' (working with men) they were stifled."[7]

A number of new women's organizations dedicated to peace or political activism either arose in Israel or expanded after the beginning of the intifada. Such groups included Women for Women Prisoners, Shani (Women Against the Occupation), The Democratic Women's Movement, and Women in Black. The largest and most informal of the groups, Women in Black, probably is the most visible and innovative. It includes Israeli and Palestinian women living within Israel's borders.

The organization started in 1987, when a group calling themselves "Women in Black" began to hold silent vigils in Jerusalem, Tel Aviv, and Haifa for an hour each Friday. Dressed in black, they held signs that said "Stop the Occupation" and "Talk to the PLO," lettered in Hebrew, Arabic, and English. The movement spread quickly. Just before the Gulf War, Women in Black was holding weekly Friday vigils in more than twenty towns throughout Israel. Despite a lull during the Gulf War, Women in Black continues today and has become one of the longest sustained protest movements within Israel to date. Currently, it is spreading around the world, and Women in Black groups are active in Italy, Canada, and the United States, as well as in Israel. The members are Jewish, Christian, and Moslem and of varied persuasions—traditional, liberal, secular, religiously orthodox. Their ages range from the very young to the very old.

For many women the bond of motherhood, the fear of losing children and husbands, was what brought them together to protest the occupation of the West Bank and the Gaza Strip. Fairuz and Leila Nagami are a Palestinian mother-daughter team who participate in Women in Black. Leila Nagami said, "God willing, if Jewish and Arab women join hand-in-hand we will really accomplish something. After all, we are the ones who bore the children, we are the ones who raise them, we will be the widows if war takes the men, and our children will be the orphans. Because of this, we want peace. We are ready to work with anybody to achieve peace. We are ready to go to every woman and say, your children are being killed and they kill our people. Let's stop this. So we support and back movements like [Women in Black]. And we ask God to give us all peace."[8] Jewish women repeated these sentiments, stating that they felt solidarity with other women, as they were going to be the widows, and their children, orphans. Thus, they, too, were obliged to take action.[9]

Solidarity with other women was also an important factor. Daphna Levy, an Israeli translator and member of Women in Black, said, "I felt something had to be done [about the continuing occupation]. And I had no illusions about changing something but I also did it out of solidarity with other women. I didn't want them to stand by themselves, so I joined. And in the beginning it was strange, just exhibiting myself, standing, displaying myself with this little sign; I felt it was a bit awkward, I felt uncomfortable. But I didn't miss even one Friday, maybe except when I was sick or something. If I'm in town I go every Friday."[10]

Many women stated that they brought a different perspective to the conflict. To them, peace was not defined just as the absence of war; but also as the equal sharing of power and resources. The grass-roots women in the peace movement have worked for years in organizations where no hierarchy exists, where power is shared. Thus, the connections women make between peace and their own lives are not surprising. These women also see that the legitimization of violence in the occupied territories has deleterious consequences elsewhere in society. At least one Israeli woman linked the increased repression in the West Bank and Gaza Strip to increased levels of violence toward women and a growing number of rapes in Israel.[11]

Judging by the length of time that Women in Black has existed, it is very successful. Why is this? The answers given by its members revealed that two significant factors are its informal structure and its accommodation to the reality of the average woman's schedule. Hannah Safran, a Jewish member, said, "We [Women in Black] are not an organization because we have no symbols of an organization. We have no address, no telephone, no list. Every woman who feels that she wants to voice her protest against the occupation, and is willing to join us, has got just to choose where she lives to walk out to the place where there is a vigil of Women in Black every Friday between one and two o'clock . . ."[12]

Members emphasized the special problems faced by women who want to be politically active: time, money, and familial obligations. Safran spoke for many women when she said: "The woman is often the person who looks after the household and the children, but also is the breadwinner, and on many occasions the one who cares for old people, sick relatives, and so on. Women simply have no extra time. Most women are also poor both in relative terms and in absolute terms. So they have not the time, the energy, or the money to participate in the usual activities suggested by conventional political movements: committee meetings, traveling to other towns and speaking in public, spending money on telephone calls, on writing letters."[13] Because that is not possible, women have discovered other ways to be active. The group meets only once a week for an hour so its members can adjust their other activities and can take their children with them, when necessary.

Women in Black, then, presents a different kind of organizational and political structure, a way for women to be active—women who are unable to voice their opposition to current politics or even to influence politics in traditional ways.

Many of the women interviewed indicated frustration with the idea that war is the only solution to crisis. The consensus was that something had to change. The Gulf War of the winter of 1991 presented a major challenge to this group of cooperating Israeli and Palestinian women.

They were able to overcome their differences because a level of trust had already been established and their members were committed to a simple slogan and loose organization. Rana Nashashibi, a Palestinian peace activist, described the organizations that fell apart during the Gulf War as having members "who joined because it was the fashion. The fashion before the Gulf War had been house visits, organizing women for conferences, and talking about the Palestinian intifada. Trust was a major problem." Nashashibi was a participant in several such groups. "I began to feel often as though they [the Israelis] did not believe me. They seemed to feel that I was telling them what they wanted to hear. This was a very disappointing experience for me."[14] Women in Black members seemed not to suffer from "faddism or lack of trust." Although many women stopped attending the vigils during the war, they continued to talk together. When the vigils began again they kept their message simple and basic. "We just agree on very simple slogans; our first slogan was 'an end to the occupation of the Gaza Strip and the West Bank.' We later added three other parts—negotiations with the PLO, two states for two people, and an international conference for peace," said Safran.[15]

If anything, surviving the Gulf War as a group has strengthened the bonds between these women, validated their work, and set an example for other groups. Dalia Tzachst, a Jewish member from Haifa, described the way the women cooperate as a "unique process" that Palestinian and Jewish Israelis go through when they try to work together for peace. "The war was very bad for us. I mean all of us [Palestinians and Israelis] stand together every week with the belief that peace is the way and not war. And then when the war broke out, we didn't like the idea, to say the least, and we were afraid. All during the war we talked together. After the war we began trying to understand what we went through. During the bombing I was very very afraid, I was very afraid that my family, my friends, my Israeli Jewish friends will be hurt. And the Palestinian women were very afraid also for us, and were afraid for themselves. But they were also afraid for the Iraqi people and Arabs like them. I think this was the main difference between us and the other groups of peace, of Israeli-Palestinian groups. We kept talking and tried to understand what each of us was going through."[16]

Did these years of standing for an hour at busy intersections bring this group any closer to achieving its goals? Leila Nagami stated her goals for the group: "I am ready and strongly determined to find a peaceful solution that can be translated into practical terms. We must live together and understand each other's problems."[17] Women in Black, numbering in the thousands in the cities and towns of Israel, *have* managed to work together and understand one another.

The two-state idea suggested by many as a viable solution to the

Israeli-Palestinian question is beginning to be discussed. However, it is not even close to being implemented. Despite a seeming lack of movement toward a resolution of the Israeli-Palestinian conflict, many of the women believed that the mere fact that they were able to agree and work together was a major achievement. Nabila Espagnoli explained, "The relationship between us in Women in Black demonstrates that cooperation is possible, that it is the only possibility. Because Women in Black was organized as a group of equals, we succeeded. This, I think, is the major thing that we can show as Women in Black, that cooperation is possible between equals."[18]

Women in Black has provided Palestinian and Israeli women with a peaceful forum within which they can meet, work together, and get to know one another as human beings. Indeed, Naomi Raz, an Israeli *kibbutz* member said, "One of the most important things for me that came out of this group of Women in Black in Akko was our meeting the Arab women that we stood with. With some of these women, particularly the ones that came regularly, we developed relations of friendship, we kept in touch all through the war and we are still in contact. There were differences of opinion, of course, but we decided that we would allow for differences of opinion. Together we stood for a particular point, to make the major point that everybody agreed with, 'an end to the occupation of the West Bank and Gaza Strip.'"[19]

Many of the women believed that the future of Israel depends on increasing understanding and strengthening ties between the Arabs and Jews because neither group will have a future if they cannot live together in the same area. According to some, it is much harder to hate and to think about killing an enemy who has a face, a name, and a personality that you know.

The women who participate in the movement see the strong response to their vigils as indications of its success. They are catching people's attention and stirring up emotions. And perhaps they make people think about the occupation. However, Women in Black receives a very gender-specific response to its weekly vigils. Almost all of the antagonistic comments directed at Women in Black by passersby are sexual in nature or attempt to try to put them in their place. Comments included "Why aren't you at home in your kitchen?" and "You sleep with Arafat!" In addition, they have been threatened physically to the extent that they have had to ask for police protection in some cities. (They have also received gestures of support—food, flowers, drinks of water.)

Daphna Levy stated: "There was a time when there were other demonstrations by other organizations which opposed the occupation. Some of their slogans and signs were much more provocative than ours and, curiously, the response to them was more moderate, not nearly as aggressive as the responses we get, simply, I think, because we are women. Women in Black has simple messages: Just stop the occupation. But people respond to that very emotionally; I think it's because we are women."[20]

Naomi Raz described her experiences: "People that drove by on the road would make all kinds of horrible remarks and they would even gesture as if they were going to shoot us. It was very difficult to stand and hear all of that, but it would get even worse. One day a bunch of criminal types tried to run us over with their car."[21]

In *Jewish Women's Call For Peace* Gila Stravinsky asks, "But why do they become so aggressive? . . . Maybe we look like witches, it occurs to me. Or like Cassandras, at least. Seers and Prophetesses with gloomy visions of death and armageddon. Death, clearly: Death is why we are frightening. We as women represent more than life and nurturing. We also represent death . . . We are not your mothers, your wives, your lovers. We are the Women in Black, the phantoms of your fear of death."[22]

In Israel and the occupied territories, as in other countries around the world, women are creating their own alternative structures through which they can work toward peace and through which they can provide alternatives to war in crisis situations. Whatever their reasons may be for joining, these women also develop a greater consciousness about their own position in society. They are able to link issues of national importance with their own positions. Frequently, they are accused of being separatists. Are they? Interestingly enough, when women discussed their frustrations with "mixed groups" they were most often talking about men and women, not Palestinians and Israelis. These women are redefining the framework and lines of collaboration. Separation from one group is leading to unity with another that is more receptive to their needs and with whom they are in closer agreement. If these new lines of alliance do indeed result in a more peaceful world, we will all benefit from them.

Notes

1. Islah Jad, "From Salons to the Popular Committees, Palestinian Women, 1919–1939," in *Intifada: Palestine at the Crossroads,* Jamal Nassar and Roger Heacock, eds. (West Bank and New York: Bir Zeit University and Praeger Publishers, 1991), 134.

2. "It Is Possible to Agree on Principles" (an interview with Hanan Mikhail Ashrawi), *New Outlook* (June/July, 1989):8.

3. Ibid.

4. Personal interview with Ghada Andoni Isaac, Palestinian schoolteacher, Beit Sahur, West Bank, March 1991.

5. Islah Jad, "From Salons to the Popular Committees," 133.

6. "The Israeli Women—Myth and Reality" (an interview with Naomi Chazan), *New Outlook* (June/July 1989) : 13.

7. Rita Falbel, Irena Klepsfisz, and Donna Nevel, eds., *Jewish Women's Call for Peace: A Handbook for Jewish Women on the Israeli-Palestinian Conflict* (Ithaca, N.Y.: Firebrand Books, 1990), 11.

8. Personal interview with Leila and Fairuz Nagami, Palestinian participants in Women in Black, Akko, March 1991.

9. "It Is Possible to Agree on Principles," 9.

10. Personal interview with Daphna Levy, Israeli translator, participant in Women in Black, Jerusalem, March 1991.

11. Falbel et al., *Jewish Women's Call for Peace*, 15, 10.

12. Personal interview with Hannah Safran, Jewish participant in Women in Black, Haifa, March 1991.

13. Ibid.

14. Personal interview with Rana Nashashibi, Palestinian peace activist, Jerusalem, March 1991.

15. Personal interview with Hannah Safran.

16. Personal interview with Dalia Tzachst, Jewish participant in Women in Black, Haifa, March 1991.

17. Personal interview with Leila Nagami.

18. Personal interview with Nabila Espagnoli, participant in Women in Black, Haifa, March 1991.

19. Personal interview with Naomi Raz, Jewish participant in Women in Black, Akko, March 1991.

20. Personal interview with Daphna Levy.

21. Personal interview with Naomi Raz.

22. Falbel et al., *Jewish Women's Call for Peace*, 9.

Note: All interviews were conducted in Israel and the West Bank as part of the production of the film, *The Struggle for Peace: Israelis and Palestinians*, March and April 1991.

Other Sources

Hall-Cathala, David. *The Peace Movement in Israel.* New York: St. Martin's Press, 1990.

Lipman, Beata. *Israel—Embattled Land: Jewish and Palestinian Women Talk about Their Lives.* Ithaca, N.Y.: Pandora Press, 1988.

Ruether, Rosemary Tadford, and Marc H. Ellis, eds. *Beyond Occupation.* Boston: Beacon Press, 1990.

Arab-Israeli Conflict at the Threshold of Negotiations[1]

Yehoshafat Harkabi is Hexter Professor of International Relations and Middle Eastern Studies at the Hebrew University of Jerusalem (Emeritus). Born in Haifa, Professor Harkabi received his M.A. and Ph.D. degrees from the Hebrew University and his M.P.A. from Harvard University. Before becoming an academic, he served in the Israeli Defense Forces as an infantry company commander in 1948, and was a member of the military delegation to negotiate the armistice agreements. He was deputy and then chief of military intelligence (1950–1959), with the rank of major general. While at the Hebrew University (1968–1989), he was seconded to serve as assistant for strategic policy to the minister of defense (1974–1975) and adviser on intelligence to the prime minister (1977).

He has held various academic positions in the United States (Brown University, Princeton University) and now teaches at the Israeli National War College. Among his publications are: *Nuclear War and Nuclear Peace; Arab Attitudes to Israel; Arab Strategies and Israel's Response; The Bar-Kokhba Syndrome; Israel's Fateful Hour;* and *War and Strategy.* He was awarded the Sadeh prize for military books in 1991.

T HIS CHAPTER WILL attempt to analyze the recent developments in the Arab-Israeli conflict, drawing first on some theoretical differentiation in terminology. It will review the changes in the adversaries' positions, examine the role of the United States and the effects of the Gulf War, and analyze the present circumstances and the possibilities of moving toward negotiations to resolve this conflict.

The recent Iraqi crisis has demonstrated the importance of the Arab-Israeli conflict for Arab public opinion. Manipulating the Palestinian issue helped Iraqi leader Saddam Hussein gain popularity among the Arab masses. Arabs may dislike the Palestinians, but still be deeply concerned with the Palestinian problem, which symbolizes a widely shared Arab grievance that the Western countries have mistreated the Arabs. Of course, the Arab-Israeli conflict is not the main cause for Middle Eastern instability. Nonetheless, it does play a pivotal role in the region's unrest. Many of the region's other problems are somehow related to it. The tensions it generates do not allow the relaxation needed for the solution of other regional problems such as economic development, reform and de-mocratization of regimes, arms control, and water distribution.

In order to analyze the conflict, I shall present the two kinds of posi-tions in a polarized fashion, as follows:

1. *Absolute,* or metaphysical, positions are autonomous, not influ-enced or developed as a response to a rival's positions, ideologies, or ac-tions. Thus, such positions are impervious to changes in the rival's posi-tion. They are metaphysical in terms of their being deeply ingrained in the value system of a political party or its ideology, or in flowing from what this party considers to be existential imperatives.

2. *Relativist* positions are partially derived from the adversary's posi-tion, serving as a response to it. Such positions evolve following changes in the adversary's position or changes in the current political environment.

The difference between these two kinds of positions resides in the amount of persuasion or pressure that is needed to cause a change in a party's position. A relativist position may change in response to a conces-sion offered by the adversary, whereas a metaphysical position may change only by unbearable costs, or by a threat of grave consequences coming mostly from a third party whose power to harm is greater than that of the direct contestants.

An absolute position may be inconvenient to present to world public opinion and may hamper diplomatic relations. Therefore, its adherents may dissimulate this feature and instead present their position as if it were relativistic and reactive to threatening features in their adversary's position or conduct. The more relativist the positions of the adversaries, the more elastic the conflict and the easier to reach a compromise. By contrast, meta-physical positions make the conflict rigid and less amenable to resolution; intransigent parties can be pushed to make concessions only under duress. This is the case in the Arab-Israeli conflict.

Ignoring the difference between absolute and relativist elements in the contestants' positions has been a major obstacle in analyzing the Arab-Israeli conflict. Absolute positions have become almost a rarity in other modern conflicts, which dims the observers' ability to perceive them here. Instead, both political scientists and journalists attribute relativist posi-tions to both sides and stress symmetries between them. Presenting a po-sition as absolute would be seen as a hasty judgment that denies contes-tants the flexibility of altering positions.

Foreign journalists may have difficulty detecting absolute positions behind rhetoric that might appear relativist. Journalists may also be appre-hensive that reporting on the absolute elements in the position of one adversary would strain their contacts with this party. In order to assure accessibility to sources, journalists may even unconsciously retouch its positions, ignoring their absolute features, thereby giving the impression that the positions are more relativist than they actually are.

Political scientists committing the same mistake could boast of an unbiased, scientific approach. However, positions in this conflict are not symmetrical, and analyzing the differences between the adversaries' positions and searching for absolute positions are major tasks in any rigorous account of this conflict. It makes the analysis more arduous and demands greater specificity than does the convenient resort of claiming that both contestants entertain positions that are "mirror images" of each other.

I am convinced that ignoring this need for specificity and overlooking the difference between absolute and relativist positions have been common mistakes in the study of the Arab-Israeli conflict, a conflict whose major feature has been its asymmetry, and in which absolute positions played a crucial role. Such a mistaken analysis might have had political implications by influencing world public opinion and governments to tolerate in the positions of the adversaries what should have been repudiated. Sparing absolute positions from criticism has helped them to take root and crystallize, as I shall stress in the following section.

The Arab Position

After the war in 1948, Arabs tended to consider the establishment of the state of Israel as the most outrageous scandal in history, an act of gross injustice. The country was not only taken from its indigenous owners, the Palestinians, as in other cases of colonialism, but the Palestinians were also dispossessed. Arabs considered this act an affront to all Arabs, epitomizing for them European disregard of Arab rights.

Rectification of this injustice could be achieved, they maintained, only by undoing the establishment of Israel, which meant the destruction of the state, an act for which I have coined the term "politicide." This position was absolute and independent of the behavior of the state of Israel. Faults in Israeli behavior were explained as necessarily arising out of its congenital depravity. Israel's existence was intolerable; Israel had to be annihilated.

Such an absolute position was at odds with the most basic norm of modern international order expressed in the United Nations' Charter, namely, the preservation of the integrity of existing states. Therefore, Arab spokesmen did their best to present their position as relativist, as an unavoidable response to Israeli expansionist designs. The state of Israel was established by an act of aggression that stamped its immutable, aggressive nature. Politicide was presented as an inexorable historical imperative.

Arabs dedicated great effort to elaborate an ideology substantiating this position for the sake of their own national indoctrination and foreign public relations.

Political scientists and journalists felt uncomfortable presenting Arab positions as absolute. Had they been willing to do so and had the metaphysical nature of Arab positions been more widely understood, pressure would have built up earlier to censure them and to force a change.

Yet the conflict is a learning process for those involved. Slowly, Arab leaders came to realize that their politicidal position enmeshed them in an impossible situation by antagonizing many circles of world public opinion and that they had to resign themselves to the existence of Israel. The justification for this change frequently offered nowadays in Arab parlance is that it has been called forth by "international legality" (*shar'iyya dawliyya*), namely, that the change has been mandated by the exigencies of the present world order. Thus, the change of position is explained not so much because of an Arab realization that the Israeli phenomenon has to be viewed differently, but because of a characteristic of the prevailing juridical order.

My first publications dealt with the absolute feature of Arab positions. At that time, Israel could do very little to placate Arab enmity, precisely because of the absolute nature of Arab positions. However, recognizing an incipient change in Arab positions, I started calling for a positive response on the part of Israel in order to encourage this change and to work toward reconciliation and peace.

The trend toward Arab resignation to the existence of Israel culminated in the Camp David accords with Egypt; in the King Hussein–Arafat agreement of February 1985, which was based on the principle of peace for territory; and in the acceptance of the two-state solution by the nineteenth Palestinian National Council (PNC) of the Palestine Liberation Organization (PLO) in November 1988. One can add to this list, although with less certainty, ambiguous stipulations in the resolutions of the Fez Summit Meeting of September 1982, in which several Arab countries joined to discuss the issue.

Many Israelis are convinced that the Palestinians' demand for a Palestinian state in the occupied territories and the Syrian demand for the return of the Golan Heights are motivated by their wish to spite Israel, or from malignity or vindictiveness. All that is wrong. Such demands emanate from an Arab conviction that these demands are fair and just, and that Israel will eventually have to accede to them by the force of equity and history. They could not subscribe to the view that because there are many Arab states, they have to cede territory to the Jews, irrespective of the fate of its Arab inhabitants.

However, present Arab relativist positions should not be projected backward, as if from the beginning they have been relativist and never called for the destruction of the state of Israel. Furthermore, among Arabs there still exist manifestations of uncompromising attitudes toward Israel, including metaphysical elements. For instance, such positions surfaced during the Gulf War in expressions of unrelenting enmity and of harboring vicious intentions toward Israel.

Absolute positions are entertained by Arab and Palestinian hard-liners, who maintain that the conflict is a war of attrition in which the Arabs, because of their numerical preponderance, will eventually prevail, and the Israelis will be forced to relinquish their state. Thus, the goals of Israel's demise will be fully achieved, and there is no need to reach a compromise solution.

Metaphysical positions are also evident in an Islamic refusal to recognize that the Jews may have a state in a territory, described as within the "Abode of Islam." This previously Islamic territory has been usurped, thereby inducing Islam to retreat. Such a retreat gives rise to a religious obligation incumbent on all Muslims to enlist in a holy war (*fard 'ein*). Thus, no coexistence with Israel, no matter its size, is acceptable.

Finally, the frequently asked question of whether the Arabs in general have really changed their position toward acceptance of Israel and living in peace with Israel is unanswerable because it depends on the "type" of Israel envisaged, namely what borders it will have. The Arab mainstream could accept Israel in its pre-1967 boundaries. UN Resolution 242 that serves as the legal underpinning for this demand is supported by the entire international community, including the United States. The Arabs will not be more forthcoming than the rest of the world. The Palestinians originally demanded 100 percent of the Palestinian territories. Subsequently, they reduced their claim to 25 percent; they can hardly be expected to go down more.

THE PALESTINE LIBERATION ORGANIZATION

After moderating its stand at the nineteenth PNC in 1988 by accepting the two-state formula, the PLO expected a positive response from Israel. U.S. President Ronald Reagan considered these changes as warranting the beginning of a "substantive dialogue" with the PLO. Israel demurred. Palestinian hard-liners admonished the PLO's leadership, saying that their concessions would be in vain because Israel would dismiss them. The hard-liners' predictions came true, the position of the PLO's leadership deteriorated, and they turned to the most pugnacious Arab country—Iraq.

During the first stage of the Iraqi invasion of Kuwait, a euphoria spread in PLO ranks, caused by a belief that the Iraqi leader, Saddam Hussein, would come out of the ordeal victorious, and that the Americans would recoil from a full-fledged war. They hoped Iraqi success would usher in a new period in the Middle East and in the Arab-Israeli conflict. Israel would then be forced to surrender to Palestinian demands.

Thus, the absence of a positive response from Israel to the PLO's overture in part caused the PLO's regression to a stance of supporting Saddam Hussein. However, it should be recognized that regardless of PLO leader Yasir Arafat's support of Saddam, he has not rescinded the PLO's adoption of the principle of a two-state settlement.

Despite the deterioration of the PLO's stature in the Arab and international arenas as a result of its stand in the Gulf War, the Palestinians persist in considering the PLO as their leadership. The strength of the PLO stems from its symbolizing the idea that the Palestinians are not inferior to the Israelis and, like them, deserve statehood. It is precisely because of this claim that Israel rejects the PLO. No Palestinian is ready to forego the PLO's basic demand for a Palestinian state. In the most basic issue of the conflict, namely, Palestinian statehood, no organization is more forthcoming than the PLO.

Thus, the search for an alternative Palestinian leadership is futile. Despite their best efforts, the Syrians and Saudis have not succeeded in contriving a new Palestinian leadership. Eventually, they will reconcile themselves with the present PLO, as the Egyptians have already done. The recent failures of the PLO's leadership may result in some personnel and structural changes. Nevertheless, for both Arabs and Palestinians, the PLO will maintain its official stature as the acknowledged sole representative of the Palestinian people.

In June 1990, the American administration suspended dialogue with the PLO because of a Palestinian terrorist operation. However, for all practical purposes, the Americans have already renewed their dialogue with the PLO, for Secretary of State James Baker has repeatedly conferred in Jerusalem with Palestinian representatives who make no bones about their loyalty to the PLO. Americans profess to supporting Palestinians of the "interior," namely, the Palestinians from the occupied territories, whose position towards Israel is pragmatic. This group knows Israel better and tends to recognize Israel as a fact and a state with which they will have to live. They take a more lenient position on the issue of the peace process, abandoning previous demands to settle in principle before the beginning of negotiations Palestinian calls for establishing a Palestinian state and dismantling the Jewish settlements.

There is some subtle competition between the "interior" and the "exterior" (the PLO's leadership), accompanied by a sentiment of mutual dependence. The PLO recognizes that the main arena of the Palestinian struggle is the territories. It gives the "interior" leadership some leverage over the PLO. Thus, the importance of the Palestinian leadership of the occupied territories versus the PLO is growing. The balance is shifting.

Still, the "interior" leadership recognizes that its legitimization in the eyes of its constituency, the Palestinians living in the occupied territories, emanates from PLO support. Paradoxically, by attesting their allegiance to the PLO, these leaders acquire some leeway in their contacts with the Americans and Israel.

The weakness of these leaders from the "interior" is twofold: their leadership has not been institutionalized, and the permanent fear of detention or expulsion by the Israeli authorities looms heavily on them, constraining their resourcefulness.

The only openly antagonistic competitor to the PLO is Hamas (the Palestinian Islamic Fundamentalist Movement). Arab states have to consider that by weakening the PLO, they strengthen Hamas, with menacing consequences not only for the Arab-Israeli conflict, but for themselves.

The Israeli Position

Zionism, from its beginnings, desired to have Palestine in its entirety. Zionism was caught in a cruel dilemma: Without hurting the Arabs, implementing the Zionist dream was impossible. Zionism, therefore, looked for means to compensate them monetarily. What facilitated the Zionist task was Palestinian collaboration; directly, for instance, by selling land and in manual work in Zionist enterprises, and indirectly, through their refusal to compromise with the Jewish community that already existed in Palestine. Thus, Zionism became an existential imperative for the Palestinian Jewish community, in order to withstand the Arabs. The Zionist mainstream recognized, however, the need to meet, although partially, some of the political aspirations of the Arab inhabitants of the country. Thus, it has been inclined to the idea of the partition of Palestine into two states ever since the British first proposed it in 1937.

The successes of the 1967 war increased Zionist, or by then, Israeli, territorial ambitions, but the incumbent Israeli governments did not abandon their main political relativist disposition. Labor governments accepted UN Resolution 242, which was based on the principle of trading territory for peace. Following David Ben-Gurion's government, successive Labor governments were indeed inspired by the Zionist ideal and ambition; yet, for the most part, they did not lose sight of the exigencies of the constraining reality.

All that changed in 1977 with the ascendancy of Menachem Begin to power. For Begin, Resolution 242 was an anathema. In August 1970 he had resigned from the Government of National Unity (which had been composed three years earlier on the eve of the Six-Day War) in protest against Prime Minister Golda Meir's acceptance of the principle of withdrawal from the territories occupied in the 1967 war, in accordance with

Resolution 242. The Likud's approach was summed up by the platform of the Likud's coalition in March 1977, which stated: "The right of the Jewish people to the land of Israel is eternal and indisputable and is linked with the right to security and peace; therefore, Judea and Samaria will not be handed to any foreign administration; between the sea and the Jordan there will only be Israeli sovereignty." Significantly, the platform's claim to eternal rights did not include to the Sinai and the Golan Heights.

The Likud's claim to Judea and Samaria is primarily ideological and absolute. Such a position is autonomous and is determined neither by what the Arabs design or do nor by Arab threats. The security objective that holding these regions serves is ancillary, although one should not deny that many Israelis are beset with security worries that naturally follow from Israel's existence within an Arab region.

A practical consideration presently reinforces the absolute aspect of the Israeli governmental position. The ideological position has been translated into action in a wide movement of implanting Jewish settlements in the occupied territories. The accelerated settlement policy was meant to produce facts that would foil the loss of these territories. The Likud ideology has been "reified" by these settlements; the realm of ideas has been transcended. Now, withdrawing from the territories and relinquishing the settlements would create an enormous national crisis. Such a move would signify a rebuff to the Zionist aspirations so much boosted in recent years. For the Likud's leadership, withdrawal would portend both a supreme bankruptcy of the Herut Party and its ideology and would constitute history's condemnation of the role of Jabotinsky's movement in Zionism.

Furthermore, many Israelis would accuse the Likud and its associates on its right for misleading the nation by fostering the belief that Israel would retain the territories. People would calculate the huge sums invested in the territories that would now have to be considered irretrievable losses. That would be especially painful, when the absorption of the Soviet Jewish immigrations is endangered because of a dearth of resources to provide housing and employment. Settlers might react violently against the Likud leaders, castigating them for betrayal.

The Likud leaders are assuredly haunted by such developments. No wonder they do their best to prevent a withdrawal, preferring the continuation of the conflict to a peace involving relinquishment of land. It is doubtful whether the Likud is humanly capable of trading territory for peace, thereby signing its own political death sentence. Furthermore, the Likud tends to identify the defeat of its policy with the defeat of Israel, rather than its own final extinction.

Some Likud members, even in the high echelons of their movement, might be groping for a way to extricate the Likud from the trap of its absolute metaphysical positions. If they can be identified, they should be encouraged and helped. It should be noticed that the annexationist policy has become the raison d'ête of the Likud. Can the Likud negate its core value? Can its members pretend that their position on the occupied territories has been different from its wording?

The attempts to draw an analogy from Begin's giving up Sinai to Yitzhak Shamir's eventual consent to give up Judea and Samaria, are specious. Begin gave up Sinai precisely in order to keep Judea and Samaria. I am ready to speculate that were Begin the present prime minister, he would not have been more forthcoming than Shamir. In the present circumstances, Shamir's quiet obduracy is more effective than Begin's bravado. Shamir and Ariel Sharon, as well as Moshe Arens, David Levy, and the rest of the Likud ministers, fully agree on the strategic goal of retaining the occupied territories; the differences among them are on means, procedure, and style, and on how their common strategic goal would be best achieved. That is widely misunderstood abroad. Once negotiations turn to the question of territory, they will all rally to support the same old policy goals. Had the leaders of the Likud, of Moledet (R. Zeevi), and of Tzomet (R. Eitan) to choose between three goals: (1) negotiations and peace; (2) Jewish immigration, which the Russians allow, provided there is movement toward peace; (3) settling the territories with Jews; they will unhesitatingly prefer the settling of the territories as the supreme national goal, and the means to cling to a greater Israel.

I do not mean that the Likud leaders do not desire peace. They want peace wholeheartedly, but they define the peace to which they will agree as a situation in which the Palestinians in the territories are content with autonomy under permanent Israeli domination. Autonomy, in this version, is not a transitional phase, but the end result. That outcome is not sheer fantasy, for Israel can determine the future of the autonomy. According to the Camp David accords, at the end of five years of autonomy, negotiations will take place on the final status of the territories and Israel's consent is required in order to pass from autonomy to independence. Israel can veto such a development.

Thus, Begin's fundamental policy guidelines (1981) state, "The autonomy agreed upon at Camp David means neither sovereignty nor self-determination. The autonomy agreements set down at Camp David are guarantees that under no condition will a Palestinian state emerge in the territories of *Eretz Yisrael*. At the end of the transition period set down in the Camp David agreements, Israel will raise its claim, and act to realize its right of sovereignty of Judea, Samaria and the Gaza Strip."

The Likud's position is based on a major assumption. Like the Arab hard-liners, the Likud considers the Arab-Israeli conflict as a war of attrition, a contest of endurance, in which the tenacity of the Israelis will prevail. As time passes, they believe, the Palestinians will get exhausted, understand that their wish for statehood will be frustrated, and will resign themselves to it. Eventually they will emigrate, leaving all the territories west of the Jordan to Israel. To achieve these purposes there is a need to procrastinate and win time. Israeli hard-liners hope that as the number of settlers increases they will attain a critical mass that will make evacuating the occupied territories an impossibility. They believe world public opinion will recoil from demanding that Israel commit national suicide and will become resigned to Israel's present boundaries. They believe that the Arabs will follow suit. And finally they believe that this outcome will be reinforced by the unconditional readiness of the Israeli population to struggle to retain the territories, no matter what sacrifices are required.

Likud leaders are confident that their policy will triumph because of their success, until very recently, in the international arena. Although the United States, Europe, the Soviet block, and the third world all oppose their policies in principle, financial subsidies continue to flow. States that severed diplomatic relations with Israel are meekly renewing them. Repeatedly, prophecies that a crisis with the United States was in the offing because of annexationist policies did not come true. Diaspora Jews' support of Likud policies has grown. The historical lessons to be deduced are that the external opposition to the Likud policies should not be considered insurmountable and that by persistence and some dexterity in tactics, Likud policies will prevail.

The Israeli government's refusal to budge from its position does not stem from its coalition brittleness, from Shamir's inferior personal stature compared with Begin's, or from Shamir's constant need to look over his shoulders to Sharon's reaction. Such explanations have been frequent in journalistic and academic analyses, but they are wrong. Journalists and political scientists failed to present the absolute nature of the Likud government's positions. They projected a more conciliatory Israeli position than was warranted and unwittingly made it easier for this position to consolidate and endure.

The explanation that Israel is ready to trade peace for the territories, but is simply disheartened by the Arab reluctance to give up their claims of belligerency and to terminate the economic boycott, thus, in the meantime, compelling Israel to implant settlements, is disingenuous. The settlements were not implanted to serve as trump cards for negotiations, and eventually be dismantled.

Begin formerly defined withdrawal from the territories and the establishment of a Palestinian state as constituting a "mortal danger" for Israel, an extremely effective allegation with Israelis and dispora Jews. What this argument overlooks is that a state can make stringent demands on its neighbor to reinforce its security. However, it cannot define its security in terms of the nonexistence of a neighbor, namely, that Israel, in order to be secure, can deny the existence of a Palestinian state.

Israeli spokesmen used to reiterate that Jordan is Palestine. However, transforming Jordan into a Palestinian state will not solve the main problem of the conflict, that of the Palestinians in the occupied territories. They will not resign themselves to the idea that their state is east of the Jordan River, and that they live west of it in a diaspora. Furthermore, the attitude toward Jordan has changed as a result of the Gulf War. The Likud leadership now recognizes the importance of having on the east a more moderate state as a buffer.

The diplomatic successes of the Likud policies are only short-range. The Likud leaders are not alive to the fact that the emerging world order does not recognize "acquisition of territory by force" and the imposition of a foreign rule on such territories and their people. This factor will decide the long-range outcomes. It was not always like that. For a long period, from the Peace of Westphalia and until this century, conquest has been considered as granting entitlement to territory, as promulgated in the eighteenth century in Emmerich Vattel's legal system. This position has largely lapsed, even if it lingers in some inconsistencies. As a result of it, the European powers had to relinquish ruling their colonies and the Baltic states achieved their independence. By clinging to the territories, Israel puts itself in an impossible position, contravening a main norm of the present legal order. Such a policy is anachronistic and parochial, hence, destined to fail.

One can argue that the Likud's goals might be realized. My answer is that the probability is small in view of opposing social and historical factors. In addition, the price for failure of the Likud policies is extremely high. The Likud central article of faith that Israel can both retain the territories and achieve peace seems to be preposterous. The Israeli position envisages only one state west of the Jordan River, whereas the official claim of the Arab mainstream is for a conciliatory, two-state solution. Therefore, the Arab position will win the support of the world community. A compromise by which the Arabs will not get all, but most, of the occupied territories will signify a terrible rebuff for Israel. This will be the outcome and bequest of the Likud policy to both Israel and Jewry.

Finally, the danger of an Arab-Israeli war seems now more remote than perhaps ever before. The Arab states are not prepared for war and do not want it. Still, if a settlement of the conflict is not achieved, war could be in the offing, according to the present Israeli chief of staff, Ehud Barak. Israel's insistence on keeping the occupied territories will convince Arabs and the world that Israel does not want peace, but conquest. Israeli rejection of Arab demands to only a quarter of the Palestinian territories, and Israeli denial that Palestinians are human beings constituting a collectivity will prove to Arabs that Israelis are inherently depraved. Such a neighbor cannot be tolerated. They will conclude that all Arabs should consider the Arab-Israeli conflict as an endless struggle culminating in wars to the bitter end, which means to achieve Israel's destruction, a course that is a pan-Arab manifest destiny. Most Arabs do not want war. Yet the Israeli position may force it on them. It is precisely such a development that should be avoided; namely, that the conflict will revert from a conflict over the occupied territories to what it once was, a conflict over the very existence of Israel.

WHY WERE ISRAELI MODERATES INEFFECTUAL?

The arguments supporting moderate Israeli positions are very persuasive. So the question then becomes, why do they fail?

Begin's coming into power changed political discourse in Israel. It began to be inspired by a variety of mythical themes such as ethnocentrism; the grandeur of the Jews; flamboyant nationalism; voluntarism (Jewish will and audacity are the factors that mold Jews' history); and blindness to the difference between calculated audacity and adventurism. Other themes include the idea that unity necessarily leads to success, so if the Israelis unite, nothing can oppose them; a belief that history is made by Promethean feats such as one-time exertions and fait accomplis;[2] an orientation toward power; downgrading of considerations of realism, because what seems unrealistic may turn out to be realistic; the allegation that realistic considerations are tedious and disheartening; the idea that readiness to offer concessions is a sign of feebleness; and the belief that all the world is against the Jews.

All these attidues constitute what I call the "Jabotinsky-Begin Ethos."[3] It is Begin's elaboration of Jabotinsky's fundamental attitudes. This ethos is composed of attitudes and emotional underpinnings of the ideas in their ideological system. The power of these attitudes stems from the fact that they are not completely senseless. In different doses, they are found in other social groups.

Once political discourse became influenced by myths promising a bigger Israel, the Labor Party became ineffectual in challenging the Likud. Israelis asked why they should resign themselves to a small state when achieving a bigger state was possible. Moreover, some members of the Labor Party became fascinated with some elements of the ethos.

The wide populist circles that supported the Herut Party were not conversant with Jabotinsky ideology but they were aroused by its ethos. That ethos inspired their historical imaginations, their basic sympathies and antipathies, their context of ideas and patterns of political outlook. Furthermore, strange as it may seem, despite the fact the Jabotinsky was secular, some of these attitudes jibe with basic attitudes in the Jewish religion stressing the uniqueness of the Jews and their "chosenness," accompanied by sentiments of self-righteousness. In religious circles, historical events are explained as miracles, the common explanation of the Israel victory in 1967 and the present period is "the beginning of redemption."

Thus, religious circles have spearheaded annexation. Paradoxically, some religious circles, for whom Zionism is sacrilegious, consider the Zionist state's conquests as holy, not to be relinquished on the behest of a religious precept.

I suspect there is a deeper cultural factor in the facile acceptance by Israelis of the Jabotinsky-Begin Ethos. The Jewish legacy developed by the sages is extremely exalting but it is limited to interpersonal matters. Jews were absent from the world of politics for many centuries and the sages and rabbis have not had experience dealing with how a Jewish state should perform in the international area.

The basic problems that face Israel have not been political, but meta-political, residing in those basic patterns of thinking that gave birth to the Likud policies. Rebutting the Likud positions could not be accomplished by politicians but should have been done by moderate Israeli intellectuals. However, when the intellectuals saw their people going astray, they did not stand in the breach. Instead, they malingered and abdicated.

The moderates also depended on the reaction of the outer world to Israeli policy. They argued that the superpowers would not allow the annexationist policy. These prophecies failed in the short run, although they may come true in the long run. In the meantime, annexationism was allowed to thrive, confirming the Likud's comforting homilies to the Israeli public. The Israeli hard-liners' position was popular because it was independent of foreign endeavors.

In general, the intellectual moderates showed an inability to produce a clear and cohesive message. They bickered over their small divergences rather than uniting on the main thrust of their position. Furthermore, they did not start from an analysis of Arab positions. They could not meet a popular argument from the Likud arsenal that the Arab positions are such that no peace is feasible. Their dovishness was mostly unilaterally derived, having little or nothing to do with Arab positions.

Their argumentation was anemic in shrinking from taking trenchant positions. For instance, their main argument justifying why Israel had to withdraw from the occupied territories was that otherwise Israel would impair its democratic regime and become ugly. Such an argument proved effete, compared with Begin's slogan that withdrawal from the territories was a "mortal danger"; namely, that Israel may die as a result. The moderates flinched from using a similar argument that staying in these territories is the mortal danger. For doves, moderation in policy mandated mildness in articulation. But the argument that the main drawback of annexation is its negative effects for Israeli democracy implied that annexation is a practical proposition. Common Israelis could justifiably argue that if ensuring the existence of the state entails some deviation from democracy, it is worth paying the price.

Many Israeli doves took equivocal midway positions that made them slide into the lap of the Likud. For instance, for years many Israeli moderates were hesitant to state clearly that there should be a Palestinian state. Some argued that such an idea was not marketable in Israel. They found refuge in such wishy-washy expressions as there should be a "Palestinian entity."[4] There the difference between them and the Likud is blurred. The Likud is not adverse to a Palestinian entity, which it perceives only in the shape of a permanent autonomy.

While the moderates hesitated, Likud positions consolidated. At present, a change in Israeli public position could hardly come from within Israeli society. True, the Israeli public is bewildered and split, not only between groups such as moderates and hard-liners; Israeli individuals are split within themselves. Many suffer from agonizing ambivalences. They recognize that Israel cannot stay for long in the occupied territories, yet they are still opposed to negotiations with the Palestinians. Typically, a research study conducted at Hebrew University concluded that Israeli eighth to twelfth graders are dovish on the issue of a conflict settlement but hostile to Arabs. Their attitudes are cognitive on the conflict and emotional on the Arab people. Unfortunately, the Israeli public has not received guidance from its molders of public opinions on what is possible and what is not possible in the world and on the implications of the basic positions in the Arab-Israeli conflict.

The American Position and Role

The United States could have called Israel to order in the 1970s long before the mass implantation of settlements. The fateful moment occurred in 1977 when Begin assumed power. His advocacy of de facto annexation of the occupied territories flew in the face of UN Resolution 242. Washington was aware of Begin's political positions when his visit to the United States was arranged. The former U.S. ambassador to Israel, Samuel Lewis, recounts: "I got to know Begin earlier, and because I was able to go back to Washington during late June and help prepare for the visit, I succeeded in changing the approach of the administration from what would have been, I think, one of the more disastrous encounters in American diplomatic history, had it taken place according to the game plan which our friends in the National Security Council had initially designed."[5]

This "game plan" presumably referred to the preparations by President Jimmy Carter's aides to challenge Begin's position. American Jews were astounded by the election of Begin to the premiership. He was not popular with them, and challenging him then would not have met with the same resistance as later, when the Jewish organizations began to like him. Begin acquitted himself well in Washington by U.S. standards by declaring that "everything is negotiable." The Americans were relieved, apparently interpreting this declaration as a sign of moderation. It really meant that everything is "talkable" and nothing more. Begin returned to Israel triumphantly.[6]

American diplomacy won over American statesmanship. From this time on, Israeli rejection of UN Resolution 242 and its claim to retain the occupied territories were no longer outlandish but became political positions, official positions of the state of Israel.[7] By not challenging Begin, the United States granted his position political respectability and made it impossible to challenge the Likud policy on the grounds of international norms and legality. American leaders lacked the foresight to grasp the importance of this encounter.

Begin's success in Washington had great importance for Israeli political life. It signaled to Israelis that they should not be too concerned with the world's opposition to expansionist policy in the occupied territories.

The Camp David accords, which Begin signed, were based on UN Resolution 242, which had been rebuffed by Begin. Previously, Israeli leaders, led by Begin, interpreted Resolution 242 as calling unequivocally for complete withdrawal on all borders, and therefore, they fiercely repudiated it. Now, with immense inconsistency, the Likud leaders claim that under this resolution further withdrawals are not called for, because the withdrawal from the Sinai dispenses with any need to withdraw elsewhere.[8] At this point, Resolution 242 has been practically discarded by Israel, as can be inferred from Secretary of State James Baker's demand for Israeli reaffirmation of its acceptance.

From time to time the United States has announced its positions, as in President Reagan's speech of September 1, 1982. However, because Israelis and Arabs could balk at them with impunity, these positions were merely declaratory. It can be said that the United States has had positions on the Arab-Israeli conflict, but hardly a policy. Arabs could wonder how the American positions that were in conflict with Israeli policies were so ineffectual. They could explain it to themselves as being caused either by the insincerity of the United States or by evoking an alleged all-powerful, muzzling influence of American Jewry.

Americans have recognized that the settlements were meant to weld the territories to Israel and prevent Israel's withdrawal, which puts a peaceful settlement out of the question. For years, however, they did not express this realization in a forthright fashion but instead used anemic expressions such as the settlements were not "helpful" for peace; later, they declared the settlements to be "an obstacle to peace." Israelis could consider this lukewarm opposition to proceed from the Americans' need to pay lip service to their friends, the Saudis; they could conclude that for the Americans the whole issue was of little concern.

American leadership could have been effective with the Israelis had they stressed that it was precisely an *Israeli* and not an American interest that demanded that Israel refrain from settlements, that the settlements were a waste of money and a squandering of national effort, and that from the perspective of the U.S. leadership, the Israelis would eventually have to withdraw from these territories. American officials said those things to me privately; why were their leaders afraid to say them publicly?

The Americans, perhaps, were apprehensive that by expressions of disapproval of Israeli policy they would expose themselves to the accusation that they had prejudiced the outcome of future peace negotiations. But why? Was it ever their evaluation that Israel would retain the West Bank if the United States did not take such a position? Does not the American leadership have a right to have a historical view and express it? Can American leaders be denounced for making an ally and its public privy to their historical evaluation?

Furthermore, the Americans' position about Israeli withdrawal from the occupied territories according to Resolution 242 has been accompanied by an aversion to elaborate a general conception of what will, or should, happen in these territories after the withdrawal. For some years, Americans could assume that these territories would revert to Jordan. However, since 1974, when Jordan joined the resolution of the 1973 Arab Summit meeting, which proclaimed that the PLO represents the Palestinians, Jordan lost Arab legitimacy to represent the Palestinians. Since then a Jordanian option has not been in the cards. Thus, no concrete alternative was conceived by the Americans to the Israeli scheme of retaining the territories, which was allowed to enjoy a monopoly. Furthermore, such an omission helped to nurture a hope in Israel that perhaps, against all odds, the occupied territories would stay Israeli.

American officials claim that the United States does not reject a Palestinian state, but as the current expression says, "will not support a Palestinian state," which they interpret as meaning that the United States will not propose it. Why should the only real superpower in whose hands the destiny of world is deposited find refuge in such a diffident expression? If the American position was that these territories would be confederated with Jordan, the territories have first to constitute a political object. In the present world order, this means first to become a state, which only then can be confederated.

One can understand that the American administration finds it now easier, because of American internal politics, to challenge Israeli settlements and not Israeli basic policy. The settlements are not meant to infuriate the Americans. They are the practical incarnation of an ideological position spawning a policy. It is first, and foremost, the underlying policy that should have been taken to task.

The settlements are not popular in the United States, even among

American Jews. But Americans fail to ask themselves why. Apparently, they oppose the settlements, either because they oppose annexationism on principle, or at least, because they consider that the territories must be subject to negotiations. Israel declares emphatically that the negotiations should be without prior conditions. However, implanting settlements constitutes a tangible prior condition designed to foreclose negotiations on withdrawal. The settlements are an organic part, rather the concrete quintessence, of the Likud policy. Honesty commands those who oppose the settlements to condemn the Likud policy, lock, stock, and barrel. But many recoil from doing so. Some find refuge in differentiating between "provocative," or new, and regular, or old, settlements. But what is the difference? They are all means to dictate to history that the territories will stay Israeli.

Challenging Israel over the settlements and its de facto annexationism could have been done many years ago, to the benefit of Israel. There has been no need to stall so long. Israel's pains in withdrawing from the territories when the Jewish population there amounted to a few thousand or less, would have been incomparably smaller than now, when the number is more than one hundred thousand, and will be multiplied shortly, in view of the current enthusiasm for building houses there.

Israel will pay heavily for American squeamishness. Israel will be accused of having brought the suffering on itself by misreading reality and disobeying international norms. Nevertheless, the United States will be guilty of irresponsibility, political and moral, for allowing Israel to follow a wrong policy and for allowing Israel to flout accepted international standards. American Jews will probably be found to bear a large share of the blame for this situation.

The Effects of the Gulf War on the Middle East and the Conflict

The Gulf War may prove to be a watershed in the history of the Middle East and may have some important, wider effects for world order. It brought into relief the basic problems of the Middle East. The Arabs feel uneasy and despondent; they feel that all national dreams have failed; they demand popular participation in the decision-making process; and they have an urge for a more equitable share of the affluence derived from oil. There are no signs that the popular demands for greater social justice will be modestly met. In a world swept by a wave of democratization, most Arab states still struggle with ugly authoritarianism, or worse, anachronistic autocracy, but only temporarily. The Arab states ask now for American military safeguards against external threats. However, their real threat is internal instability, rising from social disgruntlement, against which the foreign military safeguards will be of no avail.

The stature of the Palestinians has changed radically. On the Arab official level, the PLO has discredited itself in the eyes of the Arab anti-Iraqi coalition governments. The PLO will suffer for this politically and financially. More significant is the apparent change in Arab public attitudes to the Palestinians. The situation is radically different from what it was after the Arab military debacle in 1967. Then, Arab intellectuals felt a need to be somehow associated with the Palestinian cause, and, in many cases, volunteered to serve with Palestinian guerrilla organizations. To be a Palestinian freedom fighter was then a social distinction, a social chic.

Whereas Arab intellectuals formerly felt a need to be associated with the Palestinian cause, now there is considerable resentment concerning the Palestinians' pretense that their problem is the most important problem in the Arab world, to which all other Arab states' concerns should be subordinated. Many Arabs are tired of being reminded of the indebtedness to the Palestinians and are impatient with the Palestinians' lack of realism in indulging in dreams beyond their means to accomplish and beyond the means of the Arab world to procure for them. Palestinians are criticized for bungling their cause, and for their internal wranglings, bloody internecine disputes, and their modes of operation against Israel. Everything to do with Palestine has gone awry. Despite these new resentments, most Arabs feel they cannot forsake the Palestinians, especially those under Israeli rule.

Viewing the malaise in the Arab world, Likud leaders may consider it a vindication of the Likud position. Israel does not need to fear a war because Iraq has ceased to be a major military menace, and the other Arab states are too deeply immersed in their own predicaments. There is no hurry to start negotiations with leaders and regimes whose future is uncertain. The Likud may conclude that Israel should go on implanting settlements and should not introduce change in its policy. Furthermore, the Likud leadership can argue that the expressions of hatred against Israel that surfaced during the Iraqi crisis and the expressions of glee among Arab masses when Israel was hit by missiles prove that the old politicidal positions have not changed, that the old Arab metaphysical positions still hold sway.

These manifestations of Arab extremism, even if they can be explained, do cause worry. The refusal of Arab leaders to start negotiations with Israel made the official Arab position suspect. Their optimal diplomacy would have been to come to negotiations with alacrity to prove that Israel, faced with the alternatives of retaining the territories or achieving peace with its neighbors, prefers the territories over peace.

On the other hand, it can be argued that after the Iraqi war Arab leaders have an interest in expediting the settlement of the conflict. Otherwise, the leaders of Egypt, Syria, and Saudi Arabia will be in an awkward position. Popular opinion will blame them for conspiring with the Americans to force the Iraqi withdrawal from Kuwait, while they turn a blind eye to Israel's retaining the territories occupied in 1967. Furthermore, an enhanced Arab interest in a peace settlement may stem from the rise of the Muslim fundamentalism that may threaten the regimes of some Arab leaders. The fundamentalists use the conflict as a main vehicle to agitate and propagate their gospel. Palestinian Muslim fundamentalism, based in the occupied territories and Jordan, has recently assumed an important central position in the Muslim fundamentalist movement. Syrian leader Hafez al-Assad is well aware of the burning urge for vengeance among the fundamentalists against his regime, for the atrocities he committed against the Muslim Brotherhood.

Perhaps the most important factor in present Arab readiness to reach a settlement is greater realism as a result of the Gulf War. There are some beginnings of Arab self-criticism, of questioning nationalist dogmas. The end of the cold war deprived the small states of the possibility of playing one superpower against the other, and of using a superpower as their protector. The frustration of the Iraqi aggression and the terrible punishment visited on Iraq may have a "demonstration effect" of discouraging leaders from embarking on aggressive wars. On the whole, the mainstream Arab position is now closer to a consensus that UN Resolution 242 should serve as the basis for the settlement of the conflict by virtue of its embodying the principle of trading territory for peace.

Conclusions for the Arab-Israeli Conflict and the Peace Process

The conclusion possibly learned by the Likud from the last crisis, that there is no need to reach a compromise and peace, is perhaps plausible tactically, in the short run. It is not wise strategically, in the long run. Lack of peace will only make the lives of both Jews and Arabs a hell. The present instability in the Arab world may stymie Arab military initiative against Israel. However, on the political level, it may hamper Arabs from coming to terms with Israel's existence and concluding a peace agreement. Arab instability averts Arab *threats* against Israel, but constitutes a main source of *risks* to the whole region, including Israel. It is myopic to consider that Israel's interests are served, in the long run, by Arab instability.

The Palestinians' support of Saddam Hussein is condemnable. However, a nation does not forfeit its right to statehood by objectionable behavior. This lesson can be learned from the cases of both the Japanese and Germans in World War II. Instead of Israel trying to exclude the PLO from the negotiations, it should, preferably, invoke the PLO's recent behavior to reinforce a demand to improve Israeli conditions in the peace settlement with regard to security and territory.

Analogy between the Iraqi occupation of Kuwait and the Israeli occupation of the territories occupied in 1967 is wrong. However, that does not mean that Israel has a right to retain these territories, or that it will be allowed to do so.

I understand the Palestinians' apprehension that autonomy would be a trap hindering them from achieving independence, and that by accepting it, the Palestinians disarm themselves of the means of exerting further pressure on Israel through the *intifada*. If I could give the Palestinians and PLO a word of advice, I would urge them to lower their demands and join the negotiations, without too much ado about procedures, modalities, and results. They will gain from the negotiations and it is against their interests to impede their commencement.

The only possible solution to the Arab-Israeli conflict is partition into two states: Israel and the Palestinian state. Thus, within one homeland (*Watan* or *Moledet*) to which both Palestinians and Israelis owe sentimental allegiance—called "Palestine" or "Eretz Yisrael"—there will be two smaller states, the "State of Palestine" and "Israel," in which they will, respectively, exercise sovereignty. Having a common homeland may in the future nurture collaborative relationships between them, and with Jordan, with which the Palestinian state would be confederated. A historical irony has developed: a Palestinian state is a condition for the survival of Israel as a Jewish, and not a bi-national, state.

In any negotiations and settlement the onus of concessions between the Arabs and Israel is not symmetrical. The Israelis will have to give up real assets as territory. The Arab concessions are more of a declaratory nature, such as terminating belligerency, terminating the boycott, and agreeing to normalize relations with Israel and live in peace.

But these concessions are not enough. In any future negotiations, the Palestinians and Arabs will have to be reminded that their case is not as impeccable as some of them try to present. For a very long period, the Arabs were the main obstacle to peace. Their readiness for a compromise solution and reconciliation is only recent. The Palestinians' support of Saddam Hussein will also serve as a reminder that they need to prove the seriousness of their peaceful intentions.

They should understand that Israel cannot possibly agree to retreat exactly to the previous borders, expecially those closely around Jerusalem. Too many Jews now live outside the Green Lines there. The settlement movement is not an Israeli fault alone. Israel could not keep these territories for so long as an untouchable pawn without people starting to settle there. In maintaining a long posture of belligerency, Arabs share the blame. The treatment Palestinians got from Kuwait should present Israel to them in brighter hues.

They should give up ambiguous formulations in their documents and declarations. The Palestinians are as transparent to the Israelis as the Israelis are to them. They should announce that they do not harbor hidden agendas, that the peace settlement will be final, leaving no residual claims, and that the Palestinian "right of return" will be restricted only to the Palestinian state, as the Israeli "law of return" will apply only to Israel. They should manifest some understanding toward Israeli worries about security, and agree that the Palestinian state will accept arms control restrictions.

Many Israelis suspect that some Arab circles harbor vicious intentions and a hidden agenda of the "phases tactics," namely, to use Israel's withdrawal as a springboard to continue the struggle against Israel. This is not a paranoid figment of imagination. Arabs have articulated such intentions. However, the only way to combat against these circles and their designs is not by delaying negotiations, which will only reinforce those intentions, but by making the settlement robust enough to withstand evil designs. In general, diplomacy has not assumed that the adversary is sincere and motivated by benign intentions. Diplomacy has been the art of producing a solid settlement capable of thwarting malevolent designs and hidden agendas, which if the adversary does not entertain today, he may cultivate tomorrow. A political settlement cannot be founded on volatile moods such as congeniality, good faith, and sincerity of one's neighboring country, but on sturdy arrangements.

The tragic dilemma that faces Israel is that it is possible that Israelis would regret following their moderates' advice and allowing a Palestinian state, because of the unsettling outcomes that may surface, including manifestations of unplacated Arab enmity. By the same token, Israelis may deeply regret following the hard-liners in refusing a compromise. All human solutions are patchwork whose seams eventually start fraying. Following either policy would not allow a comparison to what might have happened had its alternative been chosen—a limitation with which historians grapple. Nevertheless, my conviction is that the first option is incomparably better. Its harmful outcomes can be prevented by the quality of the peace settlement arrangements, which can be made very robust. Appreciating that, Arab hard-liners oppose any settlement with Israel and reject the effectiveness of the "phases tactics," arguing that a peace settlement, once achieved, will become permanent, so much so that the Arabs will be unable to undermine it. In the second alternative of no peace, devastating consequences are inexorable. Indeed, risks can be found in both, in peace and in the continuation of the conflict; the choice is not between good and bad, but between bad and worse. The risks in peace are more controllable than those in the continuation of the conflict.

True, if Israel weakens after the peace settlement, Arab inimical intentions may be resuscitated, as their erstwhile "grand design" of hoping for Israel's demise may linger for sometime after their "policy" has been mod-

erated, becoming peaceful.[9] However, Israel will continue its military preparedness, and the international community will bolster the peace settlement through safeguards. As peace consolidates with the passage of time,
the inimical intentions in the "Grand Design" may be discarded altogether.

MEDIATION

Left on their own, the Arabs and Israelis are incapable of devising a
settlement. They need a mediator. All Arab-Israeli negotiations and agreements until now have been mediated. Americans as meditors will wait in
vain if they expect "new ideas" to come from the contestants themselves.
Expectations that the parties should muster the will and the vision to provide an escape from the present deadlock are complimentary for the contestants, but overly optimistic. The absolute elements in their positions
stifle any creativity on their parts.

It is only natural that a mediator will first concentrate on the modalities of "procedure," and try to prod the contestants to agree on them.
However, procedure is not detached from substance and the pressure that
will be needed to hammer out an agreement of substance may be needed
earlier in the negotiations on procedure. It is a delusion to think that the
mediator's main task is simply to get the parties to negotiate and that once
they meet, they will shed their illusions and moderate their positions. Parties will give way, not to persuasion, but to pressure.

The Americans' eagerness to see the negotiations started is understandable. Once they begin, it will be easier to apply pressure and reprove
intransigence by presenting to public opinion the metaphysical aspects of
the parties' positions. This will be a sharp weapon against Israel. It may
help the U.S. executive branch in its controversy with Congress, which has
frequently imposed constraints on the administration's policies in the
Arab-Israeli conflict. However, this avidity to arrive at the negotiation
stage can become counterproductive if the prospective mediator commits
to measures of procedure that may limit freedom of action when the negotiations arrive at the substance stage.

Israeli demand for direct negotiations means that the mediator's role
will be minimal and passive. However, once the substantive negotiations
start, the sharp antithesis between the Israeli and Arab positions will come
into the open forcefully and cause an immediate deadlock. No compromise on secondary issues can substitute for the need to come to grips with
the main, substantive, territorial bone of contention. Then the mediator
will have to pursue an active role and propose solutions to the controversies
on which the negotiations were stuck, notwithstanding a possible previous
promise to Israel not to do so. The United States will find that in order to
move the negotiations, it will have to convert its theoretical, inconsequen-
tial, and toothless positions into firm political demands.

Israeli argument that any position taken by the Americans is obnoxious, because it will inflate Arabs' claims and reinforce their intransigence, is specious. It is only a recipe to freeze the status quo. Arab positions are already made up. Their call for withdrawal and for a Palestinian state has not come into being because the Americans inflated their hopes. American positions are also not new. The Israelis claim that the Americans should refrain from challenging the settlements because of prejudicing the outcomes of the negotiations. But by the same token, Arabs may claim that by American quiescence in the face of Israeli accelerated housing construction in the occupied territories, an accomplished fact is produced that may prejudice the negotiations.

A mediator also will have to develop an idea on how and where to lead the negotiations. So long as the negotiations are within the framework of Resolution 242, the settlement's general lines are already given, and the bargaining is constricted. Because the interpretation of Resolution 242 is crucial, it may be necessary to reach an authoritative interpretation of this resolution. The mediator can either impose an interpretation or apply for an advisory ruling from the International Court in The Hague. My guess is that the court will reject the Israeli interpretation that withdrawal in the Sinai disposes of the need to withdraw elsewhere. The Americans probably will pressure Israel to implement Resolution 242 and withdraw from the occupied territories.

In the Camp David accords, Begin recognized "the legitimate rights of the Palestinian people and their just requirements." However, neither Begin nor subsequent Israeli prime minsters have been asked to define what such rights are. Rights are not an issue to be elaborated by negotiations but should precede them. A demand to define these "rights" and "requirements" may help Israelis to start to see that these contradict their design for the occupied territories. Another useful exercise for the mediators would be to ask both parties to define what they expect the position of a moderate adversary of theirs—Israeli or Palestinian—should be. It may bring to light the absurdity of the Israeli position that defines a Palestinian moderate as one who agrees that Israel will retain the territories.

The question of Palestinian representation in the regional conference is a grave stumbling block. The Palestinians consider that depriving them of the right to decide on the composition of their delegation to the negotiations is an act of egregious injustice, signifying an American submission to Israeli whims. The bitterness of the feeling of being wronged may drive people to irrational behavior. Against their interests, the Palestinians may wreck the whole process, before it starts or during the negotiations, despite their suspicion that precisely that is what Israeli leadership anticipates. Their hard-liners argue that the intention to have only a truncated Palestinian representation augurs ill as to the outcomes for the Palestinians

from such a peace process; they therefore advocate boycotting the conference. The hard-liners may, in some stage, carry the day. Taking lightly the
Palestinians' claims as if they are the weakest party may prove a grave
mistake.

The representation of the 170,000 Palestinians living in Jerusalem is
also a thorny question. Palestinians may claim that excluding them flies in
the face of any rudimentary notion of democracy. The United States recognizes that East Jerusalem is occupied territory like the rest of the West
Bank. Then why, Arabs ask, should the Jerusalem Palestinians not be en-
titled to representation like the other West Bankers? It is only a delusion
to believe that by excluding them Israel will ensure its annexation of Jerusalem. In Jerusalem there is a need to meet not only the Israeli aspirations,
but also those of the Arabs (Muslims) and the Christians.

Because of the moderate position taken by Palestinians of the occupied territories, engaging in negotiations with them may facilitate the process, relieving it of the complexities of unwieldy multilateral negotiations.
As promulgated in the resolutions of the last Arab summit meetings, the
Palestinian problem is the "nub" of the Arab-Israeli conflict. Thus, a solution of the Palestinian problem is the necessary preamble to the settlement
of the other problems between Israel and the Arab countries.

Arms control arrangements cannot precede the peace settlement and
will not be a vehicle to bring peace. Analogies should not be drawn from
the success of European arms control negotiations. There the negotiations
were conducted between states that recognized each other and maintained
diplomatic relations. These basic conditions are missing in the Arab-Israeli
case. Israel will be justifiably reluctant to disarm itself of those kinds of
weaponry that give it an edge over the Arab states unless it is first assured
of a safe peace. Excessive preoccupation with arms control could divert
attention from the real task of achieving a peace settlement. However,
arms control should be part of the settlement.

Europe and the Soviet Union have to coordinate their policies with
those of the United States and may assume the obligation to guarantee the
peace settlement by concrete safeguards. Weakening of the Soviet Union
will facilitate the Americans' task. Europe may play an important role in
enticing Israel to make concessions. For example, Europe, the main market for Israeli agricultural products, may invite Israel to be included in the
European economic space, provided peace is achieved with the Palestinians. Although the possibility for such an affiliation is unknown to the
Israeli public, the Italian minister for foreign affairs, Gianni De Michelis,
expounded this idea in an article translated from *La Stampa* that was published in *Ha'aretz,* June 30, 1991, and in speeches during his visit to Israel
in September 1991. Europe should consider offering a similar arrangement
to the Palestinian state, provided it meets the conditions of democracy and
a market economy.

Americans may hope that the blessings of peace will cast a spell on the Likud leadership and awaken fervent readiness to relinquish the occupied territories, sparing them an ugly showdown. However, such a hope will not come true. Once it becomes clear that the only possibility is a peace entailing withdrawal, the Likud leadership will become desperately strident and the whole situation will become unpleasant. For the Americans, it will be the nemesis for the historical mistake in 1977 of backing away from challenging Begin and of its U.S. "policy" in the years since then.

Settlement of the Arab-Israeli conflict may require an American showdown with the Arabs and the Israelis, although on different issues. If the Americans are reluctant to put pressure on Israel and the Arabs, they may threaten to forsake the contestants to stew in their juices, isolate the conflict from harmful repercussions, and marginalize its significance. Or they may pass the onus of mediation to the UN Security Council. The United States may announce that it would no longer straitjacket Security Council action through vetoes. The Security Council would then be free to command the parties to abide by Resolution 242. Israeli policy of banning the United Nations from participating in international deliberation on the conflict goes against the prevailing trend of involving it in major international controversies.

Once it becomes clear that withdrawal from the occupied territories is required, a governmental crisis may ensue and the present Likud-led coalition may disintegrate and fall. This would cause a slight delay in the negotiations, but only slight; a country cannot go for long without a government.

THE INFLUENCE OF PUBLIC OPINION

Governments may change positions not only in response to pressure exerted by other governments, but as a result of the pressure of their own population and the stigmatization of their positions by world public opinion. For instance, many circles in the United States are of the opinion that the American adminstration should exert pressure on the Saudi and Kuwait rulers to democratize their regimes, as they promised before the Gulf War. Lack of change in these regimes may mean that the United States went to war to make the Middle East safe, not for democracy, but for ugly monarchies.

Americans pass to the Bush administration the task of bringing about a change in these regimes. They are not alive to how much they can be effective by exerting social pressure on every Saudi and Kuwaiti they meet. Instead of drawing a distinction between these states and their citizens, they should express forthrightly their disapproval of the regimes to the citizens of these countries. The criticism of these states should thus be *personalized*. The citizens of these states should be made ashamed of their countries. For example, the Saudis should be reminded that their practice of not allowing in visitors who have passports carrying an Israeli stamp is galling and calls for a harsh international reaction. Of course, in nondemocracies individuals are not legally responsible for the corruption of the rules; still, pressure on them can help.

Once people from these countries are met everywhere with scorching criticism; once the regimes of their countries are incessantly castigated as being outside the pale of acceptability; once they feel uneasy socially; once all of them, including the highest ranks of these countries' administrations, hear the same sharp criticism from their peers in foreign governments as well as from simple citizens, a climate of opinion will be generated in these countries that eventually will force the changes.

The same applies to the influence on Israeli policy that can be exerted by diaspora Jews and, in particular, American Jews. They criticize Shamir's policy, yet, when he comes to the United States, they applaud him with ardor. Actually, they mislead him, for their acclaim may lure him to think that American Jewry is behind his policy and will defend it on Capitol Hill and at the White House. If American Jews personalized their attitude toward members of Likud visiting the United States, candidly expressing to them what they thought about their ideology and policy, they could exercise considerable influence.

We are enmeshed in some dishonest inconsistency when we denounce ideas and at the same time do not reprobate their promulgators and adherents when we meet them. Had Likud leaders known that upon coming to the United States they might be met by disconcerting excoriation of their positions, their self-confidence would have left them and doubts would have gnawed at them.

MORAL RECONCILIATION AND NATIONAL IDEOLOGIES

Within both parties, the Palestinians and the Israelis, there is a great deal of bewailing about the historical injustice that has been administered to them. Both are afflicted with a conviction that humanity is indebted to them. Some people suffer from a guilt complex; Israelis and Palestinians suffer from nonguilt complexes.

Palestinians and their sympathizers describe copiously the miseries that befell Palestinians through no fault of their own. The responsibility for their misfortunes is externalized. These circles of sympathizers are not alive to the disservice that they perform to the Palestinians by hindering their coming to grips with their situation and, indirectly, in helping them to nourish illusions.

Thus, the slogan that there should be a "just solution," brandished by Palestinians with overflowing feelings of morality, is baneful. Only an unjust solution for both the Palestinians and the Israelis is possible. Both deserve bigger states, but only mini-states are available.

Similarly, well-meaning Jews are not aware of the imperceptible link between a subtle support of the annexationism by default and the accounts of the horrible Jewish sufferings in the Holocaust and the iniquities committed against the Jews in history. The evil wrought to the Jews does not grant them license, and settlements in the occupied territories are not compensation for Jewish historical sufferings. Criticism of others should not curtail self-criticism, but, to the contrary, should make us more alive to our own failings and our need of self-criticism. I do not compare the Holocaust to Palestinian afflictions. Nevertheless, it is intrinsic to the human condition that previous collective sufferings cannot be transformed into a writ of indebtedness. Humanity and history do not recognize such a liability.

Both Israelis and Palestinians will need a great amount of introspection and self-criticism. Zionists and Israelis should acknowledge that the Zionist venture was not possible without causing injustice and suffering to the Palestinian Arabs, even if they, like myself, feel very deeply that the Zionist enterprise was justified.

National self-criticism is shallow if it only entails an acknowledgment that a previous policy was mistaken, without going further and inquiring what in the collective personality made such a mistaken policy possible. Thus, for example, the Iraqis should not only acknowledge that Saddam Hussein's policy was wrong, but should examine how the whole Saddam Hussein phenomenon was possible. Israelis should not only realize that the policies of de facto annexationism are wrong, but should question the factors in the Jewish legacy and even in the Jewish religion and culture that contributed to the adoption of such a policy, and made the Likud ethos attractive. What went wrong in the Zionist venture?

The Palestinians will have to turn to themselves and examine their national movement, and ask themselves why was it afflicted with so much internecine bloodshed and so many objectionable features.

Both Palestinians and Israelis will have to atone for the sufferings they have caused to their adversary, which they have tended to disregard. What is needed is not some ceremonial, mutual expiation, but the percolation of this awareness into their educational systems. They will have to rewrite their national histories, transcending their parochial grievances and claims to include the grievances and the claims of their adversary, who has become a neighbor and a prospective partner.

Palestinian and Israeli intellectuals will need to rethink their national ideologies and how their nations can function in the new political circumstances. Israeli intellectuals will have to address themselves to an examination of the question of Israelis' self-identification, which can no longer be left hazy and enmeshed in many contradictions. Is their hallmark a nationality? Is it a religion or Jewishness? But then, who is a Jew? Or will they come to the conclusion that what distinguishes Israelis is their Hebrew language and its culture?

Both will have to address themselves to the problem of the relationship to their respective diasporas. This relationship is not analogous. The links between the Palestinians in the Palestinian state and their diaspora brethren are mostly remembrances of a common geographical origin and recent, short history. Thus, the Palestinians define themselves geographically. Ethnically and culturally they are not different from other Arabs, and even more so, from Arabs in the neighboring countries. In contrast, the links between the Israelis and diaspora Jews are ethnic and religious.

One can venture the assumption that the bonds of common geographical origins are of a relative short longevity, especially once the political struggle is over. The assimilation of the Palestinian diasporas into their current environments will be accelerated once a Palestinian state is established.[10] On the other hand, once the Arab-Israeli conflict is settled, Israel's dependence on the Jewish diaspora will diminish.

It is not easy to project one's self and think rigorously on the circumstances after the achievement of the settlement. Both the Palestinian and Israeli societies will undergo serious crises. Palestinians will face the difficulties of establishing their small state and writhe from the disparity between the aspirations and hopes about its blessings and its reality.

For Israel, a settlement will entail a national crisis—political, social, and religious. Zionism was open-ended on the territorial configuration of the Jewish state. Withdrawal will spell dreadful finality to the Zionist dream. The Israelis suffer from a psychological closure that causes an internal resistance to considering the outcomes of the peace negotiations. Turning Israeli public attention to reflect on these outcomes is of great importance. Israeli intellectuals could fulfill an important role here. Such thinking will not only prepare the public for what is in store for them, it may also influence their present political convictions and behavior.

Israelis should address themselves to issues such as: What kind of Israel will emerge from the ordeal of the peace settlement? How will history since 1967 and 1977 be judged? What lessons can be learned from the upheaval? What changes are mandated in the political life? What are the possible economic consequences of the crisis and the settlement? It should become an all-embracing, national self-reckoning.

Both Israelis and Palestinians are gifted people and should exert themselves to develop their small states in order to distinguish themselves. The Palestinians are perhaps the Arab community most alive to democratic ideas.

I call on Israelis to develop what I term "Zionism of quality" to supersede the "Zionism of acreage" of the annexationists. The urge for excellence, without the pretense of "chosen-ness," should become a national obsession. Because Israel became such a central ingredient in the self-identification of many Jews for whom the former religious link has waned, the quality of the Israeli state has become crucial for maintaining their allegiance, not only to Israel, but to their Jewish identity itself.

Notes

1. This chapter is a revised, enlarged, and updated version of a public lecture at Princeton University on April 8, 1991, and of a paper delivered at a conference on "The Aftermath of the Persian Gulf War: Realignment in the Middle East?" at the University of Utah, May 13, 1991.

2. This is the belief that achieving success becomes easier by contracting action to a short stretch of time—an event—instead of success resulting from the long exertion of one's self in a process. In the military domain, this kind of thinking prompts the flaw of "tacticization of strategy," namely, seeing war as if it were one battle. Such thinking typified the Israeli-Lebanese war of 1982.

3. Amplification of this is in my book, *Israel's Fateful Hour* (New York: Harper & Row, 1988, 2d ed., 1989).

4. See, for instance: Z. Schiff and E. Ya'ari, *Intifada, the Palestinian Uprising—Israel's Third Front* (New York: Simon and Schuster, 1989), 338. It should be noted that previously Arabs used to refer to Israel as the "Zionist entity" (*al-kian as-Sahiuni*).

5. S. W. Lewis. "The Impact of America's Ambassadors on the Foreign Policy Process," in *U.S. Middle East Policy: the Domestic Setting*. Shai Feldman, ed. (JCSS Studies, the Jaffe Center for Strategic Studies, Tel Aviv University, and Westview Press, 1988), 27.

6. I worked then in Begin's office as "the prime minister adviser for intelligence." My evaluation was that the Americans, alive to the implications of Begin's position for the future of both the Arab-Israeli conflict and the Middle East, would take Begin to task, and unequivocally denounce his position on Resolution 242. I preferred an early clash between Begin and the United States rather than allowing him to proceed with annexation. My evaluation failed completely. A short time afterward, I resigned from office. I summed up my distress in a book: "I confess that over the last years I found myself in a Kafkaesque predicament, wishing for the sake of Israel, an early Israel-United States crises in order to prevent a later rupture which would be more damaging, perhaps irreparable. I prayed for the wisdom of nipping trends in the bud before they assumed uncontrollable dimensions. I found myself in an impossible situation, considering both the Israeli government and the American Embassy as my adversaries—the Israeli government for what it does and intends to do, and the American Embassy for what it encourages by omission." *The Bar Kokhba Syndrome: Risk and Realism in International Relations* (New York: Rossel Books, 1982), 180.

7. It raises a theoretical problem: Should not the international community react early in the event that a political party in some state takes an ideological position that contravenes international norms, and not wait until this party is in-

stalled as the government of this state and implements its position? I believe that the trend of the international community to intervene in the internal affairs of states (*vide* the Conference on Security and Cooperation in Europe), despite the principle of sovereignty, will usher in such an approach.

8. The question may be posed as to whether the Camp David accords were a positive contribution to the settlement of the Arab-Israeli conflict and peace, or whether, as I tend to suspect, their contribution was, judging their aftermath, negative. True, they constituted a great revolutionary achievement in concluding peace with a most important Arab state. However, they have been interpreted by Israel to mean that by making territorial concessions to Egypt, it could retain the other territories. The peace with one Arab state was Israel's installment in order to dispose of the need to achieve peace elsewhere. One can argue that without the peace with Egypt the pressure to achieve a comprehensive peace with all concerned would have been stronger, and perhaps more effective.

9. The differentiation between "grand design" (what one dreams or hopes for, without exerting efforts to realize) and "policy" (what one considers realistic and is ready to invest effort to achieve), is essential in analyzing this conflict. Elaboration of the distinction between these two categories is found in my book, *Israel's Fateful Hour,* chapter 1.

10. I owe this observation to Professor Ghasan Salame.

The Future in the Present:
Issues of Palestinian Statehood

Salim Tamari was born in Jaffa and received a Ph.D. from Manchester University, England. He is an associate professor of sociology at Bir Zeit University and editor of *Afaq Filistiniyya*, the Bir Zeit University Research Review. He is also editor of *Working Papers in the Social Sciences* and an associate editor of Middle East Report (MERIP), Washington, D.C. He has served as a visiting professor at the University of Michigan, Ann Arbor, and Durham University, England.

EDITORS' NOTE: The Palestinian uprising called the *intifada* erupted in December of 1987 on the West Bank and in the Gaza Strip after more than twenty years of Israeli military occupation. From within the Palestinian community a new force for self-determination emerged. The intifada not only refocused attention on the unresolved question of Palestine, it also sparked discussions about the issues and obstacles to gaining actual statehood. At the nineteenth session of the Palestine National Council (PNC), held in Algiers on November 15, 1988, a proclamation on the independent state of Palestine was issued. The intifada had reinvigorated Palestinian discussions of statehood, and now the leadership was struggling to bring together Palestinians living in the Israeli-occupied territories and those from the diaspora under a common goal of creating "Palestine." Since that proclamation was issued, the Middle East has undergone dramatic changes that will have a significant effect on Palestinian self-determination. The following article by Salim Tamari attempts to identify some of the as yet undiscussed problems that an independent Palestinian state would face.

Futurist Debates on Palestinian Statehood

The actual unfolding of events in the Middle East has not dealt kindly with futurist conceptions of Palestine. In the early 1970s, the debate centered around the economic viability of this small, landlocked entity. It later became clear that true viability had little to do with economic issues. In the 1980s, with the intensification of Jewish settlements and land confiscation, the controversy shifted to matters of demography, creating the impression on both sides that the future of the Arab-Israeli conflict would be resolved in the arena of population growth. Although the debate on demography is still alive and has become more pointed because of a massive influx of Soviet Jewish immigrants, the focus of the discussion has shifted once again over the course of the three years of the intifada. Futurist scenarios have restored the significance of the discourse from the 1970s on the nature and role of the embryonic institutions of a future Palestinian state. It is noteworthy that most participants in the debate, whether Israeli or Palestinian, assume that sovereignty—the creation of an independent Palestinian state—is an inevitable outcome of the conflict.

There is a substantive difference between the discourses of the two periods mentioned previously. Whereas early debate focused on Palestinian national institutions in the West Bank and Gaza (syndicates, universities, municipal councils, trade unions, etc.) as future *organs of power*, today, the debate stresses *process and form*. In the period following the October war of 1973, Palestinian statehood was seen as imminent and the role of the national institutions in the "transitional period" was viewed as one of preparing for the seizure of power. Following the Camp David accords, the rise of the Likud to power in Israel, and the invasion of Lebanon, this perspective was questioned and instead yielded to a more sobering reassessment of what the Palestinians could and could not accomplish. The intifada revived this debate, but it took place within a radically transformed climate. The emergence of mass organizations in public service sectors, including agriculture, health, and education, and the creation of popular committees of mobilization, challenged many of the earlier forms of Palestinian representation. They also challenged all traditional authority and created a rift—though not always acknowledged—between an implicit national consensus that established the limits of "legitimate" struggle against occupation, and new social forms of rebellion that transcended this consensus.

The Two Formations: Political and Social

The most serious subject for consideration is the manner in which the present Palestinian social formations in the West Bank and Gaza Strip are likely to incorporate, and in turn be integrated within, a third social constellation: the diaspora community and the political-bureaucratic apparatus of the Palestine Liberation Organization (PLO). Other social issues, for example, demographic imbalance, the generation gap engendered by the intifada, and the inherent class conflict of prospective beneficiaries of Palestinian statehood (those living in the occupied territories versus those dispossessed Palestinians living elsewhere) are also part of this discussion.

The so-called Palestinian "national leadership" in the occupied territories is actually a regional leadership having delineated social bases of

various strengths in each district, with a relatively weak national representation. These leaders are joined by a national network that is both party-
based and interparty (such as the United Leadership of the Uprising). Thus,
prominent leaders like Shak'a, the late Rashad Shawwa, Faisal Husseini,
Elias Freij, Shaher Sa'd, etc., are leaders within a distinctly Nabulsi, Gaz-
zan, Jerusalemite, Bethlemite, etc., political context. Although most of the
above-mentioned have national prominence and on several occasions have
spoken for the movement as a whole, their ability to mobilize people outside their region is extremely limited, as has been demonstrated on more
than one occasion during the intifada. This limitation is less a function of
their political ability than of the social formations in which they operate.
Palestine today is politically integrated by its partisan/factional network
but socially fragmented by local elites and socioeconomic structures.

The Integrating Function of the Factional Network

Much has been written about the divisive character of the factional
leadership within the occupied territories. Often forgotten is that in the
absence of a state apparatus and a national market, this same factional/
partisan network has been crucial in generating a coherent network for
integrating Palestinian communities in the West Bank and Gaza Strip at
the institutional/political level. The organizational antecedents of this
integration existed in the form of professional syndicates, trade unions,
and chambers of commerce that reflected class-based interests. However,
neither the West Bank nor Gaza Strip has a national elite (certainly, no
national hegemonic class exists that is equivalent to the urban landed notables of the 1930s and 1940s). Thus, the emergent clandestine movement
was able to function as a kind of surrogate "ruling class."

By the end of the 1970s, most corporate organizations, such as unions
and syndicates, were themselves heavily dominated by factional politics.
The 1980s saw the extension of factional politics into civil society through
the establishment of mass community organizations and popular committees. Only traditional women's organizations, charitable societies, and the
religious establishment remained somewhat outside this factional sphere.

The Internal Forces and the External Leadership

The links between this internal factional network and the external national movement are camouflaged by the rhetoric of national unity, but that
does not make those relationships any less significant. For purposes of this
analysis, I will argue that the PLO (the external leadership) is made up of
its constituent factional components (and other nonfactional corporate
bodies) and an institutionalized bureaucracy. Of the two components, the

bureaucratic/institutional component was largely developed (some would say overdeveloped) in the diaspora, whereas it was almost nonexistent in the occupied territories. The links between the internal and external leadership, therefore, were coordinated through various factional groupings and their organizational extensions in the PLO's external body. Since the mid-1970s, a program has existed which sees a minimum consensual basis of linkage with the parent body as essential.

The emergence of the United Leadership of the Uprising, a popular-based underground group, during the intifada was of qualitative importance in the coordination of these bodies, particularly because it expanded that consensual program in both political and institutional terms. But the character of the relationship between internal and external forces remained essentially the same—a relationship still ultimately articulated through factional bodies, and not through the bureaucracy of the PLO. Needless to say, Fatah, the largest of these organizations, constitutes the linchpin of this connection. Despite its size, it continues to be challenged when its political directives conflict with those of the other factions.

What has changed this dynamic is the enhanced political weight of the internal forces during the intifada. Now the internal forces collectively exercise a decisive role in the political initiatives and directions of the movement as a whole. During the first two years of the intifada, the internal forces succeeded, both as parties and as an amorphous movement, in creating a directive that imposed itself morally and organizationally on the PLO leadership in Tunis. The crowning demonstration of this new development was the political resolutions of the Algiers PNC (November 1988), in which the historic adoption of a territorial solution would have been inconceivable without the intervention of internal forces.

Even more decisive in long-term effects have been the organizational achievements of the uprising in redefining the contours of the relationship between internal and external forces. These achievements rest, in large part, on new patterns of social relationships that have affected virtually every sector of Palestinian society. Although many of the early gains that led to the creation of popular organizational networks have begun to recede in the third year of the intifada, the collective memory of those who experienced the fateful confrontations of 1988 and 1989 are bound to affect the relationship between internal and external forces.

The Two Palestinian Communities

This brings us to the initial problem of how to mend the historic rupture between the Palestinians residing in the West Bank and Gaza Strip and those in the diaspora community. This will be a crucial issue in a future state formation. The answer to this question depends on several variables:

Demographics: Who and how many members of the diaspora community will actually relocate in a Palestinian state? Their fate is largely a function of the absorptive economic capacities of that state. Even dispossessed people are unlikely to leave their unstable environments for an unknown situation based on national and sentimental attachment to the "land of their fathers." The scenario is likely to be one where the refugee populations of Lebanon and Syria will relocate in Palestine, while those in Jordan will be divided by class lines, with the middle classes remaining integrated in the Transjordanian society. It is too early to even speculate on the fate of Gulf Palestinians in the aftermath of the Iraqi occupation of Kuwait. Here we must distinguish between those who hold current West Bank/Gaza residencies (who will be able to re-establish themselves in the interim periods) and those who might emigrate to the United States or Europe after the state is established. Ultimately, the answer to this question depends on the access of the state to resources, including capital and control over land and water, and on the form of a settlement.

Form of a Settlement: What relationships will the future state have with Israel and Jordan? The fate of commuting workers, who still constitute about 40 percent of the total labor force in the West Bank and Gaza Strip, is of central importance to relationships with Israel. With Jordan, the situation depends upon the future market outlet and free movement of goods and people to the Arab world. Although cutting the links of economic dependency with the state of Israel will create the need (and incentives) for long-term planning and investments in the Palestinian manufacturing sector, the short-term scenario is likely to lead to severe unemployment, a condition that will certainly affect the influx of potential expatriates and refugees.

Gaza and the West Bank: In most of the existing literature, the future of the Gaza Strip is either subsumed under that of the West Bank or else altogether ignored (one often hears, for example, about the "future West Bank State"). This is both inaccurate and dangerous. In many respects, the social structure and topography of the West Bank is more similar to that of the Galilee than it is to Gaza; the dominance of highland peasant small holdings, population and settlement dispersal, and the marginal impact of refugee population are features of West Bank society that contrast sharply with those of the Gaza Strip. These differences will have a profound impact on the nature of future political settlement. Aside from the problem of logistic links between the two regions, integrating such disparate entities into a future state will be a challenge.

Ideological Character: Questions of the ideological content of the Palestinian state will need to be addressed. What is the broad political character of the state (secular/fundamentalist)? What socioeconomic orientation will it adopt (social-democratic/state capitalist/free enterprise)? What range of political/social freedoms does it offer its citizens? Although these questions are more pressing from the perspective of the professional middle classes, businessmen, and the intelligentsia, they nevertheless play an important role in determining the future of the state. Some examples include: the amount of private capital that will be reinvested in the public and private sector, and the nature of Palestinian diaspora intellectuals who will decide to relocate their bases from the capitals of the Middle East and Europe. (One should keep in mind that the size of these social segments among the Palestinians is large relative to equivalent groups in the Arab world.) Finally, the degree of control by fundamentalist Muslims over issues of sexual segregation in school and work will determine how attractive the state will be for future returnees.

I have posed four variables that are likely to determine the future character of the state of Palestine: demographic considerations (the volume and social composition of the returnees), the nature of links with Jordan and Israel, the nature of internal links between the Gaza Strip and the West Bank, and the ideological orientation of the hegemonic elite, including its satellite middle and professional classes. Obviously, the mix of these variables will itself determine and be determined by the manner in which the bureaucratic-administrative apparatus of the PLO addresses these questions.

Given the complex relationship between the diasporan hierarchy and the resident community in Palestine, one of the greatest challenges facing the national movement will be the actual transfer of power. In other words, how can these groups create a stable polity of Palestine from the two parallel power structures without provoking a civil conflict of the Algerian post-independence type.

The potential strains that might lead to the development of civil conflicts are likely to be:

1. The attempt by the PLO's external bureaucracy to impose itself as the exclusive state apparatus of the nation, without taking into account the fabric of local community or institutional structures developed under more than two decades of Israeli occupation. This seems an unlikely scenario because such an external bureaucracy, even if backed by an armed force, would face formidable opposition from a highly developed civil society, steeled in years of rebellion. This outcome would prove expensive, inefficient, and highly dangerous.

2. The attempt by the dominant faction in the nationalist movement to impose its will within the state apparatus on minority factions,

thus effectively ending the existing pluralistic model of the PNC. This prospect is possible, but unlikely, given the considerable strength of leftist factions and Islamic currents within the occupied territories (compared with their respective weight in Tunis, Syria, and Lebanon). What is likely to happen is that Fatah will try to co-opt some leftist factions within the executive, at the same time containing the opposition within the parliamentary council. In this case, the task of the left would be to ensure maximum constitutional guarantees for the individual and collective liberties for opposition forces. In this context, it will find common cause with Islamic forces.

At stake also is the fate of community service associations, which evolved at the behest of mass organizations in the 1980s and as forms of resistance during the intifada, but would evolve into organs of national power. Today these associations, in the fields of health, agriculture, and social welfare, and as community organizations, are seen as future embryonic state organs. Whether these associations will survive the process of state formation will depend in large part on their institutional stability and extended network, their actual professional performance, and on their factional affiliations. It will no doubt be tempting for the future power elite to replace these "archaic" institutions with "modern" state agencies. But the price of replacing them with so-called "modern" organizations will inflict a heavy blow. Internal democracy could be sacrificed and the danger incurred of straining the relationship between the diasporan community and the civil society that bore the brunt of Israeli occupation. The seeds of new strife could thus be sown.

PART IV. FUTURE POSSIBILITIES

ROBERT VITALIS

The Palestinian-Israeli Conflict: Options and Scenarios for Peace

Robert Vitalis began studying the Middle East in 1976, during a junior year abroad program in Alexandria, Egypt, and Haifa, Israel (thanks to the State University of New York at Binghampton). He returned to the region in 1980–1982 and 1984–1985 as a graduate student in political science at the Massachusetts Institute of Technology (Ph.D., 1988). He is presently an assistant professor of government and international relations at Clark University, where he is completing a book on business and politics in Egypt and beginning a study of the U.S. role in the building of Saudi Arabia.

THE PALESTINIAN-ISRAELI CONFLICT is not something mysterious, rooted in antiquity, or in some other way impossible for ordinary people—non-"experts"—to understand. The conflict is most basically about territory: two *peoples* collectively claim the same land as their *national* home. The European-based Zionist movement began a campaign of colonial settlement at the turn of the twentieth century to create a nation-state for the Jewish people in what they now call Israel. The Palestinian national movement arose in resistance to the Zionist settlement campaign and, especially, to the massive displacement of the indigenous people resulting from the 1948 war for Israeli independence. In other words, the Palestinian people claim the right of return to their land and homes, and the right of national self-determination in what they call Palestine.

Although it is easy to define, the conflict has proved hard to resolve. From the 1930s until today, every attempt to negotiate a solution has failed to meet the minimal, acceptable conditions of one or both of the two peoples or their representatives. In 1947, Palestinian leaders rejected the United Nations partition plan, arguing that, as the indigenous majority, the Arabs of Palestine had the right to self-determination in an undivided territory.[1] Once they gained control of the entire disputed territory, many Israelis adopted a similar view. Thus, in 1991, Prime Minister Yitzhak Shamir of Israel once again refused the Palestine Liberation Organization's (PLO) offer to settle the conflict, opposed to the idea of ceding Israeli control over any part of *Eretz Yisrael* (Greater Israel).

At the same time, the seventy-five year legacy of violence makes clear that the two sides have been no more successful in using force to impose a solution. There is a tragic symmetry here: in this case, to the illusions harbored at different times by members of the Palestinian and Israeli communities. For many years, the "resistance groups" led by Yasir Arafat's Fatah organization have believed that only armed struggle could achieve liberation (the destruction of the Israeli state), while Israeli governments explicitly have rejected the idea of Palestinian national rights and have used violence to suppress it.

It is in the wake of these catastrophic encounters that we find signs of the slow, uneven and, yet, unmistakable changes taking place in Palestinian and Israeli political positions, which are expressed so powerfully by the Palestinians and Israelis profiled in the film, *The Struggle for Peace*. In essence, various groups in the two communities have come to recognize that the Palestinian and Israeli people both enjoy the same collective rights and, in particular, the right to national self-determination.[2]

There is a marked asymmetry, however. Until now, the official Israeli political leadership has not matched the Palestinian National Council's (PNC) and Chairman Arafat's call for peaceful coexistence between an Israeli state and a Palestinian state—nor is it likely to do so in the near future. Yet, some Israeli political organizations have recognized the Palestinians' right to self-determination; individual intellectuals, politicians, and political activists prominent within the peace movement have called for creation of an independent Palestinian state, and the issue is now part of the contemporary political debate inside Israel.[3]

In this chapter, I examine the idea of a "two-state" solution in relation to the major existing alternative frameworks for resolving the Israeli-Palestinian conflict. Other chapters in this book focus on various aspects of the negotiating process and assess the formidable political, social, and psychological obstacles to ending the conflict. My focus, in contrast, is the broad *principles and preferences* that inform the *contending perspectives on peace*.

Virtually all major Palestinian and Israeli political factions have put forward terms for settling the conflict. I distinguish among these alternatives by examining how, if at all, they accommodate the rival national-territorial (sovereignty) claims. Historically, the two national movements adopted what might be called *exclusivist* positions. Neither the Israelis nor the Palestinians recognized the other's national claims as legitimate. More recently, in the 1970s and 1980s, in both societies there began to emerge accommodationist alternatives that propose to compromise on "historic rights" in return for security and peaceful coexistence.

Professor Herbert Kelman, the Harvard University psychologist who specializes in the problem of conflict resolution, traces the emergence of these new, pro-compromise currents to the 1967 Arab-Israeli war (the Six-

Day War) and what he calls the gradual "Palestinianization" of the conflict. The war strengthened the Palestinian national movement and, as a result of the Israeli occupation of the West Bank and the Gaza Strip, the conflict is "increasingly [being] transformed from an interstate conflict between Israel and its neighboring states to an intercommunal conflict within the post-1967 borders of Israel."[4] Thus, in this chapter, I limit the discussion to what Kelman and I agree is now the most salient dimension of the conflict, namely, the rival national-territorial claims of the two peoples.

I make no judgment here as to which, if any, of the two national movements has the more compelling or just claim to the "historic homeland." It is assumed, however, that *both* Palestinian and Israeli people have equal and unalienable rights, including the national right to self-determination. Although four different proposed solutions to the conflict are discussed, only the so-called two-state solution accommodates the currently existing majority preferences of both Israelis and Palestinians for exercising their national rights in the form of an independent state within the boundaries of the historic homeland.

As will be seen, other solutions either deny national rights to one side or the other, or else constrain the exercise of these rights in some way. For instance, the Islamic resistance organization in the occupied territories, Hamas, rejects Israeli national claims outright. The right-wing Israeli political parties, Tzomet (Crossroads), Moledet (Homeland), and Tehiya (Renaissance), argue that Palestinians should seek to exercise their national rights, if at all, in Jordan rather than in the occupied territories. And, here in the United States, the Bush administration insists that Palestinian national rights cannot be exercised in the form of an independent state.[5]

The objective of this chapter is to provide a context for understanding the full range of Palestinian and Israeli views on the conflict. Unlike most discussions of the "peace process" here in the United States, I avoid the tendency to see the universe in terms of those who want peace versus the "rejectionists." Because the many Palestinian and Israeli factions have defined and, in many cases, redefined their preferred settlement terms over the years, such blanket judgments as "the Israelis don't really want peace" or "the Palestinians refuse to compromise" make no sense. Rather, various Israeli and Palestinian parties differ significantly on the kind of peace that they seek.

The Clash Between Zionism and Palestinianism

Nationalism is, of course, the key force underlying the conflict between Israeli-Jews and Palestinian-Arabs. The state of Israel was founded in 1948 by European Jewish colonists who had migrated to Palestine with the goal of setting up an autonomous Jewish nation-state. The indigenous Arab majority population opposed the settlers' state-building project. The local population viewed Zionist claims to Palestine as a threat to their land, their identities, and their own evolving national ambitions for an independent Arab Palestine.

Between 1920 and 1948, the Arab population of Palestine developed an increasingly distinct Palestinian identity, which was reinforced in exile after 1948. Palestinian national claims have been expressed and advanced in one of two ways. After 1948, most Palestinians believed that their problem would be resolved through the concerted action of the established Arab states. In this sense a "pan-Arabism" perspective dominated Palestinian political thought in the 1950s and 1960s.

The hope that Gamal Abdel-Nasser of Egypt and other Arab nationalist regimes would liberate Palestine was destroyed in the 1967 war. In its aftermath, an alternative nationalist current, which might be thought of as Palestinianism, grew increasingly powerful in Palestinian political thought. Palestinianism embodies a sense of the need for independent Palestinian action and decision making, as well as a renewed focus on attaining national sovereignty within the historic boundaries of Palestine, as the paramount objectives of the national movement.

The rise of armed resistance organizations such as Fatah to leadership positions inside the national movement, symbolized by Yasir Arafat's election as chairman of the PLO in 1969, gave a powerful boost to the Palestinianism current. Of course, the PLO militants continued to reject all Israeli sovereignty claims, which they viewed as an illegal occupation of their homeland, and yet they recognized that the Israelis were unlikely to dismantle the Jewish state of their own volition. Hence, in the 1960s, the leadership of the PLO argued that Palestinians would have to resort to armed struggle in order to "liberate" Palestine.[6] Starting in the mid-1970s, however, key factions within the PLO moved toward accepting a negotiated, compromise settlement of the conflict, a course that led to the 1988 Palestinian declaration of independence and recognition of Israel.[7]

Like the Palestinians, at a crucial point in their history the leaders of the Zionist movement publicly and unambiguously claimed exclusive sovereignty rights in the territory of the Palestine mandate. Thus, in the May 1942 Biltmore Declaration, the future prime minister of Israel, David Ben-Gurion, and other militant Zionists demanded that all of Palestine be declared a Jewish state. Five years later, in 1947, Ben-Gurion and the majority of the Zionist leadership publicly compromised these ambitions and endorsed the UN proposal calling for the division of Palestine into two states. Some Zionists, like Menachem Begin, another future prime minister of Israel, denounced the partition plan as "illegal" and continued to claim that all of Palestine belonged exclusively to the Jewish people. The

Zionists ultimately used the UN plan to declare the creation of an independent Israeli state on May 14, 1948. In the immediate wake of independence, all the major Israeli political groupings and personalities, Ben-Gurion included, reaffirmed the historic right to all of Palestine.[8]

For most parts of the Israeli political spectrum, however, in the intervening years the concern with consolidating the new state and defending its existing borders took precedence. Only a few fringe groups openly called for the conquest of the rest of the disputed territory. The historic national-territorial claims only became salient once more following the Six-Day War in June 1967, when Israel occupied additional Palestinian majority-inhabited territories, including East Jerusalem, the West Bank (both under Jordanian control between 1949–1967) and the Gaza Strip (under Egyptian control from 1949–1967). As a result, the present Israeli political leadership now governs the entire area of the original Palestine mandate.

Since 1967, virtually all discussion of a peaceful resolution of Israel's conflicts with the surrounding Arab states, on the one hand, and the Palestinian national movement, on the other, has come to center around the territories captured in the 1967 war. The most powerful party in Israel today, the Likud, was formed in 1973 by groups who were intent on holding on to the captured territories, which they viewed as historically part of Greater Israel. The party's current leader, Israeli Prime Minister Yitzhak Shamir, along with many of his close allies, like Defense Minister Moshe Arens, opposed the 1979 peace treaty between Israel and Egypt, which returned the Sinai Peninsula to Egypt. The Likud governs Israel today in alliance with a bloc of religious and ultra-nationalist parties whose common denominator is opposition to the return of any additional territory.[9] Nonetheless, only a minority of Israelis justify keeping the occupied territories on religious or nationalist grounds.

The views of most Israeli citizens on the question of territorial compromise—"trading land for peace"—are shaped by concerns for the country's security, rather than a commitment to the ultra-nationalism of Likud's leaders and their right-wing allies. Even those who support the return of the occupied territories generally frame the issue in terms of what is in the country's long-term security interests. Thus, the leadership of the Labor Party, which governed the country between 1949–1977 and currently represents the main opposition to the Likud within the Israeli parliament, has proposed withdrawal from some area of the occupied territories as part of a general conflict settlement. Smaller parties to the left of Labor have gone further, by supporting national self-determination for Palestinians in the occupied territories.[10] (See Table 2, Alternative Solutions to the Israeli-Palestinian Conflict, later in this essay.)

For the Palestinians, the occupation of the West Bank and Gaza Strip likewise transformed the terms of debate inside the national movement. Ironically, it has made it possible to envision a political compromise with the Israelis that would permit Palestinians to exercise direct sovereignty over at least part of the historic homeland. The PLO's diplomatic initiatives in the 1980s have all been based on the proposal to create an independent Palestinian state in the Israeli-occupied West Bank and Gaza Strip, reflecting what Professor Kelman describes as Palestinians' "evolving perception of their national interest."[11]

Portions of the Palestinian political spectrum remain opposed to the idea of an independent West Bank/Gaza state on ideological grounds. Similar to the debates that took place among Zionists in the 1940s (and that continue today), some Palestinians see no reason to concede or to compromise their historic right to the entire territory, particularly when the majority of Palestinians trace their local origins to towns and villages that would have to remain under Israeli control. Other viewpoints echo the security concerns voiced by many Israeli leaders and citizens. That is, some Palestinians are reluctant to back these compromise proposals because of the fear that the project will fail, given what they see as the enemy's preponderant power in its unremitting war against the Palestinian national community.[12] Nonetheless, proponents of a two-state solution now represent the dominant current within the Palestinian national movement, and one that has obtained broad backing in the international arena.[13]

Contending Perspectives on Peace

This diversity of perspectives found inside *both* Palestinian and Israeli national communities has translated over the years into what I see as four distinct "scenarios for peace." I employ this phrase quite specifically to mean that some Palestinian or Israeli faction(s)—the PLO or its constituent parts; Israeli political parties, party factions, organizations like Yesh G'vul (There Is a Limit) and Gush Emunim (Bloc of the Faithful), or broader and looser groupings like The Peace Movement—envision one of the particular scenarios as a reasonable solution. Of course, it is precisely the wide gulf between what groups consider "reasonable" that remains a primary obstacle to negotiations.

I categorize these four scenarios along a continuum described by the terms *exclusivist* and *accommodationist,* which is based on the chapter's introductory definition of the Palestinian-Israeli conflict. I said that the conflict stems from the competing claims of the two peoples, in particular, their claim to the exclusive right of national self-determination (sovereignty rights) in the same territory. Yet, as my analysis underscores, Palestinians and Israelis have historically rejected and tried to de-legitimize the other's national-territorial claims, for instance, by challenging the "authenticity" of, and refusing to recognize, the other's national identity or existence.[14] Certain peace scenarios rest on this exclusivist conception of national rights and nationhood in Israel/Palestine. They typically advocate indivisible sovereignty (one state) over the entire territory. Other peace scenarios, by contrast, entail the re-division of the country and, *to different degrees*, recognition of the national rights of both Palestinians and Israelis.

EXCLUSIVIST SCENARIOS: THE "SINGLE-STATE" SOLUTION

The Zionists' ambitious vision for the future Israeli state was, of course, never meant to include or accommodate the large, indigenous Palestinian majority, which still comprised roughly two-thirds of the population on the eve of Israeli independence. With the exception of the ideologues in the left-Labor *kibbutz* movement, Hashomer Hatzair (Young Guard), who opposed the creation of an exclusively Jewish-national state, the Jews who settled in Palestine implausibly imagined that the non-Jewish Palestinian majority would eventually sell their land and homes, uproot their families, and move elsewhere. Until today, few Zionists have been able to recognize, much less come to terms with, the heavy toll that the effort to create and maintain a Jewish state in Palestine has exacted on the country's indigenous Arab population. That is not, however, atypical: nationalist movements are usually focused on their own people's problems and aspirations and only rarely take into account the injustices they may be doing to others.

In the 1950s and 1960s the leadership of the Palestinian national movement articulated an equally exclusivist project for the liberation of the homeland, and, like the Zionists before them, they evinced a predictable lack of concern, at least at first, for the fate of the new majority population of Israeli citizens. Until the late 1960s, most Palestinian leaders wanted to turn the clock back to before 1917 and create an Arab state in Palestine. However, the thinking of core parts of the movement changed over the course of the 1960s and 1970s, beginning with an attempt to define a plausible solution to the "problem" of the by-then millions of Jewish inhabitants who "occupied" Palestine. The PLO eventually endorsed the idea of a "democratic state" of Palestine, or a state of all those living in the disputed territories, which would be neither explicitly Arab nor explicitly Jewish but nonsectarian and democratic.[15]

Palestinians generally see the idea of a unitary, democratic state as the first of a series of historic compromises with Jewish nationalist claims, which led in turn to contacts with "progressive" groups inside Israel, to proposals in the mid-1970s for establishing an independent Palestinian state on any "part" of "liberated" Palestine, and ultimately to the two-state solution explicitly adopted in the 1980s. According to journalists Alain

Gresh and Helena Cobban, each of these positions came to be accepted in turn by a majority of Palestinians, against minorities who argued that such compromises were either tactically ill-advised or wrong in principle.[16]

At the present time, there are few, if any, influential voices within the Palestinian national movement adhering to the "classic," exclusivist PLO position, which sought to reverse the 1947–1948 partition through the use of armed force. Only the newly formed Islamic Resistance Movement, Hamas, whose leadership openly challenges the compromise course charted by the PLO in the past decades, attempts to mobilize support around a scenario of "total liberation" of "Islamic-Palestine."[17] On the other hand, minority voices within the left wing of the national movement continue to put forward the "democratic state" scenario as an alternative "ideal" to the majority-backed, two-state solution.

I argue that the democratic state scenario is exclusivist in that it rejects the Jewish people's preference for the exercise of national self-determination, although it envisions power-sharing among the citizens that in effect accords equal rights to the two communities. I contrast this with the exclusivist position of the current government of Israel. In the Greater Israel scenario favored by Prime Minister Shamir and his ideological allies, refusal to recognize the Palestinians as a national community is coupled with a commitment to uphold undivided Israeli sovereignty over the entire historic homeland. In this sense, current Israeli policy is a mirror image of the project that Palestinian guerrillas originally pursued in the 1950s and 1960s and that the Islamic Hamas movement follows today.

Greater Israel

The premises of the Greater Israel scenario are straightforward. Its proponents maintain that the Jewish nation alone has a legitimate claim to exercise sovereignty over the entire ex–British Mandate of Palestine (still defined by some ideologues to include Jordan). This project was advanced by the conquest in 1967 of Jerusalem, the West Bank ("Judea and Samaria"), and the Gaza Strip. Thus, Israeli Prime Minister Shamir has repeatedly insisted that his government will not "trade land for peace" in contravention of the Jewish people's "natural" and historic rights. Needless to say, Palestinian claims to nationhood and sovereignty rights over any part of the homeland are rejected outright.

The opposition of over 1.7 million Palestinians currently living in the occupied territories represents a dilemma for the Israeli political leadership and the major obstacle to those who seek to fulfill the Greater Israel scenario. Thus, until now, authorities have resisted pressures to formalize Israeli rule by annexing these territories, even while supporting a policy of Jewish settlements there. As of 1991, over two hundred thousand Jews have settled in East Jerusalem, the West Bank, and the Gaza Strip. Israelis have seized control of more than 50 percent of the land. The hardships of life under occupation led to the *intifada* (literally, the "shaking off"), or the Palestinian revolt against Israeli rule, and to renewed calls for an end to occupation. The irreconcilable opposition between the vision of an independent Palestinian state and the vision of Greater Israel explains the Shamir government's refusal to negotiate with the PLO. According to *The New York Times,* "that organization embodies the Palestinians' claim to an independent state and by simply talking with it, Israel would be legitimizing that claim."[18]

Committed to holding on to the territories at all costs, advocates of a Greater Israel scenario instead have proposed two different solutions to what they see as the "problem" of the Palestinian "non-Jewish" population in the territories. The first, favored by Prime Minister Shamir, is to negotiate some type of local *autonomy* accord with them. The idea is to offer Palestinians limited self-rule while ensuring Israeli control over the land and its resources.

Other proponents of the Greater Israel scenario, including the leadership of the small, ultra-nationalist Tehiya and Moledet parties, oppose the autonomy plan and negotiations with Palestinians, which they see as a step that will lead ultimately to the loss of the territories. Instead, the Moledet leader, Rahavam Zeevi, has called repeatedly for "transfer" (a euphemism for expulsion) of the Palestinians, as reported regularly in the Israeli press. For instance, in a March 1991 radio broadcast, Zeevi proposed that Palestinians "return to the countries of their forefathers," because those who remain can only be "residents, not citizens" inside Greater Israel.[19]

The Bi-National State and the Democratic State

The previous vision of inequality, dispossession, and expulsion stands in stark contrast to the vision of *coexistence* within a state where Jews and Palestinians would share equal sovereignty rights as citizens. In the 1940s, the left-wing Zionist party, Hashomer Hatzair, sought unsuccessfully to win over the Jewish community in Palestine to its idea of a "bi-national state." The party, which was one of the only Zionist groups to recognize Palestinian-Arab national rights, opposed the idea of a Jewish state where only Jews would be permitted to exercise self-determination. However, following Israeli independence in 1948, its members abandoned the dream of bi-nationalism.[20]

In 1971, the Palestinian National Council voted to accept Fatah's formula for a "democratic state in the whole of Palestine" as a basis for resolving the conflict, a proposal that shared key points with the left-Zionist bi-nationalism scenario. In particular, its proponents insisted that the democratic state provided a formula for peaceful coexistence between Jews and Palestinians. A crucial difference, however, was in the Palestinians' use of the formula generally to deny rather than affirm Zionism and the Jewish people's legitimate national rights, as Israeli and other critics pointedly noted.[21] Certainly, the Jewish people's autonomous preferences were not given consideration by this formula, particularly because the PLO assumed that such a state could only emerge through armed conflict.

At the present time, there is little, if any, organized support in the Palestinian or the Jewish community for the sharing of sovereignty within a unitary state, whether in the bi-national framework or the democratic and nonsectarian framework.[22] For most Palestinians, the democratic state formula is invoked today more as a symbol of the laudatory ideals or principles behind their peoples' drive for statehood than as a blueprint for a reasonable settlement of the conflict. Yet in the late 1960s, when Fatah's members began to debate the democratic state scenario, many Palestinians condemned the proposal as heretical because it called for coexistence in a state where Palestinians would be a minority.[23]

The proposal for the creation of a democratic state was an important turning point in the political perspective of the Palestinian national movement. It legitimized the idea of independent Palestinian sovereignty over the homeland (the pan-Arab current opposed this step) and forced the movement reluctantly to come to grips with the reality of Israeli nationalism. As a result, the movement eventually came to endorse the alternative and more unambiguously accommodationist proposal of two separate and independent states within the boundaries of the historic Palestinian homeland.

ACCOMMODATIONIST SCENARIOS

It is impossible to overstate the impact of the 1967 war on the Middle East generally and on the Palestinian-Israel conflict in particular. Israel's overwhelming victory in the war and its conquest of additional territories, including the remainder of historic Palestine, fundamentally altered the situation for all parties.

Almost immediately following the war, the United Nations launched a new attempt to settle the conflict, based on the terms of UN Security Council Resolution 242, passed in November, five months after the war. The document still serves today as the basis of a broad international consensus on the requirements for a comprehensive and just settlement, based on (1) "[w]ithdrawal of Israeli armed forces from territories occupied in the recent conflict" in return for (2) recognition of the "sovereignty . . . of every state in the area and their right to live in peace within secure and recognized boundaries."

For Israelis, the war thus opened a still unresolved debate about the wisdom of trading land for peace. As we have seen, supporters of the exclusivist, Greater Israel scenario form one side in this debate, based on their opposition to withdrawal from the occupied territories. Other Israeli political parties and factions, however, accept the principle of territorial compromise. According to 1991 opinion poll data, the population of Israel as a whole splits fairly evenly on the issue, with a slight majority "supporting the formula of territories for peace."[24] Within this accommodationist current, acute differences arise over the terms and conditions of such a compromise and, in particular, over the question of supporting Palestinian sovereignty claims. For most Israelis, the land for peace formula remains firmly coupled with rejection of an independent Palestinian state.

In the case of the Palestinians, the upheaval of the 1967 war catalyzed the shift in outlook that I called "Palestinianism" and this is evidenced in the intense and rapidly evolving debate over the conditions of an acceptable settlement scenario. Fatah first introduced the democratic state formula in 1968 as an alternative to UN Resolution 242 and other "political" solutions that did not explicitly recognize Palestinian national rights. At the same time, as the debates revealed, the Palestinians were sharply divided. Many advocated a unified Arab solution, including return of the West Bank to Jordanian sovereignty, whereas some West Bank residents appealed for a final settlement with the Israelis in return for an independent "mini" state.

By the mid-1970s, the international community had come to recognize the need to satisfy Palestinian national rights as part of any comprehensive and just settlement.[25] In turn, the PLO leadership moved closer to the prevailing consensus. In 1974, the PLO first accepted the idea of an independent state in the occupied territories, albeit through a tortuous formulation: "the people's national, independent and fighting sovereignty on every part of Palestinian land to be liberated."[26] While the "revolutionary" leadership attempted to cloak this change of position in militant rhetoric, the opposition current within the PLO (the "Rejection Front") attacked these measures as evidence that Arafat and his supporters had abandoned the cause of liberation.

Of course, the Israeli leadership rejects the Palestinians' project for a state in the occupied territories and thus has sought consistently to block any attempt by the PLO to participate in peace talks.[27] This unyielding opposition poses a basic dilemma for the pro-compromise factions inside the PLO because it appears to confirm the views of the hard-liners, who have argued since the mid-1970s that diplomatic efforts are doomed to failure. It is not hard to understand the so-called "studied ambiguities" and "prevarications" in PLO positions in the 1970s and 1980s, or the ambivalence of the leadership as it pressed in 1988 for acceptance of the two-

state scenario. For most Palestinians now scattered around the world, recognition of the legitimacy of the original 1947 partition means giving up
the dream of returning home.

Land for Peace

"Land for peace" has in essence served as the basis for the international consensus on settling the Arab-Israeli conflict since the first round
of fighting in 1947–1949. The cease-fire and armistice agreement that
ended Israel's successful "war for independence" left three basic issues unresolved: (a) Israel's borders (As a result of the war, Israelis controlled two
thousand square miles of territory beyond the boundaries established in
the UN partition plan); (b) The issue of Jerusalem (Israel annexed the
section of Jerusalem under its de facto control [West Jerusalem] and declared the city its capital, which the United States still does not recognize);
and (c) The "right of return" of the approximately 700,000 Palestinians
who fled or were expelled from Israeli-controlled territories. (The "scenario" officially promoted by most member nations of the United Nations
envisioned Israeli accommodation on these territorial questions in return
for recognition and peace treaties with the Arab states.)

Israeli leaders and political factions generally reject this territorial
compromise scenario for its failure to understand and accommodate the
nation's security needs. Professor Don Peretz explains the opposition in the
following terms. Israelis traditionally view "recognition" or "acceptance
of the Jewish state" above all else as "the key to peace." The Arab states'
recognition of Israel is believed to hinge on Israeli strength or power,
not on territorial concessions that compromise the country's security—"a
weak Israel will never be accepted."[28] Thus, whereas Arab parties early on
insisted that a settlement depended on Israeli withdrawal to the 1947 UN
borders, Israelis insisted that peace depended on recognition first, without
preconditions.[29] The reality is that no party was ready to settle on the
terms put forward in the 1940s and 1950s.

The architects of Israel's 1948 "security" policy have little trouble in
seeing the unfolding of events as having vindicated their reluctance to
bargain on the basis of territorial concessions. Israel's power has grown
significantly more formidable, while the original terms of the dispute,
for instance, the question of Israel returning territories gained in the
1947–1949 fighting, have essentially disappeared from discussion of the
broad terms for a peaceful settlement. Israelis frequently justify the logic
of their hard-line ("pragmatic") policies in the 1950s and 1960s by claiming
that Arab hostility to them was "absolute" and "metaphysical."[30]

Israel's conquest of the Sinai Peninsula, the Golan Heights, the Gaza
Strip, the West Bank, and East Jerusalem in 1967 reopened, and at the same
time redefined, the issue of territorial compromise as the basis for a con-

flict settlement. Soon after the 1967 war, the Israeli political leadership initiated the policy of seizing land, building strategic agricultural-military settlements in the occupied territories, and gradually integrating the infrastructure—power, water, new roads linking Jewish settlement areas to Israel, etc.[31] At the same time, however, the government maintained that, although Israel would not return to the pre-June 1967 borders, it was willing to consider territorial compromise as part of an overall settlement.

The Labor Party government's espousal after 1967 of the formula of land for peace is one of the defining features of Israel's increasingly polarized political discourse. Labor presents itself as a clear-cut alternative to its rivals in Likud, who have pledged to hold on to the territories at all costs.[32] The distinctiveness of Labor's stance is blurred somewhat by its role in devising policies for the settlement and integration of the occupied territories ("creating facts") that have been followed by all post-1977 Likud and Likud-Labor coalition governments. Critics and supporters alike understand the function of the settlements as the main instrument for the de facto annexation of the territories, where over half the land is now directly controlled by Jewish settlers or by the Israeli state.[33]

The Labor Party's land for peace platform appears more inconsistent than Likud's Greater Israel platform, in part because of the sharp divisions contained within Labor and its allied factions.[34] Land for peace serves as an umbrella for those from the left wing, who have pressed for reaching an accommodation with Palestinian nationalism, and the dominant core, including those who view territorial expansion as essential to the country's security (or who see a need to draw defecting voters back from Likud). As I discuss in the following pages, this polarization within the Labor Party is moving toward formation of a small but identifiable bloc of Israelis prepared to back a two-state solution.

In Israel, the debate over the territories and, by extension, the settlement of the Palestinian-Israeli conflict is defined largely in terms of security. Both the Likud and Labor base their appeals to voters on the grounds that only their policies guarantee Israel's future, while "their rival's are a threat to the nation's security."[35] Likud, of course, can also count on the votes of those who share the belief in Israel's absolute right to the territories, out of either nationalist or religious fervor. In contrast, Labor leaders argue that these extremist views, if implemented, will ultimately threaten Israel's long-term security.

Labor's security rationale centers around the "problem" of the nearly two million Palestinians residing in the territories. Annexation of the territories does not deal realistically with the likelihood that Palestinians will refuse the offer of permanent second-class status offered under the rubric of "autonomy" or self-government. If the territories' residents are granted and willingly accept full citizenship rights, including the right to vote, then, given certain projections of demographic trends and expectations about Palestinian political preferences, the "Jewishness" of Israel will come under increasing legal-political challenge. In order to protect Zionist principles, Israel will have to extend its policy of coercive and antidemocratic control of the Palestinian population indefinitely, in what some envision as an Israeli version of apartheid. Likud's policies are seen as having already fueled dangerous antidemocratic and antienlightenment tendencies within Israeli society. In essence, the argument is that Israel's survival is ultimately threatened "from within." [36]

The ex-head of Israeli military intelligence, Major General (Res.) Yehoshafat Harkabi, employs many of the same arguments to criticize the Labor Party's land for peace scenario, which proposes to resolve these dilemmas by awarding sovereignty of the Palestinian population centers to Jordan. This maverick "realist" thinks that Palestinian nationalism makes such a solution unworkable. The "logical conclusion" of a policy of territorial withdrawal is self-determination for the inhabitants, "which will be, of course, an independent state (probably eventually confederated with Jordan)." [37] Although Harkabi believes that a viable settlement depends on negotiating with the PLO and recognizing the inevitability of Palestinian statehood, this remains a politically unacceptable compromise for most of the Labor alignment leadership.

Israeli supporters of the land for peace scenario see the key element in the compromise quite differently from other parties. The disagreement is again about boundaries. The Soviet Union, the Arab states, and many other countries interpret UN Resolution 242 (the institutional anchor of the land for peace scenario) as requiring withdrawal from all the occupied territories; the United States interprets 242 as *permitting* "minor" border rectifications. Many Israelis envision *at best* minor adjustments in the areas Israeli has already annexed or will seek to acquire for security reasons as part of the compromise.

Viewed in terms of outcomes, the difference "between Labour and Likud is more one of principle than of practice," according to British analyst David McDowall.[38] Labor is willing, practically, to share sovereignty of the territories with Jordan, while Palestinians will presumably administer their own local affairs. Likud backs a version of home rule as well, at the same time insisting that sovereignty is Israel's exclusively.

Those Israelis at present willing to countenance a more far-reaching withdrawal to the 1949 armistice lines also tend to accept the alternative, two-state scenario. In contrast, the Labor leadership is as unequivocal in its rejection of an independent Palestinian state as those who steer the current Likud-led government. Together, Labor and Likud control two-thirds of the seats in the Knesset (Israel's parliament), presenting a formi-

dable obstacle to those pursuing a settlement based on mutual and recip-
rocal recognition, security need, and national rights for Palestinians as well
as Israelis.

The Two-State Solution

As General Harkabi notes, the creation of an independent Palestinian
state is the logical outcome of Israeli withdrawal from the occupied territories. This is the exact argument that Likud's leadership uses to savage
Labor. Those to the right of Likud were opposed even to Prime Minister
Shamir's plan for holding elections in the West Bank for fear that the vote
would somehow legitimate Palestinians' sovereignty claims. Unlike other
scenarios, there is no possibility for exploring the differences in the way
Palestinians and Israelis envision the implementation of a two-state solution. The terms of this compromise still remain unthinkable to most of the
present Israeli political leadership.

The idea of a settlement based on an independent Palestinian state
side-by-side with Israel was once unthinkable to most Palestinians, to
judge from the reactions that greeted Tunisian President Habib Bourgui-
ba's plea to Palestinians and Israelis, in 1965, to return to the principle of
the 1947 partition plan. Others broached the subject immediately after the
June 1967 war, including the Egyptian journalist, Ahmad Baha al-Din; in
retrospect, the most important were the minority voices in the newly occupied territories who rejected the idea of a return to the pre-war status
quo and proposed the creation of an independent West Bank state.[39] The
Arab-nationalist majority within the Palestinian national community opposed such an outcome, while the Fatah leadership began to opt for the
alternative, democratic state scenario. Israel's government, still under the
control of the Labor Party, began to elaborate its project for a possible
accommodation with Jordan over the territories.

The emerging Palestinian intellectual and political leadership in the
territories played a leading role in articulating and backing the project for
an independent state. At the same time, they provided Arafat and his allies
within the PLO with a constituency clearly in favor of a negotiated solution. Alain Gresh makes this point particularly clearly: "Having lived under
the occupation for six years, the population had no wish to see it prolonged for the sake of a more or less mythical democratic state. The liberation of the West Bank and Gaza and the setting-up of a state in these
territories were concrete objectives that met their aspirations."[40]

This current of nationalist-"realism" eventually proved decisive in the
long and often bitter debates and political conflicts that took place in the
decade that preceded the Palestinian declaration of independence. Three
basic issues were raised repeatedly around the issue of an independent

state: Was it a viable or workable solution? Could it be implemented successfully under prevailing regional and international circumstances? And, probably most important to the Palestinians outside the territories (the diaspora), was it worth the cost of, ultimately, weakening or forgoing their historic claim/right to all of Palestine?

When the Palestinian national movement formally adopted the two-state scenario in November 1988, they echoed the debates inside the Zionist movement in 1947, and not simply because Palestinians were finally accepting the UN partition plan. Some of the positions were inevitably rehearsed as well, for instance, the recognition that circumstances dictated hardheaded pragmatism, as found in Abu Iyad's plea for "decisive clarity" and "an immediate, concrete statement of . . . goals."[41] Yet, where in 1947 the realist current within the Zionist independence movement had the capacity to succeed in carrying out their project, Palestinian realists can harbor few illusions about the prospects for a negotiated two-state solution, at least in the short term.

In the wake of the Palestinian uprising (intifada) in 1987 and the independence declaration in 1988, PLO leaders reiterated their long-standing offers to meet with Israelis at the negotiating table. Although the PLO's recognition of Israel in November 1988 led to a new round of debate in the Israeli press and other venues, the government unsurprisingly dismissed the Palestinian diplomatic overtures. *The New York Times* reported that Prime Minister Shamir rejected the formulation of a two-state solution *in advance,* because in his worldview, the PLO is by definition "opposed to peace with Israel."[42] More tellingly, by 1990 the prime minister unveiled a new hard-line coalition cabinet that included all of Israel's far-right parties. In effect, the PLO's post-intifada diplomatic initiatives furthered the polarization taking place in Israeli political life around the question of the territories, leading supporters of an accommodation to contemplate more far-reaching forms of compromise, while redoubling the efforts of Israeli exclusivists to resist them.

Among Israeli political parties and organizations, the most consistent support for the two-state scenario has come from the Communist Party (Maki), which draws its support almost exclusively from Palestinian-Israelis (Palestinians living within Israel's pre-1967 borders who are citizens). Maki has held four Knesset seats (representing approximately 4 percent of the total electorate and 30 percent of the Palestinian-Israeli electorate) throughout the 1980s, and although it has stood solidly behind a two-state solution since the 1960s, its radicalism and close identification in the public's mind with Palestinian interests place it outside of the political mainstream. Maki runs as part of a coalition known as Hadash (Democratic Movement for Peace and Equality).[43] Two other small, largely Palestinian-supported parties, the Progressive List for Peace and the Arab Democratic Party, suffer the same limitation.

The other main core of support in Israel for a two-state solution is found among the small parties of the "Zionist-left," Mapam and Ratz (the Citizen's Rights Movement). These two parties, which won eight seats in the 1988 elections (representing 7 percent of the total votes cast), tend to draw swing voters away from the Labor Party. In 1988, both organizations put forward platforms that recognized Palestinians' right to self-determination and envisioned negotiations with the PLO. In addition, there is an informal grouping of Labor Party leaders ("doves") who have challenged the consensus within their own party by proposing an alternative peace plan based on the two-state scenario.[44] Many of the Israelis profiled in *The Struggle for Peace* would tend to identify with these political parties and factions.

Of course, opponents attack such views ("Arafatists," "PLO-lovers," etc.) for threatening Israel's security or, more ominously, in the frequently hyperbolic terms employed by rival political and ideological camps, Israel's "existence." One of the most common ways that the West Bank is envisioned within the prevailing security-oriented discourse is in terms of Israel's "strategic depth," that is, as a kind of buffer against attack from hostile states. Another argument regularly used to discredit the idea of Palestinian self-determination is that it will result in a hostile "rump state" from which Palestinians can directly continue their war against Israel. U.S. President George Bush endorsed this view. Yet Abba Eban, Israel's foreign minister during the 1967 war, has complained that Israel is often depicted in such scenarios as some kind of "demilitarized land like Iceland . . . or Costa Rica" while the PLO is likened to "Ghengis Khan . . . able to exterminate Israel," and he dismisses the idea of a Palestinian threat to Israel's existence as "preposterous."[45]

The debate over Israel's security is a serious one, conducted at a number of levels, because the term *security* covers a broad range of military, political, and economic concerns. Even in the case of military-oriented circles, views differ. The Jaffee Center, Israel's most prominent strategic think tank, in 1989 recommended that the government drop its opposition to talking with the PLO, while envisioning the possibility that a "highly constrained but independent Palestinian state . . . would not necessarily threaten Israel."[46] The fortunes of political parties and factions obviously also ride on their ability to capture the "security vote." The Likud's foreign minister resorted to attacking the Jaffee Center's lack of objectivity, based on the fact that its director is an ex-Labor Party cabinet minister. General Harkabi, the author of *War and Strategy*, who played a key role in Israel's national security establishment in the 1940s–1960s, claims that Likud's great success "has been its ability to present its policy of maintaining the occupation of the West Bank and Gaza *as if* it is dictated by strategic imperatives" rather than their "nationalist ideology."[47]

Most Israelis do not identify with the religious extremism and ultranationalism of right-wing ideologues like Yitzhak Shamir, Moshe Arens, Ariel Sharon (Likud), Geula Cohen, Yuval Neeman (Tehiya), Raphael Eitan (Tzomet), Rahavim Zeevi (Moledet), and the settler movement Gush Emunim. Yet they support the exclusivist positions of these leaders and the arguments that defend the occupation on security grounds, often in the exaggerated terms—the "rhetoric of weakness"—that Abba Eban deplores. Ultimately, the ideological right is able to exploit what Harvard psychologist Herbert Kelman calls the "psychological core" of the conflict: "The conflict is perceived by the two parties in zero-sum terms, not only with respect to territory but, most significantly, with respect to national identity and national existence. Each party perceives the very existence of the other—the other's status as a nation—to be a threat to its own existence and status as a nation. Each holds the view that only one can be a nation: Either we are a nation or they are. *They* can acquire national identity and rights only at the expense of *our* identity and rights."[48]

The ambiguous language of many Palestinian proposals is understandable, given the likelihood that the most far-reaching compromise will be rejected, even while leaving them vulnerable to a "process whose outcome is uncertain and potentially fatal to their cause." Israelis fear the process of accommodation as well, convinced that Palestinian nationalism is "inherently threatening." Kelman's analysis confirms what Palestinians have always believed. It is "the PLO as the embodiment and agent of Palestinian nationhood" that remains the target of Israel's formidable military power.[49]

The Peace Process

The outline I have presented about the four fairly distinct perspectives on peace obviously complicates some of the more conventional depictions of the peace process, in both its historical and its contemporary contexts. For instance, many people have internalized Israel's "official" or statesanctioned and propagated version of the past, namely, that Israel has consistently sought peace but "there has been no one to talk to."[50] The more accurate rendition would be "there was no one willing to talk on the terms Israel's government was offering." Similarly, the peace terms offered by various Arab states in the 1940s and 1950s were rejected by the Israeli leadership, an issue that Israeli historians have recently begun to examine.

In the period since 1967, the basic question remains not "who wants peace?" but "peace on what terms?". Indeed, there has been remarkable stability in the configuration of parties and positions, with one clear exception. During the 1970s–1980s, the international consensus on the terms of a lasting settlement shifted to accommodate Palestinians' rights to national self-determination. In other words, the two-state solution gained increasing diplomatic backing as part of a "comprehensive settlement." Roughly parallel with this current, the Palestinian national movement revised its position to support the two-state solution as well. At present, the governments of the United States and Israel are the two parties that remain most firmly opposed to the terms of this particular settlement scenario.

The four alternative scenarios presented here serve as the basis for the numerous peace plans, proposals, and initiatives first undertaken in the late 1940s and early 1950s and revived in the wake of the 1967 war. Table 1 lists some of the most prominent peace proposals and initiatives of the past fifty years, categorized according to the terms they offer for resolving the conflicting Palestinian and Israeli sovereignty claims. Of course, most 1949–1967 era plans neither recognized nor sought to accommodate Palestinian national claims—a fact that led Palestinians in the 1960s to oppose, for instance, UN Resolution 242. As the table helps illustrate, the emergence of the Palestinian national movement as an organized and relatively effective political force, together with the rapid evolution in its position during the 1960s–1980s, represents one of the most dynamic elements in the long-standing conflict.

The Palestinians see the intifada against Israel's occupation of the West Bank and Gaza Strip, begun in 1987, as the most powerful expression to date of their evolution as a national movement. It is also seen as a key factor in the outcome of the nineteenth Palestinian National Council held in Algiers in November 1988, where the leadership issued a declaration of independence along with a renewed call for an international conference to settle the conflict, based on the principle of two independent states. The initiative garnered widespread support abroad, leading the Reagan administration in December 1988 to reverse the long-standing refusal of the United States to recognize the PLO as an official party to the conflict. Israel's political leadership viewed the PLO's "diplomatic successes" as "serious dangers."[51]

What the last two U.S. administrations—and, hence, the U.S. mass media—have termed the peace process needs to be viewed in the historical and comparative terms that I have tried to outline here. Throughout the 1980s, Israel's Likud-dominated governments sought to implement a radically different settlement scenario, based on the vision of Greater Israel or indivisible Israeli sovereignty over the West Bank, Gaza Strip, and East Jerusalem. In response to the intifada and the domestic political backlash that it caused, the Israeli government revived the proposal to implement self-rule in the territories as a way of countering Palestinian demands for an end to the occupation. This is the essence of the 1989 Shamir plan. The

TABLE 1

Contending Perspectives on Peace, 1949–1991

DEMOCRATIC STATE	TWO-STATE SOLUTION	LAND FOR PEACE	GREATER ISRAEL
		Lausanne Conference, 1949	
		Husni Zaim (Syria) Proposal, 1949	
		Secret Israeli-Egyptian Talks, 1954	
	Bourguiba Plan, 1965	Eshkol Plan, 1965	
		Jarring Mission, 1967	
		Allon Plan, 1968	
		Hussein Plan, 1969	
		Rogers Proposal, 1970	
8th PNC Resolution, 1971			
		Geneva Conference, 1973	
	UN Resolution 3236, 1974		
	13th PNC Resolution, 1977		Begin Plan, 1977
		Camp David Accords, 1978	
	Brezhnev Plan, 1980		
	Vienna Declaration, 1980		
	Fahd Plan, 1981		Sharon Plan, 1981
	Fez Plan, 1982	Reagan Plan, 1982	
	PLO Plan, 1988		Shamir Plan, 1989
		Baker Initiative, 1991	

American administrations have chosen to advance this particular diplomatic counterinitiative, maintaining that autonomy for Palestinians is compatible with its long-standing support for the principle of territorial compromise.[52]

Table 2, which maps the positions of Israeli and Palestinian political factions in terms of the four major alternative peace scenarios, makes clear that a wide gulf continues to separate most Palestinians from most Israelis. The vote taken at the November 1988 meeting of the PNC provides a rough indicator of Palestinian support for creation of an independent, West Bank–Gaza state. The overwhelming majority of delegates, 253 out of a total 309 representatives from the guerrilla groups, Palestinian trade unions and professional groups, and delegates from the various corners of the diaspora, backed the two-state solution. Fifty-six delegates either opposed the plan or else abstained from voting. The minority position of the Palestinian-Islamic movement, Hamas, which advocates a single Islamic state of Palestine, is the only political force not represented in the voting at the nineteenth PNC.

The last Israeli election, also held in November 1988, provides an equivalent rough indicator of the divisions inside Israel. The figure shows the number of Knesset seats obtained by parties and blocs. Parties supporting the principle of Palestinian national self-determination received fourteen seats. At the other end, parties articulating a clear preference for the Greater Israel scenario gained twelve seats. The majority of Israelis divided their support evenly among the two major blocs, Labor and Likud, which gained thirty-nine and forty seats, respectively. As can be seen in the figure, there is, on the one hand, a polarization of positions, with a certain portion of voters moving to the left and right, and on the other hand, a "centrist" core willing to support some kind of territorial compromise. Nonetheless, there seems little likelihood at present that the Israeli government will cease opposing the PLO's pursuit of an independent Palestinian state.

The broad terms of the U.S.-sponsored peace process, revived in 1988 and continuing today, are therefore crucial to an understanding of the reluctance of Israelis and Palestinians to enter into negotiations or, more accurately, to accept the various implicit and explicit conditions that set the boundaries of negotiations. First, the United States continues to back the principle of land for peace embodied in UN Resolution 242, while purposely leaving the boundaries of territorial compromise undefined. Second, it has stated its opposition to the principle of national self-determination for the Palestinians, which Bush administration spokespeople have labeled a "codeword" for a Palestinian state. Third, it continues to reject the principle that Palestinians be allowed to select their own representatives to negotiations, namely, the PLO.

TABLE 2

Alternative Solutions to the Israeli-Palestinian Conflict

	BINATIONAL STATE	TWO STATES	LAND FOR PEACE	GREATER ISRAEL
	Hamas			
	PFLP→ DFLP	PNC Mainstream	← Pro-Jordanians	
		(PLO)		(Shamir Govt.)
				(Post-Shamir?) ↓
				Tehiya
				Moledet
			← Likud	Tzomet
				NRP
		Hadash	Mapam	
		PLP	Ratz	
		Arab Dem. Party	← Labor →	
Votes in 19th PNC	56	253		
Votes in 1988 Knesset Elections		6	8	39	40	12
		(Int'l Consensus)	(U.S.)		

PFLP = Popular Front for the Liberation of Palestine; DFLP = Democratic Front for the Liberation of Palestine; PLP = Progressive List for Peace; NRP = National Religious Party.

Consider the viewpoint from Israel. If a majority of Israeli citizens are willing to accept the principle of land for peace, they are nonetheless afraid that negotiations may lead to an unfair exchange, at the cost of their security. For the militant expansionists, their vision of Greater Israel is automatically threatened by any talk of territorial compromise. For both segments of the population, compromise has come to be seen as a course that may lead to Israel's destruction. Because Israelis now effectively control the entire contested territory, there are few arguments likely to convince the citizenry that the path of compromise is worth the risks.

For most Palestinians, who view the consolidation and expansion of Israel as the outcome of a long process of dispossession and occupation of their homeland, the peace process seems to be designed to force them to abandon their claim to the right of national self-determination as the cost for a seat at the negotiating table. There is a large measure of truth in this argument, which was employed against Arafat at the nineteenth PNC in Algiers, where he eventually won acceptance for a two-state solution. Many Palestinian opponents of the peace process are convinced that, given the present Israeli consensus, which has received firm U.S. backing, there is little chance of obtaining sovereignty for an independent state under the current circumstances. For others, the negotiating process holds out a slim hope for improving the grim conditions of the long Israeli occupation. Presumably, still other Palestinians exist who see negotiations as possibly altering the situation much more dramatically. At any rate, negotiations remain the only real political possibility—however dangerous—open to the national movement.

Conclusion

Although each of the four alternative solutions to the Israeli-Palestinian conflict has articulate and forceful defenders, three of them fall short of the standard that I put forward in the introduction. Only the two-state solution accommodates the principle that Palestinian and Israelis have equal, inalienable, and nonexclusive rights to national self-determination in their historic homeland. The preference of the Jewish national movement for an independent state was articulated clearly in 1942. The Palestinian national movement's preference for a state has been expressed equally clearly since at least the 1970s.

Of course, my understanding of this basic symmetry between the two peoples may be objectionable to many, given the tendency to reject or to denigrate the claims of one or the other national movement. In the past, Palestinians have spent much energy seeking (futilely) to undermine the national self-identification of the Jewish people, for instance, by equating Zionism with racism. Similarly, the power of the Israeli state is directed today against virtually all cultural and political symbols of Palestinian nationalism, and, more ominously, against the Palestinians' struggle for national self-determination.

The symmetry is painfully confirmed by Professor Kelman's description of the "zero-sum" nature of the conflict. Palestinian recognition of Israeli national rights exacts a tremendous cost, in terms of the threat to the Palestinian people's own national rights, while such a compromise alone offers little if any assurance that the national movement's minimally acceptable objectives will be obtained. It is therefore not surprising that Palestinians have set forth what they describe as a "historic compromise"—recognizing the principle of partition—in such careful and qualified terms.

Israel's leadership has rejected the claims of the Palestinian national movement as forcefully as the Palestinians once rejected Zionism. This rejection takes one of two forms. The first somehow tries to show that Palestinian national claims are illegitimate, the exact course that Israelis and others regularly condemned Palestinian and other Arab leaders for pursuing. The second argues that Palestinians have effectively forfeited their national-territorial claims by refusing to accept the UN compromise proposal when offered in 1947.

As I have tried to suggest, the most likely reason for the Israelis' reluctance to accept the legitimacy of Palestinian national claims is because they view their own "security" as overriding other principles. Thus, many Israelis raise the question, "How can we trust the Palestinians?" and view the peace process as dangerously open-ended.[53] But this is the precise logic that led the indigenous Palestinians naturally to distrust the Jewish national movement, even when the settlers, under the duress of international exigencies and with much division among their own ranks, voted to accept the UN partition proposal of 1947.

If we can sympathize now with the Israelis' reluctance to compromise, grounded in their fears of what the future holds, then we have to sympathize with the Palestinians, who, in 1947, refused to compromise. Many Israelis see acceptance of a Palestinian state as the first step in the destruction of the state of Israel, but this is exactly how Palestinians and other Arabs responded to the UN partition plan of 1947. If Israelis claim a principled right to part of Palestine, then they must accept that the same principle holds true for Palestinians now. Principles are not obviated simply because of the failings of political leaders—on either side of the Green Line.

The distinction between principle and power is worth contemplating as the peace process continues to unfold. The Palestinians, who are, objectively, the weakest party in the conflict, will be pressed hard to compromise their right to an independent state. At the same time, the PLO leadership may view the degree of indeterminacy in the political process as a factor working in its favor, but the Palestinians are unlikely to surrender their claim to statehood. After all, the tenacity of the Palestinian national movement is at least as strong as that of the Jewish nationalists, who, in the face of formidable odds, succeeded in establishing the independent state of Israel in 1948 and, rightly or wrongly, found the cost in blood and destruction to be worth the price.

Notes

Author's Acknowledgment: Although he has not read this article, my debt to Noam Chomsky is immediately apparent. I am pleased to be able to thank Zachary Lockman for his careful reading and comments on an early draft.

1. The Jewish community, which was roughly 33 percent of the population of Palestine, owned 7 percent of the land. They were alloted 55 percent of the land by the UN plan. As a result of the fighting between 1947–1949, they controlled 75–80 percent of the land. After the 1967 war, the Israelis controlled the entire territory of the ex–Palestine mandate. Figures are quoted from Ian J. Bickerton and Carla L. Klausner, *A Concise History of the Arab-Israeli Conflict* (Englewood Cliffs, N.J.: Prentice-Hall, 1991), 89, 91, 97; and David McDowall, *Palestine and Israel: The Uprising and Beyond* (Berkeley: University of California Press, 1989), 24–28, 192.

2. For example, see the text of the "Israeli-Palestinian Joint Declaration on Peace," issued in Jerusalem, August 5, 1990, following a "peace debate" between Israeli Knesset members and Palestinian political and intellectual leaders. Reprinted in the *Journal of Palestine Studies* 20, 1 (August 1990): 148.

3. See Arafat's December 14, 1988 press conference (Geneva), transcript in Ian J. Bickerton and Carla L. Klausner, *A Concise History of the Arab-Israeli Conflict* (Englewood Cliffs, N.J.: Prentice Hall, 1991), 254. See also Edward W. Said, "Intifada and Independence," 5–22, Azmy Bishara, "The Uprising's Impact on Israel," 217–229, and "Palestine National Council 'Political Communique'," appendix iv, 401–404 in Zachary Lockman and Joel Beinin, eds., *Intifada: The Palestinian Uprising against Israeli Occupation* (Boston: South End, 1989); and Don Peretz, "Israeli Peace Proposals," in Willard A. Beling, ed., *Middle East Peace Plans* (London: Croom Helm, 1986), 11–36.

4. Or, to put it slightly differently, an Israeli "struggle with the Palestinian Arab community over the control of Palestine." Herbert C. Kelman, "The Palestinianization of the Arab-Israeli Conflict," *The Jerusalem Quarterly* 46 (Spring 1988): 3–15: 5.

5. For a recent restatement of the U.S. position, see Thomas L. Friedman, "Arabs Won't Give Baker Final Word on Peace Parley," *The New York Times* (September 21, 1991): 1 and 4.

6. See the original PLO Charter promulgated in 1964 and analyzed in Yeho-

shafat Harkabi, *The Palestinian Covenant and Its Meaning* (London: Vallentine-Mitchell, 1979).

7. On the meaning of the declaration of independence, see Said, "Intifada and Independence," in Lockman and Beinin (1989); on the PNC's recognition of Israel, see the statements by American Jewish intellectuals following their December 6, 1988, meeting with PLO leader Yasir Arafat, and the "Stockholm Declaration" issued by Arafat and the Swedish Foreign Minister, 7 December 1988, texts in *The New York Times* (December 7): 6 and (December 8): 10.

8. Privately, Ben-Gurion recognized the need to gain territory beyond the borders specified by the UN and cooperated with the Jordanian King Abdullah to abort the creation of a Palestinian Arab state. See Simcha Flapan, *The Birth of Israel: Myths and Realities* (New York: Pantheon, 1987); Tom Segev, *1949: The First Israelis* (New York: Free Press, 1986); and Avi Shlaim, *Collusion across the Jordan: King Abdullah, the Zionist Movement, and the Partition of Palestine* (New York: Columbia University Press, 1988).

9. For background, see Ian Lustick, *For the Land and the Lord: Jewish Fundamentalism in Israel* (New York: Council on Foreign Relations, 1988); and Myron J. Aronoff, *Israeli Visions and Divisions: Cultural Change and Political Conflict* (New Brunswick, N.J.: Transaction Books, 1988).

10. For details, see Bishara, "The Uprising's Impact on Israel," in Lockman and Beinin (1988), 221–222.

11. Kelman (1988): 7.

12. See, for instance, Columbia University professor Edward Said's account of the position taken by George Habash, leader of the Popular Front for the Liberation of Palestine (PFLP), in the debate on the nineteenth PNC's program (1989), 16.

13. "By mid-1990, more states recognized the PLO declaration than recognized Israel." Bickerton and Klausner (1991), 238.

14. For an extended discussion of this issue, see Herbert Kelman, "The Political Psychology of the Israeli-Palestinian Conflict: How Can We Overcome the Barriers to a Negotiated Solution?" *Political Psychology* 8, 3 (1987): 347–363.

15. The PLO position is often referred to as the "democratic secular state" formula, but I follow Alain Gresh here, who argues that PLO documents never use the term "secular." It was a state of Muslims, Christians, and Jews, defined, perhaps implausibly, in religious but nonsectarian terms. See Alain Gresh, *The PLO: The Struggle Within*, rev. and updated ed. (London: Zed Books, 1988), 34–50. Israelis have generally chosen to ignore or disclaim the formula, while focusing on the standard, twinned phraseology of "liquidation of the Zionist entity," which they take as evidence of implacable hostility to Jews.

16. Gresh (1988); Helena Cobban, *The Palestinian Liberation Organization: People, Power and Politics* (New York: Cambridge University Press, 1984).

17. See Lisa Taraki, "The Islamic Resistance Movement in the Palestinian Uprising," in Lockman and Beinin (1989), 171–177.

18. Thomas L. Friedman, "Mideast Talks: Peace Might Be an Incidental Result," *The New York Times* (July 24, 1991): A8.

19. Jerusalem Domestic Service, interview with Zeevi, 4 March 1991, reported

in *Foreign Broadcast Information Service* [*FBIS*], NES-91-043 (5 March 1991): 38–39. The opposition to negotiations is reported in *Ha'aretz* (3 March 1991), translation in *FBIS*, NES-91-042 (4 March 1991): 49.

20. Joel Beinin, "The Arabists of Hashomer Hatza'ir (Mapam)," *Social Text* 28 (1991): 100–121.

21. For example, see Yehoshafat Harkabi, *Arab Attitudes To Israel*, trans. by Misha Louvish (New York: Hart, 1972). Nonetheless, the rejection of Jewish national rights was neither universal nor metaphysical. See, in particular, the statement by the prominent Fatah official, Said Hammami, published in the *Times* (London) (December 17, 1973) on the eve of the Geneva Peace Conference. Hammami used the specific term "bi-national" in describing the PLO's position, while maintaining that the key to solving the conflict was for Palestinians and Israelis to "recognize one another as peoples." Details in Gresh (1988), 144–146.

22. In the months before the Gulf War, the Israeli researcher Meron Benvenisti and the Palestinian theorist Sari Nusseibeh reiterated a controversial argument for what amounts to a new version of bi-nationalism. They argue that political and economic realities make the Israeli occupation of Palestinian territories irreversible. Thus, the Palestinians under occupation would be better off pressing for citizenship rights rather than national rights.

23. See Gresh (1988), 37.

24. Hillel Schenker, "Anyone Here for Peace," *The Nation* (July 1, 1991): 13; *Yediot Aharanot*, March 11, 1991, translated in *FBIS* NES-91-050 (March 14, 1991): 31; also see John Waterbury, ed., *Towards New Orders in the Middle East: The Role of U.S. Policy* (Center of International Studies, Monograph Series, Number 2, Princeton University, 1991), the section titled "Israel and the Palestinians," 22–26.

25. The UN General Assembly formally acknowledged the Palestinian people's right to self-determination for the first time in 1969, and has reiterated the position countless additional times. PLO chairman Yasir Arafat received the first invitation ever to a nonmember to address the General Assembly in 1974. In 1975, the Security Council allowed the PLO to participate in its debate on the Arab-Israeli conflict. American policy had shifted, at least symbolically, in 1975, by acknowledging "the legitimate interests of Palestinian Arabs;" President Jimmy Carter endorsed the idea of a Palestinian "homeland" in 1976. The joint U.S.-USSR proposal in 1977 to reconvene the Geneva Peace Conference in 1977 invited the participation of Palestinian representatives for the first time. European support for the Palestinian right to national self-determination is unambiguous. See the account of the "Venice Declaration" by the foreign ministers of the European Economic Community, details in *The New York Times* (June 13 and 14, 1980).

26. From the ten-point program of the twelfth PNC in Cairo (June–July 1974), quoted in Cobban (1984), 62.

27. William Quandt, *Decade of Decisions* (Berkeley: University of California Press, 1977); and Helena Cobban, "Palestinian Peace Plans," in Beling (1986), 37–52.

28. Peretz, "Israeli Peace Proposals," in Beling (1986), 11–12.

29. For details see Peretz in Beling (1986); Flapan (1987); and William Quandt, "American Proposals for Arab-Israeli Peace," in Beling (1986), 69–70.

30. For an interpretation of "original" Arab positions in these terms, see Ye-

hoshafat Harkabi, "Arab-Israeli Conflict after the Gulf War," a revised version of General Harkabi's paper for a conference, The Aftermath of the Persian Gulf War: Realignment in the Middle East?, May 13, 1991, University of Utah. The paper I am quoting from is dated Princeton, June 11, 1991. (Appears in revised form in this book.)

31. For details, see David McDowall, *Palestine and Israel: The Uprising and Beyond* (Berkeley: University of California Press, 1989), 93–96.

32. Myron J. Aronoff, "Political Polarization: Contradictory Interpretations of Israeli Reality," in Steven Heydemann, ed., *Issues in Contemporary Israel: The Begin Era* (Boulder: Westview, 1984), 41–52; Yochanan Peres, "Stalemate: Structural Balance in Israeli Politics," *Middle East Review* 20, 4 (Summer 1988): 37–42; and Don Peretz and Sammy Smooha, "Israel's Twelfth Knesset Election: An All-Loser Game," *Middle East Journal* 43, 3 (Summer 1989): 388–405.

33. Ian Lustick, "Israel and the West Bank after Elon Moreh: The Mechanics of the De Facto Annexation," *Middle East Journal* 35 (Autumn 1981): 557–577. The "ambiguities" in the U.S. position on settlements mirror Labor's policy. American administrations have maintained that Jewish settlements in the territories are an illegal violation of the 1949 Geneva Convention, yet until now they have taken no action to stop them.

34. Peretz, "Israeli Peace Proposals," in Beling (1986), 25–26, stresses this point.

35. Aronoff, "Political Polarization," in Heydemann (1984), 54; Abba Eban, "Israel, Hardly the Monaco of the Middle East," *The New York Times* (January 2, 1989).

36. Abba Eban, "The Threats Are from Within," *Jerusalem Post International Edition* (week ending December 3, 1988); McDowall (1989), 164–181; and David K. Shipler, "A Choice between Bad and Worse," review of *Israel's Fateful Hour* by Yehoshafat Harkabi, *The New York Times Book Review* (November 29, 1988): 7.

37. Yehoshafat Harkabi, "The Grim Realities under the Carpet," *Jerusalem Post International Edition* (week ending November 5, 1988). He develops these arguments fully in *Israel's Fateful Hour,* trans. Lenn Schramm (New York: Harper & Row, 1988).

38. McDowall, *Palestine and Israel: The Uprising and Beyond* (1989), 248.

39. Details in Gresh (1988), 63–74, 120–121.

40. Gresh (1988), 133.

41. Flapan (1987), 30–31; Said, "Israeli Peace Proposals," in Beling (1989), 16–17, for quote describing Abu Iyad's intervention.

42. *The New York Times* (November 15 and December 23, 1988); and *The Daily Texan* (University of Texas, Austin) (November 15, 1988). For PLO offers and the debate inside Israel, see Salah Khalaf [Abu Iyad], "Israel and Arafat Can Talk," *The New York Times* (March 8, 1989); and Boaz Evron, "Can We Trust Them?" *Yediot Aharonot* (April 14, 1989), translated in *Middle East International* (April 28, 1989): 20.

43. McDowall (1989), 146–149; Gresh (1988), 72–74; and Peretz and Smooha (1989), 396.

44. Peretz and Smooha (1989) for vote totals; Schenker (1991); *Yediot Aharonot* (March 3, 1991); Israeli Defense Forces Radio Broadcast, Tel Aviv

(March 2, 1991), translated in *FBIS*, NES-91-042 (March 4, 1991): 49. The key figure is Moshe Shahal, a lawyer and ex–energy minister who is originally from Iraq.

45. Abba Eban, "Israel, Hardly the Monaco of the Middle East." The article singles out *New York Times* columnists A. M. Rosenthal and William Safire, among others, for the disservice they do by feeding the "myth of Israeli weakness" and exaggerating the PLO's or the hypothetical West Bank state's military capacity.

46. Glenn Frankel, "Israeli Leaders Urge to Open Talks with PLO," *Austin [TX] American-Statesman* (March 9, 1989). The analysts described a scenario of a peacemaking process of ten to fifteen years, entailing mutual concessions and confidence building, leading to a demilitarized state.

47. Harkabi, "The Grim Realities under the Carpet," (1988), emphasis added.

48. Kelman (1988), 9.

49. Kelman (1988), 9–10.

50. See, for instance, the weekly ads placed in *The New York Times* op-ed page by the American-Israel Friendship League, during July 1991, e.g., 7/31/91.

51. John Kifner, "Israelis Install New Government," *The New York Times* (December 23, 1988).

52. On U.S. support for the Shamir initiative, see Bernard Reich, "The United States in the Middle East," and Alan Dowty, "Israel the Deadlock Persists," both in *Current History* (January 1991): 5–8, 14–17.

53. Kelman (1988); Boaz Evron, "Can We Trust Them," *Yediot Aharonot* (April 14, 1989), and translated in *Middle East International* (April 28, 1989): 20.

PART V. CONCLUDING COMMENT

Toward Enduring Peace in the Middle East

Augustus Richard Norton holds a Ph.D. from the University of Chicago and is currently a professor of political science at the U.S. Military Academy at West Point. In addition, he is director of a major project on the Middle East for the International Peace Academy, where he was the senior research fellow in 1990–1991. He has traveled, worked, and conducted academic research in Cyprus, Egypt, Israel, Jordan, Lebanon, Mozambique, the Soviet Union, Syria, and Turkey. In 1989 he was a Fulbright research professor at the Norwegian Institute of International Affairs in Oslo, where he researched and wrote about peacekeeping, particularly in Middle East settings.

He is the author of *Amal and the Shi'a: Struggle for the Soul of Lebanon,* and in 1990 he co-authored *UN Peacekeepers: Soldiers with a Difference.* He is now at work on *Rulers Under Siege: Middle East Politics in the 1990s* and *The Middle East after Desert Storm.*

THE ARAB-ISRAELI CONFLICT has confounded the best efforts of peacemakers for more than forty years. Although enduring peace in the Middle East may seem a utopian goal, it is actually a realistic one if citizens groups committed to peace and freedom enjoy the right to organize in Israel and in the Arab states. The first casualty of authoritarianism is the free and competitive exchange of ideas. Authoritarian governments are insecure, hence paranoid about protecting the government; they typically rationalize their power in terms of external threats, and therefore suspect those voices that refuse to demonize the enemy or even deny there is an enemy. Fortunately, among both the Palestinians and the Israelis there exists an unusually rich and varied collection of groups and movements espousing a nonmilitaristic approach to conflict resolution. This is a source of significant encouragement for those of us who believe that Arabs and Jews must learn to live side by side, if not together.

In the Arab world, however, authoritarian government remains the norm, and there is only limited scope for the free play of ideas. Unless these governments open up, peace will always be brittle and freedom will remain a hostage to the Arab-Israeli conflict. Movement toward a peaceful settlement of the morally wrenching conflict between Israelis and Palestinians will necessarily undermine those regimes that base their credentials for governing on anti-Israeli militance. Fortunately, there are signs of important political openings within the Arab states, however tentative those signs may be. As this development matures, the footing of Israeli hard-liners will become unsteady. Denied an enemy, both Arab and Israeli hard-liners will have to take their place in the unemployment line, and enduring peace in the Middle East may actually begin to come into view.

This is truly a remarkable moment in world history. The Soviet ogre, rotten from within, has proven to be a feeble and pitiable thing. Democracy, which has no deep roots in Russian culture, has become the motivating ideal among many citizens of the country we used to call the Soviet Union. The enormity of the changes that have occurred is signalled by the fact that we scarcely know anymore how to refer to that state, or is it states?

Democratic movements have triumphed in much of Central Europe, and in South America democracy has caught its second wind, notably in Chile, where General Augusto Pinochet increasingly came to resemble a character out of Gabriel García Márquez's *Autumn of the Patriarch*. In struggling, developing states, where conventional wisdom counsels skepticism about the vitality of democracy, popular movements espousing it have been gaining force. Witness the Philippines, where another aging dictator, Ferdinand Marcos, was felled by "people power." Or Zambia, where the autocratic Kenneth Kaunda was voted out of office in the first contested elections in nearly two decades. Even though the regime in Beijing brutally trampled the Chinese democracy movement on Tiananmen Square, the courage and tenacity of the students leaves little doubt that a latent movement is likely to reemerge.

In nearly every corner of the world, the appeal of democracy is being felt. Yet, somehow, when it comes to the Arab world there is a tendency on the part of officials in Washington, journalists, and the "experts" who descend on crises like locusts blanketing a field of wheat, to presume that the Arab world is somehow insulated from the democracy trend. It may be worth remembering that many of the same experts now propounding on the implausibility of Arab democracy earlier expressed their skepticism that the states of Eastern Europe could be transformed into democracies. Eight years ago, one of America's leading political scientists wrote that "with a few exceptions, the limits of democratic development in the world may well have been reached."[1] Since then, a veritable blossoming of democracy has occurred in Europe, Latin America, and Africa. This should chasten any rush to judgment, especially when one considers the historical novelty of the democratic ideal in Eastern Europe, not to mention Russia, where people are groping toward a freer form of political life in lands where the roots of democracy are neither thick nor deep.

This is not to argue, by any means, that all of the Arab states will metamorphose and become democracies overnight, or even that some of them will. The prospects for democratic openings vary from one state to another, and, as in Europe, some autocratic regimes will cling to power, thrashing and crushing opponents, whereas others will experiment (and "experiment" is precisely the right word) with opening up government, permitting free or semi-free elections, and even sharing, or pretending to share, power.

The global communications revolution has had a striking effect on men and women throughout the world, and the peoples of the Middle East are no exception. Governments may no longer hide behind a cloak of secrecy. With access to reliable and alternative sources of information, such as the BBC, Radio Monte Carlo, and sometimes even CNN, the people in the street enjoy access to valuable information about their government, and about the world. Coupled with education (the literacy rates for Arab adults have pushed steadily upward),[2] this information allows individuals to judge their governments in ways that would have seemed extraordinary only a few decades ago.

The phenomenon of public opinion has emerged in the Arab world. Its people are demanding a voice in decisions that affect their lives, complaining about rife corruption in government, and insisting that the leaders address their needs. Arab opinion is not monolithic, but entails a diversity of ideological perspectives and nuances, perhaps particularly on the "Islamic street," where freer political life has encouraged competition rather than solidarity.

Arab leaders feel the pressure and anyone who denies that fact has not been listening to what these leaders have been saying. There is no conversion underway to Jeffersonian democracy in the Arab world, but the pressure to open up the political systems is increasingly obvious. For their part, many Arab politicians are pragmatic; when they advocate widening political participation, they are reflecting the need to vent steam, to relieve the pressure.

Concession Versus Repression

Faced with restive and increasingly assertive populations, some governments will continue to try to pound round pegs into square holes by choosing repression over concession; others, however, have chosen to experiment with democratization. Of course, the most advanced fledgling democracy in the Arab world is Egypt, where President Hosni Mubarak has pursued a mixed strategy of co-optation—sharing the blame as well as the goodies—and reasonably free elections according to rules that make a victory by the ruling National Democratic Party (NDP) a foregone conclusion. In the December 1990 parliamentary elections, necessitated by the invalidation of the 1987 elections, both the neo-Wafd party and the Muslim Brotherhood boycotted the elections. The NDP won an overwhelming but, some would note, an empty victory in that not even the appearance of an effective parliamentary opposition was preserved (notwithstanding the six seats won by the left-wing Tagama' Party). Still, compared to the autocracy of the former president, Anwar Sadat, and the intolerance of the Gamal Abdel-Nasser period, Egypt is certainly a freer place than it has ever been.

Jordan, Algeria, Tunisia, and Yemen are also moving, in fits and starts, down the path of democratization, and the badly battered Lebanese democracy may be regaining its vitality. Incipient political liberalization has even been noted in Libya. There is the open question of Kuwait, where the opposition has demanded the reconvening of a freely elected parliament and the reestablishment of the 1962 constitution, both of which had been suspended. Prior to the Iraqi invasion in August 1990, the emir of Kuwait, Jaber al-Ahmed al-Sabah, responded to opposition demands by invoking pseudo-participation—the creation of pliant political structures through which citizens could go through the motions of participation. The regime created an Advisory National Council in June 1990 rather than reconvening the parliament, but this sort of political hokum fools no one. As with earlier ventures into pseudo-participation by the late shah of Iran and President Nasser in Egypt, the effect is simply to accentuate the absence of free political structures. After his return to Kuwait, following the country's liberation, the emir attempted to dampen enthusiasm for the opposition by bribing virtually all Kuwaitis. The emir simply forgave all commercial and mortgage loans. Whether he did any more than provide ammunition to his many critics, who were quick to note that the ease with which the emir was able to dip into the treasury illustrated their complaint, will only become clear in October 1992, when the long-demanded parliamentary elections are scheduled.[3]

Dwindling Legitimacy

Arab governments are widely viewed with disdain by their own citizens. Whereas Americans routinely refer to "our" government, an Arab hardly ever thinks in these terms. Instead, the distinction between a citizen and his or her government is a distinction between "us" and "them." In short, Arab governments are widely viewed with a mixture of contempt and fear, although that mixture varies widely from one individual to another, and, just as important, from one state to another.

In the Arab world, as elsewhere, weak, insecure, marginally legitimate rulers tend to view as a dangerous challenge any attempt to organize citizens outside the authority of government. Unless they fall under direct government control, labor unions, professional associations, civic clubs, interest groups, and the like are viewed with utmost suspicion. Collectively, these groups comprise civil society, the mélange of clubs, organizations, and groups that acts as a buffer between state power and the life of the citizen. In some settings, among the Palestinians, in Lebanon and Egypt, and in parts of Arab North Africa, civil society is vibrant and varied. In Algeria, liberalization has promoted a flourishing civil society, with a reported more than twelve thousand professional and cultural groups. But in most of the Arab world, civil society is weak and fragmented, signifying the absence of freedom. In Iraq, the government has gone out of its way to destroy any vestige of civil society that it cannot dominate, thereby making it hard to imagine any peaceful transfer of power beyond the Ba'athist regime.

Frequently, Muslims find a voice for their demands in religious movements, which are less vulnerable to government pressures and offer compelling indictments of the rulers' inability to meet the legitimate social and economic demands of citizens. In fact, where civil society has been systematically repressed, the Islamic sector has often been uniquely successful in surviving intact.

All governments must justify themselves, or stake out their right to rule. In other words, governments must establish their legitimacy. Not too many years ago, Arab leaders resorted to vague if moving references to the unity of the Arab nation, the need to bring justice to the Palestinians, and the confrontation with Israel in order to justify their rule. The old formulas by which governments justified their claim to legitimacy are wearing very thin. These themes are still present in Arab politics, but the shibboleths have lost some of their force.

In point of fact, the Arab-Israeli conflict has often been exploited to justify the creation of garrison states in which freedom and prosperity have been sacrificed in the interest of national security. Can a regime that lacks electoral legitimacy and roots its right to rule in the confrontation with Israel, the unity of the Arab nation, and a commitment to justice for the Palestinians survive a peace? This is a particularly relevant question for President Hafez al-Assad of Syria, whose dilemma became transparent at the Madrid Peace Conference, which convened in late October of 1991. The Syrian regime rests its claim to legitimacy on its role as a standard-bearer of Arabism and as the self-appointed protector of Palestine. Symptomatically, when the Syrians received $2 billion as a gratuity from Saudi Arabia for their participation in the anti-Iraq alliance, the money was spent, for the most part, on missiles, rather than for the domestic economy, which is in deep crisis.

Even as the Palestinian delegates enthusiastically pursued negotiations with Israel, rightly seeking to grab a last opportunity, the Syrians have shown great reluctance to proceed. This reluctance was not merely procedural or tactical, but reflected the tacit acknowledgment that steps toward normalizing relations with Israel necessarily undermine the regime's formula for legitimacy. Yet, the Syrians could not afford to be left out of the discussions, especially given the present dominance of the United States and the disastrous economic conditions in Syria that make further Saudi largesse essential. If the peace process does move forward, as now seems likely, it will be interesting to observe the regime's attempt to refashion its legitimacy formula.

Not only have the Arab governments failed to match action to political rhetoric on the Arab-Israeli front, outside of the rich, oil-producing states of the Arabian peninsula they have a widespread record of economic failure. In states like Algeria, where 60 percent of the population is thirty years of age or younger, the pressures of rapid population growth have exacerbated the dimensions of economic failure. The poor have become poorer and the middle class confronts a significant decline in its standard of living. Anger over empty pockets and empty plates is further stoked by widespread perceptions of corruption on the part of government officials.

The Algerian Bellwether

Important and promising experiments are under way in Algeria. All eyes in the Arab world are watching this country, where the National Liberation Front (FLN) has ruled continuously since 1962, when Algeria won its independence from France. Following bloody rioting in October 1988, when discontent stemming from unemployment and a general economic crisis erupted in Algeria's major cities, the government revised the constitution to permit the creation of political parties in the formerly one-party republic. The effect of this change, specified in Article 40, was to prompt the creation of nearly two dozen political parties to contest nationwide elections in June 1990. Benefiting from an election boycott by several of the largest of the new opposition parties, the Islamic Salvation Front (FIS), which campaigned on the platform that "Islam is the solution," won thirty-two of forty-eight provincial assemblies and over half of the 1,541 municipal councils. Even the Algerian president's hometown voted for the FIS.[4]

The FIS victory was stunning and earth-shattering. Although the FLN remained in control of the government, there was no doubt that its grip was tenuous. President Chadli Benjedid, who, along with the powerful leadership of the army, is apparently convinced that the Algerian political system must open up if it is going to survive, announced parliamentary elections for early 1991, then postponed them until June.

The old order will not go easily or quietly. Rather than riding quietly off into the sunset, the present holders of power and privilege are trying to manipulate the laws to preserve their power and they may succeed. Hence, the Algerian parliament, still an FLN preserve, passed a new electoral law on April 1 which illustrated that gerrymandering is a universal craft. Capitalizing on the FLN strength in rural districts, the new law constructed electoral districts so that a disproportionate weight was given to FLN strongholds. In the most egregious cases, pro-FLN voters in rural areas would cast votes effectively weighted to equal ten FIS votes in the cities. In addition, runoff procedures were modified so that only the top vote-winners would compete. This precluded the voters from exercising a third choice, choosing a party that might mark the middle ground between the FLN and the FIS.

By May, the new electoral law sparked demonstrations pitting the FIS against the army. The two leading figures in the FIS have been Shaikh Ali Abbasi al-Madani and Ali Belhadj, with al-Madani espousing political coexistence with other political parties and Belhadj, a firebrand, outspoken in his skepticism of pluralism. Both men blasted the election law and urged their supporters to protest. The demonstrations in late May prompted a declaration of martial law and the appointment of a new prime minister, Sid Ahmad Ghozali, who met with Shaikh al-Madani in early June and committed his government to "free and clean elections" by year's end, but tension persisted. The army jailed hundreds of FIS members and by the end of June both al-Madani and Belhadj were arrested for plotting against the government. The two leaders remain in custody, although most of their incarcerated followers have been released. The postponed elections were eventually rescheduled for December 26, 1991. In Algeria, where a group with fifteen or more members may register as a party, as many as 64 parties will compete in the December election, if it is held. FIS will have to compete with at least half a dozen serious rivals.

Following the uproar in May and June, the parliament had a chance to amend the law, but instead made it tougher. For instance, despite the request of Prime Minister Ghozali, procedures for absentee balloting, which in practice permit a man to vote for his wife, were retained. (Subsequently, the prime minister referred the matter for review to the Constitutional Council, the body empowered to overturn legislation that is not in line with the constitution. In an important exercise of this power, the Constitutional Council invalidated the section of the electoral law authorizing absentee balloting on the grounds that the right to vote is necessarily the right to cast a ballot secretly and personally.)

Algeria has become a bellwether for a genuine political opening in the Arab world, and the results of the election, if held, are likely to inspire imitation elsewhere. Whether the imitation will be a design for controlling dissent or a step toward pluralism remains to be seen.

Saudi Arabia: A Regressive Case

If Algeria may be moving forward toward pluralism, albeit hesitantly, in other Arab states autocracy is retrenching, tightening social controls after glimpses of a freer political life during the Gulf crisis. The most obvious example is Saudi Arabia.

In Saudi Arabia, certainly the most socially conservative Arab state, middle-class professionals have long pressured the regime to provide an outlet for popular participation in decision making. Since 1962 the ruling family has periodically promised to establish a *majlis al-shura* (consultative council), but the promises have never been fulfilled. Typically, the majlis al-shura promise is dusted off during a moment of popular discontent, and then promptly put back on the shelf for a few more years. The most recent use of this concept was in November 1990, in the midst of the Gulf crisis and on the heels of promises by the Kuwaiti royal family to restore parliamentary life in the emirate. Just as the Kuwaiti emir's commitment remains unfulfilled, so the Saudi majlis al-shura has predictably been returned to the prop room (although in November 1990 King Fahd Ibn Abdul Aziz al-Saud told reporters he was putting the finishing touches on the council, and he again referred to it in May and June of 1991).

As the protector of the two holiest cities of Islam—Mecca and Medina—King Fahd is especially sensitive to any charge that he is placing their sanctity or purity in jeopardy. Although the learned men (*'ulama*) of the puritanical Wahhabi sect do not rule in Saudi Arabia, they are keenly concerned with the state of public morals and they are a conservative bulwark for the monarch and the regime. In effect, a challenge to the regime's Islamic probity is a challenge to its core legitimacy. Hence, King Fahd had to be sensitive to conservative grumbling over his agreement to permit the predominantly non-Muslim and U.S.-led anti-Iraq alliance to deploy in the kingdom.

Given an opportunity to emphasize his credentials as the upholder of the faith, King Fahd grabbed it. This opportunity came on November 6, 1990, when some four dozen Saudi women audaciously dismissed their drivers in Riyadh and drove their own cars, thus violating the informal but well-known ban on women driving cars. Saudi liberals—who later petitioned the king to create a parliament and an independent judiciary to ·reduce the powers of the religious leaders and to review the status of women—were initially heartened by the demonstration; however, the regime reacted harshly to the demonstration, ostracizing the participants, firing several from teaching positions, and exploiting the incident as means to stress the regime's Wahhabi bona fides. The Supreme Council of Islamic Research lent support to the king with a *fatwa* (authoritative religious opinion), which found that "women should not be allowed to drive motor vehicles as the *shari'a* [religious law] instructs that things that degrade or harm the dignity of women must be prevented."[5]

In June 1991, in a move that was widely interpreted as an attempt by the 'ulama to collect for their wartime sufferance of the regime's welcome of Western troops to the kingdom, as well as to counter the entreaties of liberal Saudis, the 'ulama presented a memorandum urging King Fahd to install a series of conservative reforms. These reforms included the creation of an 'ulama-dominated parliament, application of consistent punishments for corruption, and the stricter application of Islamic law. Although the conservative reforms have not been applied, there is little doubt that political life in Saudi Arabia will continue to be the exclusive preserve of the regime, not its citizens.

The Islamist Movements

Recent years have seen a striking proliferation of Islamist movements in the Arab world. Enjoying a broad popular base that crosses economic classes and a populist theme—the answer is Islam—these movements have been remarkably successful in winning votes in contested elections (making them a little like the "Right to Life" movement in the United States). In Jordan, in 1989, Islamists captured thirty-four of eighty parliamentary seats and managed to construct a working majority through an alliance with leftist representatives. As noted previously, the FIS has changed the complexion of Algerian politics, and, since 1984, the venerable Muslim Brethren in Egypt have competed successfully in two national elections. In Kuwait, the Islamic Constitutional Movement (formerly the Muslim Brethren) is poised to play a leading role. Several points need to be made about these movements:

First, their vitality stems, in significant measure, from the general impoverishment of civil society. Where civil society has been repressed, the Islamic groups have often prospered. In effect, they have had the field to themselves. Religious institutions are a part of the cultural landscape of the Arab world, and the fundamental Islamic institution, the mosque, is a natural meeting place, one that is often reasonably autonomous from government control. As civil society is enlivened, it is only natural that the influence of the Islamist groups will be challenged.

Two, the Islamic groups are a symptom of the broad social and economic changes that have swept through the region. Many of the recruits to such groups are individuals who have received college educations but can't find decent jobs, people who have heard the promises of politicians but have borne the brunt of government inefficiency. It is no accident that many of the Islamic groups have cemented their solidarity by providing services that government has provided incompetently or not at all. Thus, in many countries, such as Egypt and Lebanon, we find the Islamist groups performing as quasi-governmental social-welfare and medical agencies, filling a vacuum left by government incapacity or incompetence.

Three, where the government has attempted to quell the rise of Islamic groups, they have formed a marked solidarity. However, where government has tread more lightly or at least more selectively, there has been a marked process of fissuring and competition. Examples include Algeria and Egypt, where Islamists willing to the play by the government's rules have deserted those unwilling to do so.

Four, where they have moved from opposition to positions of public responsibility, these groups submit themselves to a more prosaic evaluation standard. For instance, in the Algerian municipalities where they assumed authority, FIS officials often failed to deliver on their promises and accordingly lost some support. Obviously, it is one thing to castigate government for its incompetence and its corruption, but it is another to be able to efficiently collect the garbage.

Moreover, playing the game of politics has opened the Islamists to political exploitation, notably in Jordan. On New Year's Day, 1991, King Hussein oversaw the appointment of five Muslim Brethren and two other Islamists to cabinet posts, including the ministries of education, social development, religious affairs, and education. The monarch's motive obviously was to put a lid on the public temper, which was at a boil due to the Gulf War and the heavy economic impact of that crisis upon Jordan. When the Islamists had served their purpose, the king dismissed the government in June, appointing as prime minister Tahir Mashri, a moderate thought to be more congenial to the unfolding peace process. On June 9, 1991, a national charter was promulgated in which a multiparty political system, freedom of the press, and equal rights for women were endorsed.

Five, although the Islamist groups certainly see themselves as part of the world community of Muslims (the *'umma*), they are clearly indicating a willingness, indeed a propensity, to voice their demands within states. Some observers believe this is some sort of trick, but the evidence points in another direction, namely, a pragmatic acceptance of the reality of the state. Obviously, some Islamists like Ali Belhadj of the FIS reject pluralism and democracy, but many others do not.

Six, even during the Gulf War, when popular opinion throughout much of the Arab world often ran strongly against the U.S.-led alliance, the Islamist leaders were often forced play a difficult balancing role between their benefactors (particularly Saudi Arabia) and their followers. In general, they displayed a noteworthy capacity for pragmatism.

Thus, as the preceding points illustrate, the Islamist movements are basically social-reform movements. Yet, they retain a keen interest in Jerusalem, the third holiest city in Islam, and in the fate of Palestine as a part of the *dar-al-Islam* (roughly, the land of Islam). Of course, the Islamists have no corner on dogmatic obstinacy—one only needs to look at Israel's secular Likud party to see that—so as the peace process unfolds, it will be interesting to watch the Islamists respond to the need for compromise.

The Watershed Year: *1991*

Commentary about the Gulf War has often noted that the events surrounding it represented a watershed—that is to say, one of those moments in history when profound changes, a reconfiguring of assumptions, even more, a reconfiguration of political reality, occur. This sort of change does not just signify a rearrangement of the pieces, but the shift to an entirely new game, as from checkers to chess. Of course, some pundits were disappointed that sweeping changes did not occur instantly. Others have been overhasty in declaring that the Middle East was returning to business-as-usual. This impatience—in an age of instant news when history plays out before our eyes—is explicable, but the history of the Middle East teaches us that watersheds become apparent over months and years, not days or hours. It is likely that the events of 1990–1991 represent a particularly rich watershed, marking significant international changes and catalyzing inchoate political trends in the Middle East, especially at the level of state-society relations.

Ironically, the most significant impact of the Gulf War may have been, as one Arab scholar noted recently, that the "wall of fear" separating citizens from autocratic rulers has been broken. If this is so, George Bush and his leader-colleagues may have unleashed whirlwinds of change that will engender profound instability in the Arab world. The irony, of course, is that while the great powers applaud participation and exalt democracy, they loathe instability, yet the achievement of greater participation and democratization without accompanying instability is difficult to imagine. And, to embroider the irony, there is, of course, no necessary affinity between popular (often populist) political voices and Western governments. The contrary is often the case.

But, if some of the Arab governments are showing a new tolerance for contested elections, this is no guarantee, obviously, that the results will be free of manipulation or that the polling will be fully fair. This points out the need for the international community to be willing to supervise elections in the Middle East. Relatively free elections—under international supervision—have been conducted in countries such as Namibia, Nicaragua, and Haiti. International supervision does not prevent an election from being overturned by a coup, but it does invoke a level of international attention that inhibits tampering with the results. Certainly, in the Arab world, Kuwait and Lebanon would be obvious candidates. In Kuwait, international supervision would reduce the temptation of the regime to ignore or reverse the results; in Lebanon, supervision would be a means to facilitate the re-legitimizing of the Lebanese parliament, which last stood for election in 1972, as well as for putting some distance between Lebanon and its overly intrusive neighbors, Israel and Syria.

The phenomenon of liberalization will sometimes exacerbate tensions, rather than moderate them. But, whatever their transitional excesses, democratizing governments must eventually balance arms budgets against social policies and address the demands of those to whom they are accountable. Aggressive wars are not easily launched in political systems where leaders must win support for their policies through a process of consultation and consensus-building. Dictators, by contrast, are free of these constraints.

One yet unmeasurable, but palpable result of the Gulf War is that many Arab intellectuals *and* policy-makers now argue that the Arab malaise is precisely a product of the lack of freedom in the Arab world. *This may be the most profoundly significant effort of the war.* In the short run, loosening the grip of authoritarian regimes will be a messy process, and incrementally minded Western officials will resist encouraging liberalization of Arab politics. But, statesmen with a longer view of history will appreciate that promoting liberalization is precisely the key to preempting the emergence of absolute rulers of the Saddam Hussein ilk. And no matter what statesmen may decide, the train seems to have left the station.

Author's Note

On December 26, 1991, the first round of parliamentary elections was conducted in Algeria. Although 49 political parties competed for the votes, the turnout of over 60 percent of the eligible voters produced a landslide for FIS, the Islamist political movement, which won outright 188 of 430 seats. Trailing far behind was the Socialist Forces Front, with 20 seats, while the ruling FLN managed to win only 16 seats. The remaining seats were to be decided in a second-round run-off election on January 16, 1992, in which FIS was virtually assured of winning a majority. In the days following the election, FIS officials professed a willingness to honor the precepts of democracy and took some steps to reassure wary Algerians.

However, this experiment with the democratic process came to a quick end. On January 11, President Benjedid resigned his office, apparently under pressure from hard-liners within his regime and the leadership of the army. Although the generals tried to erect a civilian leadership facade, there was no mistaking this for anything other than a coup d'état. The sighs of relief from Western capitals were more audible than the pro forma condemnations of the coup. The run-off elections were canceled, but the fate of FIS, which still possesses a residual legitimacy from its electoral triumph, is still unfolding. To many observers, the coup seems more likely to postpone a transfer of power than to prevent one. The FIS has behaved with restraint and even dignity. There were even hints that FIS might find common cause with its secular party rivals against the newly imposed government, which promises to rule until 1993, when presidential elections are scheduled to be held.

Inevitably, the stifling of the Islamists in Algeria will enliven radical voices, which will point—with some accuracy—to the double standards of regimes of their Western supporters, and argue that if it is not possible to move to power within the system, then the only answer is to topple it. Whether the action of the Algerian army was right or wrong, justified or unjustified, the fact remains that the long-term consequences will hardly bolster moderate voices. The outcome cannot be described as encouraging.

Notes

1. Samuel P. Huntington, "Will More Countries Become Democratic?" *Political Science Quarterly* 99 (2) (Summer 1984): 218.

2. *Summary Statistics of Education in the World, 1970–1984* (UNESCO).

3. See the excellent account by Milton Viorst, "A Reporter at Large (Kuwait)," *The New Yorker* (September 30, 1991): 37–72.

4. Muhammad Abdul Wahab Bekhechi confirmed these figures, as well as other figures used in this section, in a presentation to a meeting on "Democratization in the Middle East," sponsored by the Turkish Political Science Association and held in Antalya, Turkey, November 14–16, 1991. Bekhechi is a member of the Constitutional Council, which was created as a result of the 1990 constitutional revisions referred to above. For a splendid analysis, see Robert Mortimer, "Islam and Multiparty Politics in Algeria," *Middle East Journal* 45 (4) (Autumn 1991): 575–593.

5. See Eleanor Abdella Doumato, "Women and the Stability of Saudi Arabia," *Middle East Report* (July/August 1991): 34–37.

The Editors

Elizabeth Warnock Fernea

Elizabeth Fernea is a professor of English and Middle Eastern studies at the University of Texas at Austin and is director of the educational project, "Perspectives on Peace: the Middle East," two components of which are this book of readings and the accompanying documentary film, *The Struggle for Peace: Israelis and Palestinians*. She has lived and done research for many years in the Middle East and is the author of several books about the area, including *Guests of the Sheik: An Ethnography of an Iraqi Village* and *A Street in Marrakech*. With Basima Bezirgan she edited *Middle Eastern Muslim Women Speak*. Her most recent books, written with her anthropologist husband, Robert A. Fernea, are *Nubian Ethnographies* and *The Arab World: Personal Encounters*. Films include *A Veiled Revolution* for Channel 4, London, and *Saints and Spirits* for Granada Television.

Mary Evelyn Hocking

Mary Evelyn Hocking is a writing assessment specialist at the University of Texas at Austin, where she is responsible for the evaluation of all essays written as a part of the high school equivalency exam administered in Texas. She writes and delivers presentations in the field of developmental writing techniques. She received her B.A. from Tulane University in 1962 and her M.A. from the University of Texas at Austin in 1991. She is the author of *Islam: The Religious and Political Life of a World Community* (1984), a study guide to accompany a print-audio course for National Public Radio. Since that time she has collaborated with Elizabeth Fernea on several print/media educational projects concerned with the Middle East.

Index

'Abd Allah (Abdullah): as emir, 11, 71; as
king, 25–26, 54 n.96, 81, 83, 310 n.8
al-Abdel-Qader, 22
Africa, 37
Agranat Commission, 35
al-Ahmed al-Sabah, Jaber, 320
Aker, Mahmoud, 223
Algeria, 320–326
Allon Plan, 44
American Jews: and Zionism, 11, 14, 18; in-
fluence of, 49 n.35, 259, 270; view of Is-
rael, 201, 203–204; reaction to Begin, 258;
and Israeli settlements, 261
Amin, Idi, 61 n.159
Amirav, Moshe, 171–173
Andoni, Ghassan, 164, 168–170
Anti-Semitism, 8, 200
Arab Democratic Party, 301
Arab Higher Committee, 12, 16, 17, 19, 20
Arab-Israeli wars (1956–1973), 27–38. See
also Israeli-Palestinian conflict
Arab League, 19, 25, 52 n.62
Arab North Africa, 321
Arabs: reaction to Zionism, 9–13; violence
against Jews in Palestine, 9–10, 13, 15, 16,
17, 19; rising nationalism of, 10, 11; British
support for, 11, 16; during British Mandate over Palestine, 13–19, 21–22; leadership during British Mandate, 14; and establishment of Israel, 19–20; and 1948
war, 21–27, 247–248; Arab-Israeli wars
from 1956–1973, 27–38; Soviet support
for, 27, 28, 30, 31, 33–34, 56 n.105, 58 n.133,
58 n.137; oil embargo by, 37, 60 n.151;
chronology of, 87–91. See also Israeli-
Palestinian conflict; Palestinians; and
names of specific countries
Arafat, Yasir: and Fatah, 41; withdrawal
from Lebanon, 42, 61 n.161; and two-state
solution, 46, 286, 295, 299, 307; need to

negotiate with, 188; and King Hussein,
248; support of Saddam Hussein, 250; as
chairman of the PLO, 288; address before
UN General Assembly, 311 n.25
Arens, Moshe, 253, 289, 302
"Army of Salvation," 22, 24
al-Assad, Hafez, 263, 321
Ateek, Naim, 165–167
Abu Ayyash, Radwan, 232–234
al-Azm, Haqqi Bey, 48 n.24
Azuri, Najib, 11

Ba'ath party, 29
Baker, James, 149, 250, 259
Balfour Declaration, 11, 12, 13, 18, 48 n.18, 62,
63, 71
Bardin, Hillel, 177–179
Bar-Lev Line, 34, 36
Baruch, Bernard, 49 n.35
Bateson, Mary Catherine, 123–124
Beeman, William O., 123–124
Begin, Menachem: as minister in Labor
cabinet, 31; peace talks with Egypt, 38;
military strikes against Syria, 42; resignation of, 43, 44; Herut party of, 50 n.39; as
commander of ETZEL, 82; terrorist acts
of, 188; position on UN Resolution
#242, 251, 273 n.6; political policy of, 253,
256–259, 269; compared with Shamir,
254; visit to United States, 258–259; and
1947 partition plan, 288
Belhadj, Ali, 323, 326
Ben-Gurion, David: military policy of, 18,
23, 28, 29, 53–54 nn.84–85, 64, 83; on creation of Jewish state, 21, 51 n.60, 52–
53 n.74, 289; and Nasser, 28, 56 n.109; as
prime minister, 48 n.15, 251; on Bernadotte's assassination, 54 n.88; and 1947
partition plan, 288; and King Abdullah,
310 n.8